FORGED IN FIRE

FORGED IN FIRE

The History of
The Fire Brigades Union

Edited by
VICTOR BAILEY

LAWRENCE & WISHART
LONDON

Lawrence & Wishart Limited
144a Old South Lambeth Road
London SW8 1XX

First published 1992

Cover photograph of FBU banner
courtesy John Gorman collection

Photoset in North Wales by
Derek Doyle and Associates, Mold, Clwyd
Printed and bound in Great Britain by
Billing & Sons, Worcester

In memory of all firemen and firewomen
killed in the line of duty

Contents

Part III Memoirs

Illustrations

Abbreviations

AEU	Amalgamated Engineering Union
AFS	Auxiliary Fire Service
ARP	Air Raid Precautions
ASLEF	Amalgamated Society of Locomotive Engineers and Firemen
ATS	Auxiliary Territorial Service
COHSE	Confederation of Health Service Employees
CP	Communist Party
DHSS	Department of Health and Social Security
EC	Executive Council (of the Fire Brigades Union)
FBC	Fire Brigade Committee (London County Council)
FBU	Fire Brigades Union
FTU	Firemen's Trade Union
GLC	Greater London Council
GMBATU	General Municipal Boilermakers and Allied Trade Union
ILO	International Labour Organisation
IMF	International Monetary Fund
JCC	Joint Consultative Committee for Civil Defence Workers
JFOA	Junior Fire Officers' Association
LCC	London County Council
LFB	London Fire Brigade
LTC	London Trades Council
MEA	Municipal Employees Association
NAFO	National Association of Fire Officers
NALGO	National and Local Government Officers Association

NATO	North Atlantic Treaty Organisation
NBPI	National Board for Prices and Incomes
NCLC	National Council of Labour Colleges
NFBTO	National Federation of Building Trade Operatives
NFS	National Fire Service
NFSOA	National Fire Service Officers' Association
NIFA	Northern Ireland Fire Authority
NILP	Northern Ireland Labour Party
NJC	National Joint Council for Local Authorities' Fire Brigades
NUAF	National Union of Auxiliary Firemen
NUCW	National Union of Corporation Workers
NUGMW	National Union of General and Municipal Workers
NUM	National Union of Mineworkers
NUPE	National Union of Public Employees
RB	Representative Body (London Fire Brigade)
SEATO	South East Asian Treaty Organisation
SNP	Scottish National Party
STUC	Scottish Trades Union Congress
TGWU	Transport and General Workers Union
TUC	Trades Union Congress
WAFS	Women's Auxiliary Fire Service
WRNS	Women's Royal Naval Service
WVS	Women's Voluntary Services

Acknowledgements

Many people have contributed in formative ways to this book. I have tried to acknowledge these contributions in what follows; if I have failed in this endeavour I trust the actual publication of the book will provide compensation to those whom I have inadvertently overlooked.

I am greatly indebted to the following officials and members, past and present, of the Fire Brigades Union. General secretary Ken Cameron and national officer Dave Higgs oversaw the project from start to finish. Without their advice, help with documents and Job-like patience the book never would have rolled off the stocks. I am also indebted to Dr Terry Segars, who contributed to the initial decision to commission a new history of the FBU, and unselfishly made available his wide knowledge of, and research into, firemen's trade unionism. He also offered valuable criticisms of my own written contributions. I benefited immeasurably from the impassioned personal recollections, tendered at day-long meetings in Bradley House, Kingston-upon-Thames, in 1987, of John Horner, Enoch Humphries, John Macdonald and Tom Harris. Their enduring commitment to, and obvious affection for, the union they did so much to shape was truly infectious. Personal recollections and documents were also helpfully provided by Bob Bagley, Charles Best, Herbert Birkwood, John Cormack, Norman Greenfield, Sir Peter Pain, Jim Raphael, R.C. Shaw, Norman Stevens and Glyn Williams. Memories of the national strike of 1977-78 were submitted by many participants, and in this regard I would like to thank James Alexander, Bill Craig, Brian Critchlow, John Curran, Paul Kleinman, R. McQueen, Colin

Middleton, Pete Rockley, R.J. Roxburgh and Alistair Spence. My understanding of the strike was also greatly assisted by Ronnie Scott and David Shephard. Finally, I am grateful to the members of the Executive Council, 1987-1991, for their continued and unconditional support of the project.

I have also incurred debts beyond the confines of the FBU. The largest debt I owe to Professor John Saville. He it was who recommended me to the union as a possible editor, and who readily agreed to act as editorial adviser. At the cost of delaying his own research on post-war foreign policy, he contributed in numerous essential ways to the book, only a few of which are obviously apparent in the pages that follow. Most importantly, he convinced me of the need to break out of the standard framework of trade union histories, and was instrumental in shaping the format we eventually settled upon. It was a great privilege for me to work with, and learn from, this most eminent of economic and social historians.

In locating the sources of firemen's trade unionism, I was helped by my good friends and former colleagues, Dr Joyce Bellamy, Dr Douglas Reid, Dr David Rubinstein and Dr Michael Turner. Dr Owen Ashton also kindly helped me with the history of the Staffordshire Fire Brigade. I was greatly assisted by the following custodians of archives: Stephen Bird of the Labour Party archives in Walworth Road, Ms C. Coates of the Trades Union Congress Library in Great Russell Street, Richard Storey of the Modern Records Centre, University of Warwick and Patrick Baird of the Local Studies Department, Birmingham Public Library. I would also like to thank the staffs of the Greater London Record Office, the Public Record Office, and the Brynmor Jones Library, University of Hull. I received valuable criticisms of early drafts of my chapters from members of the economic and social history seminar at the University of Kansas. My thanks go to the seminar participants, and to the organisers, John Clark and Tom Weiss. None of these people, of course, bears any responsibility for the errors which doubtless remain.

The Joyce and Elizabeth Hall Center for the Humanities at the University of Kansas generously awarded me a travel grant with which to complete my research. The project was also supported by University of Kansas General Research allocation No. 3925-XX-0038. I would like to thank Catherine S. Evans for indexing the book, and Irene Baldwin and Barbara Brown for secretarial assistance. Finally, I am indebted to Stephen Hayward, the most dextrous and uplifting of publishers.

On the personal side, I must thank my mother for her constant encouragement, at great personal sacrifice, of my studies; and Wilfriede, Megan, and Matt for doing so much to smooth my passage to the heartland of America. Lastly, I owe a special debt of gratitude to Patricia Fidler for the encouragement which helped me to complete the book, and for a love borne out by gladly learning more about firemen's trade unionism than an art historian could conceivably need.

Victor Bailey
Keighley, Yorkshire
July 1991

Foreword

This history of our union takes the reader through its formative years to one of the most traumatic periods in that history, the first national fire service strike. The participation in, and the outcome of that strike have had a tremendous impact, economically, politically and industrially on the membership.

The pay formula won as a direct result of that strike, which compares a qualified firefighter after four years' service with the upper quartile of male manual workers, has maintained the earnings of all of the membership from its inception up to the time of writing.

The lessons learned from that strike, both political and industrial, have assisted in ensuring that two attempts by Conservative governments to end that agreement have been thwarted due to the solidarity of the membership. In this same period workers in the fire service as in other parts of the public and private sector, experienced attacks on staffing and funding of the service. The response from the membership was to carry unanimously a policy of action at the union's 1981 Annual Conference that in the event of any wholetime member being made redundant the Executive Council would recall the union's Conference with a recommendation for national strike action, a policy reiterated on a number of occasions since then.

This policy in conjunction with national and local lobbies and marches, has resulted, to-date, in all threats of physical redundancy being withdrawn. This has not meant however that there have not been job losses through natural wastage which have led to fire station closures and fire appliances coming off the run in some parts of the country.

These cut-backs have taken place against a background of a decade of disasters, the like of which had not been experienced in post-war Britain – major incidents such as the Bradford City football stadium fire and the Hillsborough tragedy, accidents on our railways and underground at Kings Cross, Clapham and Purley, and air disasters such as Lockerbie and the M1 air crash – were but a few which strained the fire service to its limit.

Despite the prevailing political climate the union, unlike many other TUC affiliates, continued to grow in strength throughout the 1980s. The membership at the end of the strike in 1978 stood at 39,097 and at the end of 1990 had risen to 47,801, an increase of over 20 per cent.

I am certain that with the continued education and involvement of the rank and file, the union will progress with confidence into the next century.

I would like to express both my personal appreciation and that of the Executive Council to all those who have contributed to this history. Particular thanks must be paid to John Horner, without whose major piece such a complete history would not have been possible, and to all the other authors for their fascinating contributions. Victor Bailey and John Saville have both given very generously of their time, expertise and imagination to make this the readable and well-rounded book it is, and we owe them a great debt of gratitude.

Unlike most such books, this history is both *of* and, in large part, *by* members of our union, and so in a wider sense is the property of all our members, and their families, who over the years have made great sacrifices both for the union and the community at large.

Ken Cameron,
General Secretary
Fire Brigades Union
October 1991

Introduction

In 1987 the Executive Council of the Fire Brigades Union decided to commission a new history of the organisation. An earlier official history, *Fetch the Engine*, by F.H. Radford, had stopped in 1950; since then many changes had taken place in the fire service and the union. The EC turned to Professor John Saville to get the project off the ground. He agreed to act as editorial adviser and recommended me, then his colleague at Hull University, to be the editor. From the start he and I were determined to get away from what may be called the traditional history of trade unions, usually a dull and detailed chronological account of the internal evolution of the organisation; and instead provide a volume which both trade unionists and the 'guild' of labour historians would be eager to read.

To this end we divided *Forged in Fire* into three very different sections. The first presents a straightforward account of the first thirty years of the FBU, from 1918 to 1948, though one that tries to assess work-place social relations and the impact on union evolution of changes in economic structure, technology and the labour market. These were critical years in which the FBU changed out of all recognition, from a small, insular, London-dominated body into a sizeable, extrovert, national trade union. War and its demands had a considerable part to play in this transformation.

The middle section of the book departs from the strictly chronological form, and documents the union's development since the Second World War by way of special themes and topics. A number of labour historians contributed to this section. Their essays bring a breadth and diversity to the union's history which no single-handed chronicle could achieve. They also focus attention on themes – the role of women, the position in Northern Ireland – which trade union histories have a tendency to overlook. However, while the subject of these essays is varied, many of them point towards the National Strike of 1977-78, an event in the making from 1948, when the National Fire Service was dismantled and the local authorities reassumed control of fire brigades, and an event which posed the greatest challenge to firemen and their union. To a degree, the strike still promotes controversy among firemen who took the painful decision to withdraw their labour; and I know my analysis of the strike will not receive universal assent. For that reason, we urged members to offer their own recollections of the strike, and promised to include a sample of them in the final section of the book.

The third and final section of the book takes full advantage of the consultation with FBU members, past and present, which the union was pleased to arrange, and which we were keen to develop. We were committed, moreover, to recording the voice of firemen trade unionists in the volume. That we have succeeded in doing. Pride of place goes to the vivid account by John Horner of his eventful career as active fireman and general secretary. In addition, Chapters 13 to 19 contain an edited selection of union members' individual stories, comments and reflections on their experiences of the nine weeks the National Strike lasted. These memoirs have the added merit of revealing some of the sharp differences and hard argument which characterise relations between fellow unionists, and which make trade unions such crucibles of democratic life.

But enough of our attempt to design a more appealing shape for trade union histories. It is unlikely, of course, that this alone would deflect academic reviewers from their general tendency to savage officially-commissioned union histories. Labour history has moved on, they cry; no one now reads detailed histories of single unions. How, then, do we justify this trade union history?

Introduction

Only Rip van Winkle could be unaware of the important advances which have taken place in the history of labour in the past twenty years. Traditionally, the history of the institutions of labour – political parties, co-operative societies, trade unions – were placed at the centre of labour history. The history of labour was the record of organised struggle. Yet, as we know, trade unions only ever recruited a minority of the workforce, and rarely sought to influence every dimension of people's lives. Political parties of the left invariably had difficulty attracting the allegiance of working people, many of whom accepted rather than contested their position in the economic and political order. In recent years, therefore, an exclusive focus on institutions, leadership and militancy has been replaced by a broader investigation of the social history of the working class, of the unorganised as well as the unionised; of women and minorities as much as skilled male craftsmen; of beliefs and culture instead of material conditions; of workplace, family and community rather than the strategies of union head office. In short, historians have turned from tending the formal representative institutions to tilling the ground in which those institutions are rooted.

This historical scholarship is well known to the authors of the present volume, and, I would suggest, has left its mark on their contributions. But if we applaud this sea-change in the direction and range of labour history, we cannot agree that the organisation and strategies of trade unions deserve the undervaluation they seem increasingly to receive. Trade unions were and are the most critical agency of working-class self-defence and self-betterment, vital to the improvement of wages and the working environment, to the structure of industrial relations and to the social and political framework of all working people. This is particularly true of the present century. The struggle for trade union organisation was and is one of the most influential means through which working people develop collective identity and mount collective action. Changes in the outlook of working people, in other words, can result from changes in trade union organisation.

More specifically, the history of the Fire Brigades Union deserves attention for a number of reasons. Firstly, the FBU is a rare example of broad-based and effective trade unionism flourishing in the unlikely soil of a uniformed and disciplined occupation. This book should alert historians to the larger story, which remains untold, of the efforts, however short-lived, to secure a right of representation and improved conditions for the disciplined services. Secondly, the union displays the fascinating paradox, which is difficult to explain, of a body of men accustomed to semi-military ranks and disciplinary procedures agreeing to be led by radical and, for a decade, Communist leaders, whose stance on foreign policy, incomes policies and nuclear disarmament was well to the left of the organised labour movement. The FBU is hardly unique in having leaders more militant than its members, but for a union in a security service it is rather remarkable. Thirdly, in an economy and labour market ever more dominated by service industries, it is important to explore trade unionism in particular regions of that service sector. Finally, the structure of the fire service compels the examination of the influence on industrial relations of the attitudes and strategies of employers and the state, institutional forces which labour historians have commonly neglected.

Over and above the volume's contribution to the history of the labour movement, *Forged in Fire* is a record of the struggles waged, the privations and sacrifices endured by ordinary firemen in the cause of better working and living conditions. It is also a testimony to the union's substantial contribution, against considerable resistance from national and local government, to the modernisation of the British fire service. In this, we all, as citizens, have a stake.

One of my most vivid childhood memories is of a day in late February 1956, packed into a noisy, double-decker school bus, passing the woollen mills of Worth Village, Keighley. One mill had become a raging inferno. Our excitement at seeing the flames and the fire engines reluctantly gave way to the thought that some of us had mothers working inside those mills. We were right to be anxious, for eight young mill workers lost their lives in the blaze. The fire spread rapidly across oil-soaked timber floors, trapping the women in lavatories and on upper floors. Contrary to the regulations of the Factories Act, 1937, the mill had no fire alarm system, the fire escape did not reach all floors and the door of the fire exit was tightly fastened. The Factory Inspectorate had visited the mill in 1951, and drawn attention to the breaches of the Act, but nothing had been put right. Alas, this factory was not alone. A national survey of 60,000 factories carried out in the wake of the tragedy found that only half had the required fire alarms, and only half had the necessary fire escape certificates. The Keighley tragedy did at least produce the 1959 Factories Act, which increased the responsibility of fire authorities for implementing and enforcing fire prevention legislation. The FBU had been pressing for this for many a long year; for the union has always done much more than protect the living standards and safety of its membership. Indeed, the FBU is largely responsible for the conversion of the antediluvian fire brigades of the Victorian era into the modern fire service that Britain boasts. The Fire Brigades Union is, therefore, much more than an organisation dedicated solely to the promotion of its members' sectional interests. As the contributors to this volume hope to demonstrate, it is a union whose history mirrors the selflessness of the firefighter's work, and one which has made a unique contribution to British trade unionism.

I The Early Days

1 The Early History of the Fire Brigades Union

Victor Bailey

This chapter is a detailed history of the emergence, and struggle for acceptance, of the Fire Brigades Union.* It traces firemen's trade unionism from 1906, or thereabouts, when employers in the shape of local councils still considered trade unionism incompatible with, indeed subversive of, their disciplined, uniformed fire brigades, to 1948, by which date the FBU had become the nationally recognised negotiating body for most firemen and many officers. If there was one factor instrumental both in the union's initial appearance, and in the dramatic sea-change in the union's fortunes, it was, as we shall see, the forcing-house of war. The social and political discontent aroused by the running sore of the First World War impelled firemen to unionise in 1918; the massive recruitment of men and women into the fire service, to combat the destruction of the blitz during the Second World War, hugely augmented the membership, influence and aspirations of the FBU. If the 1914-18 war incubated firemen's trade unionism, the 1939-45 war enforced the union's maturity.

Inevitably, the chapter largely investigates when, why and under what circumstances firemen resorted to, and exploited, collective organisation to improve their pay, pensions, duty hours and working conditions. Too many trade union histories, however, consider the organisation's effectiveness in changing the terms and conditions of work, to the detriment of the actual working experience of the union membership. This volume begins, therefore, with an estimate of the working conditions and culture of professional firemen, both in London and the provinces, in the years straddling the First World War.

Ships on Dry Land

At the beginning of the 1920s there were about 3,400 full-time professional firefighters in Britain. The largest brigade was the London Fire Brigade (LFB), with a strength of roughly 1,300 officers and men, manning 65 land stations and three river stations. Candidates for enrolment into the LFB had to be over nineteen and under 31 years of age, at least 5 feet 5 inches tall, not less than 37 inches in chest measurement and able to read well and write legibly. They also had to be British subjects of pure British descent.[1] As for previous training, ever since the days of Captain Eyre-Massey Shaw, the legendary head of the Metropolitan Fire Brigade in the Victorian years, ex-seamen were thought to make the best candidates. Indeed, until 1899 recruitment was entirely restricted to seamen. Veterans of the Royal Navy were supposedly inured to rigid discipline and devotion to duty, well-versed in the use of knots and splices in ropes, and accustomed to going aloft, to the loneliness of serving a long watch and to the need for 'all hands on deck' at critical moments.[2]

The preference for seamen persisted into the inter-war period. As Sir Aylmer Firebrace, a former navy commander, who joined the LFB as a principal officer in 1919 (and how could he fail to join with a name like that), recorded:

> Sons followed fathers into the Service, and many were sent early into the Merchant Navy so as to increase their chances of being accepted for the Brigade at an early age ... The maximum recruiting age was specially fixed at thirty-one in order to leave the door wide open for those sailors who left the Navy at the expiration of their first period of service.[3]

The figures tell the same story. Of the 1,391 officers and men serving in the LFB in 1920, almost one-third, 444 were ex-members of the Royal Navy. In addition, 454 had been in the Merchant Marine, and 261 had served in the Army. Only 232 were from other trades and callings.

The naval influence went well beyond the point of recruitment. The language, lore and social rules of the job, indeed the entire work culture, was redolent of salt water. The pattern of life in a fire station (as on board ship) was dictated less by efficiency, by the training of an effective fire-fighting force, than by drill and discipline, what Firebrace termed 'the well-disciplined ship' and the men knew as 'bull'. 'Spit and polish' took precedence over training in firemanship. Station houses were swabbed and polished to a state of naval smartness. Firemen – at least the 'junior buck' or newest recruit – were even expected to clean the floors of the senior officers' homes. Little wonder that the vernacular of the fire service reflected this naval heritage: 'ship', 'crew', 'watch' and 'mess'. Fire stations were simply ships on dry land. Appropriately, firemen were expected to be available for 'continuous duty'.[4]

Every fireman was on duty for 24 hours a day for fourteen days and nights, except when sick. Every fifteenth day was technically free, although it was not unknown for the day off to be suddenly cancelled because of a fire call or a drill. This meant, for example, that men who had been engaged at a serious fire during the night would have to work cleaning and testing the engines and equipment the next morning, and be ready to turn out if another fire occurred that day, inevitably in a tired and worn-out condition. This compares with a working week of 54 hours for other trades, with the possibility of a further reduction to 50 hours. Firemen were allowed 'short leave' of two or three hours each week, and annual leave of seven days. Otherwise, for about 330 days in the year, firemen were confined to quarters in small fire stations, under strict discipline. No inspection work or other out-duties broke the monotony of waiting for a fire call and of cleaning the station and appliances.[5]

Discipline in the brigade was both arbitrary and severe. A

system of heavy fines for small infractions, such as straying a few yards from the station, gave the power of God to station officers. The position had deteriorated with the change from horse-drawn appliances to motors. It took longer to turn out with the horses, so men had time to return from a pub near the fire station when the bells went down. Motors turned out too quickly for this to be allowed. It was also harder to hear the bells, since the fire stations were now closed in order to keep the engines warm. Unless the station officer allowed the public, or 'strangers', to frequent the recreation room of the fire station, the men, as Jim Bradley told a Departmental Committee in 1920, 'are just as much isolated as if they were at sea'. He went on: 'The men themselves will tell you that they get sick and tired of one another's society ... of seeing one another's faces and hearing the same yarn over and over again.' Nor was the fireman's family immune from this severe regimen. Bradley claimed that wives were as much under discipline as the firemen: 'If you take a woman into a London fire station ... it is practically condemning her to penal servitude ...'[6] Few families would have been unaffected by the bells going off or by firemen returning soaking wet.

The insular life of firemen and their families was aggravated by the direct consequences of continuous duty: residence in quarters in or attached to the fire station. Until 1920 all London firemen lived on the station, single men in dormitories, for which 1 shilling per week was charged, married men with families in small two-room flats, with scullery and bathroom on a communal basis, for which they were charged according to length of service. Firemen with up to ten years' service paid 4 shillings per week rent; after twenty years' service quarters came free. But there were many anomalies in the provision of accommodation. Those for whom no married quarters were available, the 'single-married', had to live in the station, but maintain a wife and family elsewhere (for which they received a rent allowance of 4s. 6d. per week). The son of a fireman, on reaching the age of eighteen, had to be turned out of brigade quarters to ensure that the meagre accommodation sufficed for large families. Sons returning from war service were often not allowed to re-enter the home. In the event of a married man becoming a widower he had to board his children out and himself revert to single men's quarters. Accommodation was thus a real bone of contention between firemen and the London County Council.[7]

In the provincial fire brigades conditions of service were remarkably similar, whether one examines the police brigades (notably Bristol, Hull, Leeds, Liverpool and Sheffield), where the professional firemen were technically part of the police force, or the non-police brigades (such as Birmingham, Bradford, Edinburgh, Glasgow, Leicester and West Ham). The Manchester brigade was independent of the police between 1897 and 1920, but was then reconstituted as part of the police force.[8]

The naval influence in the composition of provincial fire brigades was again evident, without being as dominant as in London. Seamen were acceptable to A.R. Tozer, Chief Officer of Birmingham Fire Brigade, and about half the brigade had come from the navy. Many of the Manchester brigade had been sailors. But provincial brigades, like the police brigade of Newcastle-upon-Tyne (which consisted of both permanent and auxiliary firemen) often liked to recruit tradesmen – fitters, joiners, plumbers, motor mechanics – who were employed on the repairs to machinery and buildings. Such repair work was done in Birmingham and Manchester, for which extra pay was given, though the Painters' Trade Union had put a stop to painting and decorating in both brigades. In Scotland, in contrast, where non-police brigades predominated, few sailors were recruited, with the exception of Edinburgh, where a good number were seamen. Skilled mechanics and tradesmen were much preferred: they knew better the interior of a building, which could improve fire fighting, and when not answering a fire call they could work in the engineers', joiners' and painting shops, doing their ordinary trade work. In Glasgow, for example, four shoemakers made the boots, belts and helmets for the brigade.[9]

The continuous duty system prevailed in the majority of

provincial brigades until 1920. Salford firemen were accordingly described by the *Manchester Courier* as 'municipal slaves', imprisoned for fourteen days at a time. Firemen in Cardiff (a police brigade) were, however, in the envious position of having one day's rest in seven. As in London, men were usually resident, in either single or married quarters, on the bell. In Birmingham and Manchester firemen did at least have free quarters. Provincial firemen also had to suffer the petty tyranny of station life. Norman Greenfield's vivid description of life as 'a glorified charlady' in the Manchester brigade could be applied to many other brigades at this time: polishing brasswork, scrubbing floors, sawing up disused telegraph poles, a task worthy of prison labour.[10]

The worst off among professional firemen, however, were those in the smaller brigades, usually part-professional and part-retained, such as Southampton and Gloucester. Here the rigours of continuous employment were aggravated by the lack of pension arrangements and by a reduction in pay during sickness. In London firemen were entitled to a pension, based on length of service (although awards relating to retirement for reasons of injury or ill health were entirely discretionary and could prove extremely niggardly). Many provincial brigades still had no superannuation scheme of any nature. Though some local authorities gave an *ex gratia* retirement allowance when a man was considered to be no longer efficient, the problem remained that in brigades without a pension scheme, employers were reluctant to turn firemen out into the street and so kept them in the service when they were long past the work. The treatment of firemen while sick varied. In the London Fire Brigade men were given full pay when absent from duty owing to injury or illness from any cause. In some brigades 1 shilling a day was deducted from the man's pay, while in Southampton firemen were put on half-pay directly they were sick.[11]

Not surprisingly, not everyone who joined stayed in the service. In the pre-war years, according to Bradley, 'the difficulty was to retain the men in the fire brigade when they found the conditions under which they had to serve'. Over

200 firemen left the service in the space of twelve months in 1912-13, all of them men with less than two years' service.[12]

Yet the outlook for firemen was not entirely bleak. In most of the large brigades firemen's pay was on a par with that of policemen. In police brigades firemen generally received the pay and pension of the police, albeit for longer hours of work. Wages of firemen were close to the national average wage for adult men, if below the wage of a skilled craftsman. Pension schemes or *ex gratia* allowances on retirement were an undoubted advantage, still denied many other workers, who had the anxiety of surviving during old age. In addition to pay and pension (where available), firemen could sometimes get a free uniform, free or subsidised rent and full pay while sick. The job was secure from periods of unemployment and short time, and it had its exciting and life-saving moments. It was never too difficult, therefore, for the employers to fill vacancies in the ranks. There were usually numerous applications for each position advertised.[13]

These, then, were the service conditions of professional firemen, which were far from conducive to the development of trade unionism, at the time of the First World War, and for many years following the war. Professional firemen were few in number, scattered across the country, shut up in small fire stations, residentially and occupationally segregated from other work groups. Habits of obedience and sentiments of loyalty to the service were instilled by para-military regimes, whether in professional or police brigades. In such an occupational culture firemen did not readily think in collective terms. They tended to avoid political discussion lest it result in conflict and ill-feeling. They were more likely to define the union organiser as agitator, to reject as alien an appeal to collective or class solidarity, to view the union member as social deviant.[14]

Firemen were encouraged in these patterns of thought by employers, whose prevailing view was that allegiance to an organisation outside the brigade would inevitably interfere with the workings of a disciplined, uniformed and hierarchical service. While local councils recognised trade unions for other of their manual workers, when it came to firemen they adopted the military mind-set of the senior officers. For the latter, effective discipline meant unquestioning obedience. Senior officers insisted that direct, democratic representation would sap the command structure of the fire service, divide the men's loyalty and jeopardise the fire service's supplementary role as a security force. In all, employer opposition to firemen's unionism rested on a military model of the appropriate form of service organisation.[15]

Yet if these working conditions conspired to stop firemen *thinking* in collective terms, the self-same conditions conduced to firemen *acting* in collective ways. The interminably long hours of duty, the shared workspace and male camaraderie together with the high level of team work enforced by a dangerous job all nurtured a strong group solidarity. Ironically, the very consciousness of a separate identity from other workers, the very caste divisions of officers and men (as pronounced in the fire service as in the navy), disposed firemen towards industrial and political radicalism. Ratings 'moving straight across from the navy to the LFB might not be thought of as the most promising of trades union material', says John Horner, FBU general secretary from 1939 to 1964. 'But I came to realise', he goes on, 'that the strong bond of mutual reliance which characterised "the job", could be a powerful element in forging a special kind of trade union for a special kind of service.'[16]

Battle for Trade Union Recognition

It was inevitable, given the size and relative concentration of the London Fire Brigade that the battle for trade union recognition would be fought first and most fiercely within the metropolis. The Municipal Employees' Association (MEA), which grew out of the London County Council (LCC) employees' organisation in 1894, took the initiative. As a result of its attempts to recruit the uniformed sections of municipal employment, the MEA enrolled a number of LCC firemen early in 1905, and in September pressed the Fire Brigade Committee (FBC) of the LCC to amend the lodging regulations so as to enlarge the number of married firemen entitled to two rooms each. An application of this kind, the Chief Officer fumed, 'is extremely prejudicial to the discipline of the Brigade', and the MEA was instructed that the proper course in matters of staff welfare was for firemen to apply to their superior officers. To nip trade unionism in the bud the FBC further proposed, and the LCC accepted, the 1906 regulation which required, on threat of dismissal, that any complaint for the attention of the FBC had to come via the Chief Officer. Representations from a trade union would not be received. The threat had little effect, since the MEA boasted a branch of some 500 London firemen by the end of 1906.[17]

Events became confused in 1907 with the formation of a rival union to the MEA, the National Union of Corporation Workers (NUCW), later to become the National Union of Public Employees. LCC employees were prominent in this new union, and some LCC firemen formed a branch of the union. Eventually the entire London firemen's branch of the MEA (close on 500 men) transferred to the NUCW. The scent of trade unionism goes cold, however, until 1913. In November and December of that year the Fire Brigade branch of the NUCW grew to 1,100 members, out of a total of 1,300 London firemen. The branch secretary was sub-officer E.W. Southgate, who now stood in danger of dismissal. To protect fireman-secretary Southgate, the union nominated executive council member, Jim Bradley, a London park-keeper, to take over as branch secretary. The growth of membership was doubtless influenced by the 'Labour Unrest' (the upsurge of militant trade unionism in pre-war Britain), by an increase in the wages of the metropolitan police force and by the feeling that the Chief Officer, Lieutenant-Commander Sladen, had not effectively represented the firemen's case.[18]

Chief Officer Sladen believed firemen were a 'privileged class', in terms of wage rates and conditions of service, but he accepted that some form of collective representation would provide an outlet for grievances. He thus proposed the creation of a London Fire Brigade Staff Committee of twelve members, to be chosen by the men of the brigade, including a secretary who would have direct access to the Chief Officer, all of whom would be on the permanent staff of the fire brigade. This would mean that collective representation would be made to the Chief Officer, who would remain the men's representative before the fire brigade committee of the LCC. The Chief Officer could, however, arrange for a deputation to attend before the fire brigade committee of the LCC.[19]

The LCC endorsed the scheme with the added concession that firemen would not be required to leave any union in which they had benefit rights. While sub-officers and station officers pressed for a similar staff committee for each grade, the firemen rejected the scheme, insisting upon the recognition of the Fire Brigade branch of the NUCW. Commander Sladen saw the mutinous hand of the union in all this, but Sir George Askwith, Chief Industrial Commissioner of the Board of Trade, whose help the LCC requested, insisted that most firemen were opposed to the staff committee. As stubborn as ever, the LCC reiterated the 1906 regulation and continued to set its face against any outside organisation intervening between the council and the brigade. Trade union representation would, the LCC believed, subvert the strict discipline required of firemen.[20]

Firemen in every London fire station were, by now, close to open revolt. The union had not only pressed for recognition but had also petitioned for one day's rest in eight (in place of one in fifteen) to shorten the excessive hours of duty, for the reduction of service for pensions from 28 to 25 years, for the withdrawal of the regulation under which sons of firemen were compelled to leave their fire station homes at eighteen years of age, for widowers to retain the quarters assigned them as married men and for a pay increase. Firemen started at a wage of 26s. 6d. a week, which amounted to little more than 2d. per hour, with an annual increase of 1 shilling up to a maximum of 35 shillings. Their wages were on average below those of mechanics. Still, in July 1914 the fire brigade committee rejected the firemen's demands. The union and the FBC were now on a collision course.[21]

The immediate outbreak of war stemmed the mounting wave of industrial unrest in the country, and momentarily braked the momentum of the London firemen. Over 200 were recalled to the army and navy reserves; many younger men volunteered for the armed services. Some of the gaps were filled by men who, ever after, were cruelly known as the 'Kitchener dodgers', but soon the London brigade was seriously under strength, particularly in the face of such incidents as the munitions factory explosion in Silvertown, West Ham, in January 1917.[22]

Shortly after the war began, a 30 shilling minimum weekly wage was conceded (with 38s. 6d. as the maximum), and war bonuses were granted amounting, by July 1918, to 25 shillings a week. The war wages, however, were neither permanent nor pensionable, nor did they keep pace with the inexorable rise in living costs. By 1917 the wage status of firemen had sunk to the level of industrial labourers. As if this were not bad enough, a woman tramway conductor's weekly wages, after one year's service, were higher at 54s. 3d. than the maximum rate of pay of a fireman, after eight years' service, at 53s. 6d. (inclusive of war wage). In all, the war led neither to improvement in the real wages and conditions of service of London's firemen, nor to union recognition. Throughout 1917 Jim Bradley pressed G.H. Roberts, Minister of Labour, to install a channel of communication (other than the staff committee) between firemen and the fire brigade committee, but in vain.[23] By 1918 the firemen's despair could be contained no longer.

Before dealing with this formative moment for firemen's trade unionism, it is well to look beyond London, if only fleetingly, to record the few additional advances in collective organisation. In Aberdeen the town council agreed in October 1914 to receive a deputation of firemen, members of the Gasworkers and General Labourers' Union (later the General and Municipal Workers' Union), to press for an improvement in the length of annual holidays and in the time allowed for meals. The deputation did not come away empty-handed. In Belfast the Municipal Employees' Association, which claimed to represent two-thirds of the brigade, demanded a pay increase and improved conditions in 1912. In pre-war Manchester, according to Norman Greenfield, a number of firemen joined the MEA. In April 1918 the Manchester Fire Brigade Branch of the Workers' Union (forerunner of the Transport and General Workers' Union) was formed and soon had more than 100 members. The union immediately demanded an eight-hour day. To stop the rot the council in October 1920 conceded the two-shift system of twelve hours each, and then merged the brigade with the police force, thus outlawing trade unionism.[24]

Strike Threat

By 1918 Britain was war-weary and afflicted by industrial unrest. Even the disciplined services began to crack. Discontent among sailors at prices out-pacing pay led in July 1918 to proposals for a strike of the Lower Deck. Given the close connections between the fire service and the navy this move toward collective organisation could not but influence firemen.[25] The police, too, were no longer prepared to tolerate low pay and the authorities' refusal to recognise the Police and Prison Officers Union, formed in 1913. The Metropolitan Police force went on strike on 29 August and the following day won improvements in pay. The police stirred up a hornets' nest, and the day after their victory Jim Bradley, secretary of the Fire Brigade branch of the National Union of Corporation Workers, again asked the Ministry of Labour to help get the union officially recognised. If no reply was received within a week, Bradley threatened, the men would strike, despite the fact that such a breach of discipline was an offence under the wartime Defence of the Realm Act. Meanwhile, a secret ballot of firemen was held on the issue of strike action. A vote of two-thirds of the men affected was needed for a strike. Bradley never fully disclosed the results of the ballot, but reliable sources indicate that feeling was running high in favour of strike action.[26]

Commander Sladen was disturbed by events which, he believed, only weakened his authority over the brigade. To make matters worse, a deputation on behalf of station officers demanded, in early September, both official recognition of their staff committee and that their pay and pensions come into line with those conceded to the police. Sladen began to doubt whether the officers could be depended upon in the event of a firemen's strike. He also received confidential information that Germany was preparing to attack London with incendiary bombs on a larger scale than before. To cap it all, Scotland Yard made it clear that it wanted to use the police (as opposed to the military) to protect fire stations and working firemen during the strike in order to see if the police intended to carry out their duty in the jittery aftermath of the police strike.[27]

Sladen was out of his depth and failed to provide the kind of leadership and advice the fire brigade committee expected. The committee was even more nonplussed when, on 7 September, Sladen met the elected representatives of the firemen at brigade headquarters and immediately put his cards on the table. He told them of the imminent incendiary attack, of his fear that the public would respond to a strike by reducing the size of the London fire service to provincial levels and of his own active support for the firemen's wartime wage claims. He also told the men that he was not taking any side in the matter. Little wonder the branch executive committee, made up of two firemen from each district of the brigade, pressed for its slate of demands: that the branch secretary be recognised as the men's representative; that firemen be given the right to choose an outsider as their secretary; that £1 of the £1 5s. war bonus be made permanent and pensionable; that one day's leave in ten be allowed to all men (with one day in seven to be granted after the war); and that the council promise to introduce eight-hour shifts of duty within twelve months of the war's end.[28]

The Ministry of Labour reacted to these adverse events by hosting a conference in mid-September of union representatives and the fire brigade committee, which the government asked Sir George Askwith to chair. At the conference the FBC was prepared to offer either a representative body akin to the station-officers committee, or a body similar to that accepted by the police. The firemen held out for trade union recognition, although Bradley, in an unwise and premature step, gave an assurance that the fire brigade branch of the union (which, he claimed, was a fully autonomous section of the NUCW) would get involved neither in labour disputes outside the fire service nor in disputes in the fire service outside London. Yet even this considerable concession failed to move the FBC, and hence both parties agreed to refer the dispute to the Chief Industrial Commissioner for arbitration. Any question of a strike was removed for the time being. A few days later, in a significant development for firemen's trade unionism, a group of sub-officers, led by George Hayes, informed the LCC that they too wished to be represented by the NUCW and that they would abide by the arbitration award.[29]

The hearing took place on 18 September 1918 before Sir George Askwith. Commander Sladen declined to appear, not wishing to stand in opposition to what the men considered a point of principle. Jim Bradley presented the firemen's case for the right to make collective representations via the union of their choice. He did not, however, insist that the Fire Brigade branch of the NUCW be that union. He also restated the concession concerning involvement in outside labour disputes. The firemen did not want 'to break down another Fire Brigade, nor ... be involved in any industrial union'. Bradley did, however, float the idea of a National Fire Brigade Union, so unique were the conditions of firemen's work. Such a union, he said, would better secure the improvement of the entire country's fire brigade services.

For the LCC, G.H. Hume emphasised that no union, especially a branch of an industrial trade union, should have anything to do with a force, on whose discipline the security of London from fire depended. When, however, Bradley asked if the LCC would agree to an independent firemen's trade union, with a secretary chosen from outside their own ranks, Hume replied that it would.

Askwith's award on the firemen's claim for recognition of their union was a study in compromise. He ruled that London firemen could have a 'representative body', the committee of which would consist of and be chosen by only London firemen, but the 'spokesman' of which need not be a member of the brigade. At the Home Office's bidding Askwith inserted extra conditions: the representative body was to restrict itself to the welfare and conditions of service of the brigade, it could take no part in any labour dispute, it could not induce its members to withdraw their labour and it could not interfere with 'the regulations and discipline of the service or methods of management'. As an *alternative* Askwith offered firemen the option of forming a 'London Fire Brigade Union', composed of firemen only, to which would be applied the extra conditions above. In fact, London firemen subsequently decided to accept the representative body, thereby remaining members of the fire brigade section of the NUCW.[30]

We now know, from the recent history of the National Union of Public Employees (of which the NUCW was a forerunner), that Bradley was already promoting 'the secession of the Fire Brigade branch [of the NUCW] into the small Firemen's Trade Union', basically a friendly society catering for 200 men in private brigades, led by George Gamble.[31] Without either informing the NUCW or getting their agreement, and with some ill-feeling (as was shown by the libel case in November 1919 between Bradley and Albin Taylor of the NUCW), the firemen broke away from their long-standing parent body and threw in their lot with Gamble.[32] Bradley became assistant secretary of the new union.

Given the obvious desire on Bradley's part to form an independent union to serve the distinct needs, as he saw them, of firemen, it is hard to explain why he accepted the Askwith alternative of a representative body, rather than the

'London Fire Brigade Union'. The latter option had the decided virtue that a union, which ultimately had to be recognised by the LCC, would be acting on behalf of firemen. The chosen option, in contrast, established a most unsatisfactory framework of trade unionism in the London Fire Brigade, which prevailed for the next twenty years. The firemen's independent union remained unrecognised by the LCC, even though the general secretary of the union acted as the 'spokesman' of the representative body. The Firemen's Trade Union occupied a nether world, able only to abet covertly the actions of the representative body. What can be said in favour of the chosen option is that the 'outsider', Jim Bradley, could continue to lead the fight (from which, as a non-fireman, he would have been excluded under the alternative option), and the union was not restricted to London firemen but free to recruit firemen in other brigades. It was felt most probably that these benefits outweighed the disadvantages of the representative body. A link with the outside, however tenuous, was the obvious choice.

Whichever option had been chosen, however, the Askwith award ensured that London firemen would be bound to a no-strike clause, and would be prevented from supporting industrial action by firemen in other parts of the country or by other public sector workers. This served only further to isolate London firemen, the most effectively organised of any brigade, from all other uniformed firefighters.

If London firemen emerged from the 1918 dispute with less than what seemed possible in the heady days of the threatened strike, Jim Bradley had to his enormous credit extracted from the Leviathan of the Home Office, Ministry of Labour and the LCC, a channel of collective representation. An unintended side-effect was a change in command of the London fire brigade. As the First World War ended in November 1918, Chief Officer Sladen was pressed to resign, guilty, among other things, of too large a sympathy with the men's aspirations.[33]

The Askwith award made no attempt to deal with the firemen's other demands, now addressed by the twelve-member representative body, entering the lists against the

LCC to play its small part in creating a 'land fit for heroes'. Success attended its first joust. In December 1918 the LCC granted firemen one day's leave in ten (down from one in fifteen), with one day in seven likely once the brigade was back to normal strength. In addition, 15 shillings of the war bonus (not £1 as the men demanded) was to be made permanent and pensionable.[34] The representative body then forced the pace, protesting that consideration of the request for an eight-hour shift system had been deferred until at least March 1919. According to 'spokesman' Bradley, the men wanted an eight-hour, non-residential shift system to allow them to get away from the fire station and to bring similar conditions of service to those of the police.[35]

A serious situation confronted the LCC. Pay and conditions of service were evidently creating profound unrest among London firemen in early 1919. This was bound to be aggravated by the improvement in police pay and conditions that Lord Desborough's Committee on the Police Service was about to recommend, since London firemen's pay was based on the pay of the Metropolitan Police. For firemen to get not only pay parity but also the same hours of work as the police, was, said both the Home Office and the LCC, preposterous. Given the average number of 'call outs' per station, firemen would, it was claimed, spend most of the eight hours sitting about waiting or simply cleaning appliances. The argument was lost on the men, who, by July, were threatening strike action.[36]

The LCC got off the hook temporarily, thanks to the Home Office, which proposed the establishment of a departmental committee to examine the hours and pay of professional firemen.[37] Meanwhile the council accepted the proposal that uniformed staff be allowed one day's leave in seven. Much more surprisingly, in December 1919, in a move that could not fail to pre-empt the recommendations of the departmental committee, the LCC followed Birkenhead's lead in agreeing to a system of two shifts of twelve hours each for all firemen and sub-officers, which, on a six-day week, meant a 72-hour week.

This was granted on the understanding that the

representative body would make no application for eight-hour shifts, or a 48-hour week, before June 1922. Upon the introduction of a two-shift system, scheduled for June 1920, firemen would be granted an allowance of 8s. 6d. a week in lieu of quarters and permitted to live wherever they wished. The brigade would thus be organised on a non-residential basis. In addition, the council agreed to revised pay scales on the basis of police pay. Firemen would now get 70 shillings a week, rising by annual increments to a maximum of 93 shillings. Sub-officers would receive 97s. 6d. a week, with a maximum of 110 shillings.[38]

The urgency which the LCC displayed in reaching a settlement reflected concern that serious disturbance in the fire brigade was brewing, but, more importantly, the view that better a two-shift system of 72 hours than a three-shift system of 48 hours, which might well be forced on the council by either the firemen or the departmental committee, or a combination of the two. Fortunately for the LCC, the men accepted the offer on hours and pay, wrongly believing that it was a package deal and because they were reluctant to lose the new police rates of pay (including nine months' back pay in one lump sum).[39] If failing to secure the whole loaf of a 48-hour week, the representative body improved considerably the pay and hours of work of London firemen in the post-war years. Of much greater significance, firemen below the rank of station officer cast off the chains of tied housing and 'continuous duty', under which they were on duty for 24 hours a day for 330 days a year. Senior officers lost the round-the-clock hold over firemen and families on which their military regimen depended.

The inauguration of the 72-hour week, on the 'two platoon' system (nine hours a day shift, fifteen hours a night), made it necessary to increase substantially the size of the London fire brigade. During 1920 the authorised strength of the brigade rose from 1,290 to just over 1,900. The task of recruiting the 600 new firemen fell to the newly-appointed principal officer, Aylmer Firebrace. He later described the long queue of men, three and four deep, stretching down Southwark Bridge Road. According to

Firebrace the standard for entry was set high and so only one applicant in every 100 was accepted. The newcomers, eventually 800 of them, although known by the veterans of the brigade as 'The Hungry Thousand', were not typical service types from the navy. They were young men who had survived the horrors of the Flanders trenches. As such, they brought a transfusion of radical blood into the brigade and union.[40]

Middlebrook

All eyes now turned to the Departmental Committee 'to inquire into the hours, pay and conditions of service of firemen in professional fire brigades ...', the first such investigation on a national scale. The committee, chaired by Sir William Middlebrook, Liberal MP for South Leeds and experienced local government hand, took evidence between February and April 1920, submitting its report in May.[41] Three issues figured prominently in both evidence and report: pay, pensions and hours of duty. Police-firemen had been automatically granted the new rates of police pay awarded by Desborough, and many of the largest non-police brigades had followed suit. But enormous variations and complexities in pay remained, and in the majority of brigades the rate of pay was below that paid to the police. In his evidence, Jim Bradley, now representing union members in 35 brigades, asked that all firemen be paid alike for similar work. Other witnesses advocated pay parity between firemen and the police. Middlebrook recommended, therefore, that the pay of firemen should closely follow that of the police in cases where the men were available for duty for twelve hours or more a day (as opposed to the police eight-hour system), and that rates of pay should be standardised throughout the country.[42]

The evidence laid before Middlebrook concerning a pension or superannuation scheme was unanimously in favour. About 2,500 full-time professional firemen (out of 3,400) already enjoyed the benefits of a pension scheme.

These were men in the police brigades, in the LFB and in provincial brigades like Manchester, Birmingham, Leicester and Edinburgh. But there were still brigades like Glasgow, where men, old and weakened by years of arduous fire-fighting, relied upon the corporation's largesse. In consequence, the chief officer deposed, 'They hang on till they are ready for tumbling into the grave almost before they are superannuated,' with all the inhumanity and inefficiency to which this was heir.[43] Not surprisingly, Middlebrook recommended that all firemen should have the benefit of a pension scheme, based on that for the police service.[44]

Middlebrook was much less helpful when it came to hours of duty. A good part of the problem was the inconsistent evidence from firemen's representatives. Jim Bradley furiously condemned the 24 hours' continuous duty system, the existing practice in most brigades, and rejected Middlebrook's fall-back position of the 'stand-by' duty system of eight hours duty, eight hours stand-by and eight hours free, on the grounds that this led, in effect, to a sixteen-hour working day, with men still resident in fire stations.[45] Firemen in Manchester and Birmingham, still on continuous duty, also rejected 'stand-by', insisting on an eight-hour, three-shift system. Unfortunately, firemen representatives from Leicester, Glasgow, Edinburgh and Aberdeen clung to continuous duty in the hope that this would be improved by a bit of extra leave and pay.[46]

This disunity allowed Middlebrook to indulge its prejudices and recommend that the continuous duty system – in its view 'the most efficient and most economical' – be continued, but a more generous amount of leave granted. As an alternative the committee suggested that local authorities might adopt the 'stand-by' system, which would require little additional accommodation and an increase in manpower of only 50 per cent. The committee simply ignored the fact that most witnesses, whether representing firemen, officers or the local authorities, had nothing positive to say of the 'stand-by' system. Middlebrook categorically rejected both the eight-hour, three-shift system, and the two-platoon system (the LCC's choice), since they required a tripling and a doubling, respectively, of brigade strength and cost, and gave men insufficient fire-fighting experience.[47]

Perhaps nothing would have persuaded Middlebrook to recommend a universal departure from continuous duty. It is a pity, however, that a more united and concerted effort was not made by firemen's representatives to rid the service of this most vicious of systems, particularly since in the immediate post-war period continuous duty was reeling, hit by the conviction, shared by many echelons of the service, that in modern industrial society men could not always be at the employer's beck and call, even if residential quarters were provided.[48] That so many firemen held fast to continuous duty is explicable only by the inertia of 'better the devil you know', by the fear of losing quarters at a time of severe housing shortage, by the hope that long hours of duty would lead to pay in excess of police rates (as in Birkenhead) and by the preference for night duty in family quarters as opposed to the fire station.

The failure to exploit Middlebrook fully was a reflection of the still limited and diverse unionisation of the fire service. For a start, police-firemen were represented by the 'in-house' Police Federation, formed after the second police strike of 31 July 1919, as embodied in the Police Act of that year. It meant that police-firemen, who constituted over half of the professional fire service in the provinces, were strictly prohibited from membership of a trade union. The Firemen's Trade Union, led by Gamble and Bradley, represented around 1,000 firemen from 35 brigades, including the London Fire Brigade, the brigades around London (namely Acton, Beckenham, Bromley, Croydon, Ealing, Finchley, Hendon, Hornsey, Hounslow, Isleworth, Richmond, Walthamstow, Willesden, Wimbledon and Wood Green), the Bank of England and Beckton chemical brigades, and firemen privately employed by music halls, hotels and theatres. The FTU was affiliated to the London Trades Council, and expected soon to affiliate to the Trades Union Congress.[49]

Most professional firemen in the provinces, where in a union, were members either of the Municipal Employees'

Association (as in Glasgow), or the NUCW (as in Edinburgh, where, in addition, skilled men among the firemen commonly stayed with their craft union), or the Workers' Union. The latter body, more strictly known as the fire brigade branch of the Amalgamated Society of Gas, Municipal and General Workers, represented two-thirds of the 200 men of the Birmingham brigade, and around 100 Manchester firemen, in negotiations with the respective Watch Committees.[50] As we have already seen, Manchester council outflanked the demand of the Workers' Union for an eight-hour day by merging firemen with the police force. From November 1920 the welfare of Manchester firemen lay with the Police Federation.

The collective representation of firemen was further complicated by the existence of two organisations which long predated the Firemen's Trade Union, and were recognised by the Home Office and the local authorities. They were the National Fire Brigades Association (until 1919 the National Fire Brigades Union) and the Professional Fire Brigades Association (until 1920 the Association of Professional Fire Brigade Officers). Both bodies felt competent to discuss the wages, hours and pensions of firemen, and hence opposed the call for trade union recognition in 1918. Indeed, the National Fire Brigades Union, representing officers and men in the voluntary brigades, offered its strike-breaking services to the Chief Officer of the London Fire Brigade in September 1918. In the post-war years, however, the Professional Fire Brigades Association actively pressed for a government committee to investigate conditions of service throughout the country, and subsequently pressed the Home Secretary and local councils to move quickly towards implementation of the Middlebrook recommendations.[51]

The FTU participated in this campaign to get the Middlebrook recommendations implemented. In July 1920 Jim Bradley informed the Home Secretary, Edward Shortt, that firemen were in a state of serious unrest in many parts of the country, through the failure of local authorities to adopt Middlebrook. He urged the Home Secretary to make the granting of the recommended rate of pay 'compulsory upon the Authorities'. Other than despatching the report to local authorities, however, the Home Office declined to act, arguing that the fire service was a purely local one, that it was for the local authorities to decide whether or not to implement Middlebrook and that it was not for central government to introduce legislation requiring local councils to adopt a particular scale of pay or pension scheme. The position adopted by the Home Office wrecked any chance of improving pay and conditions across the board. Implementation of Middlebrook was very patchy. Some provincial brigades received a pay increase; some brigades gained a pension scheme under the 1922 Local Government Superannuation Act. As for hours of work, continuous duty remained the standard system of most non-police brigades. Yet the Middlebrook award did serve as a platform on which the union could attract firemen in the small, non-police brigades in the inter-war years.[52]

By the early 1920s securing improvements in conditions of service had to take a back seat to resisting attacks upon wage rates, particularly in London. The Lloyd George government, in an attempt to reverse the war-induced inflation in prices and wages, appointed a committee, chaired by Sir Eric Geddes, to find economies in public expenditure. One result of the Geddes Axe was that in July 1922 the London County Council enforced a contribution of 2.5 per cent towards pension, to be deducted from the pay of uniformed staff. This in no way contravened parity with the police, since the latter already paid a similar contribution. A year later the LCC was back at the door, asking for a 20 per cent reduction in the pay of the 1,800 firemen and sub-officers, which was commensurate with the fall in the cost of living since December 1919 when the existing wage rates had been fixed. The LCC denied having pledged always to follow police rates, and insisted upon reviewing fire brigade pay 'independently of any comparison with that of the police'. The Representative Body countered by declaring that 'there was no reason to make any reduction in their pay so long as none was made in the pay of the police'. In June 1923 the issue was referred to the Industrial Court, which called on

Middlebrook in defence of its judgment. 'It is too soon yet to make a break with the scheme which places the London fire brigade and the police more or less on an equality ...'[53]

By its stand the Representative Body of the London Fire Brigade resisted wage cuts more effectively than other groups of firemen. Too many provincial councils succeeded in reducing wages and other costs with little regard to the efficiency of the fire service. No greater proof appeared of the deleterious impact of the cuts and the continued inadequacies of fire cover than the events in January 1922 in West Hartlepool, Durham (population 24,000), where a timber-yard fire jumped the surrounding road and went on to destroy 60 houses, rendering over 100 families homeless. The single motorised fire engine (with its superintendent and six men) was quickly overwhelmed, and antediluvian, horse-drawn steamers had to be used. Reinforcing brigades arrived, but found difficulty in attaching their pipes to local hydrants. This parlous state of affairs was not peculiar to West Hartlepool, as was borne out by the evidence given to the Royal Commission on Fire Brigades and Fire Prevention, whose sadly verbose and equivocal report of August 1923 was predictably pigeon-holed.[54]

The Firemen's Trade Union

These years were, in consequence, an uphill struggle for the limited membership and slender resources of the Firemen's Trade Union, which now requires a fuller assessment. The union was unavoidably dominated by the London Fire Brigade branch and hence had a somewhat lop-sided and disjointed appearance. This was reflected in the composition of the executive council. In addition to the general secretary and assistant secretary, seven members were of, and elected by, the London Fire Brigade, two members came from the other public brigades (such as East and West Ham, Bradford and Birmingham) and three members represented privately employed firemen. In 1922, however, a falling out with the private firemen's section, probably over the very object of trade unionism, led to the departure of the men who had sired the union.[55] Jim Bradley eventually took Gamble's place as general secretary.

In London, of course, the union was fettered by the fact that the LCC dealt only with the Representative Body and, in its relations with the uniformed staff recognised no union. The position was only further weakened by Bradley's agreement in October 1921 with the Chief Officer, A.R. Dyer, to keep the business of the union distinct from that of the Representative Body. This was expected to obtain, also, when firemen and sub-officers were given leave to attend meetings of the Representative Body. It seems, moreover, that this agreement was made without the endorsement or even the knowledge, to begin with, of the executive council.[56]

Matters improved, however, when the London station officers made advances to the union. The officers were determined to restore their sphere of influence, which the union had seemingly eroded. By casting off their ineffective staff committee and by joining the Representative Body and the union (of which 62 of the 79 station officers were members by April 1922) they hoped to forge a more cordial relationship with the lower ranks. Not surprisingly, the Fire Brigade Committee of the LCC objected that this would be subversive to discipline, and consistently declined to allow station officers to become part of the Representative Body. By the end of 1923 all station officers had resigned from the union, despite the efforts of Herbert Morrison, secretary of the London Labour Party, who tried unsuccessfully to get the LCC to remind station officers that, despite their exclusion from the Representative Body, they could remain members of a trade union.[57]

In the preface to the early rules of the FTU the stated aim of the organisation was decidedly inoffensive: 'Our object is not to do anything either indiscreet or illegal, but to protect and advance the interests of members of the Union ...' Political activity was not an object, and the first ballot on the creation of a political fund failed to gain the required two-thirds majority. In 1922, however, another ballot on political action carried by a majority of 676 (1,029 for, 353 against). The political levy would, it was hoped, allow the union to advance the question of compulsory pensions in parliament and to support candidates for election to local councils.[58]

Most whole-time firemen in the country were covered by a superannuation scheme, either under the Police Pensions Act, 1921, in the case of police-firemen, or under powers conferred by local acts, as in the case of the London Fire Brigade. Yet some 800 of the 4,000 professional firemen in non-police brigades still had no pension rights. The union wished to rectify this anomaly, but the Professional Fire Brigades Association was, in truth, the organisation that secured the Fire Brigade Pensions Act, 1925, which provided a half-pay pension after 25 years' service, two-thirds pay after 30 years. Pensions were also to be given to men injured on duty and invalided out and to widows of men killed on duty.[59]

The union then turned to direct representation at the local level. In 1925 the FTU paid the election expenses of George Mills, who stood as Labour candidate for the LCC seat of South Poplar. Mills was not a fireman, but he promised to uphold the firemen's interests. Potentially more significant, in 1928 the union's general secretary, Jim Bradley, was nominated to contest the Bethnal Green seat. Bradley had by now, however, parted company with the Labour Party, believing it to have abandoned the road to socialism. He had become a member of the Advisory Council of the National Left Wing Movement, the body established by the Communist Party to reverse the Labour Party's opposition to CP affiliation. In the LCC election, therefore, Bradley stood as one of the two unofficial candidates supported by the Communist Party. Inevitably, he fell foul of the determination on the part of the national and the London Labour Party to avoid all association with Communist councillors or fellow-travellers, to scotch the CP initiative of the United Front. A deputation from the London Labour Party, headed by Herbert Morrison, persuaded the union's executive council to withdraw its support for Bradley. In the next annual report, the EC euphemistically stated that 'certain matters militated most strongly against [Bradley's] successful return.' Shortly afterwards, however, Bradley returned to the Labour Party fold.[60]

In the most significant political event of the trade union world, the General Strike of 1926, firemen took no direct part. The Askwith award had, of course, prohibited firemen in the London Fire Brigade from taking part in an industrial dispute, so all firemen were granted exemption by the TUC from withdrawing their labour. However, when the government-run *British Gazette* incorrectly reported that the union was opposed to the strike (and that firemen had used water hoses on other trade unionists), firemen decided to assist the strike financially by volunteering a 5 per cent levy on their wages.[61]

For the leadership of the FTU it must at times have seemed that the union was proceeding on the principle of 'one step forward, two steps back'. The membership of the union fluctuated during the 1920s, but what the executive council termed 'a distinct downward tendency' sent membership to a new low in 1927. Lack of contributions even led to publication of *Firefighter*, the union paper, being suspended for the December quarter. A Special Conference in October appointed J.H. Desmond to the post of national organiser, his job being to increase membership. At the 1928 annual conference, Bro. Hanson (Bradford) urged Desmond to visit Yorkshire, where brigades like Halifax and Keighley were ripe for organisation. The Special Conference also extended the scope of membership by admitting auxiliary volunteer and retained firemen to the union.[62]

As the executive council faced the difficult task of building up the union, it lost Jim Bradley, who died on 17 March 1929. What obituary should we write for this pioneer of firemen's trade unionism? James Joseph William Bradley, born on 6 May 1867, in a Marylebone fire station, was the son of a London Fire Brigade engineer and station officer.[63] Little is known of his early contact with the labour movement, though it is claimed he was briefly a member of the Social Democratic Federation, a Marxist body whose dismissal of the trade unions as bastions of capitalism

Bradley could not accept. He mixed with some of the most prominent union leaders and political agitators of the day: Tom Mann, Ben Tillett, John Burns, Keir Hardie and Eleanor Marx. Subsequent contact with the SDF came, ironically, through his job as park-keeper in Victoria Park, enforcing the LCC by-laws against public speaking.

In the early 1900s Bradley was secretary of the Bethnal Green branch of the Municipal Employees' Association, and a member of the MEA executive. In 1907 he helped launch the National Union of Corporation Workers, in which he played a prominent part, eventually becoming president. He it was who recruited the first firemen into the NUCW and who agreed to be secretary of their fire brigade branch, testimony to his knowledge and understanding of the firemen's job. It is in the presidential address to the NUCW's annual conference in 1912, moreover, that we glimpse a rare piece of evidence of Bradley's authentic radical voice. 'There is a fierce conflict going on between Capital and Labour', said Bradley, referring to the 'Labour Unrest' of the pre-war years. Through it all, continued Bradley,

> there runs a grand display of solidarity, that new-born spirit and cohesion among the different grades of workers that few people thought possible. These examples of this great spirit will teach the capitalist that the workers are not so insignificant as they have imagined them to be ... This revolt of the workers has driven the capitalist class into such a fit of alarm that is so great that they are trying various methods to kill the new born strength of the workers. The country has been subjected to martial law; troops with ball cartridges sent to all parts of the Kingdom to overawe the workers ... but in spite of it all the workers are not overawed, and are determined not to return to work until peace is proclaimed – a peace which must mean increased wages, shorter hours, better conditions, a greater share of life's comforts and the right of combination ...[64]

Stirring stuff for the NUCW, which generally shied away from industrial action.

Bradley was active in labour politics, too. He was a founder member of Bethnal Green Labour Party, and in February 1908 he stood as 'Trade Union Labour Candidate who has no interests but labour to serve ...' for the Bethnal Green council. He failed to get elected on that occasion, but was successful just after the war. He was also successful in elections to the local Board of Guardians, the body which dispensed poor relief to the unemployed, the sick and the widowed. Finally, as we have seen, he tried to secure election to the LCC in 1928 with Communist assistance. His main contribution to the labour movement, however, rests with the Firemen's Trade Union, which he championed for ten arduous years.

During this time, he combated the ingrained resistance to trade unionism and collective action on the part of a uniformed, disciplined workforce recruited largely from the armed services. He contested the arguments presented by the LCC to block the introduction of a negotiating body between itself and the brigade. If Bradley does on occasion seem too conciliatory towards the LCC, particularly in his acceptance of a no-strike clause, in his renunciation of supportive industrial action and in his willingness to distance the union further from the deliberations of the Representative Body, he did ensure that not all firemen were debarred, as were all policemen, from being trade unionists, and he kept alive a civilian alternative to the prevailing semi-military model of fire service organisation.

The FBU in the 1930s

Bradley's place as general secretary of the union and 'spokesman' of the London Representative Body was taken by former president Percy Kingdom, a one-time seaman, veteran of the Corporation Workers' Union and a retired London sub-officer. Kingdom was a dour, blunt gladiator. He was much less the canny trade union negotiator than Bradley and his links with the political labour movement more tenuous. As leader of the union, re-named the Fire Brigades Union in 1930 (to end the confusion with railway and ships' firemen), and as 'spokesman' in London, Kingdom had a baptism of fire. 1931 was a year of heavy unemployment, financial crisis and a National Government pledged to financial austerity. Under the Economy Act, 1931, the Home Office reduced the pay of police forces for a period of one year.[65] It was only a matter of time before the LCC would require an equivalent sacrifice from the firemen, for there was no greater defender of police parity than the Council when it came to *reducing* pay!

In November 1931 the LCC demanded temporary reductions of 5s. 6d. a week and 4s. 3d. a week in the pay of sub-officers and firemen, respectively, for one year, a deduction of around 5 per cent. Kingdom informed the Chief Officer that such reductions were acceptable only if the council introduced the same rates of pay and hours of duty as obtained in the Metropolitan Police force. If you want parity in pay, said the firemen, we want parity in hours, to wit a three eight-hour shift system, already operative in some fifty provincial police brigades. The Industrial Court's ruling went against the firemen, however, the court stating in February 1932:

> While ... in determining the wages of men in the London Fire Brigade regard may well be had to the wages paid in the Metropolitan Police Force it does not follow that in this or other respects the conditions of employment should be uniform in the two services.[66]

In short, conditions of employment were similar but not identical; wages did, but hours of duty did not, come within the principle of parity. A few months later the court again upheld the council, when the latter fixed rates for new entrants to the brigade related to rates fixed for police new entrants. For the 1,800 sub-officers and firemen of the London Fire Brigade a fighting retreat was on.[67]

A year later, again in line with further reductions in police pay, the LCC demanded that the reduction in firemen's pay be set at 10 per cent, or 11 shillings a week for sub-officers and 8s. 6d. a week for firemen. Once more the Representative Body requested the *quid pro quo* of a three-shift system and improved rent allowances. And once more the Industrial Court found for the council.[68] The pattern held when the LCC asked for the 10 per cent reduction to continue beyond February 1934. On this occasion, however, the council got more than it bargained for.

A board of arbitration, chaired by the former Chief Inspector of Mines, Sir Richard Redmayne, decided the issue. When the nominees for the opposing sides, Frank Pick for the Council and A.M. Wall (secretary to the London Trades Council) for the men, failed to agree on the terms of the award, Redmayne played umpire and upheld the council's case. The award came, however, on the understanding:

> that the parity with the Metropolitan Police force will be maintained in respect both of increments and reductions in rates of pay, without reservation, and that should this practice not be adhered to by the London County Council the whole question of the rates of pay of the fire brigade shall be immediately open to revision.[69]

Here was an unambiguous assertion that parity applied to increases as well as reductions of pay, and the Redmayne Award, as it became known, was to act as sheet anchor of the firemen's case in many subsequent battles with the LCC. It was not much to show for years of reduced pay, but it was a harbinger of better times.

In 1934 the Economy Act, 1931, was rescinded. When half the police pay cuts was restored the principle of parity obliged the LCC to do the same for firemen. Rent allowances were also increased slightly. In late 1934 the Representative Body signalled the next major tussle when it asked for early consideration of a 48-hour week, in place of the existing 72-hour week. The incentive to increase the stake came from the fact that the Labour Party had, for the first time in its history, won control of the LCC. Labour had wrested control from the conservative Municipal Reform Party. A Labour-controlled Council would, it was widely assumed, surely be more sympathetic to the firemen than its predecessor. It boded well when Edward Cruse, a former trade union secretary, was appointed chairman of the Fire Brigade Committee.[70]

Claims for a 48-hour week dated back to 1918, when the fire brigade branch of the NUCW asked the LCC to institute shifts of eight hours' duty within twelve months of the Armistice. The question had then been resolved by the compromise of extra pay and a two-shift system (or a 72-hour week), on the proviso that no further application for a 48-hour week would be put prior to June 1922. Before that date was reached the Middlebrook Committee muddied the water with its statement that the eight-hour, three-shift system was too costly and unsuitable for the fire service; and that police rates should apply to a brigade only where the men were available for duty for twelve hours or more.[71] But Middlebrook had reported nearly fifteen years before, and so in June 1934 the Representative Body considered it was high time to discuss a three-shift system again.

Kingdom reminded the Chief Officer, Major C.C.B. Morris, that while the work load of firemen had increased no change had been made in the brigade's hours of duty. Yet working hours throughout the country had continued to decline, and both the river pilot section of the brigade and the LCC ambulance service worked a 48-hour week. Health and efficiency considerations warranted a shorter week, concluded Kingdom, as witness the large amount of sickness in the brigade.

The arguments against change were the cost of a three-shift system, approximately £200,000 a year (although money was found for a new headquarters and new appliances), and the fact that there was no precedent for such a system. Taking the fire brigades adjacent to the London County area, while some (East Ham, West Ham, Walthamstow and Tottenham) had adopted a two-shift system since the war, most (including Croydon, Willesden, Kingston and Ealing) were still on the continuous-duty system. Edinburgh, too, with a population of half a million and a brigade 104 strong, was on continuous duty. Finally, as for the police brigades (in, say, Bristol, Liverpool, Manchester and Hull), while the ordinary police worked an eight-hour shift, those engaged on fire brigade duty did not work less than an average of twelve hours a day. In

December 1934, therefore, the council came in with its decision to make no change in duty hours.[72]

Labour council or no, the Representative Body was not prepared to accept this decision, and wheeled out the big guns of the London Trades Council. A delegate meeting of the LTC passed a resolution, asking Herbert Morrison, leader of the LCC and secretary of the London Labour Party, to allow a deputation to go before the Policy Committee of the LCC Labour Party, respecting firemen's hours of duty. Morrison was irritated by this appeal to the wider labour movement, bypassing the council's established machinery for the discussion of grievances. He penned a hard-hitting letter to *London News*, the monthly paper of the London Labour Party, in which he questioned why the LCC had been singled out for attack, when the union had nowhere established the 48-hour week, even in districts with Labour councils, and had not yet won the 72-hour week in many brigades.[73]

Morrison added insult to injury, however, by suggesting that the weekly average of 'working' time was 29 out of the 72 duty hours. As for the night shift, the average 'working' time was under 25 per cent, with firemen allowed to sleep in their clothes on trestles in or close to the appliance room. As such, a fireman's duties did not bear comparison with those of a policeman – and Morrison, as a policeman's son, claimed to speak with some authority in this respect. The final straw was Morrison's nostalgic reference to the responsible methods of general secretary Jim Bradley (whom Morrison had ousted as LCC candidate), in contrast to the hostility displayed by Kingdom.

Kingdom was stung into replying in the next month's *London News*. Basic working hours were not less than 40 hours out of 72, he declared. More to the point, 'firemen do not want to rest on trestles; they do not want to remain at work to "play games" [a response to Morrison's remark about firemen on the day shift playing billiards]. They want to go home like other workers when they have completed eight hours.' Kingdom concluded by reminding Morrison that the labour movement was committed to a 40-hour week for all workers, in view of which, 'a most unreasonable and even hostile attitude has been adopted towards both the union and the movement of which it is part'.[74]

The entire episode was an unfortunate, although probably inevitable, clash between the FBU and the leader of the Labour group on the LCC. Above and beyond the industrial issue of duty hours, however, politics figured. Herbert Morrison came up through local government, not the trade union movement. His political goal was to create an electoral machine in the London Labour Party and a brand of municipal socialism (efficient, economical and responsible) capable of winning and keeping control of the London County Council. No trade union, much less one which sheltered Communist Party sympathisers, could be allowed to impair this strategy. While money was found for dual purpose fire engines – or 'pump escapes' – none was made available for improvements in firemen's conditions of service. Firemen were sacrificed on the altar of Morrison's moderate caucus politics.[75]

The Representative Body could, of course, have put the matter before the Industrial Court under the Askwith Award. Were the decision to go against the 48-hour week, however, it would be written down and might be used in evidence against them. Hence it was not until 1937 and the advent of a new council, still Labour-controlled, that the FBU tried again. By this date the issue had got caught up in the air raid defence of London. Kingdom argued, therefore, that by establishing a three-shift system the LCC would gain a further 900 trained men, making 2,700 firemen available in time of war. An enlarged permanent staff would, in turn, facilitate the training of auxiliary firemen. With war clouds building up, Morrison conceded that the new council would look closely at the question of a reduction of duty hours.[76]

Even so, it was early 1939 before the Representative Body was offered a 60-hour week, still on a system of two shifts, and with strings attached concerning the training of, and secondment to, the Auxiliary Fire Service. The reduction from 72 to 60 hours would be made by granting an extra leave day. By May the Representative Body had accepted the offer, though still chafing at the strings; implementation of the 60-hour week was set for 1 January 1940.[77] But fate was cruel: the long-delayed improvement in hours crashed into the Second World War. Not only was the 60-hour week put into cold storage but the 72-hour week was replaced by continuous duty!

Before examining the war years, however, we should examine the activity of the Fire Brigades Union in the country at large in the 1930s. Membership figures were on the rise again: 2,279 in 1934, 2,386 in 1935, 2,500 in 1937, and 2,800 in 1938 (1,700 of whom were in the London Fire Brigade). On the outbreak of war over 3,000 firemen were in the FBU. Only about a quarter of these members contributed to the political fund. Through the work of George Hayes, the assistant general secretary, many new branches were formed: Blackpool, Bolton, Stoke-on-Trent, Swindon, Warrington and West Hartlepool. By May 1938 there were union members in 62 brigades in addition to the LFB. The Birmingham brigade, which proved an extremely tough nut to crack, had FBU members in its ranks by the late 1930s.[78]

The union still faced the frustrating problem of the General and Municipal Workers' Union, the Transport and General Workers' Union and the Public Employees' Union recruiting firemen as members. When a young John Horner raised this issue at the annual conference in 1937 Kingdom was pessimistic about getting the big battalions to stop poaching: 'your prospects of getting them to agree that you, and you alone, shall organise firemen, is as remote as the chance of a celluloid dog trying to get through hell ...'[79] In London, however, the union was close to securing 100 per cent membership in the brigade. This was made possible by an increase in the recruitment of sub-officers: practically all 200 sub-officers in the LFB were in the union in 1936. They did, however, insist upon being organised as a separate branch of the Representative Body. The union agreed, rather than lose them.[80]

In the provinces, the FBU struggled to get the economy cuts of the early 1930s eliminated, to negotiate the

Middlebrook rates of pay where councils still dragged their feet (as in Gloucester, Warrington and Greenock) and to replace continuous duty with a two-shift system. The annual conference in 1937 was told of success, in this latter regard, in Bolton and Willesden, while pressure was being applied to the councils of Stoke, Bournemouth and Southampton. The essential problem of winning provincial improvements lay with the Trades Disputes and Trades Unions Act of 1927, imposed in the wake of the General Strike, which put restrictions on trade unions representing municipal workers. The result was that few local authorities had recognised machinery for settling firemen's wages and working conditions. Nor was there any statutory right, as existed in London, to refer disputes to an independent tribunal. Failing a system of arbitration firemen had no alternative but to accept council decisions.[81]

The FBU finally began to devote more attention to the larger political questions of the labour movement. In 1936 union funds went to the Spanish Republicans. At the annual conference of that year, in a resolution concerning the steps required to safeguard peace and democracy against fascist governments, ultra-pacifism came under attack. In a radical speech, Harry Short, a delegate from East Ham, warned against trusting their own National Government to fight for peace and democracy. Short's views were seconded by John Horner, of the LFB, who called for a 'Peace front' against the fascist countries made up of the British Labour Party, French Socialists and Russian Communists. The resolution was carried overwhelmingly.[82]

At the next annual conference Harry Short and S.J. (Chick) Merrells pressed the executive to organise an educational scheme through the National Council of Labour Colleges. Horner supported the resolution on the grounds that firemen, at least in London, had a limited class consciousness: 'They do not understand that when one section of the working class moves forward, whether it be the London 'busmen or the Haworth miners ... it helps them with their demands on the London County Council.'[83] This time, however, opposition came from Kingdom and the assistant general secretary, Harold Gibbs, who felt the union's education ought not to be restricted to a Marxist educational body like the NCLC. At the same conference, indeed, Kingdom urged delegates not to become involved in any political sect; consideration of union problems, he said, should never be conditioned by such external influences.[84]

These political differences reflected a growing separation between an 'old guard' of union officials, headed by Percy Kingdom, concerned exclusively with firemen's pay and pensions, and increasingly discomfited by the thought of the disruptions that war would bring, and a group of slightly younger Executive Council members whose minds were occupied increasingly by whether the union (and whether they as firemen) would survive the war at all. The war acted as wedge between these two contingents until the 'old guard' simply fled the field, leaving the union in the hands of Harry Short, Chick Merrells, Jim Bradley (son of the former general secretary) and John Horner.[85]

The 'new guard' inherited a union still dominated by firemen from the thoroughly insular London Fire Brigade, men who considered themselves the elite of the fire service and assumed an attitude of *de haut en bas* towards provincial firemen. In outer London and the provinces, with police brigades off-limits to recruitment, the union struggled to hold its bridgehead in brigades like East Ham, Stoke-on-Trent and Bradford where age-old problems persisted. A scattered, isolated workforce, often still tied to the rack of continuous duty, schooled in the 'service code' of drill, discipline and duty, was poor soil for the plant of trade unionism. The FBU, moreover, was not alone in seeking to recruit this workforce, and the large general unions also peddled their wares. Local councils preferred to deal with firemen's grievances through the conduit of senior officers, not trade union officials. Most councils declined to establish negotiating machinery through which collective representation could function.

Ten years later, however, the Fire Brigades Union was the prime representative for professional firemen and the Home Office accepted that the union had an integral part to play in the development of the post-war fire service. For this sea change in the fortunes of the FBU the Second World War was directly responsible.

The Road to War

The fire hazards of war were massively transformed by the increased range of aircraft and the development of the incendiary bomb. Government preparations for defence had inevitably to include a large fire-fighting organisation. The first step towards the planning of emergency fire-fighting measures was the May 1936 report of the Departmental Committee on Fire Brigade Services. The Riverdale Committee report dealt both with the planning of emergency measures and the improvement of peace-time fire services, on which an emergency organisation would be built, and which left considerable room for improvement.

Britain had only 4,000 whole-time firemen, a good half of whom were in the London area, plus 2,000 police-firemen, and about 12,000 part-time retained and volunteer firemen. This motley crew was attached to hundreds of separate fire authorities in England and Wales, ranging from the large and efficient London Fire Brigade to the inadequately-manned and poorly-equipped parish brigade, the legendary 'parish pump'. With the exception of the London County Council, no fire authority was under any statutory obligation to maintain a brigade. There was no central supervision of local provision and thus no national standard of manning, equipment or efficiency. And few brigades had made arrangements with neighbouring outfits for mutual support. Riverdale sought to improve this ramshackle and archaic organisation. The FBU, it should be added, refused to appear before the committee, reflecting the traditional attitude of the union's leadership which wanted no part in shaping national fire service policy, no part in management.[86]

Many of Riverdale's recommendations were implemented in the Fire Brigades Act, 1938. For the first time a general duty was imposed on local authorities to provide fire protection. A Fire Service Commission, appointed by the Home Secretary, was to review the provision of fire cover. No central grant was given to fire authorities, contrary to Riverdale. Nor was any attempt made to provide for standard conditions with regard to pay, accommodation and duty hours. The Middlebrook recommendations, written on paper discoloured by age, were as permissive as before. In spite of the fact, moreover, that parish councils were deprived of their fire brigade powers, and that police brigades were to be phased out, there were still 1,440 separate fire authorities in England and Wales, 228 in Scotland. The fire service remained a patchwork quilt of small, under-resourced units.[87]

How effective the 1938 Act would have been in improving peace-time services, it is impossible to say. War overtook it. The Air Raid Precautions Act, 1937, was activated, charging local authorities with the duty of recruiting and training a volunteer force of auxiliaries to supplement the peace-time resources. On 1 September 1939 the Auxiliary Fire Service was mobilised: 89,000 men and 6,000 women grafted on to and soon overshadowing the regular fire brigades.[88]

The size of many brigades multiplied tenfold. No fewer than 23,000 auxiliaries smothered the few thousand regulars in the London Fire Brigade. They came from all walks of life: from factories, offices, boardrooms, courts of law and universities.[89] A large number of London taxi-drivers joined up, proffering their cabs as towing vehicles for the trailer pumps.[90] Aged between 25 and 50, many were well educated, with executive experience in business or the professions. The regulars, along with reservists (or retired firemen), had the task of training this immense, heterogeneous influx of recruits to handle power appliances, to get into the centre of the fire (a London fire-fighting tradition), to withstand the heat and smoke and to rescue the trapped. AFS men long remembered these well-meaning instructors. Stephen Spender recalled language of 'great idiomatic allusive richness'. ' "Now sometimes we 'as ter use evil ter expel evil," ' prefaced the demonstration of a carbon-tetra-chloride extinguisher, emitting phosgenous gas. ' "In other words, when using this extinguisher, use yer common or garden, use yer loaf." '[91]

The auxiliaries were considered by the authorities to be incapable of officering themselves, having no experience of fire-fighting. Large numbers of regular firemen, particularly in London, were therefore promoted to the rank of sub-officer and put in charge of a sub-station. Some rose to the occasion, but many more found it difficult to gain the respect of the auxiliaries. Officers were eventually drawn from the London AFS, but were allowed little say in the organisation and control of auxiliary firemen. Only in smaller brigades were the auxiliaries run as a separate unit under their own AFS officers.

The administrative arrangements for the pay, uniform and accommodation of auxiliaries were woefully inadequate. Basic pay was £3 a week for men, £2 a week for women. This was lower than the regular fireman's wage, and meant, at least for those from highly paid jobs, a serious fall in living standards. The newcomers were handed a steel helmet, rubber boots and overalls, but had a long wait for tunic, trousers and waterproof leggings. Sub-station accommodation ranged from cramped and ill-equipped for cooking or sleeping at best, to insanitary and rat-infested at worst. Early in the war some auxiliaries had to sleep under railway arches. London auxiliaries were incarcerated in such conditions for two days and two nights, under the duty system of 48 hours on, 24 hours off, which quickly replaced the continuous duty system. Finally, the Personal Injuries (Civilian) Scheme was a pitiful insurance scheme. After two weeks' injury pay or three weeks' sick pay, auxiliaries were discharged and forced to apply for the means-tested benefits of the Unemployment Assistance Board.

In a word, the auxiliaries were, as the historian of the Fire Service observed, 'worse paid, worse equipped and worse clothed than the regulars to whom they were attached'.[92] Little wonder that auxiliaries left the service for the armed forces or for the higher wages increasingly to be found in industry. The wastage of trained firemen grew to serious proportions when, during the phoney war, the press, public and parliament made hostile reference to 'army dodgers' and 'the darts brigade'. By June 1940 the government had to deny firemen, regular or auxiliary, the right to resign without permission. Little wonder, too, that relations between the AFS and the regular service were, to say the least, strained. The auxiliaries bridled at subordination to better paid regulars, whose leadership was at times found wanting. The regulars resented having their stations overrun by auxiliarics, all of whom needed training (for which the professionals got little or no extra pay) and who were exempt from the standing discipline code.[93]

The behaviour of the regulars, if ostrich-like, was understandable. They had fought long and hard to secure better conditions of service, and in London were promised a 60-hour week. Then came the war and continuous duty. The 60-hour week disappeared, as the London regulars saw it, into Herbert Morrison's fridge for the war's duration.[94] When, a week after the outbreak of war, continuous duty was replaced by an 112-hour week, it hardly seemed cause for celebration. On top of this came the untrained, underpaid and unorganised auxiliaries. The natural reaction was to treat them as dilutees who threatened to depress the pay and conditions of service of regular firefighters. London firemen, in particular, stood on their professional dignity and wanted nothing to do with these greenhorns.

The 'old guard' of the Fire Brigades Union shared these sentiments. The guard, however, was changing. The change of leadership and union direction was not the result of any sustained and policy-based campaign. What simply started as a way of bringing to the fore the question of the union's policy (or lack thereof) towards the AFS, turned into a fight to save the union from total collapse. In early 1939 Bradley, Randall and Merrells, all London firemen recruited with 'The Hungry Thousand', nominated the 27 year-old John Horner for the post of general secretary. Horner had joined the LFB in 1933, after service in the Merchant Navy. At this stage the nomination was a protest at poor leadership on the issue of the AFS, not a serious attempt to subvert that leadership. No member could stand for election except on the say-so of the executive council; this was now denied to Horner on account of his inexperience and radical politics. Unexpectedly, the general secretary, Percy Kingdom, then resigned, without explanation, and the executive council approved the unopposed nomination of assistant general secretary, Harold Gibbs. When the London branch objected to this executive self-recruitment, Gibbs agreed to stand for election, and Horner was again nominated, this time securing executive council approval. The scene was set for the annual conference at Finsbury Town Hall in May.

Horner immediately signified his disagreement with union policy by calling upon the executive council to respond positively to the challenge of the AFS. After this resolution was carried, and after full-time officials were deprived of their power to nominate candidates for official positions, the remaining leadership resigned. In less than one month all the union officials had, in effect, disappeared; the war, which would put all and everything to the test, was a couple of months away. Head office in City Road was locked up. Robert Willis, Secretary of the London Trades Council, then stepped in and organised an election for general secretary on 1 June, when Horner convincingly defeated Harold Gibbs and George Hayes. A month later, Harry Short and 'Chick' Merrells were elected assistant secretary and organising secretary respectively. In significant juxtaposition, Horner took up the reins of office two weeks after the Duke and Duchess of Kent, accompanied by Commander Firebrace, now Regional Fire Officer for London, reviewed 20,000 auxiliaries in Hyde Park.[95]

'This Transient Horde of Wartime Auxiliaries'

John Horner's attitude to the AFS was not that of the 'old regulars' (which makes his election as general secretary all the more puzzling, since for most regulars this was the only issue). On the outbreak of war he telegraphed each member of the executive council asking for permission to set up a separate section of the union for the AFS. The result of this irregular ballot remains a secret, but Horner acted as if he had a mandate to organise what Sir Walter Citrine, general secretary of the TUC, pessimistically dubbed 'this transient horde of wartime auxiliaries', whose lack of common bond, Citrine contended, made them impossible to organise.[96] Endorsement of this unconstitutional procedure was sought at the first wartime conference of the regular section of the union in May 1940. Horner had his work cut out to win over hostile anti-AFS delegates and to heal the union's divisive wounds.

Horner stressed that speed had been of the essence. The executive council took the view, said Horner, that the AFS could neither be left unorganised, nor left to any other group to organise. The executive felt 'that if the Fire Brigades Union was to be saved, if its identity was to be preserved, if the union were to survive the onslaught of the war, then the AFS would have to be organised *in* this union'.[97] He also emphasised, however, that each section of the union, professional and AFS, would have its own management committee, and that each committee would deal with the affairs of that section alone. An enlarged executive council, moreover, would include six representatives from the AFS management committee, thereby leaving the regulars' representatives in a majority. He appealed to delegates, finally, to vote for unity between the two sections of the new fire service. Delegates then spoke for and against the resolution, but the vote went unanimously in Horner's favour.[98]

By enrolling large numbers of war auxiliaries, membership of the Fire Brigades Union leaped from 3,500 in 1939 to 66,500 (including 1,000 women) in 1940. This staggering increase was due not solely to the enrollment of auxiliaries; it included over 1,000 new members recruited into the professional section, many from previously unorganised brigades in the Midlands and the North (including Scotland), a testimony to the efforts of organising secretary Merrells, and of the two provincial organisers, Tom Murray and John McHugh. But for every one regular in the FBU, there were now fifteen auxiliaries. The official union figures, however, exaggerate recruitment in the first year of the war, since a large proportion of auxiliaries, as we have seen, left the fire service in the first six months of 1940. In consequence AFS membership of the union fell to 30,000 by November 1940. Fortunately, this was only a temporary drop, and by the summer of 1941 the FBU had 5,500 regular firemen and 66,000 auxiliaries (including 4,000 women).[99]

Most of the new recruits had no trade union experience. A few, however, had been union members, like the insurance agent who wrote to Frank Crump in October 1940. His insurance business in the East End hit by the blitz, the agent, a member of the National Amalgamated Union of Life Assurance, became a trainee in the AFS. As he told Crump:

> I don't know that I have any great ambitions to be a fireman but the pay is at least reasonable and one does keep in reasonable touch with home, even if you do only see it one day in three ... I realise, of course, that fire fighting is not going to be a picnic but I think I would rather do this than stick a bayonet in someone's guts.[100]

Many of the London cabbies brought both their taxis and experience in the TGWU. The impulse among the Hull auxiliaries to join the union came largely from experienced ex-dockers. A few other recruits were more hardened campaigners. Jack Dash, a future leader of the London dockers, volunteered for the AFS when faced with delay in joining the Navy. He was stationed in an LCC school in Bow Road, Stepney. Dash had been a member of the National Unemployed Workers' Movement, the body responsible for a series of hunger marches in the inter-war period, and was a member of the Communist Party. Before long he was elected union delegate for his fire station and represented the men in negotiations with the station officer. Bob Bagley had been an active trade unionist in the Bleachers, Dyers and Finishers Union in Lancashire and had joined the Communist Party in 1938. He refused to fight for the 'jingoists', so he joined the Oldham AFS. With help from McHugh, the FBU provincial organiser, Bagley began to recruit members on each of the

AFS stations. He went on to become a prominent member of the FBU, both during and after the war.[101]

The first task of the AFS section of the FBU was to secure official recognition. The attitude of some chief officers and local councils remained hostile. Police fire brigades were the worst offenders in this respect. In Oldham the chief officer, Mr Bellamy, refused to have anything to do with Bob Bagley until John Horner arranged a meeting between Bagley and McHugh for the FBU, and the Chief Constable, a Mr Killick (the Labour Mayor) and chief officer Bellamy. The result was that Bellamy was instructed to meet members of the Oldham area committee, given proper notice and an agreed date for the meeting. By December 1940 some 500 of the 520 Oldham auxiliaries were in the union. But by no means all nuts were so easy to crack as Oldham.[102]

The Birmingham regulars had been demanding union recognition for twenty years, but the Conservative-controlled council had consistently stonewalled. In 1939 the council deferred a decision on recognition until after the war, although it did resuscitate the Representative Committee (dead since 1922) to represent the 240 firemen before the Watch Committee. In April 1941 the Birmingham council finally agreed to recognise the union; membership among both regulars and AFS grew quickly, and a union branch office was established. Glasgow city council refused to recognise the union, despite the fact that over 90 per cent of the AFS were organised. Only nationalisation of the fire service changed the situation.[103] The biggest fight, however, took place in Manchester.

The attempt by Manchester auxiliaries to secure the promised wage of 10 shillings per day (or £3 a week), having received only 8s. 7d. per day in their first wage packet, led to instant dismissal at the hands of the Chief Constable, Sir John Maxwell. Auxiliaries were treated poorly in other respects, too. The AFS men on night duty at the Headquarters station in London Road, in order to keep them awake, were made to shovel coke stored in the basement into the middle of the floor, whitewash the brick tiles, and then throw the coke back up against the washed walls. The balloon went up in November 1940 when a police fireman, Norman Greenfield, forbidden from joining the union himself, helped the auxiliaries to organise. As secretary of the police brigade swimming club, Greenfield had seen at first hand the appalling conditions prevailing at many AFS sub-stations. One station was a bug-infested room seventeen feet long, six feet wide at one end, tapering to three feet at the other end. Eighteen men were expected to sleep there.

Greenfield sent the application forms of 28 auxiliaries, and a description of their living conditions, to union headquarters in London. Blitz damage had enforced a change of address for headquarters, however, and the undelivered forms were returned to Manchester, where they fell into Maxwell's hands. Greenfield was instantly dismissed for acting in a manner likely to bring discredit on the force, and for divulging brigade matters to someone not connected with the brigade. The Chief Constable also refused to return the application forms to the union. This was the cause of Maxwell's downfall. In February 1941 the FBU successfully sued him in Manchester County Court for the return of the forms. The case aroused widespread criticism of the police brigade system, and of Sir John Maxwell, who resigned shortly afterwards. It also promoted discussion on the city council about the right of men to improve their conditions by joining a trade union.[104]

By this date, however, the FBU had won the right to negotiate with the Home Office and with local authorities on behalf of auxiliary firemen and firewomen. Every large city except Manchester had an AFS branch of the union. This right had been won by linking with the other unions catering for civil defence workers, notably the National Federation of Building Trade Operatives (whose members were involved in rescue work) and the Transport and General Workers' Union. The general secretaries of these two unions, Richard Coppock and Ernest Bevin, together with John Horner, went to see Sir John Anderson, the Home Secretary. Anderson had been regarded as one of the very ablest of civil servants in the inter-war years, although of a pontifical bearing. In fact, Anderson could not attend, but a Deputy Under Secretary told the delegation that the Home Secretary was unimpressed by the notion of trade union organisers, potential fifth columnists, visiting fire stations and civil defence depots. According to Horner, in a story he still loves to recount, Bevin exploded at this class-prejudiced suggestion of sabotage:

> Bevin's great neck reddened and swelled. 'Tell the Government,' he said, 'that it was their class which betrayed France and Norway. Just as some of them would dig up the ground from under our feet and sell it abroad if they could get 2.5 per cent profit. It was not the workers that betrayed Norway.'[105]

Anderson withdrew his opposition and recognised the unions.

In June 1940 a National Joint Committee for Civil Defence Workers was set up, on which the FBU was the recognised spokesman for the AFS. Moreover, local authorities were formally advised to deal with firemen through their trade union. Soon, therefore, most of the 1,400 local authority areas had a branch committee of regular firemen and a branch committee of AFS men. Most issues were settled between branch committee and chief officer, more difficult complaints were passed to the appropriate committee of the local authority. In London a larger number of district committees did the job of the branch.[106] It became possible, in short, for the FBU to negotiate centrally and locally for the improvement of both AFS and regular conditions of service.

The fire of hostility between the professional and the auxiliary sections of the union was, however, still burning. It was only fully extinguished in the common fight against the blitz. In the meantime the union tried to counter the threat of dilution by bringing AFS conditions closer to those of the regulars. The issue was expressed most graphically by Horner at the first annual conference of regulars in May 1940 when he recounted his response to a London fireman dismayed at the idea of a young 'red rider' (the name for an auxiliary who rode with the regulars) getting the same rate of pay. 'I said that if that man was blind, deaf, dumb, a permanent cripple, a 100 years of age and an imbecile into the bargain, if the LCC expected that man to do a professional fireman's job, then I was prepared to claim that he should get professional rate of pay.'[107]

At the first AFS National Conference, a few days later, the union's policy was laid down in a ten-point programme. It is useful to record the more important points, and to present a progress report as of mid-1941, prior to the nationalisation of the fire service. The first point was full pay while sick or injured. The FBU led the attack against the Personal Injuries (Civilians) Scheme, which allowed two weeks' injury pay and three weeks' sick pay, by way of pamphlets, mass meetings and parliamentary lobbying. By mid-1941 thirteen weeks' injury pay and thirteen weeks' sick pay had been granted.[108] Regular firemen, in contrast, generally got full pay while sick or injured. The second point concerned an increase in basic pension rates. The third point was for wages to rise in accordance with the rise in the cost of living.

Early in 1940 the National Joint Consultative Committee submitted a claim for a 10 shilling wage increase; the government conceded 5 shillings. Four months later another claim for 10 shillings went in; another 5 shillings was granted. An auxiliary's wage was now £3 10s. a week, still below that of most regular firemen. The latter secured wage increases and additional duty bonuses from some, though by no means all, local councils. London regulars, for example, received 10 shillings additional duty and 10 shillings cost of living allowances. In London, too, over 800 'red riders', plugging the gaps caused by the recall of regulars to the colours, gained the pay and conditions of service of regulars.[109]

The fourth AFS demand concerned hours: 24 on and 24 off for London firemen, with one leave day in the week, making a 72-hour week. The AFS was the only section of the Air Raid Precautions' organisation which worked 112 hours a week, even during the 'lull' period before the blitz, and it took a heavy toll in sickness. Even so, the government declined to reduce hours in view of the shortage of personnel. The remaining points dealt with uniform, living conditions, feeding and travel vouchers. A second uniform, for example, was eventually provided, but only after the blitz had led to men going about in wet clothes for weeks. The union also continued to press for proper bedding, washing facilities, messrooms and kitchens, with varying degrees of success in different parts of the country.[110]

Issues which formed no part of the AFS programme were also tackled by the FBU. One such was the decision of the London County Council to 'unify' the London Fire Service. In March 1940 a special committee under John Wilmot, MP, chairman of the fire brigade committee, had been given the task of lowering the tension in the AFS caused by the fact that London regulars, however junior, always took charge at sub-stations. The unification scheme, adopted in 1940, created a single grade of officer. Those now appointed got London Fire Brigade rank, pay and conditions, and they commanded juniors of either regular or auxiliary service. The scheme met considerable opposition from regulars, who resented being commanded by men of AFS origin, and from auxiliaries, who felt that most of the new appointments went to regulars and to a few incompetent auxiliaries, none of whom was either examined or interviewed.[111] But since the LCC chose not to consult the FBU there was little the union could do to improve the scheme.

When the blitz arrived the union brought press and public attention to the grim fact that eight London auxiliaries, killed while fighting fires in air raids, were delivered to their widows in canvas sacks on a council lorry and that the AFS had been forced to have a whip-round to pay for the funerals, without which the men would have gone to paupers' graves. Not even the Home Office could drag its feet on this issue. In October 1940 the funeral allowance of £7 10s., which was paid to London regulars, was extended to all civil defence workers. The union was less successful in modifying the harsh features of the discipline code for auxiliaries, sent out to local authorities by the Home Office in December 1940. Any one offence by an auxiliary could be penalised by a substantial deduction from basic pay or an increase in working hours.[112]

On balance, however, the first eighteen months of the war breathed new life into the Fire Brigades Union. The AFS was solidly organised in the union, providing a massive transfusion of new blood. Union membership leaped from 3,500 in 1939 to over 70,000 two years later. Union recognition was forced on the Home Office and on practically every local authority which did not receive representations on behalf of firemen through the channel of the union. The FBU was no longer the 'Cinderella' of the trade union world. If the two sections of the service had their differences, the blitz was about to blow away all dispute. In that baptism of fire volunteers and regulars merged into one citizen army, discovering a camaraderie that laid the base for a single united union. A bigger, bolder FBU arose, Phoenix-like, from the ashes of the blitz.

The Blitz and the National Fire Service

A year after the outbreak of the war the large fire-raising raids began. The onslaught started in late August 1940 with attacks on oil installations at Pembroke Dock and Thameshaven. On 7 September the attack on London opened, affecting the commercial docks and the Woolwich Arsenal, a huge ammunition storehouse. Between 7 September and 2 November London was bombed for 57 consecutive nights by an average of 200 bombers each night. During November raids took place on all except three nights. At the end of December the City of London was the target of an enormous incendiary raid. Within the square mile of the City over 1,400 fires were reported, requiring almost 3,000 pumps from London and surrounding regions. Sixteen firemen lost their lives, and 250 were hospitalised in the City raid alone. London was attacked again in the spring of 1941, notably on the night of 16-17 April, with the last major fire-raising raid on 10-11 May.[113]

The scene during the attack on the City, with St Paul's

cathedral ringed with fires, was later described by AFS poet and journalist, Philip Henderson:

> The roads are choked with pumps, strange intestinal coils of hose and huge turntable ladders backing and manoeuvring into position. Isolated groups of men in yellow anti-gas capes and gas-shields hanging from their tin hats to keep the water from running down their necks, looking like Bedouin Arabs, others like porpoises in their glistening oily black mackintoshes, stand directing jets of water through shattered shop fronts and gaping windows on to the chaos of flaming debris within.[114]

Firemen led an exhausting life during the raid periods: drenched to the skin night after night in the middle of winter, working in the very eye of the storm for fifteen hours at a stretch, an illuminated target for the high explosive bombs which followed on the heels of the incendiaries. Firewomen, too, in the control units, the mobile offices essential to operational control, were set down in the front line of the attack.[115]

Despite the hardships, however, morale remained high. Even the blitz was better than the long months of waiting with firemen the object of public scorn. When the raids came firemen rode out in a mood of exhilaration with a point to prove. If exhausted by the night's activities, they knew they had risen above themselves. And the public responded. As Blackstone observes, there was an about-turn in the public attitude to firemen: 'Pump crews returning wet and dirty from fires were cheered by passers-by in the street, cinema audiences applauded when firemen appeared on newsreels, strangers stood them drinks in public houses.' Bouquets were thrown in place of brickbats.[116]

In November 1940 the main objective of the Luftwaffe changed from London to the ports and munition and engineering centres: Merseyside, Birmingham, Coventry, Bristol, Manchester, Sheffield, Glasgow, Hull, Portsmouth, Plymouth, Southampton, Cardiff, Swansea and Belfast. The worst attack on Coventry took place on 14-15 November; in eleven hours, 30,000 incendiaries and 500 tons of high explosive fell from the sky. An earthquake could have done no greater damage. This concentrated and destructive attack gave a new verb to the language: 'to coventrate'. However, according to Herbert Morrison, who had been made Home Secretary in October, 'the town that suffered most was Kingston-upon-Hull', the worst raids coming on 31 March and on two nights in early May 1941 when 839 separate fires were reported in the town.[117]

The sheer size and awful intensity of the war-time fire-fighting problem came as a shock. Cities like Coventry and Plymouth were physically and morally shattered by the German air assault; in Southampton the civil defence services reached the point of collapse, promoting an exodus of population into surrounding rural areas. The emergency fire brigade organisation bravely weathered the fury, but the blitzes searched out the cracks in the edifice, notably deficiencies in personnel, equipment and water supplies. The reinforcement system did not work well, afflicted by differences in organisation, equipment and even service terminology between brigades. The main shortcoming, however, was the fragmentation of command among the more than 1,400 local fire authorities.[118]

By early 1941 parliament and the press urged the regionalisation or nationalisation of the fire service, and officials in the Home Office were already considering whether the time had come for a smaller number of larger brigades under a unified command. Lady Astor, witness to the Plymouth blitz, launched a series of letters to the *Times* in April, with one lambasting the inadequacies of local fire services. Herbert Morrison, author of the phrase 'the fire services are the brightest jewel in the local authorities' crown', was predictably loathe to countenance nationalisation. But following further heavy raids on London and Plymouth he bowed to the inevitable. Morrison secured the War Cabinet's approval on 8 May for 'a national fire-fighting machine'. There began a hectic series of meetings with the local authorities, which (Glasgow and Birmingham apart) responded well to the proposals.[119]

On 20 May 1941 the Home Secretary moved the second reading of the Fire Services (Emergency Provisions) Bill. In his speech Morrison explained that 'the work of fighting fire has ... become a military operation and not a municipal operation.' He assured the local authorities, however, that after the war, 'the fire-fighting forces should again be a local authority service'. All firemen were to come under direct state control. 'Their pay, conditions of service and discipline', said Morrison, 'will be regulated by the state.' Labour MP, Philip Noel-Baker, took this opportunity to press for an equalisation of conditions of both regular and auxiliary firemen. Pressed also to clarify the position of the trade unions under nationalisation, Morrison seemed to accept a continued consultative role for the FBU.[120]

Morrison could now use the sweeping powers the Bill gave him to establish the National Fire Service (NFS). England and Wales were to be divided, at least initially, into 33 Fire Areas, Scotland into six, each under the supervision of a Fire Force Commander, and each bringing a distinct urban or industrial fire hazard under a single command. Fire cover for the entire country would thus be secured by an organisation of around forty Fire Forces.

The next essential was to select officers and prescribe conditions of service for all firemen, regulars and auxiliaries. There was to be a single promotion ladder for the NFS. Selection boards organised by the Regional Commissioners of Civil Defence and by Fire Force Commanders were to appoint to the ranks of Divisional Officer and below. They began from scratch. A non-worsening clause ensured that no officer could be paid less than he was getting in his former brigade, but he could, in effect, be demoted. Indeed, there were examples of precipitate falls, from Deputy Chief Officer to Section Leader (the equivalent of the old sub-officer). Many a direct-entry 'silver helmet' officer was passed over for an AFS man. A better officer class undoubtedly emerged, and its training was improved by the establishment of the Fire Service College at Saltdean, near Brighton. Both the provision for proper training of officers, and the adoption of non-military titles for officer ranks, it should be added, owed much to Horner and the FBU.[121]

As for the rank and file, hours of duty were to be

standardised by adopting the system of 48 hours on, 24 hours off. Pay was fixed at the Civil Defence rate of £3 10s. a week, although regular firemen continued to get the old rate if it exceeded the new one. Personnel was also to be increased. The total strength of the NFS, at its peak in early 1943, was almost 350,000 men, women and youths. 100,000 were wholetime firemen; nearly 30,000 were wholetime firewomen, serving in control rooms and kitchens, and acting as clerks, car drivers and despatch riders. The remaining 220,000 were part-timers, including 48,000 women.[122]

Morrison gave the new Fire Service Department of the Home Office, headed by Sir Arthur Dixon, just three months to make the vast transition from local to national fire service. So fast was the change effected that the department neglected to lay the fire service regulations before parliament. In 1944 Morrison had to present a 'forgiving' Act to Parliament to legalise all action taken since August 1941.[123] No one had any idea, of course, when air attacks would begin again. It was a bold political decision on Morrison's part to form the NFS, ignoring the adage about not swapping horses in mid-stream. Fortunately, incendiary raids never again assumed the number or intensity of the previous blitzes.

The FBU hailed Morrison's decision to take the fire service out of 'the realm of parish pump politics' as an essential step towards efficiency and victory. At the annual conference in June, however, John Horner, on behalf of the management committee (regular section), moved a composite resolution which welcomed nationalisation but asked the Home Secretary to finish the job. For a start, the union wanted a guaranteed right to represent firemen on conditions of service. Horner reminded delegates of the significant fact that the fire brigades were 'the first disciplined, uniformed, state-controlled organisation ...' which had a union affiliated to the TUC and the Labour Party, 'part and parcel of the working class movement'.[124] Secondly, the union wanted a national minimum rate of pay, based on the Middlebrook Committee's Report, although adapted to the needs of 1941.

The union also pressed for Appeals Committees to deal with the problems posed by transfer of men from one area to another and a sickness and injury scheme for the entire service based on that obtaining in the London Fire Brigade. Finally, the union maintained its opposition to a discipline code that used stoppages from pay as a form of punishment, and demanded both the right of appeal to an independent tribunal and the right to union representation for those charged with offences under the code. As an addendum, the union called for the two-platoon system (24 hours on, 24 hours off, or a 72-hour week) to give firemen more opportunity for rest. The entire resolution was then overwhelmingly accepted by conference.[125]

In this way the FBU gave notice to the Home Office that the war had killed the principle that the management of the fire service was outside the union's province. Many experienced firemen and firewomen belonged to the union, people with ideas of how to create a well equipped, effectively trained and disciplined fire force. This well of experience was now placed at the government's disposal. Conference also took the opportunity to decentralise the union by increasing the number of provincial representatives on the governing executive body. For some time an executive dominated by London and outer London had rankled with members from the Midlands, Northern and Scottish branches. This was preface to a thorough reorganisation of the union's administrative structure, involving the formation of Branch, Fire Force Area and Regional committees, thus bringing the union's structure into line with that of the National Fire Service.[126]

The Charter Campaign

The preliminary discussions with the Home Office on conditions of service in the NFS were very disappointing. No headway was made on the FBU's major demands. The government refused, for example, to pay auxiliaries the same wage rate as regulars. Nationalisation had improved administration and control, but had left firemen's conditions untouched. The executive council decided, therefore, to organise a national campaign, the Firemen's Charter Campaign. The charter was a term which struck a chord in the labour movement, reaching back a hundred years. The Firemen's Charter was a redrafting of the Ten Points of the AFS, similarly designed to standardise firemen's conditions. The charter campaign was a campaign for all firemen, however, ex-regulars and ex-auxiliaries alike. By levelling up the general standard of conditions in the NFS, the FBU sought to improve the efficiency of all firemen in the service.

The five points of the charter were: a national minimum wage of £4 per week, full pay while sick or injured, a just discipline code, the two-platoon system (or a maximum working week of 72 hours, enemy action excluded) and promotion on merit. The remarkable feature of the campaign was that a force of uniformed men and women, including conscripts, were appealing directly to the country. As the charter concluded: 'In this people's war we ask you, the people, to take a hand with us to make a New Model fire-fighting army ...' In return the union pledged to those in the forces, in the workshops and 'our comrades on the Eastern Front',

> that when the bombers return not one bale of raw material brought through the Battle of the Atlantic, not one spare part for one aeroplane built by our comrades in the factories, shall be destroyed by fire if it is within the powers of our members to prevent it.[127]

The campaign took place in October and November 1941, a week in each district, culminating in a large London demonstration and a parliamentary debate on the charter. Hundreds of mass meetings were held to gain endorsement for the charter, MPs of all parties were sent a copy of the charter and invited to address branch meetings; and leaflets and pamphlets were written, the most effective being *The Struggle of the AFS* by national officer and former barrister, Peter Pain. There were, in addition, concerts, film shows, flag days, dances and public expressions of support from public figures including playwrights George Bernard Shaw and Sean O'Casey.[128]

Herbert Morrison was far from impressed by the charter campaign. He and his officials considered the campaign went beyond reasonable propaganda to the point of spreading disaffection at a time of national emergency. They could not, however, gainsay the public support won by the campaign. This support probably helped the union to win a pay increase of 4 shillings and an improvement in the sickness and injury scheme in February 1942. Civil defence workers were to be treated like other servicemen: full injury pay for up to 26 weeks, plus improvements in the administration of sick pay. The campaign also helped to bring more firemen into the union. The FBU now represented over 90 per cent of professional firemen and close to 70 per cent of the 100,000 wholetime auxiliaries.[129]

The FBU also championed the cause of women firefighters. Firewomen won their spurs during the blitz: staffing mobile kitchens and control rooms, acting as motor-cycle dispatch riders, driving the heavy equipment and joining mobile reinforcement units sent to heavily-raided towns.[130] Their numbers increased considerably in the National Fire Service. By September 1942 there were 30,000 wholetime firewomen and 50,000 part-timers. And there was much for the union to attack in the women's branch of the NFS.

Firewomen were always paid less than their male comrades, had an inferior injury compensation scheme and no replacement uniform to speak of.[131] In addition, the hours, conditions of service and nature of a firewoman's duty varied around the country. In some places (Grimsby, Worthing) there were even women pump crews. John Horner and Marjorie Herd, National Women's Organiser, therefore, raised firewomen's duties and conditions with the Home Office in March 1942. It was then agreed that women would be employed as crews only for light pumps in rural and suburban districts.[132] Thereafter the main aim of the Women's National Advisory Council, composed of women FBU delegates from the regions, was to get more women organised in the union (and by 1943 over 8,000 women were members of the FBU), to see to it that women were represented on all the union committees (Constance Tudor-Hart was elected onto the executive council in late 1942) and to hammer out a Firewomen's Charter.[133]

The turning point in the drafting of a Charter (and in the part played by women in the FBU) came in London in March 1943 at the National Women's Conference. There it was agreed to fight for equal pay for equal work, for proper training for firewomen and for an improvement in conditions of service. Long hours of duty in poorly ventilated control rooms were taking their toll in ill-health. The pallor of some women, it was claimed, was that of long-term prisoners. Women workers were penalised for motherhood, often being discharged at the announcement of pregnancy. The Home Office, however, considered there was little substance in these complaints, and the smallest improvements in wages, sick and injury pay, uniforms and short leave were always hard fought.[134]

Morrison, Horner and the Politics of the Left

Over and above the demands of the charter, the FBU demanded full trade union recognition. At first there was cause for optimism. Major F.W. Jackson, Chief Commander of the London Fire Force, assured representatives of the district committee in September 1941 that the path of trade unionism in the new service would be smooth. The union thus established provisional committees to negotiate with Fire Force Commanders. This was all conditional, however, on agreement being reached with the Home Office.

Other Chief Regional Fire Officers and Fire Force Commanders were urging the Home Office to allow them to deal with firemen directly, not through an outside body. Commander Firebrace, Chief of the Fire Staff, advised the same. Eventually, the Home Secretary proposed the setting up of Representative Boards in each Fire Force area. The executive council of the FBU was aghast. A new organisation, bearing an unhealthy resemblance to the Police Federation, was to run alongside the trade union machinery. Firemen were being offered what very much looked like 'company unionism'. The fight for union recognition was joined once more.[135]

In December the full executive committee, along with Arthur Deakin, in his role as convenor of union representatives on the Joint Consultative Committee, met the Home Secretary. When pressed on the representative boards, Morrison tried to assure the deputation that the boards would not deal with basic conditions of service. They would simply allow officers to meet the rank and file, particularly part-timers, to discuss local welfare matters. Morrison insisted that he had no intention of using the boards 'as a means of ousting the Fire Brigades Union'.[136] Furthermore, the Consultative Committee, of which the FBU was part, would still be recognised for purposes of discussing wages and conditions; district organisers would have the right of approach to Fire Force Commanders. This did little to pacify the FBU, especially since Morrison would not agree to restrict nomination for the representative boards to union members.

A deputation from the TUC followed in February 1942. The proposal for representative boards, Sir Walter Citrine told Morrison, 'was a nucleus which might in certain circumstances be converted into a substitute organisation for trade unionism'.[137] Consultation should thus be limited to organised trade unions. Morrison promised to reach a decision soon. In the meantime the FBU had extended its membership and its influence in the NFS. Whether for this reason, or as a result of the TUC's continued support of the FBU, Morrison abandoned the scheme for representative boards, and in May 1942 granted recognition to trade unionism. 'And so, for the first time,' stated the *Firefighter*, 'the principle of trade unionism has been accepted in a uniformed, disciplined, and conscripted force.'[138]

There was, however, a sting in the tail of this climb-down. The right to hold trade union meetings in fire stations was withheld, and the union was denied the right to make collective representation on behalf of officer members. In November 1941 the Home Office had recognised the Fire Officers' Association (an outgrowth of the Chief Fire Officers' Association). The association's membership was then extended to include company officers, and the re-titled National Fire Service Officers' Association (NFSOA), with Commander Firebrace as President, was recognised in May 1942 as representing all male officers, and in due course all female officers.

To the FBU, the NFSOA was to all intents and purposes a 'company union', developed with the connivance of the department as a way of combating the growing force of the union. Moreover, since nationalisation had resulted in the promotion of some of the FBU's best activists, the union was more determined than ever to make collective representation on behalf of officers. In June, therefore, the FBU formed an autonomous Officers' Section and asked the Home Office to recognise it. This was denied, despite considerable pressure from the General Council of the TUC, on the grounds that it would impair discipline to recognise the Officers' Section, and that it would be difficult for the department to have to deal with two organisations. There was no substance, as far as the FBU could see, in either argument. Nevertheless, the position remained that while officers were not debarred from joining the union, and the FBU was allowed to speak on behalf of individual members, the union was precluded from making any representation on conditions of service. Foiled in his attempt to introduce representative boards into the National Fire Service, Morrison retaliated by restricting the FBU to the junior ranks of the service, thereby for some considerable time blocking the road leading to a 'closed shop'.[139]

Morrison proved more amenable to the holding of trade union meetings on fire brigade premises. The FBU's campaign to this end began in June 1942 when Arthur Deakin, on behalf of the trade union side of the Joint Consultative Committee, pressed Morrison to remove the ban on meetings. The ban had been implemented by all regions, with the exception of London, though since the ban was practically unenforceable, most branches continued to hold meetings on the stations. Home Office opinion recognised the practical difficulty, given the 48/24 hour duty system, of holding meetings other than on fire service premises. Having recognised the union, moreover, the department could not logically maintain a ban on all trade union meetings.

For Morrison, the stumbling block was what he termed 'the technique and mood of the leadership'. As he told a conference of senior fire officers in August, the FBU was 'persistently attempting to extend the scope and authority of their activities beyond their proper sphere'. He feared that fire station meetings would go beyond trade union purposes, to deal with policy issues, even military strategy, and would be used to recruit non-unionists. Commander Firebrace conjured up a more frightening scenario: a strong union representative, a weak Leading Fireman, also a member of the union, in charge of the station. Inevitably, he said, the union would run the station. And where would this all end?

> We might easily slip into a state of affairs – as at one time in the Russian Army – where every unit had a member of the 'party' attached to it who 'watched' the officer-in-charge. The order by the officer to advance had to be countersigned by the political member.[140]

Firebrace's fertile, not to say febrile, imagination did not ultimately stand in the way of Morrison's decision in April 1943 to allow trade union meetings at fire stations. Horner was, after all, threatening TUC action. But permission was granted as a privilege, not a right, and hence could be withdrawn if the privilege was abused. Meetings were allowed on the condition that they were not used 'for political purposes or propaganda'. All union notices and circulars for station bulletin boards had to be approved by the officer in charge. And this in the third year of a war to save democracy![141]

Politics again bulked large in Morrison's relations with the FBU. In late 1941, as the blitz was dying down, a handful of firemen began gathering in their spare time to discuss current affairs. By mid-1942 more than 15,000 men and women were meeting weekly in hundreds of groups of between ten and 30 people in the fire stations in and around London. The groups undoubtedly helped to develop trade union and political consciousness, since they tended, according to Stephen Spender, a discussion group leader and organiser, 'to become demonstrations of the politics of the Left'. Indeed, the scheme quickly came under the direction of the FBU.[142]

More ominously still for Morrison, the war years were a period of heightened influence for the Communist Party, and notably in the ranks of civil defence. From the beginning of the war, CP members were urged to join ARP, Rescue Squads, and the Fire Service. Bob Darke, for instance, 'answered the Party instructions to join the Fire Service ...' The aim was not alone to recruit members of the National Fire Service, but to win over the FBU. In August 1940 Darke was called to a meeting of Communist firemen in the vicinity of Gray's Inn Road at which it was agreed that 'strong Communist fractions in every Fire Station' be established and that the FBU be 'completely captured by the Party'.[143] While Darke may not be the most objective of sources, quitting the party in 1951 and penning a scathing indictment of Communist practices, his account of the war years seems to be an accurate one.

Communists were soon to be found at every level of the union. Darke himself was elected onto the executive within a matter of months. Bob Bagley was an EC member and later Vice-President. Jack Grahl was active in the union in Scotland and the Northern counties, Sid Withers in the South-West. Party members dominated the Scottish Area Committee. General Secretary Horner took out a Communist Party card only after the war ended, but on his own admission he was a crypto-Communist during the war, attending both Labour Party conferences and meetings of CP members in the union. It was this duplicity, a feature of the period, which so incensed Morrison, who frequently referred to 'the strange company' Horner kept.

The Communist fraction in the FBU, moreover, exploited

its position to campaign for the opening of the Second Front in Europe, the aim of which was to take the strain off the Red Army. Slogans were daubed on walls and railway arches, resolutions went from every union branch to MPs and the War Office, speakers at annual conference and the TUC demanded the opening of the Second Front. When the government set up an overseas unit of the fire service, to aid the armed forces during the Second Front, both Darke and Bagley were told to volunteer, though neither was selected to go overseas. In all, the Communist Party succeeded in winning control of the FBU, much to the chagrin of Home Secretary Morrison, who had long assailed Communist infiltration of the labour movement.[144]

The Second Front, Productive Work and Duty Systems

If the struggle for the Fireman's Charter and for full union recognition brought Morrison and the FBU into conflict, relations deteriorated further over the opening of the Second Front, industrial work at fire stations and the introduction of a 48/24 hour duty system. For the union these three issues were closely connected. The argument ran thus. If victory in the war was to be achieved in 1942, the Soviet Union's lonely fight against fascism had to be bolstered by the opening of a Second Front in Western Europe. At the 1942 Trades Union Congress, therefore, the FBU delegation seconded the Engineers' resolution which called for the immediate opening of a Second Front.[145] Firemen could not demand a Second Front, however, unless they were prepared to do all they could to help. In particular, they should take advantage of the lull in air raids and open a 'Second Front of Production'. Firemen, that is, should become industrial out-workers in their stand-by and off-duty hours. The duty system which most facilitated production, according to the union, was the 24/24 hour system. Thus Morrison's decision to standardise duty hours on the 48/24 hour system came as a blow to the union's campaign for the Second Front.

The productive work scheme began in a small way in the

London Fire Force. Firemen used blitzed materials to make toys and equipment for wartime nurseries while on stand-by duty. The main impetus came, however, from the fact that fire raids effectively stopped. As the lull continued, the National Fire Service was cut by releasing one-sixth of the wholetime force to the fighting services. In addition, the government accepted the union's suggestion of releasing a few thousand firemen to industry for an indefinite period. That still left 100,000 firefighters kicking their heels. There was a limit to how much drill, exercise and spit and polish they could be expected to do. At station level, therefore, firemen began to seek productive work, at times seconded by Fire Force Commanders, who felt the activity would improve the men's morale and efficiency. In early 1942 the FBU decided to co-ordinate this rank and file activity. Branch secretaries began to canvass local factories for work, making or assembling simple components: boxes to hold ammunition and food, ambulance seats, dinghy paddles and radio parts. Plesseys of Ilford farmed out work, soldering and wiring radio sets, to 45 fire stations in East London. Some firemen reclaimed rubber from old tyres and cables. Others volunteered to work in munitions factories or in timber yards on their off-days. Pay was given according to a rate for the job negotiated by the union.[146]

Herbert Morrison's initial response was hostile in the extreme. As he saw it, the scheme was entirely unofficial, it raised the issue of a secondary wage and could well sacrifice operational efficiency. Payment led to profound disagreement between the union and the Home Office. Some money found its way into firemen's pay packets, especially in the early days of the scheme, but the department eventually ensured that most went to the Treasury and to fund improvements in station amenities. The union never allowed the acrimony about payment, however, to detract from the main issue of opening a Second Front of Production. 'When we talk about productive work for firemen', Horner explained, 'we mean work for victory over fascism, and not necessarily work bringing home an extra quid at the end of the week.'[147] The union also mobilised trade union opinion in defence of the scheme. Morrison backed down. Union members were officially recognised as 'productive work organisers', their job to drum up contracts and fix rates in conjunction with management and shop stewards' committees. 'The Fire Brigades Union have entered into the capitalist world ...' said a sullen Labour Home Secretary. 'It was an extraordinary example', replied Horner, 'of creative industrial democracy.'[148]

The enormous efforts made to give firemen a more productive role in industry seemed nullified, however, by the Home Office's decision, in June 1942, to standardise the 48/24 hour duty system throughout the National Fire Service. This duty system of 112 hours, the FBU protested, was less suitable than the 24/24 system (or 84 hours) for outside industrial work, since it increased the number of unproductive hours. Furthermore, accommodation was too poor at many stations for the longer tour of duty, and the sickness rate of men employed on the 48/24 system was higher, to judge from returns in the London Region. A number of senior officers in the Service agreed with the union; the Home Office disagreed.

The 48/24 system, the department argued, provided the highest operational efficiency. Two-thirds of the entire personnel were always at the stations in readiness. The 24/24 system, however, encouraged the fireman to regard his secondary job in industry as the main occupation, his fire-fighting job as a secondary one. Station accommodation was admittedly poor in some areas, but Morrison agreed to refrain from implementing the new system, wherever accommodation was inadequate.[149]

Implementation of the scheme was destined to be stormy. In the industrial areas of the Midlands and the North-West firemen were on the 24/24 system, enabling them to make a contribution to the war effort, and to earn extra money. The new system meant an increased tour of duty, a thinner pay packet and damage to the productive work arrangements. In the Midlands, indeed, it was widely believed that the 48/24 was calculated to sabotage productive work. Protest meetings of firemen were organised in Birmingham; a deputation of the city's MPs interviewed Morrison to stress the advantages of the 24/24 to the service and to the munitions industry.[150] The centre of resistance to the 48/24, however, was in Lancashire, particularly Merseyside, from late August 1942, when the change over to the new system took place. There is evidence, moreover, that the FBU leadership lost control of the agitation in this region.

In Liverpool, for example, a demonstration march of firemen was planned. It was instigated not by the FBU, however, but by the National Union of Auxiliary Firemen, a rival organisation. Indeed, Harry Short, assistant general secretary, and Jack Grahl, worked hard on behalf of the FBU to prevent direct action, instructing firemen to obey orders. As a gesture to the FBU's constitutional line, moreover, the Regional Commissioner postponed the change over in the nearby city of Manchester, pending improvement to station accommodation. But direct action would not go away; there were reports of threatened strikes in Blackpool and Bolton. And the FBU leadership was penalised for what many members considered a half-hearted fight against the change of duty system. In the Lancashire and Cheshire Region, 7,000 members left the union in the space of a few months.[151] At the Annual Congress of the ex-AFS section in Leeds in October 1942 the union's management committee had a bumpy ride during the key debate on hours.

Speaking for the management committee, Tom Haston reminded delegates of the nation-wide campaign to compel the Home Office to change its policy on hours. Yet favourable press publicity, parliamentary activity and the support of the Joint Consultative Committee had failed to change the view of Morrison and the Fire Service Department. To allow the hours issue to develop into a personal duel with the Minister, said Haston, would only undermine the union's efforts to improve the efficiency and morale of the service. Nor did it seem politic, at a time of military reverses, to launch a vigorous attack upon the government. The two Birmingham delegates, however, moved an amendment to the motion, which instructed the management committee to continue vigorously the campaign against the 48/24. The amendment carried, and hence the ball was back in the executive's side of the court.[152]

The executive council again met Morrison in November 1942, but deadlock was reached. At this juncture, according to John Horner's statement to the historic 'fusion' conference of 1943 (when the ex-regular and ex-AFS sections merged into a single union), the Executive felt compelled to throw in the towel. 'There was no further action which our Executive Council saw open to it,' said Horner, 'that would not bring into question the operation of trade unionism within a disciplined Service.'[153] The executive asked Conference, therefore, to support the resolution which simply demanded that the 48/24 as a standard system of duty be withdrawn.

In the ensuing debate, Bro. Kavanagh criticised the leadership for failing to mount a vigorous campaign, as the Leeds conference had instructed, and for failing to recognise the strength of feeling on this issue to be found still in provincial regions. Bro. Bagley, a member of the EC, supported the resolution, advising delegates that winning the war required working the hours the Service called for. As for getting rid of the 48/24, said Bagley, the union would need first to enroll a larger proportion of its membership into the political fund on behalf of the Labour Party. With that, the resolution carried.[154] For the time being the union admitted defeat in the battle over hours.

For over two years the FBU and the Home Secretary had locked horns. In the struggle for the Fireman's Charter (and for the firewoman's equivalent) the two sides disagreed essentially about the rectitude of a campaign to win public support for improved conditions of service. Morrison felt the union pushed criticism of the service and its administration beyond what was acceptable during wartime. The FBU felt strongly that a Labour minister should have moved more rapidly to improve wages, duty hours and sick and injury pay. In default, the union felt justified in using the considerable literary and legal talent in its swollen ranks to mobilise public, press and parliamentary opinion.

In the struggle for full union recognition the two sides disagreed essentially about the presence and role of trade unionism in the fire service. The FBU was determined to prove that democratic representation and discipline could go hand-in-hand. First, however, it had to rally the public and trade union support received in the charter campaign, to fight off Morrison's attempt to install company unionism in the service. Morrison had serious reservations about a strong trade union element in a disciplined, uniformed service. He doubtless realised that if the FBU got hold of the National Fire Service the union would be difficult to budge once the war was over and the service went back to the local authorities. Morrison feared, moreover, that the leadership, heavily Communist in political affiliation, would move beyond the trade union sphere of welfare and conditions of service.

The FBU went well beyond their legitimate sphere, in Morrison's view, in the fight for the Second Front, in the propaganda on the subject of industrial work at fire stations and in the campaign to forestall the introduction of the 48/24 hour duty system. The FBU saw matters differently. At the outbreak of war the spirit of the Askwith Award still determined the rights of the union. It restricted trade union activity to the winning of improvements in conditions of service; it put concern with discipline and methods of management beyond the pale. The war had changed all that.

'We regard this as our war,' said Peter Pain, AFS National Organiser, 'and the Fire Service as our Service.'[155] Traditional sectional demands were not alone the union's concern. The efficiency and morale of the service were equally relevant considerations, since they were vital to the fight against fascism. The duty of the union, as the leadership saw it, was to use their organised strength responsibly to help create a new type of fire service, one which would take its place in the new Britain that would arise from the ashes of war.

The Early History of the Fire Brigades Union

'What Kind of Fire Service?'

In a statement to the House of Commons on 13 June 1943 Herbert Morrison reiterated his pledge to the local authorities that the fire service would go back to them after hostilities, but he added the significant rider that no undertaking had been made to return the service to the *same* local authorities as were in charge in 1939. The Annual Conference of the FBU responded to this reference to the post-war service by instructing the executive council to demand a set of minimum conditions in any post-war scheme, including an eight-hour day, a standard wage equal to that of a skilled industrial worker and a new pensions Act. In other words, the union refused to return to the continuous-duty system, and rejected the prevailing civil defence wage of £3 18s. 6d. for professional firemen. As yet the union had no detailed blueprint for the future structure of the service, and simply demanded representation on the official committees considering plans for the post-war service.[156]

It boded well for the future when Morrison used the union's Silver Jubilee 'austerity' dinner in August 1943 to make a speech of reconciliation between himself and the Home Office on one hand and the union on the other. A month later firemen's pay rose to £4 0s. 6d., with firewomen receiving two-thirds (where the union had asked for 80 per cent) of the men's rate. Finally, the long battle of the hours ended in a victory of sorts for the FBU, when an 84-hour week (24 hours on and 24 hours off duty) was introduced in October 1944.[157] It was a false dawn, however. Relations between Morrison and the union deteriorated once more, with the department failing to offer any clear-cut policy for the post-war fire service, and refusing to consult the union until conditions of service were under discussion.

The FBU found Morrison's behaviour inexplicable. Plans were afoot to cut the National Fire Service establishment of 110,000 men and women by about half. In time the NFS would be reduced to about 36,000 (or double the expected post-war, wholetime strength of 18,000 firemen), from which the professional firemen of the future service would be selected. In this transition to peace-time strength the service would undergo immense changes, which the union could surely assist. The FBU was particularly concerned to ensure that those members who were demobilised found employment (to assist which the union formed the Firemen's League), and that those who remained in the service were guaranteed a decent standard of employment, one which would also induce good young recruits to join.[158] Continued indecision on the part of the Home Office, however, seriously hindered the union's efforts. Firemen became deeply suspicious of the department's plans; the service became a rumour mill. In an attempt to force Morrison to adopt an open and democratic policy, the FBU submitted detailed proposals for the post-war fire service.

In early December 1943 the FBU published *What Kind of Fire Service?* The pamphlet recognised that many firemen thought the service should go back to the local authorities who controlled it prior to nationalisation. This the executive council could not accept. A return to the 1,500 or so authorities would mean a return to the ineffective provisions of the Fire Brigades Act, 1938. Neither was nationalisation seen as the answer. The National Fire Service was a rigid, centralised war measure, unsuited to peace-time conditions. 'We need a Service', declared the EC, 'fitted to local needs, close to the people whom we serve, but free from the drag on efficiency which would result from every rural and urban district council maintaining its own brigade.'[159]

To this end the executive council proposed as a post-war scheme large brigades covering the main urban and industrial areas, each brigade administered by a committee of the local authorities within the area. This would guarantee democratic control of the fire service. A central advisory council would, however, ensure that uniform standards and efficiency were maintained. In a word, the union proposed regionalisation. The existing London civil defence region, for example, would form the basis of a unified Fire Brigade of Greater London, replacing the 67 peace-time brigades, including the London Fire Brigade. The memorandum concluded with a demand for better conditions of service: a 48-hour week, a national minimum rate ('comparable at least with the Police scales of pay'), a new pension scheme and an improved discipline code.[160] Copies of the pamphlet were put before the department and the local authorities, with a request that the union be brought into discussions on the future of the service.

The request fell on deaf ears. Not until March 1943 did Morrison and Thomas Johnston, Secretary of State for Scotland, appoint an internal committee to consider the organisation of the fire service after the war.[161] Sir Arthur Dixon was chairman and Commander Firebrace a member. The committee solicited no outside opinion; its report was a review of the problem strictly from the angles of service and department. On fire service organisation the committee simply reviewed the pros and cons of the main forms of control. The principle of local control was not ruled out, but a return to the pre-war diversity was considered unsound, so a measure of central supervision was recommended.

Turning to conditions of service, the committee proposed a two-shift (9/15 hours) 72-hour week for the big cities and a continuous-duty system of 72/24 hours for areas with a lower incidence of fires. A personal reservation was entered by Firebrace, to his credit, against the continuous-duty system and against a shift system of 72 hours. He favoured the FBU's proposal of a three-shift 48-hour week, at least for the busy fire stations in big cities. Basic pay was to be standard, irrespective of duty system or locality, and fixed on a scale identical with that of a constable. Almost immediately, however, Morrison sought to break the recommended link between fire service and police conditions:

> ... I have never been convinced that the work of firemen and policemen is analogous, and if police-fire brigades cease, the point is less applicable. A policeman's work is more difficult and responsible than that of firemen.[162]

Can the leopard change its spots?

A frustrating year followed for the FBU. The union continued to press the department for information as to the shape of the post-war fire service and kept telling the department that officers and men were disillusioned and suspicious that decisions were being taken behind their backs. In September 1944, however, Dixon assured a union deputation that the department was working to no pattern for the post-war service. Discussions were continuing with the local authorities, many of whom wanted the pre-war service restored intact.[163]

Although much less concerned with service opinion, Home Office indecision was probably reinforced by the difference of view among firemen as to the form of the future service. While many of the most capable ex-auxiliaries, officers and men, were interested in making a career of the NFS, the ex-regular firemen were decidedly opposed to nationalisation and were eager to return to the old brigade system, despite its known flaws. The *Firefighter* for September also alerted the department to the fact that leading members of the FBU (in this instance, former president John Burns and vice-president H.S. Richardson) were still not agreed on the future of the service.[164]

The Home Office displayed a more co-operative spirit in 1944 in the launching of the Second Front. Allied preparations to storm the Continent led to the concentration of vehicles, equipment and stores along the South Coast. Operation 'Colour Scheme' followed: the transfer of over 11,000 firemen and firewomen with 1,240 appliances from the North and the Midlands to protect this vast armed camp from fire. With Home Office approval the welfare aspects of the transfer and billeting of these firefighting columns were handled by union liaison officers.

It was also agreed before D-Day that an overseas contingent of 2,000 firemen, organised into five columns, would be made ready to cross the Channel, to provide fire cover in base areas. Tom Murray became the union's Overseas Organiser. Only one column of 540 firemen actually joined the invasion force, attached to the US Army. Uniquely for a unit attached to the armed forces, the men were unionists to a man, branch meetings continued to be held, the *Firefighter* was delivered and a column committee, chaired by John Forsyth, negotiated directly with the divisional officer in charge of the column.[165] Given the FBU's determined advocacy of the opening of the Second Front, it was appropriate that at least a small contingent of the union's members should be in at the end of fascism.

On 23 May 1945 Winston Churchill resigned as leader of the Coalition, and was re-apppointed as head of a 'caretaker' government of Conservatives and National Liberals. At the same time a general election was scheduled for July. Herbert Morrison made way for Sir Donald Somervell, who did what his predecessor signally failed to do: state the department's developing policy for the future fire service. The local authorities would be involved in the control of the fire service, Somervell announced, but there would be no complete return to the pre-war position. Few FBU members mourned the departure of Herbert Morrison. Instead, they waited expectantly for a Labour victory in the election and for the appointment of a Home Secretary who would restore the firefighters' shattered morale by realising an efficient post-war service and by allowing the union to play a full part in its creation.

The union donated £1,000 to the Labour Party's election fund and gave financial support to five Labour candidates, all former or present members of the FBU. Willie Hannan was returned as MP for Maryhill in Scotland, and eventually became a junior minister.[166] More significantly, the first majority Labour government climbed into the political saddle. James Chuter Ede became Home Secretary. The union seemed unsure how to respond.

Chuter Ede's political reputation rested on his wartime appointment as parliamentary secretary in the Ministry of Education, where he effectively partnered the minister, R.A. Butler, during the passage of the 1944 Education Act.[167] Chuter Ede had no experience of the Home Office before taking office, but he was a well-balanced and sensible politician, familiar with the ways of local government and sympathetic to the idea of a partnership with the FBU in creating the post-war fire service. A new and better chapter opened in the relations between the Home Office and the

FBU. Following the first meeting with Chuter Ede on 8 October 1945 John Horner wrote a word of thanks on behalf of the General Purposes Committee:

> I am to say that the nature of their reception and your expressed opinions as to the relationship which should exist between your Department and the Union, is in keeping with what they feel should be the attitude of a Labour Home Secretary.[168]

The implied contrast with the Morrison years was entirely intentional.

The end of hostilities made it necessary for the Home Office to reach quick decisions on the linked problems of recruitment and pay. If the National Fire Service was to be 'unfrozen', thus allowing those who had joined or were conscripted for emergency service to return to their normal occupations, voluntary recruiting had to begin. About 600 ex-professional firemen were in the armed forces and steps were taken to secure their early release. About 12,000 of those serving in the NFS were thought suitable and willing to remain in the service. That left 8,000 places to fill from outside the service. Men coming out of the armed services were targeted. Recruiting literature and agents were despatched in December 1945 to the main theatres of war: Europe, the Middle East and India. John Burns, the union's president, broadcast on the Forces' Educational Programme, telling servicemen about firefighting (and about the union!)[169] The 'unfreezing' of the fire service was set for April 1946.

Those eventually taken on for permanent employment in the fire service were divided evenly between ex-service men and men who were already serving in the NFS. The response from the demobilisation centres, however, was less enthusiastic than expected. Most servicemen, it seems, had had their fill of uniformed, disciplined life, and sought a higher wage than that of the fireman. Even so, of those who did enter the service at this time, many were union-minded. Indeed, two of the recruits were Terry Parry and Enoch Humphries, future general secretary and president respectively, of the FBU.[170]

Recruitment from within the service led to a good deal more controversy. Insistence by senior officers on pre-war London age limits and physical standards (in respect of height and chest measurements) led to many instances of firemen rejected for permanent service (although then offered short-term contracts) who had years of war-time experience under their belts. There was also evidence, notably in the case of Bro. Willis, an executive council member from Newcastle, that medical unfitness was a cover for victimisation of union militants. The union informed Chuter Ede of the absurdity of these 're-assessment' decisions, and the Home Secretary agreed to issue fresh instructions, making it clear that men who did not quite reach the recognised physical standards should not be debarred from permanent service, unless they posed a danger to their companions when fighting fires. He also established appeal machinery whereby 'blitz heroes' could appeal against their rejection for permanent engagement.[171]

The recruiting appeal for the post-war service was prefaced by negotiations for 'assimilation' of pay. The FBU was already pressing for former auxiliary firemen to be given the rate for the job, to be assimilated, that is, to a regular fire brigade scale. In addition, the department recognised that without assimilation of pay it would be difficult to recruit, or to ascertain which of the serving firemen were willing to stay. Hence, a standard rate of pay was laid down, starting at £4 10s. a week, identical with that of police constables, plus 5 shillings per week single and 10 shillings per week married men's allowance. The union wanted a starting wage of £6 per week, and a pay scale independent of comparisons with other local government workers. But they accepted assimilation in the knowledge that it marked the end of a six-year struggle to bring equality between the auxiliaries and the regulars.[172]

Local Control: Central Supervision

Over the entire recruitment process hung the cloud of the future control of the service. The recruitment literature stressed, for example, that the conditions of service set out were necessarily provisional. With the post-war organisation of the fire service Chuter Ede ran up against the same problem which had confronted Morrison, that of getting the local authority associations to agree to modification of the pre-war structure. Eventually it became apparent that the Labour government would have to frame its own scheme, and face down the inevitable opposition. The Home Secretary thus proposed that the fire service be transferred to the control of the county councils and county borough councils in England and Wales, and of councils of counties and large burghs in Scotland.[173]

This kept faith with Morrison's pledge to hand the service back to the local authorities, while at the same time creating larger units of organisation. The Home Secretary also proposed a larger measure of central supervision to ensure general efficiency and national standards of pay and conditions of service. The *quid pro quo* of central direction was some form of Exchequer assistance. Despite the FBU's disappointment at not being party to the discussions with the local authorities, and the fact that their own joint board proposals found no favour, they went along with Chuter Ede's solution. A Bill to give effect to these proposals was promised. Unfortunately, the press of government legislation delayed the introduction of the Fire Services Bill until March 1947. The National Fire Service got yet another stay of execution.

In preparation for the change-over the Home Secretary wound up the wartime Joint Consultative Committee for Civil Defence Workers and established the National Joint Council for the Junior Ranks of the National Fire Service. The council consisted of 21 members on the official side (fourteen for the various local authority associations) and sixteen members on the trade union side (ten for the FBU, and two each for the TGWU, the NUGMW and NUPE). The most significant feature of the new council was the right to arbitration, a right lost through nationalisation. Should council fail to agree, the difference could be referred to the Ministry of Labour's Industrial Court.[174] The FBU was quick to take advantage of this restored right.

At the first meeting of the council in autumn 1946 the FBU tabled two main demands: a reduction in hours and a pay increase. They registered the union's determination in the post-war period to have firemen accepted as

> workers entitled to all the improvements which the trade union movement will be obtaining for the working class as a whole. We are determined to break away from the old tradition which regarded firemen as something separate from the general body of workpeople.[175]

Firemen had always worked hours of duty far in excess of the normal working day in industry. In view of the agreement signed seven years earlier for the introduction of the 60-hour week in London fire brigades, and in view of the introduction of the 40-hour week in a number of large industries, the FBU felt justified in demanding a 60-hour week immediately, as the first step towards the 40-hour week. The official side of the Council favoured a 72-hour week, but conceded the union's demand on 16 October. Strictly speaking, the duty system was an 840-hour tour of duty spread over fourteen weeks.[176] The worsening economic situation and manpower shortage in Britain caused the union to refrain from pushing immediately for either the 40- or the 48-hour week.

The economic position did not, however, deter the union from pressing its claim for a new scale of pay of £6 per week (inclusive of allowances) on recruitment. In presenting this claim the union sought a scale of pay based on an assessment of a fireman's unique services, not on a comparison with the police force. In November 1946, however, policemen received a further pay increase, leading the FBU to ask that the rates of pay for firemen be increased to the new police rates (with a starting wage of £5 5s. a week), and that the rent allowance for married men be increased from 10 shillings to

17s. 6d. The official side of the National Joint Council offered an increase of 10 shillings in the standard rate (which would bring the fireman's starting wage to £5), with no increase in the rent allowance. Following union rejection of this offer, the claim was heard by the Industrial Court on 13 December 1946. The FBU made the first of its many post-war appearances before this Court.

Before a courtroom crowded with firemen and officers, the union demanded a 15 shilling pay rise for firemen (22 shillings for Section Leaders) and an increase to 17s. 6d. in the married man's allowance. The claim affected 16,500 firemen and 2,300 Section Leaders. John Horner's case for the union was built largely on the history of the London County Council's acceptance of police analogy in matters of pay, as upheld by the arbitration awards of 1923 and 1934.

For the official side, A.S. Hutchinson, Assistant Under Secretary of State at the Home Office, argued that the fire service would shortly be transferred to local authority control, and thus a pay settlement should be delayed until the independent committee, appointed by the Joint Council, had inquired into the value of the firemen's services to the community and the principles on which their pay should be fixed. In addition, the introduction of the 60-hour week without any pay reduction had to be taken into account. Later on a member of the court asked Horner if the union felt that the responsibilities of a fireman were as great as those of a policeman. The gallery holding more than 100 firemen gasped audibly. A few days later the court issued its Award.

The Industrial Court conceded the claim in respect of pay, and gave married firemen an allowance at the same rate as the rent allowance of married constables. Immediately, the government agreed to give effect to the Award, as from 1 January 1947.[177] The union rightly claimed a remarkable victory. A substantial pay increase had been won, and the principle of police parity had again been upheld. It was greatly hoped that these conditions of service would prevail when the local authorities took over.

Chuter Ede placed the Fire Services Bill before the House

of Commons in February 1947. The main object of the Bill was to break the National Fire Service in England and Wales into 146 units, each under the control of a county council or county borough council. Scotland was to have eleven fire brigade authorities. Among other things, police brigades and police-firemen were to be objects of the past. The National Joint Council for Local Authorities' Fire Brigades was to be established, with representatives of the local authorities and of the trade unions, to hammer out conditions of service, including a central pension scheme, which would have to be observed by every authority.

A Central Fire Brigades Advisory Council was also envisaged, again with union representation, to advise the Home Secretary on such matters as the transfer of men from the NFS to the new fire brigades. Finally, an Exchequer grant of 25 per cent was to be paid. This last item was the main topic of debate in the Second Reading, with many MPs arguing the case for a 50 per cent grant.[178] Behind the scenes a thornier question had concerned the negotiating machinery for the future service and the linked question of recognition for the officers' section of the FBU.

During the discussions on the Fire Services Bill in early 1947 the union advanced the idea of a single negotiating body embracing all ranks below that of Chief Officer. Local authority representatives, in contrast, supported the maintenance of two separate bodies, one for officers and one for the lower ranks. In this they were at one with the National Fire Service Officers' Association, the 'company union' established by Herbert Morrison to represent the officer ranks. Discipline would suffer, argued Reader Harris, general secretary of the Association, if officers' questions were dealt with by the same body that dealt with the conditions of lower ranks. Not even the FBU's suggestion of a sub-committee or panel to deal with officer matters, on which the NFSOA would have majority representation, lessened their objections to a single negotiating body.

Fortunately for the FBU, the Home Office agreed that the setting up of two councils for the fire service would not be practical. Gradually the department broke down the opposition of the local authorities, which by August 1947 had agreed to the formation of a single council with separate panels for the officers and the junior ranks. This became the National Joint Council. The Home Secretary also insisted that, since the officers section of the FBU had a membership of over 350 (around one-quarter of all NFS officers), the union could not be excluded from representation on the officers' panel, whatever the local authorities thought about the union. The FBU had at last won the long struggle for trade union recognition for its officer members. Thanks to TUC support, and Chuter Ede's political skill, the FBU became the one organisation recognised as competent to negotiate on behalf of all ranks.[179]

On All Fools Day 1948 firemen took up their duties in the local authority fire brigades. At a ceremony at Lambeth to mark the end of the National Fire Service Horner remarked that it was, in some ways, a 'sad occasion', to which Chuter Ede replied; 'The union might have prevented it'.[180] The implication, presumably, is that had the union come out strongly in favour of the NFS, the Labour government would have included the fire service in its programme of nationalisation. Maybe so, but this view underestimates the determination of the local authorities, at least in England and Wales (many of the Scottish authorities were more favourable to the NFS) to force central government to return the fire service to local control.

It is a moot point, anyway, since the regular firemen added their voices to the clamour for local control. Better the devil they knew than the impersonal monster run by central officials, whose bureaucratic reign they had suffered for six years. Even regulars from pre-war brigades with the very worst conditions of service wished to return to the fold. The FBU followed the lead of the professional firemen, although working for a replacement of the hundreds of small brigades by larger units. The union took comfort from the fact that, while the service would be returning to its local, quasi-democratic roots, conditions of employment would be settled nationally. As Horner told the International Firemen's Conference in September 1947:

> We will not have the position where firemen in one city earn less than the firemen in another; we shall not have the position where firemen in one Brigade work many more hours, or are on duty for a longer period, than firemen in another Brigade. National conditions of service for the British firemen have come to stay.[181]

Achievements

In other regards, too, a great distance had been travelled since 1939. The union was represented on every committee dealing with the National Fire Service, and would be likewise represented in the new fire service. Nor was the National Joint Council, say, an advance in bargaining power alone. It marked the union's accepted role in building a professional fire service, skilled in fire prevention and fire fighting, staffed by a competent and contented fire force. In fact, the FBU had brought off one of the most remarkable achievements in the trade union movement.

In a highly disciplined and uniformed social service, at a time of war, thousands of firemen and firewomen had been organised within the working-class movement. The union was in sight of 100 per cent membership of the FBU, and the 1947 Conference looked forward to the closed shop.[182] For the FBU to be the sole trade union for firemen also looked imminent, as the TUC asked competing unions to quit the field. No longer were firemen shut up in their fire stations, isolated from other workers and from the affairs of the trade union and political world. Under the politically conscious leadership of John Horner, the FBU began to play its part on the wider stage. Support was given to the India League, to the Greek partisans and to the Beveridge Plan for social security. The union opposed Morrison's decision in 1943 to release Oswald Mosley, leader of the British Union of Fascists. The FBU also pressed time and again for the affiliation of the Communist Party to the Labour Party, in the cause of working-class unity.[183]

If we require an explanation of the dramatic change in the size and significance of the FBU, we need look no further than the war and its impact. A few thousand inward-looking professional firemen were suddenly faced with an Auxiliary Fire Service of 100,000 men and women, doing the job on conditions of employment inferior to those enjoyed by regulars. No other union of the size of the FBU confronted the consequent dilemma: should the 'dilutees' be told to fend for themselves or should regulars and auxiliaries unite to secure uniform and improved conditions of service? It is to John Horner's immense credit that the second course was followed. As a result union membership exploded, the aspirations of the workforce changed and union objectives expanded from 'market' questions of hours and wage rates to 'managerial' issues of manpower, equipment and organisational structure.

The singular contribution of that remarkable personality, John Horner, deserves separate mention. His caring, committed and charismatic leadership were evident to all who made up the post-war fire service. He combined a deep solicitude for the welfare and wages of serving firemen, with a shrewd and clear-sighted appreciation of the political and economic framework in which the firemen's struggle was set. His memorable general secretaryship, however, was shaped on the anvil of war. In 1939 Horner inherited a set of problems the like of which would have dispirited the most experienced trade unionist. The FBU was a minnow of a trade union, its development limited by the sectarian concerns of the London regulars, its membership swamped by shoals of auxiliary firemen. In the critical early months of the war Horner succeeded in keeping the support of the regulars, bravely entering the lion's den of professional fire stations, and even convinced them of the need to organise the AFS. In scrupulously democratic fashion he then arranged the union of regulars and auxiliaries. The marriage of the two bodies of firefighters was, without question, the most decisive step in the history of firemen's trade unionism up to that point. Horner now had the weight of numbers when negotiating with the local authorities and the Home Office, and a much larger pool of legal and political talent to draw upon.

It in no way detracts from Horner's impressive contribution to recognise that without the skills and outlook of many of the new recruits his task would have been much more difficult. Union membership, as we have seen, rose from around 3,000 in 1939 to 85,000 at the peak of the National Fire Service. The number of ex-regular firemen enrolled in the union increased, but the vast bulk of new members were auxiliaries. Few had prior trade union or political experience, but many measured the reality of their work situation against a higher set of expectations than those of regular firemen. Conditions of employment that ex-seamen put up with in the inter-war years were considered intolerable by men from different walks of life. From these circumstances arose the long struggle to bring auxiliary firemen up to the level of regular firemen and to raise regular firemen to the level of skilled industrial workers.

Union objectives changed, too. From 1941 to 1947 the fire service was in an almost constant state of flux. Nationalisation, demobilisation and de-nationalisation enforced enormous periodic changes in the membership and administrative structure of the service (not to mention the union). Men were sieved and re-sieved as the number of officers and firemen changed; men and women of all ranks were moved around the country as the needs of war dictated. In this period of flux the union was an important element of stability, providing much-needed information on discipline, promotion, pensions and pay. And it constantly insisted upon a bigger say in the running and regulation of the service.

The war years, in fact, witnessed the transition from complete detachment to complete involvement in the management of the service. In his first annual report for the executive council, Horner wrote:

> It has never been the policy of this union to interfere in any way with the management of the fire service. We all readily appreciate that if we start telling Chief Officers how to run their brigades, it may not be long before they try to tell us how to run the FBU.

Yet in December 1943, in *What Kind of Fire Service?*, the FBU publicly evaluated the requirements of the post-war service. In February 1945, still awaiting an official announcement on the future of the NFS, the union convened a public conference on 'Fire Protection', chaired by Lewis Silkin, MP. More than 100 delegates attended from local authorities and their associations, from the technical and professional bodies associated with the fire service, and from trade unions and industrial organisations. The union was clearly intent on making its voice heard on the methods of firefighting, on the treatment of firefighters and on the manner in which the fire service was being handled. One of the main strengths of the FBU, indeed, was the way in which the affairs of the union and the fire service had become deeply interwoven.[184]

As influential as the pragmatic requirements of war, was the war-induced politics of social equality. In a People's War affairs of state could not be left in the hands of 'the man who knows'. As Peter Pain, a barrister and auxiliary fireman, stated in 1941, in a passage which heralded a new kind of trade unionism in the fire service:

> By the end of war much will be in ruins, ideas as well as buildings. The power of the bankers must lie buried in the debris of the City of London, the ghosts of vested interest must stalk disconsolate through the gutted warehouses, the abuses of the big monopolies must have been washed down the sewers by our jets. The old capitalist system, like the captive Samson, must perish in the ruins which it has pulled down on itself.
>
> The people alone will survive – the tough, invincible working people ... When peace comes, this people will build a Brave New World ... The firemen will be there, again in front rank. We shall have learnt in the Fire Brigades Union the lessons which must be applied to society as a whole. We shall know the value of unity and loyalty, of persistence against tremendous odds, of self-discipline and of democratic discussion. By virtue of our knowledge we shall take the lead.[185]

The FBU's politically-committed and forceful trade unionism chimed in with a People's War, with the Soviet Union as bold ally. It was in harmony with the spirit of the post-war years, as Labour embarked on the construction of a socialist Britain. By 1951, however, the times had changed, and the union was back on the defensive. The Labour government had been turned out of office. The return of a Conservative government invigorated the campaign of the County Councils Association to break the link between firefighters' pay and police pay. And the influence of Cold War ideology was to be felt in the charge that Communist Party influence was considerable in the Fire Brigades Union. The union would need all its organisational strength and tactical experience to combat these fresh challenges to fire service trade unionism.

Notes

* I am grateful to John Horner, John Saville and Terry Segars, who kindly read and criticised an earlier version of this chapter.

1. See evidence of A.R. Dyer, Chief Officer of the London Fire Brigade (LFB), to the Departmental Committee on the Hours, Pay and Conditions of Service of Firemen in Professional Fire Brigades in Great Britain (Middlebrook Committee), contained in London County Council (LCC), FB/STA/1/38.
2. See Sally Holloway, *London's Noble Fire Brigades 1833-1904*, London 1973, passim; Greater London Council, *In the Service of London: Origins and Development of Council Employment from 1889*, London 1986, p. 41; Ronald Cox, *Oh, Captain Shaw. The Life Story of the First and Most Famous Chief of the London Fire Brigade*, London 1984. Shaw was London's fire chief from 1861-91. See also John Horner, Ch. 10 below, pp. 280, 286 and 290; Terry Segars, 'Working for London's Fire Brigade, 1889-1939', in Andrew Saint (ed.), *Politics and the People of London*, London 1989, pp. 172-3.
3. Commander Sir Aylmer Firebrace, *Fire Service Memories*, London n.d. p. 115.
4. See Dyer's evidence to Middlebrook in LCC, FB/STA/1/38; 'Discipline', a lecture delivered by Firebrace, March 1934, p. 10, in LCC, FB/STA/3/3; A. Carew, *The Lower Deck of the Royal Navy, 1900-39*, Manchester 1981, p. 18; Segars in Saint (ed.), *Politics and the People*, p. 174; Horner, Ch. 10 below. See also LCC, MIN/6209 for the armed services background of firemen appointed in 1939.
5. See G.V. Blackstone, *A History of the British Fire Service*, London 1957, p. 309.
6. For Bradley, see Minutes of Evidence to the Committee on the Hours, Pay and Conditions of Service of Firemen in Professional Fire Brigades in Great Britain (Middlebrook Committee), PP 1920, XVI (Cmnd 876) p. 13, q. 188; p. 18, q. 294. See also Public Record Office (PRO), HO45/10899/370662/1, cutting from *Daily News*, 4 Sept 1918; Frederick H. Radford,

'Fetch the Engine': The Official History of the Fire Brigades Union, London 1951, p. 46; Segars in Saint (ed.), *Politics and the People*, p. 180; D. Englander, Ch. 2 below, pp. 102-3.
7. See *Evidence to Middlebrook*, p. 4, q. 6 (Col Guy Symonds, late member of the Fire Advisory Committee of the Ministry of Munitions); p. 54, q. 1187 (Superintendent R. Burt, London Fire Brigade). See also Firebrace, *Memories*, p. 20; LCC, CL/FB/1/153, cutting from *West London Observer*, 26 June 1914.
8. There were five main categories of Fire Brigade before 1939. 1) The first main category were the *police brigades* in which whole-time firemen were technically part of the police force, and who received the same pay and pension as the police. In this category were many of the important brigades in the North of England: Leeds, Doncaster, Hull, Sheffield, Newcastle and Liverpool, but also Bristol and Cardiff in the West and Wales. In Scotland, however, there was only one police brigade, Lanarkshire County Police Brigade. The picture is confused by the existence of police *part-time* brigades, in which firemen were found from constables who were off duty in quarters near the fire station (e.g., Norwich, Lincoln, Plymouth and Lanarkshire.) Local authorities favoured police brigades on grounds of economy, especially since local police expenditure attracted a 50 per cent government grant. 2) The second main category were *professional brigades* of whole-time, permanent firemen. The largest such brigades were London (with 1,300 men in 1920), Birmingham (200 men) and Manchester (130 men). In the same category were Glasgow, Edinburgh, Bradford, Leicester, Tottenham and West Ham. 3) The majority of the brigades in England and Wales and in Scotland were an amalgam of professional whole-time firemen and retained men, the latter receiving a retaining fee for their services and payment for each attendance at a fire. Some police brigades and many more non-police brigades (e.g., Folkestone) were of this type; they were particularly common in small towns and country districts. 4) *Volunteer brigades* consisted of volunteer firemen, although some included one or more professional firemen and retained staff. These brigades were, in theory, independent of local authority control, but some volunteer brigades received an annual subsidy or grant of buildings from the council. 5) Finally, firms and government departments maintained works brigades or *private brigades*. The Great Western Railway had a brigade at their main Swindon works, as did Cadbury's at Bournville and Lever Brothers at Port Sunlight. There were also colliery brigades, and brigades to protect naval and military property. See *Report of the Royal Commission on Fire Brigades and Fire Prevention*, PP 1923, XI (Cmnd. 1945) pp. 125-34.
9. See *Evidence to Middlebrook*, p. 38, q. 700 (A.R. Tozer); p. 85, q. 2398 (Councillor James Johnson, Manchester Watch Committee); p. 99, q. 2800 (Dr James Brown Wright, Newcastle-u-Tyne); p. 111, q. 3271 (Arthur Pordage, Firemaster, Edinburgh); p. 34, q. 568 and p. 36, q. 607 (William Waddell, Chief Officer, Glasgow F.B.)
10. See *Evidence to Middlebrook*, p. 85, q. 2398 (James Johnson); p. 68, q. 1755 and p. 71, q. 1871 (Arthur Corlett, Chief Officer, Manchester F.B.) See also Norman Greenfield, interview, May 1987; Charles Best (Wallasey fire station), correspondence, April-December 1987; Radford, *Official History*, p. 51; PRO, HO187/130 (Corlett letter, July 1919);

Blackstone, *History*, p. 309. Blackstone compared the position of firemen to that of domestic servants, never allowed out in case they were wanted.
11. See *Evidence to Middlebrook*, p. 61, q. 1439 (Alfred Collins, Southampton F.B.); Blackstone, *History*, p. 353.
12. *Evidence to Middlebrook*, p. 12, qq. 178-80.
13. See *Report of the Committee on the Hours, Pay and Conditions of Service of Firemen in Professional Fire Brigades in Great Britain* (Middlebrook Committee), PP 1920, XVI (Cmnd 710) p. 6; W. Eric Jackson, *London's Fire Brigades*, London 1966, p. 79.
14. Cf. G. Alderman, 'The Railway Companies and the Growth of Trade Unionism in the late Nineteenth and Early Twentieth Centuries', *Historical Journal*, Vol.XIV (1971), pp. 129-31; Richard Hyman, *The Workers' Union*, Oxford 1971, conclusions.
15. See Phoenix, *The Decay of London's Fire Brigade*, London 1902, p. 55. Cf. Carew, *The Lower Deck*, pp. 86 and 197-202.
16. Horner, Ch. 10 below, pp. 289-90. Cf. K. Newton, *The Sociology of British Communism*, London 1969, pp. 47-8; M. Moran, *The Union of Post Office Workers. A Study in Political Sociology*, London 1974, pp. 19-20.
17. See LCC, MIN/5989, p. 791; LCC, MIN/5990, p. 251. See also, Bernard Dix and Stephen Williams, *Serving the Public: Building the Union. The History of the National Union of Public Employees*, Vol.1: The Forerunners 1889-1928, London 1987, p. 107.
18. See LCC, MIN/5997, p. 837; LCC, MIN/6146; Terry Segars, 'The Fire Service: the social history of a uniformed working-class occupation' (Essex University PhD., 1989) p. 128. See also Dix and Williams, *Serving the Public*, pp. 134, 162 & 165. For the 'Labour Unrest', see H.A. Clegg, *A History of British Trade Unions since 1889*, Vol. II, Oxford 1985, Ch. 2.
19. LCC, CL/FB/1/153.
20. See LCC, MIN/5997, p. 857; LCC, MIN/5998, pp. 94 & 96; LCC, *Minutes of Proceedings*, p. 1409 (9 December 1913), p. 1452 (17 December 1913). See also Dix & Williams, *Serving the Public*, p. 165.
21. See LCC, CL/FB/1/153, cutting from *Daily Graphic*, 14 July 1914. See also, Radford, *Official History*, p. 57.
22. See Blackstone, *History*, pp. 324 and 332.
23. See PRO, LAB2/268/13/7039/1-3; PRO, HO45/10899/370662/1, cutting from the *Times*, 4 September 1918. For increases in rates of wages in several occupations, including police constables, see A.L. Bowley, *Prices and Wages in the United Kingdom, 1914-1920*, Oxford 1921, p. 103.
24. See Radford, *Official History*, p. 61; Blackstone, *History*, p. 311; Greenfield, interview, May 1987; Segars, 'The Fire Service', pp. 175-6. Developments in Belfast are discussed in K.D. Brown, Ch. 5 below. In September 1919 the National Amalgamated Workers' Union (Municipal Employees' Section) claimed to have members in the Belfast and Londonderry brigades: PRO, HO187/130.
25. See W. Kendall, *The Revolutionary Movement in Britain 1900-1921*, London 1969, pp. 190-1; D. Englander and J. Osborne, 'Jack, Tommy, and Henry Dubb: the Armed Forces and the Working Class', *Historical Journal*, Vol.21 (1978), pp. 614-18; Carew, *The Lower Deck*, pp. xii, 90 and 196.
26. See Gerald Reynolds and Anthony Judge, *The Night the Police Went on Strike*, London 1968, pp. 23-4; John Horner, *Studies in Industrial Democracy*,

London 1973, p. 164; PRO, LAB 2/268/13/7039/1-3; General Sir N. Macready, *Annals of an Active Life*, London 1924, Vol.1, pp. 301-09, Vol.2, pp. 406-10. Unrest in the police force persisted until August 1919, when a second strike, to save the National Union of Police and Prison Officers, and to stop the establishment of the Police Federation, was defeated. See V.L. Allen, 'The National Union of Police and Prison Officers', *Economic History Review*, 2nd.ser., Vol.XI (August 1958) pp. 133-43; Robert Reiner, *The Blue-Coated Worker. A Sociological Study of Police Unionism*, Cambridge 1978, pp. 19-25.
27. LCC, MIN/6146, Sladen's memo, 9 September 1918.
28. Ibid., Sladen's report to Fire Brigade Committee, 31 October 1918. See also LCC, *Mins. of Proceedings*, p. 887 (15 October 1918), p. 1177 (10 December 1918).
29. See LCC, CL/FB/1/153.
30. For the hearing and its outcome, see Lord Askwith, *Industrial Problems and Disputes*, London 1920, pp. 451-2; LCC, MIN/6146; LCC, *Mins. of Proceedings*, pp. 885-91 (15 October 1918), p. 1064 (12 November 1918).
31. Dix and Williams, *Serving the Public*, p. 176.
32. Ibid., pp. 177-8. Bradley agreed to withdraw the allegation of incompetence, on Taylor's part, in dealing with fire brigade issues, and to pay £100 legal costs.
33. See LCC, MIN/6146; Blackstone, *History*, p. 338.
34. Blackstone, p. 338.
35. LCC, *Mins. of Proceedings*, 4 March 1919.
36. See LCC, MIN/6148 (Dyer, Chief Officer of the London Fire Brigade, to Fire Brigade Committee, 13 June 1919); PRO, HO187/130 (internal memo, 4 June 1919).
37. PRO, HO187/130.
38. Ibid. See also, LCC, FB/STA/1/38; LCC, *Mins. of Proceedings*, p. 1198 (14 October 1919), p. 1681 (16 December 1919), p. 1759 (19 December 1919).
39. LCC, *Mins. of Proceedings*, p. 134 (3 February 1920). See also Radford, *Official History*, p. 91.
40. See Firebrace, *Memories*, p. 21; LCC, *Mins. of Proceedings*, p. 603 (3 February 1920); *Evidence to Middlebrook*, p. 54, q. 1195 (Superintendent Burt).
41. See Radford, *Official History*, p. 92. The Home Secretary declined to include Northern Ireland in the scope of the enquiry: PRO, HO187/130.
42. *Middlebrook Report*, pp. 5-6.
43. *Evidence*, p. 38, q. 690 (William Waddell, Chief Officer, Glasgow F.B.).
44. *Report*, pp. 9-10.
45. *Evidence*, p. 11, q. 145 (Bradley).
46. *Evidence*, p. 71, q. 1872 (Arthur Corlett, Chief Officer, Manchester); p. 59, q. 1366 (John Callaghan, Birmingham); p. 65, q. 1596 (Arthur Henry Wright, Leicester); p. 62, q. 1487 (John Banks, Glasgow); p. 34, q. 575A (Waddell, Glasgow).
47. *Report*, pp. 4-5.
48. See, e.g., *Evidence*, p. 3, q. 1 (Symonds).
49. See LCC, CL/FB/1/153 (Bradley, 17 April 1919).
50. *Evidence*, p. 113, q. 3388 (James Stewart, Glasgow); p. 109, q. 3209 (Arthur Pordage, Edinburgh); p. 57, q. 1311 (Callaghan, Birmingham).

See also PRO, HO187/130 (G. Titt, The Workers' Union, to Corlett, Chief Officer, Manchester, 7 April 1919).
51. See *Fire* (October 1918) pp. 65-6, (February 1920) p. 123; Blackstone, *History*, pp. 250, 311, 347 and 356.
52. See PRO, HO187/130; Blackstone, *History*, p. 355.
53. Ibid. See also LCC, CL/FB/1/154; Radford, *Official History*, pp. 94-5.
54. See Executive Council's Report in *Third Annual Report of the Firemen's Trade Union*, 1921, p. 3; Firebrace, *Memories*, p. 80; Blackstone, *History*, pp. 370-1. For the Royal Commission, see Blackstone, pp. 357-66.
55. *Third Annual Report*, pp. 8-9; Radford, *Official History*, p. 79.
56. LCC, CL/FB/1/153 (meeting between Dyer and Bradley, 12 October 1921). The executive council found out about this agreement in August 1922, when Bradley was away from Head Office with acute diabetes.
57. Ibid. See also LCC, FB/STA/1/18 (correspondence between Morrison and Lt Col E. Ball, chairman of Fire Brigade Committee, December 1923 to March 1924).
58. See *Revised Rules*, 1922, p. 3; *Third Annual Report*, p. 4; Executive Council's Report in *Ninth Annual Report of the Firemen's Trade Union*, 1928, p. 5.
59. See *Report of the Royal Commission on Fire Brigades and Fire Prevention*, PP 1923, XI (Cmnd 1945) pp. 194-5; *Ninth Annual Report*, pp. 3-4; Jackson, *London's Fire Brigades*, p. 79; Blackstone, *History*, pp. 374-5.
60. See *Ninth Annual Report*, pp. 5-6; Radford, *Official History*, p. 98; Segars, 'The Fire Service', pp. 328-34.
61. See Blackstone, *History*, p. 375; LCC, FB/GEN/1/77.
62. *Ninth Annual Report*, pp. 2-3 & 7-8.
63. The following biographical sketch is based on Dix and Williams, *Serving the Public*, p. 147; *Firefighter*, February 1954, p. 9; Radford, *Official History*, pp. 86-8; Segars, 'The Fire Service', pp. 129-30 and 325-35.
64. Quoted in Dix and Williams, *Serving the Public*, p. 152.
65. See Blackstone, *History*, p. 378.
66. See LCC, CL/FB/1/155 and 156; Industrial Court, Award No. 1527, 6 February 1932, p. 3; LCC, CL/ESTAB/1/114.
67. Industrial Court, Award No. 1539, 27 July 1932.
68. Industrial Court, Award No. 1562, 6 April 1933.
69. For the Redmayne Award, 10 January 1934, see LCC, CL/ESTAB/1/246. For a later evaluation of Redmayne, see *Minutes of Proceedings before a Board of Arbitration ... 8 January 1952*, pp. 58-60. See also LCC, CL/FB/1/157; Blackstone, *History*, p. 378.
70. See LCC, *Mins. of Proceedings*, p. 82 (10 July 1934); LCC, MIN/6192 (Chief Officer's report, 12 October 1934); Major C.C.B. Morris, *Fire!* (London, 1939) p. 21; Radford, *Official History*, p. 97.
71. For these earlier claims, see text above, pp. 19-20 and 22-3.
72. See LCC FB/STA/1/137; LCC, *Mins. of Proceedings*, 11 December 1934, pp. 734-5.
73. See *Firefighter* (Report of the 17th Annual Conference), 1936, pp. 74-5; *London News*, March 1935, p. 7.
74. *London News*, June 1935, p. 6. See also Radford, *Official History*, pp. 103-5.
75. Horner insists that there were few, if any, Communist Party members in the FBU before the war: correspondence, August 1990. See GLC, *In the*

Service of London, p. 44; Bernard Donoughue & G.W. Jones, *Herbert Morrison. Portrait of a Politician*, London 1973, pp. 193 and 202; DNB 1961-70, pp. 769-73; N. Branson, *Poplarism, 1919-1925*, London 1979, pp. 55-6 and 166; K.O. Morgan, *Labour People*, Oxford 1987, pp. 176-8; M. Clapson, 'Localism, the London Labour Party and the LCC between the Wars' in Saint (ed.), *Politics and the People*, p. 129.
76. See LCC, CL/ESTAB/1/236; *The Firefighter* (Report of the 18th Annual Conference), 1937, p. 54.
77. Ibid. See also LCC, CL/ESTAB/1/244; LCC, *Mins. of Proceedings*, 23 May 1939, pp. 523-4.
78. See *The Firefighter*, 1936, pp. 21-2 and 78-9; *The Firefighter*, 1937, p. 57; LCC, FB/STA/1/37. In 1936 a new member of the union paid a 2s. entrance fee, then 4d. weekly. The contribution to the political fund was 1s. quarterly.
79. *Firefighter*, 1937, pp. 11 and 14.
80. See LCC, MIN/6192 (Chief Officer's report, 12 October 1934); LCC, FB/STA/1/37 (Chief Officer's report, 21 November 1934); LCC, CL/FB/1/153; *The Firefighter*, 1936, pp. 55-6.
81. See *Firefighter*, 1936, p. 76, and 1937, pp. 31-2, 47 and 53; LCC, FB/STA/1/37 (Association of Municipal Corporations, 5 October 1938).
82. See *Firefighter*, 1936, pp. 42-6, and 1937, p. 19.
83. *Firefighter*, 1937, pp. 39-40 and 45.
84. Ibid., pp. 40-2.
85. For more on these remarkable events, see below, pp. 43-4.
86. See *Report of the Departmental Committee on Fire Brigade Services* (Riverdale Committee), PP 1935-6, X (Cmnd 5224). For the Committee's composition, deliberations and recommendations, see Blackstone, *History*, pp. 384-5; Terence O'Brien, *Civil Defence*, London 1955, pp. 85 and 239-40.
87. *Hansard*, Vol. 335, 10 May 1938, col.1429, 2nd. Reading of Fire Brigades Bill; O'Brien, *Civil Defence*, pp. 249-50; Blackstone, *History*, pp. 392-3.
88. O'Brien, *Civil Defence*, pp. 145-6.
89. John S. Cormack, formerly a gardener, found bosses, office boys, clerks and dockers in the Hull AFS: interview, January 1987. For the social background of women auxiliaries, see Segars, Ch. 3 below, pp. 140-1.
90. See, e.g., Maurice Levinson, *The Trouble with Yesterday*, London 1946.
91. William Sansom et al, *Jim Braidy. The Story of Britain's Firemen*, London 1943, p. 50. See also LCC, *London's Auxiliary Fire Service* (information for intending candidates); O'Brien, *Civil Defence*, p. 241; Horner, *Studies*, p. 40.
92. Blackstone, *History*, p. 400. See also O'Brien, *Civil Defence*, pp. 253, 255 and 445-6.
93. See Michael Wassey, *Ordeal by Fire*, London 1941, p. 55; O'Brien, *Civil Defence*, pp. 447 and 449.
94. For the cartoon of Morrison putting the 60-hour week into an unplugged fridge, see *Firefighter* (Report of the 21st Annual Conference), 1940, p. 61.
95. Ibid., p. 54; FBU, *The Fire Brigade Union's Fifty Years of Service, 1918-1968*, 'AFS splits Union'; Horner, Ch. 10 below, pp. 307-8.
96. FBU, *Fifty Years*, 'Regulars vs AFS'; Horner, Ch. 10 below,

pp. 311-2.
97. *Firefighter*, 1940, p. 31.
98. Ibid., pp. 33 and 57-59. H.S. Richardson, for one, spoke in favour of the resolution.
99. Ibid., pp. 15, 44 and 56-7. See also, FBU (AFS section), *An Object Lesson for Trade Unionists*, 20 November 1940, enclosed in LCC, FB/WAR/1/178; John Horner to E. Stevens (Newport), 27 November 1939, for an example of recruitment into the regular section (document loaned by Norman Stevens, sub officer, Gwent Fire Brigade); Radford, *Official History*, p. 114.
100. E.E.S. to Frank Crump, MSS.144/87/56/Misc., National Amalgamated Union of Life Assurance Workers (Crump papers), Modern Records Centre, Warwick. See also Peter Pain (AFS National Officer in 1941), personal communication, 6 October 1987.
101. Jack Dash, *Good Morning Brothers!*, London 1969, p. 49; Horner, *Studies*, pp. 169-70; Horner, Ch. 10 below, pp. 317-9; Bob Bagley, personal communication, September 1987. Bagley was elected to attend the National Conference of the AFS section; later elected to the executive council of the union. Other AFS recruits became prominent union workers. Fred Willey, a Cambridge graduate and barrister, was in the East London AFS; he became the union's London Regional Officer. He became Labour MP for Sunderland in 1945. William Hannan, a former shop assistant and insurance agent, became Divisional Welfare Officer in the National Fire Service. He was elected Labour MP for Glasgow (Maryhill) in 1945. Jack Grahl had been a unionist since 1928 (in the National Operative Plumbers and Domestic Engineers' Association) and was a member of the Communist Party. He first became Edinburgh Area Secretary of the union; later appointed to assist Tom Murray in Edinburgh. Brett had been a shop steward and a branch president in the Municipal & General Workers' Union in Bradford. He assisted McHugh in the FBU's Bradford office.
102. Bagley, personal communication, September 1987.
103. See Peter Pain, *The Struggle of the AFS*, London 1941?, p. 5; *The Firefighter*, 1940, pp. 7-9 and 54; *The Bulletin* (of the AFS section of the FBU), May 1941, No.12, p. 3; Segars, 'The Fire Service', pp. 164-5.
104. See *The Bulletin*, No.10, March 1941, p. 6; Pain, *Struggle*, pp. 5-6; *Firefighter*, March 1941, pp. 1-2 and 10-11; *Annual Report of the Management Committee (Regular Section) to be presented at the Annual Conference*, June 1941, p. 16; *Fire* (April 1941) p. 188; Horner to Greenfield, 1 and 29 January, and 3 March 1941, seen with kind permission of N. Greenfield.
105. FBU, *Fifty Years*; Horner, *Studies*, pp. 167-8; Horner, Ch. 10 below, pp. 321-2. For Anderson, see John W. Wheeler-Bennett, *John Anderson, Viscount Waverley*, New York 1962.
106. Pain, *Struggle*, pp. 4-5.
107. *The Firefighter*, 1940, p. 37. See also Pain, *Struggle*, p. 2; Radford, *Official History*, p. 111.
108. For the ten points, see Pain, *Struggle*, p. 4. See also John Horner, *AFS. Your Rights to Compensation*, London 1939.
109. Ibid., pp. 11-13. See also *Firefighter*, 1940, pp. 26-7; LCC, CL/ESTAB/1/237 (Horner to Deputy Chief Officer, LFB, 28 November 1939).

110. Ibid., pp. 14-20. See also LCC, MIN/6209 (memo from Representative Body of LFB, February 1940); LCC, CL/CD/1/43.
111. See Blackstone, *History*, p. 404; Wassey, *Ordeal*, pp. 171-3. Wassey was the General Secretary of the breakaway union, the National Union of Auxiliary Firemen, formed in November 1940. This union, according to Peter Pain, posed a serious threat to the FBU's recruitment of auxiliaries, living off the tensions aroused between regulars and auxiliaries by sick and injury pay and by the unification scheme: Pain, personal communication, 6 October 1987; LCC, CL/CD/1/69.
112. See PRO, HO187/166 (funeral expenses); *The Bulletin*, No.8, January 1941. When, however, two auxiliaries were charged with looting and sentenced to a month's imprisonment for scrounging unwanted building materials with which to improve their fire station, with the knowledge of their LFB sub-officer, provoking a near-strike of auxiliary firemen, the FBU secured their acquittal. The union's success in this case resulted in floods of new members: James W. Kenyon, *The Fourth Arm*, London 1948, p. 22; *The Bulletin*, No.10, March 1941.
113. See O'Brien, *Civil Defence*, pp. 453-7; LCC, *Fire Over London. The Story of the London Fire Service 1940-41*, enclosed in LCC, FB/WAR/4/1; Firebrace, *Memories*, pp. 165-93, passim. In the course of the war 793 firemen and 25 firewomen lost their lives, and over 7,000 firefighters were injured.
114. Harold S. Ingham (ed.), *Fire and Water. An Anthology by Members of the NFS*, London 1942, p. 91. Ingham was an FBU area official in north-west London; he was awarded the MBE for his organisation of Productive Work, for which see below. For more prosaic and realistic passages on what blitz fire fighting was like, see Cyril Demarne, *The London Blitz. A Fireman's Tale*, London 1980, pp. 7-30. Demarne had been a regular fireman in the West Ham brigade since 1925.
115. See O'Brien, *Civil Defence*, pp. 458-60; Firebrace, *Memories*, p. 177; Segars, Ch. 3 below. There were a few lighter moments. Walter Gander got a tour of duty at London Zoo, his job to fight fires and to put back into cages any animals that escaped! See *I Can Remember*, compiled by N. Crowther, London 1976, p. 42.
116. Maurice Levinson spoke of the period before the blitz as follows: 'I had a feeling of being part of a large orchestra tuning up for a lengthy crescendo that was never going to begin.' See *The Trouble*, p. 156. For the *Daily Mirror* cartoon, 14 September 1940, which registered the change in public attitude to the auxiliaries, see Blackstone, *History*, p. 415. See also Sansom, *Jim Braidy*, p. 21.
117. See Firebrace, *Memories*, pp. 194-202, passim; Harry Klopper, *The Fight Against Fire*, Birmingham 1954, pp. 92-99, passim; T. Geraghty, '*A North-East Coast Town'. Ordeal and Triumph. The Story of Kingston Upon Hull*, Hull 1978, passim; Lord Morrison of Lambeth, *Herbert Morrison. An Autobiography*, London 1960, p. 187; Donoughue and Jones, *Morrison*, p. 291; N. Longmate, *Air Raid. The Bombing of Coventry, 1940*, New York 1978, ch. 8.
118. See O'Brien, *Civil Defence*, pp. 460-1 and 467-8; Donoughue and Jones, *Morrison*, p. 292.
119. Ibid., p. 469; Donoughue and Jones, *Morrison*, pp. 294-6; Blackstone, *History*, pp. 425-7; PRO, CAB 65/18, War Cabinet 48 (41), 8 May 1941;

War Cabinet 49 (41), 12 May 1941; *Betwixt*, May 1942.
120. *Hansard*, Vol.371, 13 May 1941, cols. 1082-3; 20 May 1941, cols. 1413-39, passim.
121. Blackstone, *History*, pp. 431-3. See also D. Englander, Ch. 2 below, pp. 19-23, for the FBU's determination to resist the militarisation of the NFS.
122. Ibid., pp. 435-6. See also O'Brien, *Civil Defence*, p. 481; Frank Eyre and E.C.R. Hadfield, *The Fire Service To-Day*, London 1953, 2nd. ed., p. 30.
123. Morrison, *Autobiography*, p. 184; O'Brien, *Civil Defence*, p. 472.
124. *Report of the Proceedings at the 22nd Annual Conference*, June 1941, pp. 32-49, passim; *The Bulletin*, No.12, May 1941.
125. Ibid. See also *Annual Report of the Management Committee (Regular Section) for Annual Conference*, 1941, pp. 22-5; Pain, *Struggle*, pp. 22-3. Englander, Ch. 2 below, pp. 113-7, provides further discussion of the NFS discipline code.
126. See *Firefighter*, August 1941, p. 1, enclosed in PRO, HO187/434; Horner, *Studies*, p. 169. For the organisational structure of the National Fire Service, see O'Brien, *Civil Defence*, pp. 475-90.
127. See FBU, *The Firemen's Charter*, enclosed in PRO, HO187/435. See also Pain, *Struggle*, pp. 30-1; *Firefighter*, October 1941, p. 1.
128. See PRO, HO187/435; *Hansard*, Vol.376, 20 November 1941, col. 473; Horner, Ch. 10 below, p. 344.
129. Radford, *Official History*, pp. 137-8. In 1943 union membership stabilised around the 60,000 mark, 5,500 of whom were in the regular section.
130. Firebrace, *Memories*, p. 271.
131. A firewoman's wage was £2 7s. in February 1942, £2 15s. in August 1943.
132. PRO, HO187/445. Horner had no objection to women pump operators, but opposed the use of firewomen at the end of a branch.
133. *Firefighter*, November 1942, p. 4. Tudor-Hart was also vice-chairman of the AFS Management Committee, a staunch worker for the Labour Party and a member of the Poole Trades Council.
134. See PRO, HO187/445; LCC, FB/WAR/4/15; *Firefighter*, March 1943, pp. 1 and 4, June 1943, p. 4. See also FBU, *Should Women Fight?* (1943?); idem., *Calling All Firewomen* (1943?). For a fuller discussion of women in the service and the union, see Segars, Ch. 3 below.
135. See PRO, HO187/425, 435 and 450; LCC, FB/WAR/1/178; *Firefighter*, October 1941.
136. PRO,HO187/450 (meeting, 5 December 1941). It is worth recalling, as an undercurrent to the relationship between Home Secretary Morrison and the Joint Consultative Committee, that Arthur Deakin, as well as being convenor of the workers' side of the JCC, was acting General Secretary of the Transport and General Workers' Union, as a result of Ernest Bevin's appointment as Minister of Labour. Bevin hated the sight and sound of Herbert Morrison, and Deakin, as Bevin's man, could not have been unaffected by Bevin's animosity: see Alan Bullock, *The Life and Times of Ernest Bevin*, Vol.II, London, 1967.
137. Ibid., deputation from TUC, 26 February 1942.
138. See *Firefighter*, July 1942, p. 3; General Fire Force Instruction, No.3/1942: Relations with Trade Unions, 8 May 1942.

139. See PRO, HO187/1082 and HO187/453; General Fire Force Instruction, No.5/1943: Relations with Organisations representing National Fire Service Officers.
140. PRO, HO187/451 (conference, 17 August 1942); HO187/940 (Firebrace's memo, 9 March 1943). Firebrace's argument impressed Herbert Morrison.
141. PRO, HO187/940; General Fire Force Instruction, No.5/1943: Relations with Trade Unions, 19 April 1943.
142. See Walter Evans in *News Chronicle*, 25 June 1942, p. 2; Sansom, *Jim Braidy*, p. 61; P. Addison, *The Road to 1945. British Politics and the Second World War*, London 1982, p. 150.
143. See J. Attfield and S. Williams (eds.), *1939: The Communist Party of Great Britain and the War*, London 1984, p. 87; Bob Darke, *The Communist Technique in Britain*, London 1953, pp. 74-5. Cf. Neal Wood, *Communism and British Intellectuals*, London 1959, pp. 162-3.
144. Darke, *The Communist Technique*, pp. 76-8; Bob Bagley, correspondence, October 1987; John Horner, correspondence, August 1990; Segars, 'The Fire Service', pp. 278 and 433. On the overseas contingent, see below, p. 74. For the wider debate on the Second Front, see A. Calder, *The People's War*, London 1982, pp. 343-44; Addison, *The Road to 1945*, pp. 137, 139, 141 and 153.
145. *Firefighter*, November 1942; Dash, *Brothers*, p. 50.
146. See *Firefighter*, May, July and August 1942; MSS/121/NS/3/3/1-13, Lady Allen of Hurtwood papers, Modern Records Centre, Warwick; *Eastern Star*, Bulletin to branches in No.4 Region, May 1942; *Betwixt*, Midland NFS Report, No.11, June 1942; *Fire*, July 1942, enclosed in PRO, HO187/448.
147. *Firefighter*, July 1942; *Report of the 24th Annual Conference*, 1943, pp. 22-3; PRO, HO187/448.
148. See Radford, *Official History*, pp. 145-9; Horner, *Studies*, p. 173; Sansom, *Jim Braidy*, p. 59; FBU, *Firemen in Production!*, 1942.
149. See PRO, HO187/448; *Firefighter*, August 1942, p. 1.
150. Ibid., deputation of Birmingham MPs, 28 July 1942; *Betwixt*, No.13, August-September 1942; No.14, October-November 1942; *Hansard*, Vol.381, 16 July 1942, col.1369; Vol.382, 23 July 1942, col.157.
151. PRO, HO187/448; Radford, *Official History*, p. 164. For the National Union of Auxiliary Firemen, see HO187/451; *Alert*, monthly organ of the NUAF, May-June 1943.
152. *Firefighter*, November 1942.
153. *Report of the 24th Annual Conference*, 1943, p. 56.
154. Ibid., pp. 57-8.
155. Pain, *Struggle*, p. 31.
156. *Report of the 24th Annual Conference*, 1943, pp. 8-9.
157. *Firefighter*, September 1943 and December 1944.
158. *Firefighter*, September and October 1944.
159. FBU, *What Kind of Fire Service? A Post-War Scheme* (1943) p. 9, enclosed in PRO, HO187/1176.
160. PRO, HO187/1176 (Horner to Sir Arthur Dixon, 8 December 1943).
161. See PRO, HO186/1594.
162. PRO, HO187/822 (Morrison, 16 March 1944).
163. See PRO, HO187/1176 (correspondence between FBU and Home

Office, March to June, 1944). See also FBU, *Eight Hours a Shift! The Union's post-war duty system for the Fire Service*, 1944.
164. Ibid. (Dixon's memo following meeting with FBU, 26 September 1944); *Firefighter*, September 1944, p. 7.
165. See O'Brien, *Civil Defence*, pp. 497-8; Firebrace, *Memories*, p. 231; Horner, *Studies*, pp. 173-4; FBU, *What the Second Front Has Meant to Us*, 1944.
166. *Report of the 27th Annual Conference*, 1946, p. 182.
167. Ibid., p. 169. See also DNB, 1961-70, pp. 216-7; *Times*, 12 November 1965 (obituary); R.A. Butler, *The Art of the Possible. The Memoirs of Lord Butler*, London 1971, p. 93.
168. PRO, HO187/1176 (Horner to Chuter Ede, 16 October 1945).
169. See PRO, HO187/1329; *Report of the 27th Annual Conference*, 1946, p. 177; Kenyon, *Fourth Arm*, p. 49. See also General Fire Force Instruction, No.25/1945: Recruitment of serving members of the National Fire Service for permanent appointment or short-term service, 20 December 1945.
170. Blackstone, *History*, p. 448. For post-war recruitment, see Enoch Humphries, Ch. 11 below.
171. *Report of the 28th Annual Conference*, 1947, p. 250; LCC, CL/ESTAB/1/242.
172. *Report of the 27th Annual Conference*, 1946, p. 18 (address by Chuter Ede). The union's executive committee also supported the employment of women in the future fire service, and the principle of the rate for the job: Report of Conference, 1946, pp. 119-25.
173. PRO, HO187/1008 (Cabinet paper, 13 February 1946); HO187/1176 (FBU deputation to Home Office, 18 March 1946).
174. *Report of the 28th Annual Conference*, 1947, pp. 221-2.
175. *Firefighter*, Autumn 1946, p. 2.
176. *International Firemen's Conference*, London, 16-18 September 1947, p. 16.
177. *Report of the 28th Annual Conference*, 1947, pp. 228-30; PRO, HO187/1065; LCC, CL/ESTAB/1/247; Industrial Court (2076), the National Fire Service, 18 December 1946.
178. Ibid., pp. 218-20; *Hansard*, Vol.435, 27 March 1947, col.1422; 31 March 1947, col.1807.
179. Ibid., p. 244; PRO, HO187/1082 and 1379.
180. FBU, *Fifty Years*.
181. *International Firemen's Conference*, pp. 13-14.
182. *Report of the 28th Annual Conference*, 1947, p. 271. Cf. *Firefighter*, January 1948.
183. See Donoughue and Jones, *Morrison*, p. 304. For John Horner, see M. Stenton and S. Lees (eds.), *Who's Who of British MPs*, Brighton 1981, Vol.IV, p. 173.
184. Horner, correspondence, August 1990. Even the London County Council finally recognised the FBU, thus ending the euphemistic nonsense of the Representative Body.
185. Pain, *Struggle*, p. 34.

II People, Places and Politics

2 The Fire Brigades Union and its Members

David Englander

'It is the element of risk and the demand for courage which set the fireman's job apart from others.'[1] As a summary of the peculiarities of their calling, the statement of the Cunningham Inquiry of 1971 embodies the consensus among operational firemen. 'You look forward to going out,' said one. 'Don't get me wrong. I'm not a sadist, but it's what I joined for.' Survey research, conducted in the 1960s and 70s, confirm his comments. The excitement, the emergency, the thrill and the skill, the exercise of initiative, the saving of persons and property – these, by general consent, supply the principal source of job satisfaction.[2] For firemen, as for soldiers, though, the emergency orientation of work produces additional sources of differentiation.

Continuous cover, an operational imperative, imparts a special character to the organisation of work and the social relations that arise from it. The fire station, unlike the factory, is the focal point of an occupational community in which the domains of work and non-work, private and public, are inextricably entwined; for firemen must work together and play together. With a work-cycle consisting of lengthy periods of inactivity punctuated by brief encounters of great intensity, the fireman is inevitably preoccupied with the ennui of routine duties and the relief therefrom.[3] 'If anyone came in the dining room some nights, they'd think everyone was potty,' said one fireman, describing the evening 'stand down' in a northern fire station. 'Grown men sat there with roulette, roll-a-penny ... and one of the blokes with a scraper saying ... "Next please, roll up, let's have your money".' The role-confusion which this engenders serves to separate firemen from factory workers. 'A lot of outsiders, workers in factories, look down on it,' said one fireman. 'They think we sit all day playing snooker ...' These perceptions, though collected in the late 1970s, were widespread within the fire service for as long as any one could remember. 'There is,' said a Home Office enquiry of 1944, 'a common impression that a fireman spends the greater part of his time idly waiting for a fire call.'[4]

The intrusiveness of work adds a further distinction. Family factors weigh heavily with firemen, for now, as in the past, the fire service includes a higher proportion of married men than in the general population.[5] Operational requirements, which compel the fireman to be available (though not necessarily on duty) for exceptionally long hours, affect the character of housing provision and the quality of home life.

'Of necessity, a fireman's life is subject to a degree of domestic disturbance that is relatively rare in the civil economy.'[6] Fire-fighting disrupts households and limits the scope of personal relations. Until the introduction of individual teletracers in the 1970s families living in fire service accommodation were disturbed day and night by the bells that summoned the fireman to an emergency.[7] Before the war, when all fire service families lived in or close to the fire station, work was to private life as an army of occupation is to a defeated people. The socially isolating and intellectually deadening effects of the 72-hour week which was then the norm, were summarised thus:

> The fireman on 72 hours rarely sees his children. If he is at home from 10 a.m. until 5 p.m. on the one shift, then they are at school; if he is at home on the other shift from 7 p.m. until 8 a.m. they are for the most part in bed. A fireman on 72 hours has no time for self-education, social activities, or politics. He has only every other Saturday or Sunday off and, therefore, cannot meet his friends as often as he would like to.[8]

It was not the only form of deprivation. Personal and professional matters were the common property of a claustrophobic community where, as one fireman put it, 'everyone knows everyone else's business and talks of little else'. The expectation then was that a fireman should live on the fire station as a sailor on his ship. This Victorian vision was, however, based on a false analogy which ignored the fact that the wives and children of seamen did not as a rule live on board ship or sail with their husbands.

The closed community of the fire station represented an extraordinary attempt to replicate the order and ethos of an all-male total institution in an inappropriate setting. There must have been comparatively few work environments in which the wives and children of employees possessed such a high profile. For management their presence was a nightmare. 'It leads to trouble where wives see their husbands at work and at drill – being "smartened up" and reprimanded in the open yard by other wives' husbands,' said one experienced officer. Their progeny, he added, were equally dreaded. 'Children living on fire stations are difficult to manage – to keep away from appliance rooms and the drill yard. When they are shooed off, trouble arises with their mothers.'[9] The non-separation of home and work is not the least of the peculiarities of fire-fighting, however.

Its singularity as a profession derives in large part from its status as a uniformed and disciplined service. Fire-fighting is a hazardous occupation in which death and injury are not infrequent. Its paramilitary character registers the necessity for self-control, orderliness and obedience both to protect the individual fireman and sustain him in the primary work groups through which his dangerous duties are performed. It is within these close-knit and highly cohesive workgroups – 'the watches' – that loyalties are formed – to the brigade, the service and to one's mates. The fireman's uniform, with its insignia of rank, is the outward expression of a special service and his place within it.

Discipline is more than a functional requirement, however; it also imparts a particular character to the development of collective bargaining within the fire service;

for in the mind of management there has existed a hopeless confusion between the discipline necessary to secure life and limb and that enforced as an instrument of control in the workplace. This confusion, though, was not unique to the fire service. Ordinary trade union methods, which in Britain are still not available to members of the armed forces, policemen and certain Crown servants, were for many years withheld from municipal and public service workers on grounds of order and efficiency. Third party interventions were considered subversive; trade union representation, it was argued, placed a barrier between officers and their subordinates; trade union machinery tended to become a substitute for a proper relationship between those who gave orders and those who received them. Grievances might be ventilated through personal approaches to immediate superiors or through the privilege of petition; either way, outside interference was deemed intolerable.[10] In the eyes of management, combination created a conflict of loyalties, and that would never do. As one senior officer put it: 'A fireman at a station must never be allowed to have a dual personality.'[11]

The obstacles to union growth, though real, were not insuperable. Fire-fighting these days is a well-organised service with an exceptionally high density of trade union organisation. From a London-based outfit with a handful of members, the FBU has grown into a nation-wide body which organises all but a fraction of fire-fighters in the public sector.[12] The modern fireman, by comparison with his pre-war predecessor, is not only better organised, but more militant. Between the wars mass unemployment limited the scope for militancy. 'In the past', the Chief of the Fire Staff told the Committee on the Post War Fire Service, 'we have been able to recruit good men ... and work them long hours because unemployment was rife. We should hardly rely on possible unemployment after the war when forming our plans for the future.'[13] The fireman of the 1940s and 50s, unconstrained by ever-lengthening dole queues, was decidedly less docile.

The FBU, following the election of John Horner as

general secretary, became markedly more political in orientation. By the close of 1941 the Home Secretary, who deplored the development, felt that 'a crisis in relations with the Fire Brigades Union might be approaching'; sixteen months later his department was still vainly trying to restrain the union and restrict fire station meetings to their proper sphere. 'If any local officers of the Fire Brigades Union attempt to ... use these meetings ... to press the claims of the Communist Party, or to agitate in favour of the Second Front or to canvass for the Union,' said the draft of a National Fire Service Instruction of March 1943, 'they must be dealt with firmly.'[14] Ten years later FBU radicalism seemed undiminished; among trade unions the firemen's union remained outstanding for its energy and commitment, its willingness to engage with defence and foreign policy questions and address non-industrial issues.[15] By the late 1960s, however, industrial issues were uppermost. 'The year has again been beset with industrial action,' wrote the Chief Inspector of Fire Services in his report for 1975.[16] But by then conflict seemed endemic; relations between firemen and their employers had so deteriorated that it was the absence of unrest that was considered noteworthy.[17] 'Perhaps,' said the *Times*, 'the long night watches waiting for the alarm to ring encourages brooding over discontents, whatever the reason firemen are often in dispute.'[18]

This disposition towards industrial and political militancy has been variously explained; some industrial sociologists present it as a function of mass society; others, by contrast, identify the increasing integration of the firemen into the mainstream labour movement as the principal source of occupational radicalism.[19] For more conservative observers, strikes and stoppages within the fire service represent a hydra-headed conspiracy, organised by the Communist Party in the 1940s and 50s and by other dangerous dissidents more recently. Firemen themselves rightly treat this kind of explanation with scepticism and contempt. 'The fellow travellers have been along of course,' said one picket during the strike of 1977, 'There's Trots down here every morning trying to sell their papers. We just tell them to piss off, and they pisses off.'[20] In this chapter, then, we shall try to relate changes in the material condition of the fireman to those changes in outlook that made possible the first national strike of 1977. Specifically, we shall examine the social composition of the fire service, the discipline code, the system of promotion and remuneration, and the relations between officers and ordinary firemen.

Personnel

Between the close of the First World War and the outbreak of the Second World War the fire service more than doubled its strength. In that time the number of permanent (police or non-police) firemen in the public service rose from an estimated 3,200 to 6,600. These were largely distributed throughout the large cities and populous districts and ranged in size from the London Fire Brigade, with about 2,000 men, to small units, five or six strong, that were just capable of manning a single appliance. Conditions were equally varied. Between brigades there was little uniformity in the recruitment, selection or training of personnel; promotion and pension schemes were dissimilar; duty systems and discipline no less so. This was inevitable in the absence of a general statutory provision for regulating the powers and duties of fire authorities. The Fire Brigades Act of 1938, which for the first time made such provision, allowed a full two years for the local authorities to adjust to newly-prescribed standards of efficiency. Until the end of the 1930s, then, the size of the fire service was determined by local priorities. Growth, appreciable but slow, rose markedly with the approach of war. Within professional non-police brigades numbers increased during the period 1936-39 by some 15 per cent largely to replace the regulars who were required for instructional purposes with the Auxiliary Fire Service. Police brigades experienced a comparable expansion. At the end of the war emergency period the permanent fire service was almost three times the size of the peace-time profession. On the eve of denationalisation, the established strength stood at 18,606.[21]

The expansion in fire service personnel at the end of the 1930s reflected the preparations for war. The continued post-war growth, by contrast, was the product of rising standards of fire cover and revised duty systems. The reports of HM Chief Inspector of Fire Service chart the broadening base of fire service employment. From the late 1950s it grew by leaps and bounds. Between 1958 and 1966 the establishment of wholetime firemen in England and Wales rose from 20,586 to 27,487, an increase of a third; between 1966 and 1976 the authorised establishment grew by more than a quarter, from 27,487 to 34,690.

The growth in union membership was equally spectacular. Before the war fire service unionism was largely confined to London; through the 1920s and 30s the FBU and its predecessor the Firemen's Union maintained a steady membership of between 2,000 and 3,000 and organised less than half the available firemen. Since de-nationalisation in 1947 trade union density within the fire service has increased from around 80 per cent to more than 90 per cent of all uniformed personnel in local authority fire brigades in Great Britain and Northern Ireland.[22]

The post-war fire service was not only bigger than that of the inter-war years; with respect to occupational background and industrial experience, it was both wider and more varied. By the end of the 1930s it was clear that firemen required a broader knowledge-base than that produced by service with the armed forces. Motorization and improvements in the science of fire-fighting exposed the deficiencies of a fire service which selected its recruits more for their physical than their intellectual capacities. Conditions of service, framed for a race of automatons, were unequal to the demands of a single-entry profession in which fire prevention and fire extinction were to be of comparable importance. Of these shortcomings the authorities were fully aware. The need to attract men of reasonable educational attainments, capable of in-service training in the technical and scientific elements of firemanship was public policy before the outbreak of war made it an urgent necessity.

Within Whitehall the diminished importance of the armed

forces in relation to fire service recruitment was readily conceded. The Home Office, which had once commended ex-regulars for fire service employment, had, by the close of the conflict, come to accept the need to broaden the basis of selection. Naval reservists, the backbone of the Victorian fire service, were now deemed unsuitable for a permanent position within the reconstructed service. 'The class of men,' said one official, 'was not essential to the Service.'[23] 'Men recruited after a period with one of the Armed Forces,' wrote another, 'were not found in practice to be so satisfactory as younger men coming in from civilian life.'[24] The Committee on the Post War Fire Service, which reported in 1944, fixed the age of entry with a view to their exclusion.[25]

Service influences diminished slowly, however. Second World War veterans inevitably supplied the bulk of the post-war intake. In terms of fire service personnel, war had been an ageing experience. Recruitment to the regular fire service ranks had ceased on the outbreak of hostilities so that, by 1945, more than two-thirds of professional firemen were over 35; wartime recruits to the NFS, being drawn from the older age-groups, were scarcely capable of rejuvenating an enlarged peace-time service. The armed forces, then, contributed the bulk of the younger men below the age of 25 and in all accounted for something like half the post-war NFS. And the armed services remained important as a supplier of fire service recruits. The over-representation of ex-servicemen in local authority fire brigades was noted by the Government Social Survey which found that 60 per cent of the junior ranks and 68 per cent of the senior ranks had done military service; and that about one-fifth of the junior ranks had been regular servicemen. The Cunningham Inquiry, too, noted the forces background of fire service personnel.[26]

Ex-service firemen, however, declined sharply in the early 1970s as the war generation came up for retirement. Revised conditions of service to enable previous duty in the armed forces to count for pensionable service further reduced ex-servicemen within the fire service – so much so that there was some concern at the number of retirements among the more experienced personnel. 'In some areas,' the Chief Inspector of Fire Services wrote in his report for 1975, 'the percentage of personnel with less than 5 years' service is as high as 55 per cent'.[27] It seems unlikely that the dilution of the ex-service element was significant in relation to the industrial unrest of the 1970s. Recruits to the post-war fire service, whether they had served in the armed forces or not, were largely skilled workers who had previously been employed in a range of industries that were fairly similar to those of the active population at large.[28] In short, post-war firemen, like the conscripts of the 1940s and 50s, remained incorrigibly civilian in outlook.

Within the fire service, then, the pace of change varied. In relation to sex-composition and work-culture it was glacial. Women first entered fire service employment during the Second World War. At its peak, in 1943, the NFS included 30,000 wholetime firewomen and 48,000 part-timers; these made up 30 per cent of the wholetime and 47 per cent of the part-time members of the force.[29] Some were employed as despatch riders and car drivers; the vast majority, though, served in a non-operational capacity.[30] As telephone operators, mobilising officers, clerks and cooks, they were deemed to have performed with distinction. 'By the services they have rendered,' declared the Post War Committee on the Fire Service, 'women have gained for themselves the right to be considered for continued employment.'[31]

A fat lot of good it did them! The authorities along with the mass of professional firemen continued to think of fire fighting as man's work. The Home Office, in seeking recruits to the permanent fire service, pitched its appeal at men of good physique 'who prefer a life of action, with some promise of excitement and adventure, to work at an office desk'.[32] The Ministry of Labour cultivated the cult of masculinity in even stronger terms; its booklet on fire service employment, issued in 1945, was entitled 'A Man's Job'.[33] In the post-war period women accounted for less than 4 per cent of the wholetime strength of fire brigades in England and Wales. The vast majority of firewomen were concentrated in non-operational support roles in which shift work was obligatory and the scope for advancement limited. Not surprisingly, wastage among firewomen was reported to be 'rather high'.[34]

Post-war and pre-war fire brigades also differed with respect to hours and duty systems. Before the war the inordinately long hours were a distinctive feature of fire service employment; most brigades operated a continuous duty system, with from four to six days and nights continuous duty followed by one day free. The men were provided with residential accommodation for themselves and their families in or close to the fire station, worked a normal day at the station on routine duties and, during the whole of their remaining duty, were required to be at home on stand-by for a fire call.

The advantages of the continuous duty system and the 72-hour week lay almost wholly with the employers. Manning costs were kept to a minimum, top-down management sustained and growth in fire service unionism checked. An internal document stated:

> Such a system does play its part in the development of a Fire Service consciousness. Officers gain a greater sense of responsibility towards the men under their charge and the men develop a better morale and Service traditions in much the way that officers and men of a ship's company develop these qualities.

Comparisons with working conditions in private sector industry, it concluded, were neither pertinent nor desirable. 'The status of the Fire Service as a service under discipline, the servant of the community, must be prejudiced by their introduction.'[35] Not surprisingly the trend among pre-war fire authorities was to develop their fire brigades on residential continuous duty lines.[36]

The FBU and its predecessor, though concerned to bring conditions of employment into closer relation with those in industry, were handicapped by continued mass unemployment. Even so, the campaign for shorter hours was not entirely ineffective. By the eve of war the employers had been persuaded to concede a 60-hour week for the London Fire Brigade.

The war experience accelerated the downward trend. The National Fire Service, which operated a non-residential system of shift work, with bunks or beds provided for the men during their 48-hour duty periods, made it hard to restore the status quo ante. As a senior official within the Fire Service Department put it: 'The argument that men must work long hours because the country cannot afford to bear the cost of shorter hours will be an extremely difficult one to use at the end of a war in which money has been spent freely and which is regarded as the prelude to better social conditions.'[37] It was not the only argument. The terms of employment, if unchanged, would make the post-war fire service uncompetitive in the labour market. 'The Fire Service will only get the "left-overs" from other professions if we offer worse terms,' wrote Commander Firebrace in November 1943.[38]

Such arguments were advanced by the FBU in support of its campaign for a shorter working week. But the union went further. 'The ultimate aim', said *Fire*, in December 1945, 'is that the fireman shall enjoy the same amenities as the average skilled worker outside the Service, namely, a 40-hour week.' This was to be achieved in stages. The FBU, aware of the nation's difficulties, was flexible about the timing. A 60-hour week was to be introduced immediately with an agreed schedule for the establishment of a 48-hour week leading to 40-hours as it became the norm in industry as a whole.

The 40-hour week, however, was not an end in itself. Long hours, low pay and low manning levels were seen by the executive as sources of division and deprivation which undermined the collective strength of firemen and the cohesion of the working class. 'For firemen it will mean the return of social life, the removal of themselves and their families from the narrowness of the fire station and the tyranny of the bells.' In a period of full employment, the *Firefighter* declared, 'the best recruits will not be retained by imposing a tour of duty which will prevent their sharing in the social and cultural advances which will be the lot of the workers after the war, or even actually from reaching the level generally enjoyed before the war.'[39]

Cost considerations, though, were not easily ignored.

Improved standards of cover, as proposed by the Committee on the Post War Fire Service, entailed an estimated average rate of 8d. (3p) in the pound as compared with 3d. (1p) or less before the war. The introduction of a 60-hour week on top of this raised man-power requirements by a third and involved expenditure equal to a 1¼d. rate over the whole country. The Fire Service Department, reviewing the position in 1946, declined to commit the ratepayers in advance of the resumption of local authority control.[40] The matter was remitted to the newly-created National Joint Council for Local Authorities' Fire Brigades.

Negotiations between the union and the employers throughout the post-war period have brought working hours within the fire service into closer alignment with those in industry. In 1956 the weekly availability of operational firemen was reduced from 60 to 56 hours and in 1961 was further reduced to 48 hours. By the close of the 1960s the FBU argument that, as in most other employments, there should be a basic rate of pay for a 40-hour week, with a premium rate for additional hours, had become irresistible.[41] The 40-hour week was under active consideration when the first national strike began. The agreement which ended the strike provided for the introduction of a 42-hour week by 1 April 1979.

Discipline and Authority

The enlarged fire service that emerged from the Second World War was also a more unified and professional service than its pre-war predecessor. Gone was the multiplicity of statutory authorities which previously administered the nation's fire service. Gone were the enormous disparities in ranks, remuneration and general conditions of service which the fragmentation of authority encouraged. Gone, too, were the police brigades, which a generation earlier had comprised one-fifth of wholetime firemen, and from which trade unions were excluded. Equally significant was the altered relationship between the permanent and auxiliary fire service. The retained and volunteer fire brigades, which before the war accounted for the majority of firemen, became a complement to rather than a substitute for professional fire fighters. The post-war fireman was a more specialised being than his pre-war predecessor. In short, total war transformed the fire service. The standardisation of training, duty systems, uniforms, appliances and equipment and the introduction of standard procedures for appointments, promotions, discipline, pay and administration, were retained when, in 1947, control was restored to the local authorities. The 1940s, then, were the formative years in the making of the modern fire service. A previous chapter outlined the FBU's role in that process.[42] Here the focus is upon discipline and authority in the period of war and reconstruction.

The organisation of the war economy, as we have seen, raised fundamental questions about the status and structure of the fire service and the place of the union within it. State regulation of the labour market, for example, made discipline in the emergency services a matter of paramount importance. Pre-war disciplinary codes, which assumed freedom of movement and career-minded recruits, were thought to be insufficiently punitive. The discipline code, said Lord Dudley, Regional Commissioner (Midland Region), 'would have to be drawn in fairly strict terms in view of the introduction of a conscript element in the Force'.[43] Indeed, as disparities grew between the civil defence service and the better paid metal trades, firemen became increasingly restive. 'At present', wrote one member of the Fire Service Division of the Home Office, 'many of the undisciplined members of the Service look upon dismissal as their goal.'[44] The severity of punishment, though, was not the sole consideration. The process of review and revision had wider implications. The war emergency provided the occasion for the first systematic attempt to formulate a uniform code of discipline for the fire service.[45] By 1944 the Home Office was satisfied that war-time disciplinary arrangements supplied a suitable basis for the peace-time service.

Definition and codification, could not, however, be settled by administrative fiat. 'No one questions the need of discipline,' said one professional journal, 'but it must be the right kind of discipline in accord with British ideals.'[46] Trade union and official conceptions of those ideals were clearly at odds. 'Discipline,' wrote an official of the Fire Service Department, 'may sometimes find itself at variance with legal formalism, since discipline concerns itself more with the good of the Service than with the individual.'[47] Horner and his members thought otherwise. The FBU, while recognising the special requirements of the service, took exception to penalties that were unduly harsh and to procedures that infringed the rules of natural justice and trade union practice. Disciplinary measures of a managerial rather than an operational character were likewise contested. Saluting, with its militarist and class connotations, was just such an issue.

'One of the ways in which the discipline and smartness of a fire force can be told is by its punctiliousness in regard to saluting,' ran the text of a draft instruction of 1941. Rank recognition, though, was more than that; for status-conscious officers it satisfied their desire for parity of prestige with the armed forces. On the eve of the blitz the Fire Service Department was preoccupied with the niceties of saluting and engaged in an almost surreal search for a euphonious set of titles to correspond with those applied to military personnel. The proposed rank structure for the NFS, with a range of titles that ran from 'Fire Colonel' to 'Fire Corporal' and included 'Fire Major-General' and 'Fire Brigadier', was thought to be good for the *amour propre* of senior officers and a tonic for their subordinates. 'Military and naval titles have about them an atmosphere of command and discipline which would have a salutary effect upon the morale of the Service.'[48]

Grandiloquent titles, however, were more likely to provoke ridicule than command respect. 'Fire General' and other clumsy composites were thus tested and discarded in a Rumpelstiltskin-style search that reduced Fire Council proceedings to a farce. 'We are on the verge of pantomime,'

Morrison warned its members in June 1941.[49] But it was the growing opposition of the trade union movement and the uncompromising hostility of the Scottish Office under Tom Johnston that brought the show to a close. Sir George Cater, a one-time advocate of rank designation based upon the military hierarchy, told the Fire Service Council that it was the opposition of the FBU to 'anything savouring of militarisation' that persuaded him to reconsider; Johnston bluntly warned Morrison that Scotland would go its own way if functional titles were not adopted.[50]

On the question of rank designation concession was unavoidable. On the question of rank recognition the Fire Service Department contemplated nothing beyond cosmetic changes. The army style of salute, which was said to be 'less obsequious than the navy type', was adopted and presented to the service not as a recognition of rank but as the outward expression of its *esprit de corps*. 'Saluting,' said Secretary of State Morrison, 'was not a sign of servitude, but a comradely greeting.' Civil defence unions, to whom such practices were alien, were appalled. Professional firemen, by contrast, who were accustomed to salute senior officers, viewed the downward extension of the requirement to company commanders with grave misgivings. 'This is just another move by our little Hitlers to make puppets of our firemen,' an official of the FBU told the *Daily Herald*.[51]

'Nazi methods' in the maintenance of discipline were also resisted.[52] The proposed code of discipline for the emergency fire service, based upon a comparison of police and army codes, was condemned outright; in Deakin's blunt prose, it was 'far too drastic and far reaching and … in no way acceptable to the trade union side'.[53] Indefinite suspension, summary punishments, the imposition of extra duties without pay and denial of rights of representation were more than unjust; such measures impaired the fire-fighting efficiency of the service. Penalties which inflicted hardship upon the defaulter's dependents, as, for example, with deductions from the basic wage, were more provocative than punitive. 'In the army allowances to the wife and children of a defaulter are not deducted and there is both humanity and good sense in this,' observed the FBU. 'Only bitterness inimical to good discipline can result from a man's knowledge that his wife and children are going short.' Similarly, the imposition of additional hours of duty was 'to punish the men at the expense of his capacity as a fire fighter'. 'We therefore urge that peace-time preconceptions of the police force should not be allowed to interfere with the paramount importance of enabling men to get proper rest in wartime conditions.' Suspension of pay pending the outcome of proceedings was equally odious. Not only did it penalise a man before guilt was established, it also prejudiced a fair consideration of the case since the man suspended with loss of pay was more likely to accept a punishment than appeal. The absence of any safeguards against delay in appeals – of critical importance to the would-be appellant whose pay might be suspended from the time when the alleged offence was committed until its final determination – the withholding of trade union rights of representation and the lack of an independent tribunal to consider the appeal were likewise foreign to the principles and procedures of the trade union movement.

FBU representations were not without effect. 'The position,' wrote one official, 'is that most of the points raised by the Union on the Discipline Code were in fact agreed by the Department and the implementation of such points has been made in the Instructions to Fire Force Commanders on the subject ...'[54] In consequence the accused was granted reasonable facilities to prepare his defence with access to premises and other firemen to obtain evidence and arrange for witnesses; appeals procedure was improved and rights of representation conceded; a proviso against an officer acting as prosecutor and chief witness in a case over which he was presiding was included and provision made against oppressive conduct by officers. These concrete concessions, embodied in the Code of Discipline of the NFS, represented a triumph for collective action and a signal advance for firemen at war. But they were more than that. The manner in which they had been won established a precedent for a wider participation in the management of the fire service. As

Horner put it: 'It has been a cardinal principle that "methods of management" have been outside our province. But war changes many things.'[55]

FBU efforts to moderate the discipline code were materially assisted by the restoration of peace. With the departure of contumacious conscripts a rapid fall off in the amount of indiscipline was confidently predicted '... as the firemen remaining in the service will regard it as a profession and will be unlikely to run away to sea, or absent themselves in order to work in a munitions factory as has happened during the war'.[56] In a free fire service job commitment backed up by the discipline of the market would suffice. 'The volume of disciplinary cases in the post-war fire service should, therefore, be much smaller than it is today, not only in the aggregate but also in proportion to the total strength.'[57] These predictions appear to have been fully justified.

The table on p. 118 shows the number of charges brought against violators of the code of discipline in the post-war period. With respect to England and Wales it will be seen that proceedings were abandoned in about two-fifths of cases and that most offences were of a minor nature, punishable by reprimand, caution or stoppage in pay. Such penalties, in fact, accounted for 96 per cent of the punishments awarded. In general terms the standard of discipline was maintained at a high level. In 1950, a year of industrial unrest in which indiscipline reached a peak, the number of charges represented less than 3 per cent of the wholetime strength; and for most of the post-war period it was less than one per cent. Its comparative absence owed much to the relative autonomy of the watch within the command structure. Station Officers, like the men they supervised, remained operational fire-fighters with work patterns that, structurally and substantively, were remote from senior management. Station Officers, as leaders and members of the watch, are by force of circumstance compelled to rely upon the personal and the informal rather than the rule book to safeguard the efficiency of the unit and their position within it.[58] The solidarity of the watch affected indiscipline in other ways.

Discipline in the Fire Service (England and Wales) 1950-1978

Year	No. of Cases	Dismissals	Required to Resign	Reduction in Rank	Stoppage in Pay	Reprimand	Caution
1950	494	5	2	6	–	–	–
1951	445	2	5	2	–	–	–
1952	401	2	2	2	113	84	102
1953	313	–	–	2	87	64	94
1954	280	1	3	2	62	41	58
1955	161	–	2	1	63	28	39
1956	147	1	1	1	43	26	40
1957	116	–	–	1	28	28	31
1958	118	1	–	–	27	30	39
1959	113	1	1	1	35	22	27
1960	113	–	–	2	40	19	32
1961	103	1	2	1	30	21	25
1962	128	–	2	1	42	17	42
1963	147	–	–	–	47	34	40
1964	138	–	2	–	50	35	25
1965	107	–	2	1	43	21	24
1966	128	–	1	3	49	17	41
1967	131	–	–	1	54	21	35
1968	92	–	3	1	32	13	29
1969	111	–	1	3	54	16	14
1970	116	–	2	1	55	13	25
1971	104	1	–	1	35	40	11
1972	68	–	1	–	31	17	10
1973	52	–	2	1	10	8	7
1974	44	–	3	–	24	7	6
1975	75	1	2	4	15	11	18
1976	48	–	2	–	21	6	6
1977	77	1	3	3	14	9	25
1978	113	13	5	1	34	19	17

Source: *Report of HM Chief Inspector of Fire Services*, 1950-1978.

The loyalties which it encouraged made it difficult to initiate proceedings and even more difficult to secure conviction.[59] Indiscipline does not, then, supply a reliable measure of authority relations within the fire service. Relations between officers and men were, in fact, far from satisfactory, and these difficulties were of long standing.

Officer-Men Relations

The inadequacies of officer selection and training were noted by the three enquiries that reported on the fire service between 1924 and 1944. The last and most searching of them, the Departmental Committee on the Post-War Fire Service, identified the prevalent system of local control as the main obstacle to the creation of an efficient officer cadre. It declared that:

> Small local authorities can never secure the efficient officering of the service. Inevitably, since the commands they can offer are small, they cannot hold out prospects likely to attract able and energetic men into the service; nor can they secure that the best and ablest men gain advancement to positions where their abilities can be used to the benefit of the service as a whole. Nor indeed under such a system is there any real chance of discovering the comparative merits of individual officers when there are so few occasions on which they are brought into contact and comparisons made.

The decentralised and fragmented system had served the nation badly. 'The outbreak of war', the committee concluded, 'found the Fire Service lamentably deficient in good officers.'[60]

The Luftwaffe disclosed its shortcomings. The sheer lack of professionalism among regular fire officers was startling. The want of training, knowledge and executive authority, said the review of the post-war fire service, constituted a danger to which the nation should never again be exposed. 'The days are over when firemanship could be acquired spasmodically by officers thrust into posts of command without preliminary training and left to pick up the elements of their profession on the fire ground.'[61] Deficiencies were particularly acute in the art of man-management. Like the Metropolitan Police, the fire service eschewed the personnel selection procedures adopted by the military in wartime. Officers for the war emergency fire services, drawn from the ranks of the regulars, were often unsuited to exercise powers of command. Summary procedure outside the Code of Discipline, to which the FBU strongly objected, was in consequence held in abeyance because, as one official minuted, 'it was doubted whether the quality of the officers who would have to apply it was high enough to deal with the cases justly.'[62] Senior officers, too, left much to be desired. The oppressive manner in which discipline was administered in some regions brought protests from Horner and a cautionary minute from the head of the Fire Service Division counselling colleagues upon 'the necessity of using the power with judgement and reason'.[63]

Within Whitehall the want of confidence between officers and men was quietly conceded.[64] Junior officers, in particular, were frequently unable or unwilling to supply the leadership which the situation required. In the eyes of superiors they often appeared to be fickle and flaccid, lacking the strength of character to withstand peer group pressure or the encroachments of strong-minded trade unionists; too many station officers, it was feared, were ready to transfer disagreeable disciplinary duties to union officials for settlement at higher level.[65] For this reason, if no other, direct FBU representation at station level seemed ill-advised. Firebrace, who viewed the prospect with horror, foresaw a situation in which power would pass from the professionals in the NFS to the commissars in the FBU. Imagine the train of events provoked by a necessary but unpopular order, a colleague conjectured. 'Immediately the men at the station ask for a meeting to discuss the order. Finally, the Fire Brigades Union representative asks to see the station officer as a result of the meeting. This, of course, would be ... unsuited to a disciplined service.'[66] The ban imposed on trade union meetings on fire service premises in 1941 was an attempt to secure through administrative action that which could not be obtained through the authority of officers exercising their ordinary powers of command.

The Fire Service Department, though, was not alone in its concern to improve relations between fire brigade officers and rank and file firemen. The FBU, too, was 'almost anxious' to promote mutual confidence and trust between those who gave orders and those who received them. 'This confidence and trust', it added, 'can only be fostered if the men and women of the service believe that their welfare is of prime concern to the officers immediately superior to them.' Restrictions upon levels of representation, the union argued, did nothing for the contentment of the service, while the ban on union meetings on fire service premises was a positive source of antagonism.[67]

The ban, which was not lifted until 1943, was designed to prevent the penetration of the rapidly expanding fire force by a Communist-controlled union which conflated professional and political considerations and conducted itself in a manner that was deemed to be inconsistent with the requirements of a disciplined Crown service. It was not only the campaign for the opening of a Second Front that was unacceptable: equally offensive were FBU interventions into management, discipline and other prohibited areas. What made this tendency to trespass alarming, however, was that it reflected and reinforced an effective recruitment drive among fire service personnel. The embargo on fire station meetings was in these circumstances more provocative than effective. Alternative policies, however, did not readily present themselves. The Scottish model of consultation bypassed the FBU but did not provide a paradigm for England and Wales.[68] A.H. Hammond of the Fire Service Department who railed against 'a union which persists in showing how irresponsible it is ... [and] ... goes right outside its scope as a service organisation', confessed that his preference for 'a representative system within the service in which every man would have his place' was impractical.[69] Morrison, who also considered the creation of an approved representative body in place of the FBU, concluded that, politically and logistically, such a course was unrealistic.

Among competing unions, the National Union of Auxiliary Firemen was considered to be 'an unsatisfactory and untrustworthy body' and much less representative than the FBU.[70] Moreover, any initiative that appeared to supplant the FBU with a company union would, he feared, inflame the firemen and the trade union movement as a whole. There was no option but to concede.

Any improvement in officer-men relations was, however, offset by Home Office refusal to recognise the Officers' Section of the FBU as the proper channel for the submission of representations on behalf of those ranks. 'The good of the service,' wrote the Chief of the Fire Staff, 'requires completely separate representation of the officers to the men.' The good of the men, he conceded, was a secondary consideration. 'The officers, through the FBU, might gain materially but would lose position and dignity; and the status of their Service would be depressed.' A unionised officer cadre could never secure parity of esteem with its counterpart in the armed forces. 'Officers,' he wrote, 'undoubtedly wish to lift their service towards the fighting services. Officers of the Army, Navy and Air Force do not have a union or an association ... But if they did, it would manifestly be an impossible state of affairs for them to join the same union as their men.'[71]

Snobbery was not the sole or even the most important consideration, for the military supplied more than a claim to social standing: it also provided a model of authority, a hierarchy of ranks and a principle of command that were alien to trade union ideals and practices. And herein lay the major attraction. From the point of view of the Home Office the more the civilian character of the service was eroded, and the more the situation of the fireman came to resemble that of the policeman and the soldier, the less the scope for free collective bargaining, agitation and unrest. FBU claims to represent officers as a collectivity were therefore seen as a threat to public policy which had to be resisted; for to vest sole bargaining rights in the FBU was to sanction the introduction of a closed shop into the fire service and thereby to make an unruly union even less manageable.

Pressure from without, though, was considerable.[72] But for the existence of a house-trained alternative it might have proved irresistible.

The National Fire Service Officers Association (NFSOA), the successor of the Chief Fire Officers Association of 1941, was a body which, not without some official encouragement, had enlarged its scope and broadened its membership so as to emerge as another medium for consultation on all matters affecting the welfare and conditions of service of its ranks. The decision, taken unilaterally by the Home Office in 1943 to confer exclusive negotiating rights upon this 'useful and desirable institution' set a precedent, which was endorsed by post-war employers, and which served to isolate officers from other ranks within the bargaining process.[73] On the eve of de-nationalisation the FBU claimed to organise about 25 per cent of the officer ranks compared with the 60 per cent enrolled by the NFSOA.[74]

The institutional separation of officers and men expressed a conception of authority relations which firemen found unacceptable. The NFSOA, described as a creature of 'the police-obsessed mind' of the Home Office and 'a near-replica of ... [its] ... cherished but spineless Police Federation', was condemned as the very antithesis of industrial democracy. 'It seems to aim at the wrong kind of leadership, the creation of Fuhrers directing from above, instead of conforming with the wishes of the majority from below, and representing that majority in its decisions.'[75] Horner and associates were quick to see that the position of the union depended in no small part upon the degree to which the police-military model prevailed in the post-war fire service. From this perspective, the status of officers in the NFS was a matter of vital importance, with implications for the future of collective bargaining and the relations between firemen and the organised working class. The Officers' Section, announced in July 1942, must be seen as evidence of the FBU's concern about the character of the peacetime service and its determination to resist those authoritarian impulses that tended to separate officers from firemen and firemen from workers.[76]

These concerns compelled the union to interest itself in the selection and training of officers as well as in their conduct and relations with the other ranks. The 'New Model fire-fighting army', the ideal formation in which discipline and democracy were happily combined, depended upon the adoption of a strictly meritocratic approach to the selection of officers. Promotions, the union insisted, should 'be made solely on merit in accordance with the best theoretical, practical and administrative knowledge of the personnel'. The favouritism, so prevalent in the past, was unfair and inefficient and out of place in a people's fire service. Equality of opportunity was essential to secure the leadership of the reconstructed service that must follow the defeat of fascism.[77]

In this, at any rate, union and management were of one mind. In the post-war fire service appointments and promotions have come entirely from within the ranks of the service. The single-tier entry system, established in 1947, requires all recruits to enter at the basic rank of operational firemen and complete a minimum number of years of operational service before seeking advancement. To qualify for promotion to the next rank the candidate has, first, to pass a written and practical examination, and, then, having secured a satisfactory reference from his (or her) superior officers, await a suitable vacancy. These vary from brigade to brigade depending upon its size, location and age structure. In general terms prospects for career development in the post-war fire service have been satisfactory. In England and Wales opportunities for advancement improved. In 1966 those in the ranks of Station Officer and above made up about 11 per cent of the establishment, whereas by 1970 these ranks accounted for 13 per cent of the established strength. And while the rank structure changed little, the years between 1967 and 1970 saw the appointment of approximately 12 per cent more Station Officers (2,116 against 1,892) and 16 per cent more Assistant Divisional Officers (600 against 515).[78] The single-entry tier system, moreover, has meant that the lines of authority at work do not follow social class divisions as they once did in the police and as they still do in the armed forces.

Officer selection, though, has not given complete satisfaction. The FBU, for one, felt that the base of promotion to the higher ranks was too narrow and that men who had qualified as Leading Firemen were not being promoted in sufficient numbers.[79] Operational firemen were more critical still. For all its meritocratic gloss, promotion procedure was perceived by many rank and file firemen as unequal, unfair and discriminatory. The Government Social Survey, which examined attitudes and opinions of uniformed male personnel in the late 1960s, identified a deep undercurrent of resentment against a system that undervalued practical experience and relied too much upon favouritism and influence in making appointments. 'I've seen so many creepers and crawlers made up, and if that's the type of person they want, I want none of it,' said one fed-up fireman. 'The system is all wrong and I disagree with it,' said another. 'In a small brigade if you are the blue-eyed boy you're in, and I'm not.' 'They are only interested in promoting officers' sons,' a colleague added. In all, 57 per cent of junior ranks felt that there was something wrong with the system of promotion in their brigade.[80]

Criticism, though, was not confined to officer selection procedures; deficiencies in management were also found to be a significant source of unrest. The importance of a consensual rather than a coercive approach to the supervision of fire service personnel had long been understood. Speaking to a conference of Chief Fire Officers in 1943, the Home Secretary said that 'every officer must feel that he had a responsibility to make his orders intelligible to his men, and must take them into his confidence, not only in the conduct of operations but in all their Service activities'. A 'friendly interchange of views and ideas', he added, was 'of vital importance to the maintenance of healthy discipline, initiative and morale'.[81]

The same speech might just as easily have been delivered at any time during the next 25 years without any loss of force. Indeed, social investigation in 1967-68 identified the want of communication between supervisors and those under them as one of the principal impediments to improved relations between officers and men. 'I think the approach of some of the officers leaves a lot to be desired,' said one malcontent. 'In fact some of them treat the men like objects and not like human beings.' 'They should stop treating the firemen as kids,' added a sharp-tongued colleague. 'It would be an improvement if officers treated you as one of them, they are a bit clannish.'[82]

These difficulties were structural as much as personal. The assumption of administrative and executive functions in addition to regular operational duties affected the role of the officer cadre and the character of command in the post-war fire service. Changes in the fire service organisation in the forty years since de-nationalisation have increased bureaucracy, reduced accessibility and made it more difficult for officers to secure the confidence and trust of the rank-and-file. Officers themselves readily conceded the need for an improvement in personal communication between senior and junior ranks. 'Appoint a welfare officer like they have in factories,' said one when interviewed by the Government Social Survey. 'Someone they can go to and say this is wrong, instead of going to the union, who will make a major issue of everything.' Current practice, the respondent admitted, tended to conceal rather than resolve difficulties. 'Now they take problems to various officers, and they get passed from one officer to another and shelved if it is a dicey complaint.' The bureaucratisation of authority relations was, indeed, a sore point. 'There should be more co-operation between officers and men without everything having to be written down on paper,' said one frustrated fireman. 'With this lot you have to write out a submit, and you should be able to go to the station officer and ask him. With these submits, it goes through about four blokes before it goes to the Chief. I don't think it should be like that.' Desk-bound commanders preoccupied with paperwork were, however, more than just remote; they were an affront to the ethos of a work-culture in which officers were expected to perform as action-men rather than apparatchiks. To firemen, recruited largely from the construction and transport industries and the armed forces, non-manual work was both unproductive and unmanly. 'Station officers and sub-officers sit in an office and look at bits of paper and pretend to be doing something,' said one critic. 'It seems to me that you get a rank and tell people what to do, and you do nothing. A bloke who is respected will get the blokes to work.'[83]

Respect, though, had to be earned. Securing it and retaining it were among the principal difficulties encountered by leading firemen and those in the ranks above them. Junior officers wanting experience and understanding were thought to be the least capable managers of men. Their difficulties, however, were multiplied by the persistence of drills, station cleaning and unpopular maintenance duties. These duties, though, were more than a simple expression of the spit and polish tradition of the Victorian fire service. The 'main object', a senior official observed, was 'to keep men employed to the extent that they will not be able to undertake employment in their off duty hours.'[84] Cleaning and station duties were condemned by younger men and those interested in promotion as a waste of time; older men held drill in comparable contempt. Enforcement of these unconstructive work-routines was equally unrewarding. Supervisors, with little authority and not enough to do with it, fell prey to barrack-room excess; morale suffered.

'It was a trivial thing,' said one despondent fireman. 'I was asked to wipe dust from a machine by a leading fireman, seeing as I had done the job once I walked away in disgust. I went back soon after and the leading fireman said, "There, it looks a lot better now doesn't it?" and I hadn't touched the machine. These things really get me mad.' Some were 'just sick of all these petty details they keep throwing at you'; others despaired of the 'silly little orders coming in from the officers to do things more for the look of them than for the efficiency of the thing'. The boorish parade-ground manner which these officers affected was equally offensive. 'All these young lads made up to be leading firemen, the way they talk to you like animals,' said one old sweat. Many merely followed in the footsteps of their superiors. 'The Chief Officer had a nasty way of dealing with things,' said one disgruntled fireman. 'He found fault with everything and talked to you as if you were lower in social scale.' 'Officers think once they're made up that they are a different class than you,' a colleague added. Apart from pay, disagreeable officers, with what one analyst called 'a superior antagonistic attitude', were the principal reason why men seriously considered resigning from the service.[85]

FBU criticisms were difficult to deny. Cleaning and station duties, which in the early 1970s occupied 25 per cent of the fireman's day, were increasingly recognised as inefficient and inexcusable. 'The argument that it helps to instil discipline', said the Cunningham Inquiry, 'is unconvincing.' 'Cleaning requires little skill, and certainly none of the skills in which the fireman has been trained.' These routine non-emergency duties offended the fireman's image of himself as a skilled worker performing a public service and made him feel undervalued and unloved.

The employment of civilian station cleaners in place of firemen was not, however, a sufficient response to pressure from below. The need for further reform was readily acknowledged. 'More attention should be paid to the dissatisfaction within some brigades about present communication and the relationships between officers and men,' declared the Departmental Committee on the Fire Service. 'We recommend that supervisory ranks at all levels should be given more supervisory and management training, with particular emphasis on the skills of effective communicators and the handling of human relations.' More specifically, it called for establishment of brigade level consultative committees, with the trade union's participation, for 'the local discussion of all aspects of management other than pay and conditions of service'.[86]

Personnel management, however, was only a part of the problem. Also required were measures to compensate those who failed to secure promotion. The exceptionally low pass rate in the national written examination for Station Officer and Sub-Officer suggested that their numbers were considerable. In many such cases it was argued, disappointment led to disaffection. As the Cunningham Inquiry put it:

'The nature of the fireman's occupation makes it difficult for him, after a period of time, to change it, so that discontent which might in other occupations be reflected in the rate of premature resignations may tend to fester within the fire service and, at the extreme, find expression in militant action, such as has occurred in the last year or two in some brigades.'[87] The introduction of a long-service increment was in these circumstances said to be 'of particular value in providing recognition and encouragement for the large numbers of extremely competent firemen who do not seek promotion or who are unlikely to gain it'.[88] Sound or not, neither the analysis nor the recommendation that followed from it answered the crisis in the making.

Remuneration

The authorities, though keen to raise standards, were unwilling or unable to offer levels of remuneration to attract men of officer calibre into the service. During the 1960s the problem became acute as fire service pay failed to keep pace with those in comparable callings. Indeed, the growing discrepancy between fire service pay and the average level of industrial earnings often made it difficult to retain recruits let alone improve the intake.[89] By the end of the decade the fire service was seething. Strikes or threatened strikes were becoming a regular occurrence. As we shall see, it was the destruction of traditional wage relativities at the beginning of the 1950s which left firemen uncertain as to what position they should occupy in the hierarchy of skilled and semi-skilled workers. From such uncertainties grew the unrest that culminated in the strike of 1977.

Until the break-up of the NFS the pay of the fireman was pegged to that of the policeman. Emerging in Victorian times, parity between the rates of pay of policemen and firemen became the basis of numerous wage settlements and trade union policy. Police-parity, which had been accepted in principle in a number of authoritative pronouncements and rulings, was also acknowledged by the local authorities who in general maintained a close correspondence between the two services. 'I think,' counsel for the employers told the Industrial Court, 'that we rightly all relate the sub-officer in the fire brigade to the sergeant in the police force and the fireman in the fire brigade to the constable in the police force.'[90] The Fire Brigade Pensions Acts, too, were modelled upon police pensions legislation.[91]

The claim for equality of treatment rested upon observed similarities in the work and status of the police and fire services. The case for the FBU was that equal work should be equally rewarded: 'The physical and educational standards for recruitment are the same, the period of training is the same, both are security services, both undertake physical risks and deal with emergencies, both have strict disciplinary codes and equally suffer from very awkward shift systems of duty.'[92] Police parity, though, was more than a wages referent; it was also a source of social differentiation. As the only other uniformed and disciplined service of a non-military and non-naval character, firemen laid claim to better pay and a social standing superior to that of non-craft manual workers in local authority employment. Nothing was more demeaning than to be treated as mere labourers. To firemen, who considered themselves a cut above such people, police parity served to distance them from the lower-waged local authority manual workers with whom they might otherwise have been aligned.

Police parity, as the customary standard, attained its maximum influence in the late 1940s. The assimilation of police-firemen into the wholetime regular fire brigades brought an influx of new, and hitherto unavailable, members into the union who were led to expect police scales of pay. These expectations, a central feature of the post-war recruitment drive launched by the Home Office in December 1945, were heightened by the substantial increases in pay and emoluments obtained by the police in 1949. But by then the foundations on which policy parity rested had shifted.

War and reconstruction had destroyed the deferential fire service as it had existed since Victorian times; relations between employer and employee were henceforth mediated by an energetic, autonomous, critical and civilian-minded trade union which acted as a political as well as an industrial agent. That in itself was sufficient to set it apart from the police. Employers unable to command obedience, except by negotiation, were in consequence less prone to seek a special relationship with firemen and more inclined to regard them as ordinary public service workers whose rewards were determined by the relative scarcity-value of skilled and semi-skilled labour. Changes in work practices and in the organisation of work, in any case, supplied a set of arguments for the wholesale revision of fire service pay which post-war employers found irresistible.

The contention was that, with regard to hours of duty and conditions of service, the position and obligations of the fireman had so changed as to render police comparability irrelevant. The replacement of continuous duty by a shift-work system meant that firemen had no longer to live on the fire station like a sailor on his ship, and relieved the fire authority of the obligation to house its workforce. The post-war fireman, unlike the policeman, was not compelled to reside in quarters provided by the employer or live in approved accommodation; nor was he liable to be recalled to duty once his shift had finished. In these respects his position was comparable with that of industrial workers. 'You are not thinking in terms of barracks any more, where people really were expected to live upon the fire station all their working life,' said Sir Cyril Radcliffe for the employers. The modern fireman, he told the Industrial Court in April 1948, 'is just like the man working in a factory who has to clock in at the right time in the morning, to be there on his job, and when his time of duty has gone he clocks off and away he goes'.[93] 'The loss of their traditional standing in relation to the police is naturally difficult for firemen to accept,' said the *Times*, in a leader on the unrest in the fire service provoked by the disruption of its traditional place on the wages ladder. 'The view that relative rates of remuneration can never be changed', it continued, 'is not one that can be accepted. If the firemen are to establish their claim to parity, they will have to show that it is justified by the responsibilities, burdens and dangers involved in their job now.'[94]

In 1952 the Board of Arbitration under Sir David Ross concluded that no such case had been made. The Ross Report, a landmark in the industrial history of the fire service, was the culmination of a consistent campaign to sever the connection between police and fire service pay that had been waged by the employers ever since the restoration of local authority control five years earlier. Henceforth local authorities were empowered to decide fire service pay policy solely 'on its merits'. In the absence of an agreed link between firemen's pay and that of other kinds of worker, said the *Times*, 'there is no surer way of judging their rates than to ask whether recruits are still coming forward in adequate numbers'.[95] And so it was for twenty years and more. So long as recruitment held up, the reform of pay-bargaining within the fire service lacked urgency. Shortages in particular brigades were regarded as matters for local adjustment. The introduction of local area payments in excess of nationally agreed rates, however, merely created anomalies that further distorted the pay structure and so fuelled the very unrest it was designed to forestall. Incomes policy made matters worse. The decade of discontent which began in the 1960s was in essence a rank-and-file revolt against the long-term failure to develop an effective basis of pay comparability.[96] No exercise in job evaluation was undertaken previous to the report of the Cunningham Inquiry of 1971. The outburst of unrest that prompted its appointment led thereafter to an increased awareness of the growing crisis within the fire service. Strikes and protests against undermanning and excessive overtime in both Glasgow and London during 1973 registered the case for reform without, however, producing the basis for a lasting settlement. That, it seemed, depended upon the introduction of an independent pay review procedure and the restoration of free collective bargaining. Meanwhile tension grew. In 1977 a fireman's pay of £65.70 a week was £12.90 behind average male earnings, while six years earlier firemen had earned £2.58 more than the average wage. A no-strike pact in return for a guaranteed position in the wages league, to be fixed by some form of pay research exercise analogous with that pioneered by the civil service, was seen by many commentators to be the way forward. 'By agreeing a point in the hierarchy of wages and then fixing the firemen on it permanently, they could be removed from the wages struggle,' said the *Sunday Times*, on 27 November 1977. 'As servants of the Crown,' it concluded, 'it is entirely proper that they should be taken out of politics like the Queen herself.' But by then, the first national firemen's strike had entered its third week.

Conclusion

Fire services can be civilian or military in character. The British case is an example of the former, the German of the latter. Fire service unionism was a child of war: the firemen's union emerged from the disruptive effects of the Kaiser's war, and in the struggle against fascism it grew to maturity. The Second World War created the conditions in which the character and scope of collective bargaining were redefined and firemen brought into closer relation with the non-uniformed working class. From this perspective the contest between the FBU and the Fire Service Department must be seen as less a discrete series of disputes over terms and conditions and more a battle over fundamentally different conceptions of the status of a disciplined service and its place in the social order. Arguments about duty systems, for example, had a socio-political dimension which both parties understood. FBU demands for a shorter working week were thus to be resisted not only on grounds of economy; the effects of reduced hours upon social hierarchies were equally compelling. The 48-hour week, if conceded, implied higher manning levels, a stronger union and a more homogeneous working class. The latter, in particular, was regrettable. 'In all the discussions of post-war duty systems', said a member of the Fire Service Department, 'too much play was being made with industrial analogies ...

The influence of the Fire Brigades Union in this connection has been most unfortunate.'[97] The FBU itself, though loth to abandon customary wage relativities, never lost sight of the general interests of fire fighters as wage workers within a capitalist system. Its conception of the fire fighter as the average skilled worker in uniform addressed work-based sources of division which, in the pre-war service, excluded firemen from meaningful participation in the cultural and social advances of the organised working class. As suggested above, post-war firemen are, by comparison with their predecessors, less inclined to think of themselves as a class apart. Since 1947 they have become more like ordinary industrial workers. The differences which remain are clearly significant but overall the dissimilarities have diminished. The national firemen's strike registered the long-term change in the character of fire service employment.

Notes

1. *Report of the Cunningham Inquiry into the Work of the Fire Service*, Cmnd 4807, 1971, p. 22.
2. Harry Deakin, 'Firemen on the Job', *New Society*, 1 December 1977, pp. 465-66.
3. A sample analysis showed that in 1970, standing time accounted on average for 60 per cent of the working week, while operational calls absorbed 3 per cent of total available time. *Cunningham Inquiry*, pp. 19, 21.
4. Harry Deakin, 'Firemen on the Job', p. 466; Report of the Committee on the Post-War Fire Service (1944), p. 19, in PRO, HO 45/23198/890164/13.
5. Margaret Thomas, *The Fire Service and its Personnel*, Government Social Survey, SS 417/B, London 1969, p. 36.
6. *Cunningham Inquiry*, p. 50.
7. Ibid., p. 73.
8. Commander Firebrace, 'The Pros and Cons of the 3-Shift System', 25 November 1943, HO 187/821.
9. Minutes of Fourteenth Meeting of Sub-Committee A of Committee on the Post-war Fire Services, 29 December 1943, HO 187/815.
10. B.V. Humphries, *Clerical Unions in the Civil Service*, Oxford 1954; David Englander and James Osborne, 'Jack, Tommy and Henry Dubb; the Armed Forces and the Working Class', *Historical Journal*, XXI (1978); A. Carew, *The Royal Navy and the Lower Deck 1919-39*, Manchester 1981.
11. Minute of A.[ylmer] F.[irebrace] to Sir Arthur Dixon, 18 February 1943, HO 187/451.
12. Memorandum of J.J. Bradley to Chief Industrial Commissioner, 7

May 1919, PRO, Lab. 2/268/15; *Firefighter*, May 1955.
13. Minutes of Fourteenth Meeting of Sub-Committee A of Committee on the Post War Fire Service, 29 December 1943, HO 187/815.
14. Extract from Draft Minutes of the Fire Service Council, 7 November 1941, HO 187/451; Representative Machinery: note of Points which might be mentioned at the Meeting with Fire Force Commanders, March 1943, HO 187/451.
15. Martin Harrison, *Trade Unions and the Labour Party Since 1945*, London 1960, pp. 70, 90, 125-6, 204-7, 213, 237. See also Graham Johnson, Chapter 6, below.
16. *Report of HM Chief Inspector of Fire Services for 1975 for England and Wales*, Cmnd 6598, 1976, p. 2.
17. Cf. *Report of H.M. Chief Inspector of Fire Services for 1976 for England and Wales*, Cmnd 6859, 1977, p. 2.
18. *Times*, 8 November 1977.
19. K. Newton, *The Sociology of British Communism*, London 1969, pp. 47-8; F.H. Radford, *Fetch the Engine, The Official History of the Fire Brigades Union*, London 1951, emphasises integration.
20. *New Society*, 24 November 1977, p. 395.
21. *Minutes of Evidence of Departmental Committee on the Hours, Pay and Conditions of Service of Firemen in Professional Fire Brigades in Great Britain*, Cmnd 876, 1920, p. 17, q. 293 (J.J.W. Bradley); Report of Committee on Post-War Fire Service (1944), p. 12, HO 45/23198/890164/13; *Report of HM Chief Inspector of Fire Services for 1948 for England and Wales*, Cmnd 7763, 1949, p. 14; G.V. Blackstone, *A History of the British Fire Service*, London 1957, p. 448.
22. Trades Union Congress, *Seventy Years of Trade Unionism 1868-1938*, London 1938, p. 260; Radford, *Fetch the Engine*, p. 186; Arthur Marsh, *Trades Union Handbook*, Aldershot 1984, p. 201.
23. Minutes of Second Meeting of Sub-Committee B – Committee on the Post-War Fire Service, 3 September 1943, HO 187/830.
24. Minute of S.J.B[aker] to Commander Firebrace, 24 June 1943, HO 187/823.
25. See First Interim Report of Sub-Committee B, 23 October 1943, HO 187/815; and Report of Committee on Post-War Fire Service (1944). On the exclusion of reservists, see HO 187/1182. These were subsequently revised in favour of recruits from the armed forces, *Report of Departmental Committee on the Fire Service*, Cmnd 4371, 1970, p. 87.
26. *The Fire Service and its Personnel*, pp. 16-17; *Cunningham Inquiry*, pp. 103, 107.
27. *Cunningham Inquiry*, p. 61; *Report of Her Majesty's Chief Inspector of Fire Services for the Year 1975*, Cmnd 6598, 1976, p. 2.
28. *The Fire Service and its Personnel*, pp. 15-16.
29. T.H. O'Brien, *Civil Defence*, HMSO, London 1955, pp. 495, 690.
30. On the role of women in NFS, see O'Brien, *Civil Defence*, p. 487; on fire service work-culture, see Graeme Salaman, *Working*, Chichester 1986, pp. 35-54.
31. HO 187/815, p. 15. See also Terry Segars, Ch. 3 below.
32. HO 187/1177.
33. HO 187/1107.
34. *Report of H.M. Chief Inspector of Fire Services for England and Wales for*

1950, Cmnd 8388, 1951 p. 5. See also Segars, Ch. 3 below.
35. HO 187/821, p. 52.
36. Residential accommodation was included in all but 14 of the 94 major fire stations built in England and Wales in the ten years before the war. Extract from Report to Secretary of State of Committee on the Post-War Fire Service, HO 187/822.
37. C.C. Cunningham to A.L. Dixon, 16 October 1943, in Minutes of the Thirteenth Meeting of Sub-Committee A of Committee on Post-War Fire Service, HO 187/821.
38. Commander Firebrace, 'The Pros and Cons of the 3-Shift System', 25 November 1943, HO 187/821.
39. *Firefighter*, December 1945-January 1946, p. 8.
40. 'The National Fire Service Duty System': Memorandum by A.I.T[udor], 1 February 1946, HO 187/1277.
41. *Cunningham Inquiry*, p. 67.
42. See above, 'The Early History of the Fire Brigades Union', pp. 44-71.
43. Re-organisation of the Fire Service; Extract from Conference with Regional Commissioners held at the Home Office, 28 May 1941, HO 187/1107. See too, HO 187/911.
44. Minute of Claud Bicknell, 26 January 1944, HO 187/1335; see too, *Fire Protection*, June 1947, pp. 200-1.
45. Discipline in pre-war professional non-police brigades was variable or non-existent; formal codes were in force only in the London, Birmingham and Croydon brigades.
46. *Fire*, October 1941.
47. Minute of G.M. Tucker to Mr Cornish, 9 September 1944, HO 187/1355.
48. 'Designation of Ranks', Memorandum by Fire Service Department, 11 June 1941, HO 187/1082.
49. Minute to Sir George Cater and Minister, 18 June 1941, HO 187/1082.
50. Minutes of Fire Service Council, 1 July 1941; Johnston to Morrison, 24 July 1941, HO 187/1082.
51. HO 187/646.
52. *News Chronicle*, 23 March 1941.
53. Deakin to Dixon, 14 October 1940, HO 187/33.
54. Minute of F.J., 28 August 1941, HO 187/1107.
55. *Firefighter*, August 1941.
56. Minute of W.A. Roper to Mr McGregor, 15 September 1943, HO 187/1335.
57. 'The Code of Discipline in the Post-War Fire Service', 11 February 1944, HO 187/1335.
58. Salaman, *Working*, pp. 48-51.
59. See for example, Aylmer Firebrace, *Fire Service Memories*, London 1949, pp. 122-3.
60. First Interim Report of Sub-Committee A of Committee on the Post-war Fire Services, Appendix II, HO 187/829; and for earlier references see *Report of the Royal Commission on Fire Brigades and Fire Prevention*, Cmnd 1945, 1923, pp. 186-190; *Report of the Departmental Committee on Fire Brigade Services*, Cmnd 5224, 1936, p. 44.

61. First Interim Report of Sub-Committee A of the Committee on the Post-War Fire Service, Appendix II, HO 187/829.
62. Minute of Claud Bicknell, 26 January 1944, HO 187/1335.
63. Minute of A.L. Dixon, 8 September 1941, HO 187/1107; and for FBU complaints, see *Report of Annual Conference of the Fire Brigades' Union*, 1941.
64. See, for example, R.N. Duke to E.A. Armstrong, 20 April 1940, HO 187/33.
65. Minute of S.J.B.[aker], 3 July 1942, HO 187/940.
66. Minute of Firebrace to Sir Arthur Dixon, 9 March 1943, HO 187/451.
67. Horner to Dixon, 17 March 1943, HO 187/940.
68. In Scotland, where the FBU was not officially recognised, the authorities had proceeded to develop a national system of committees from the station level upwards which were 'rather strictly confined' to recreational, social and educational activities. These, though superficially attractive, were, on reflection, found to be inappropriate to the situation south of the border: see 'Development of Welfare Organisation in the National Fire Service in Scotland', enclosed in A.A. Donnelly to A.W. Peterson, 26 July 1943, HO 187/940.
69. Minute of A.H.H.[ammond] to Sir Harold Scott, 6 July 1942, HO 187/940.
70. On representation in the service, see HO 187/33; HO 187/434; quotation from Meetings on Stations: Note of Points which might be mentioned in Discussion with Fire Force Commanders, February 1943, HO 187/451.
71. Minute of A.[ylmer] F.[irebrace] to Secretary of State, 19 July 1944, HO 187/1082.
72. The General Council of the TUC, for example, told the Home Secretary that the FBU had 'an inherent right' to negotiate on behalf of fire officers: Recognition of the Officers' Section of the Fire Brigades Union: Deputation from the General Council of the Trades Union Congress, 7 October 1946, HO 187/1082.
73. FBU claims to represent officers in negotiations over pay and conditions of service were not recognised as a 'legitimate right' until the close of the sixties: see *Report of the Departmental Committee on the Fire Service*, Cmnd 4371, 1970, pp. 148-9.
74. Home Office calculations suggest that officer members of the FBU accounted for 16 per cent of those ranks: see Minutes of A.H. Hammond to Mr Hutchinson, 10 October 1946, HO 187/1082.
75. *Fire*, October 1946.
76. *Fire*, July 1942. The FBU never relinquished its claim to represent all grades of fire fighters. The first national conference of officer members took place in 1956, and ten years later the FBU had in excess of 1,000 officer members: *Firefighter*, June 1966.
77. *The Firemen's Charter* (FBU, 1942) enclosed in HO 187/1277.
78. National Board for Prices and Incomes, Report No. 32, *Fire Service Pay*, Cmnd 3287, 1967, p. 4; *Cunningham Inquiry*, pp. 9-12.
79. *Cunningham Inquiry*, p. 42.
80. *The Fire Service and its Personnel*, pp. 8, 53-4.
81. 'Note of a Fire Service Department Conference held ... at the Home Office on Friday, 12th March, 1943', HO 187/940.
82. *The Fire Service and its Personnel*, p. 65.

83. Ibid., pp. 65-7.
84. Minute of H.G. Stillern to Mr Bittern, 18 May 1945, HO 187/1277. From a rather different perspective, the FBU has been critical of secondary employment on the grounds that it depresses fire service pay. See 'The Off-Duty Job', *Firefighter*, October-November 1956.
85. *The Fire Service and its Personnel*, pp. 76-83. Subsequent investigation showed that the 'attitude of officers' remained an important source of premature wastage within the Service: *Cunningham Inquiry*, pp. 56, 109.
86. *Report of Departmental Committee on the Fire Service*, Cmnd 4371, 1970, pp. 16, 156-7.
87. *Cunningham Inquiry*, p. 60. On examination pass rates, see *Report of Departmental Committee on the Fire Service*, pp. 128-33.
88. *Report of Departmental Committee on the Fire Service*, p. 152.
89. See *Report of Departmental Committee on the Fire Service*, p. 91.
90. National Joint Industrial Council for Local Authorities Fire Brigades in England and Wales, Employees' Side v. Employers' Side: Minutes of Proceedings before the Industrial Court, 29 April 1948, HO 187/1407.
91. Letter to E.W.H. Millar, 12 April 1939, HO 45/18127.
92. *The Industrial Court*, Fire Brigades in England and Wales, 24 May 1948 (2156), p. 6.
93. Minutes of Proceedings of Industrial Court, pp. 9, 44-5.
94. *Times*, 24 October 1951.
95. Ibid., 29 November 1977.
96. Speech of Neil Kinnock, *Hansard*, Vol. 938, 15 November 1977, col. 326.
97. HO 187/821, p. 42.

3 War, Women and the FBU

Terry Segars

Trade union histories tend to be written about men, largely no doubt because men have always made up the overwhelming majority of organised workers. Even the histories of unions which have recruited women members, however, are male-oriented. Women entered the Fire Brigades Union (FBU) for the first time when the union was experiencing a very rapid growth in numbers, and under the very special conditions and circumstances of the Second World War. They played an important and significant role in both the Auxiliary Fire Service (AFS) and National Fire Service (NFS), and it is to be regretted that their activities have gone largely unrecorded. It is to remedy, at least in part, the neglect of their role that this chapter has been written, and it must be emphasised that a more extensive collection of oral testimony would be of considerable historical value.

Through a mixture of conservatism and a refusal to believe that war would come, FBU members were initially united in their opposition to the setting up in 1937 of the Auxiliary Fire Service. Furthermore, the recruitment of the auxiliaries into the union was unthinkable. It took a complete change of the union's national leadership before a new policy, accepting that the AFS was there to stay, was adopted. Part of the problem was the sheer size of the AFS and the pace at which it was established. In the mid-1930s there were only 4,272 professional firemen in the whole country, and nearly half of them were members of the London Fire

Brigade. In addition, there were just over 2,000 policemen who could be called upon for fire duties.[1] In contrast to this tiny regular fire service, the AFS was 100,000-strong when war was declared in September 1939. No wonder regular firemen were worried at the prospect of AFS members outweighing them by sheer force of numbers.[2]

The AFS was built upon the base of the existing regular service, but where no service existed a new one had to be built. The process had to be completed very quickly and accommodation found, albeit on a temporary basis, for the new recruits. A further blow to the regular firemen's world of routine came when they realised that among these new recruits there would be women. Masie Gillard recalled the regulars' response: 'They didn't like the idea of women going in the fire service at all. Some of those old LFB men were quite rude.'[3] For most regulars the service had gone too far; for them firefighting was a man's job.[4]

Senior fire officers were no less opposed. Chief Officer Hall of the Leyton Fire Brigade in East London refused outright to admit women into the AFS, saying, 'I would rather resign than be made to drill young girls and women to be firemen.' He thought that the only place for women to work in wartime was in hospitals as nurses.[5]

During the war, in fact, firewomen did control-room work, as well as the more traditional women's work of typing and cooking. Their most active jobs were as drivers and dispatch riders, though in some places they were pump operators, and, on a very limited scale indeed, fire fighters.

The men who volunteered for the AFS quite often came from middle-class backgrounds, unlike peacetime recruits; some had been solicitors, shopkeepers and musicians, for example.[6] This was true also of the women who joined the service: Mary Robinson had been a trainee textile designer, Ivy O'Byrne a hotel manager. Shorthand typists were suddenly needed on a scale unimaginable in peace-time.[7] Gwen Kemp went to join the AFS at East London's Barking fire station and took her friend, Alice Flurer, along with her. Although Alice was not intending to join, when the recruiting officers found out she did shorthand they persuaded her to enlist as well.[8] Adelaide McCormick had a similar experience in May 1941 when she applied to join up at the Vine Street fire station in Liverpool. She was prepared to do shift work on the switchboard, but as soon as her shorthand and typing skills were mentioned she was put on days only.[9]

Alice and Gwen learnt their shorthand at the Park Modern School in Barking where they went until they were seventeen years old, although girls usually left school at fourteen.[10] Pat Thompson also had some commercial training and worked in offices before the war, while Adelaide McCormick went to Everton Valley Convent School until she was seventeen. Her father, the Commercial Attaché at the American Consulate in Liverpool, sent her to learn shorthand typing at a commercial training college after she left the convent school.[11] Masie Gillard had worked in Barker's department store, Kensington; she thought that learning shorthand was more of a middle-class thing to do. 'You didn't get to do that unless you had money where your parents could probably send you to Pitman's ... '[12] Others who were interviewed, however, had working-class jobs. Hilda Clark had been a cinema cashier and Anne Oakes worked behind the counter in a grocer's shop while working part-time in the control room.[13]

Masie Gillard thought that the women officers tended to come from a 'better-off' background. She remembered one who had been a ballet dancer, another a Salvation Army officer and another whose family had run a patisserie business. A secretarial background was not uncommon, but also 'we had a lot of women who ... came from the upper classes and never worked.'[14] Pat Thompson could not remember meeting any working-class women officers.[15] Mary Robinson was equally certain that the officers, male and female, tended to be 'definitely County types', though she echoed a common theme when she implied that favouritism also played a part in the more senior promotions of the women.[16]

The build-up of women in the AFS was slow, and even declined slightly from 5,400 in March 1940 to 4,500 a year later.[17] The government was not convinced that women had a significant role to play, for despite the labour shortage women's unemployment actually rose in the early part of the war.[18] These figures jumped dramatically from June 1941 onwards, however, when the number of wholetime firewomen increased from 5,400 to nearly 20,000 six months later.[19] The peak for wholetime women's membership of the AFS/NFS came in March 1943, when there were 32,200; for part-timers it came a year later, June 1944, at 54,600.[20] The ever-increasing demand for labour convinced the new coalition government, with Ernest Bevin as Minister of Labour, of the need to extend the scope of women's work.

Defining the role of women in the fire service had been the subject of some debate in the Home Office, and it seems that the civil servants were prepared to be more radical than the uniformed members of the Fire Department. An internal memorandum in July 1941 specified women's general duties as telephone and watchroom work, driving and possibly clerical and canteen work, and accepted that, 'it is not inconceivable that ultimately women may be accepted for observation duties and even as pump operators.'[21] In September it was officially announced that Fire Force Commanders were instructed to recruit women for 'all kinds of dangerous jobs connected with the NFS'.[22]

Even so, change came slowly and by the beginning of 1942 the Home Office estimated that only about 300 women were employed on firefighting duties.[23] The civil servants wanted to speed this up: '... if women were to be recruited in numbers sufficient to man the 10,690 light pumps which cannot now be manned by personnel on duty we should require a force of 50,000–60,000 women.'[24]

According to the 1951 history of the FBU, *Fetch the Engine*, there were already some cases of firewomen 'unofficially turning out with men to fight fires'.[25] This was not the experience of Sid Withers in the South-West, who was quite certain that women only 'drove canteen vans and they used to deliver the food round all the stations every day. Control room work ... they certainly didn't do any firefighting.'[26]

The reality, however, was that firewomen were more

widely involved in active work than is generally acknowledged, and they could often be found in the midst of things during the blitz, whether helping out on the pumps, in control rooms close to the centre of the severest air raids or delivering supplies to firefighters. Twenty-five firewomen were killed during the war as a result of enemy action, as well as 793 firemen.[27] One of Pat Thompson's women friends was killed in a direct hit on the Cavendish Road School, Balham sub-station, an incident that made her realise how vulnerable she was.[28] Masie Gillard vividly remembers an aerial torpedo dropping on a building only six houses along from the control room.[29]

In London women had to know something about the operational side of the service, so they could do elementary fire-fighting if their control room was hit. Pat Thompson's initial training at Tooting was 'as much about technical aspects of fire-fighting as about any work that we would get involved in ... our training ... certainly involved pump work and drills ... '[30] The fortnight's training that Agnes Shacklady was given in November 1941 when she joined the NFS in Liverpool contained nothing on administration and was so biased towards the practical side of the job that 'I really thought I was going into action.' She was mightily relieved when posted to the establishments office at the Divisional Headquarters in Bootle.[31] She had been called up after the Liverpool blitzes and it may have been then that the authorities in Liverpool accepted the idea of women firefighters. Hilda Clark received no training at all before being posted to the Hatton Garden Control Room at the end of 1940, learning the job as she went along. But after the blitzes of May 1941 control-room women started going to the fire service school in Sefton Park where they were shown how to couple hoses.[32]

Noreen Pope enjoyed a wide variety of jobs in the AFS, none of them in the control room:

> I drove a staff car – but also motor cycles and – believe it or not – a fire tender! Women were mostly concerned with the admin. side – telephonists, clerks, teleprinter operators and storekeepers. Regarding fire fighting, during the raids we

> were with the vehicles, reading gauges on vehicles and generally helping out where we could, and taking injured to ambulances or hospital.[33]

Another woman, Section Officer Pennington, recalled that even taking the canteen van out could be hazardous during the blitz:

> We went in convoy preceded by dispatch rider and control car and followed by the canteen van from HQ. We sat on the front seat by Batt [the driver] and proceeded into a darkness which was sometimes brilliantly lit by gun flashes and searchlights which was decidedly helpful when we had to lurch and wriggle our way round bomb craters. Of course, bombs were dropping around us all the time, and every now and then we had the further light of fires.[34]

In January 1941 the women's AFS magazine carried details of honours bestowed upon several women. The report on Gillian Tanner underlined how slow attitudes were to change:

> Tanner, one of 61's drivers, has been awarded the George Medal for taking out a petrol van on a night of 'Blitz' – though to read some newspaper accounts one would think it was almost equally due to her capacity for knitting without dropping stitches during a raid.[35]

Within the NFS women's role was by no means clearly defined. FBU general secretary, John Horner, wrote to the Home Office early in 1942 voicing concern about the widespread confusion then existing over the '... hours, conditions and the nature of a firewoman's duty'.[36] Women's willingness to take on different work was not without its problems as far as the union was concerned. Horner was worried

> ... about women being used for pump drill. It is a moot point whether women are capable of fire fighting under blitz conditions but I think you will agree that they should at least be put through a stringent medical test. Even part-time men who are taken on for fire fighting duties are put through a fairly severe test. Yet it appears to be the case that women are sometimes required to volunteer and sometimes detailed off for pump drill on heavy trailer pumps.[37]

Appliances and ambulance at the Henderson's department store fire, Liverpool, 1960, in which eleven people died, which led to the strengthening of fire regulations by Act of Parliament three years later

James Bradley

John Horner

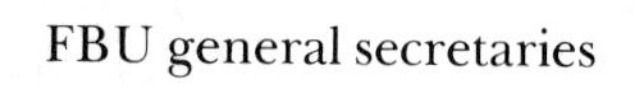

FBU general secretaries

Terry Parry

Ken Cameron

Firefighters in action during the blitz

The aftermath of the Broad Street goods depot tragedy in which three firemen died, December 1951

FBU demonstration Edinburgh, September 1961

A picket line during the national strike of 1977-78

In Grimsby, Horner had been told, there were a number of firewomen pump operators. He wanted a General Instruction laying down the limits of firewomen's duties.[38]

The Home Office claimed to be preparing such a directive, recognising they were open to criticism over women's conditions. Both Commander Firebrace, Chief of Fire Staff, and Sir Arthur Dixon, Principal Assistant Under Secretary of State in the Home Office Fire Department, wanted to ban women from pump crews. The union had come out in opposition to women firefighters early on in the war on the grounds that they lacked the necessary stamina, and, although Horner indicated that there was no objection to women pump operators, the union 'strongly deprecated the use of firewomen at the end of a branch'.[39] Marjorie Herd, the union's women's national organiser, asked for a medical standard, proper equipment, for women not to be employed on heavy pumps and, importantly, for 'equal pay to the men for similar work'.[40]

Dixon was forced to find out precisely what the situation was throughout the country, and in July 1942 he called for a report on the numbers and activities of 'women only' fire stations. The report highlighted, among other things, the shortage of working women, on the South coast at least.

At a station in Rochester the towing vehicle and light trailer pump had been run for a month by women, but 'due to [a] shortage of women they have had to be taken into control'.[41] The fire station in Worthing High Street had women pump crews and operators who

> have attended a large number of fires, and have proved themselves to be efficient and enthusiastic ... It has ... been an irksome task to have to abandon the Women Pump Crews ... The firewomen are most unhappy about the change which has had to be made: which is due to the urgent need of women in this Area for Control work, and driving where possible.[42]

Mary Robinson and Fred Wells remembered these crews and could not recall any resentment from the men about the women doing the job.[43] At the Withdean Lodge Fire Station, Brighton, fourteen firewomen worked on more traditional duties, hose-repairing, cooking and cleaning for the training school.[44] Further along the coast at the Moreton House station, Hastings, there were eight firewomen doing all those duties as well as operating the pump.[45]

When the need became urgent women were being assigned to these 'masculine' duties. The point is further illustrated by the example of Bamburgh, a tiny village in Northumberland, which boasted the only all-female fire station in the Northern Region. It happened quite simply because 'there are no available men ... These women have attended several fires in the village area and dealt with them efficiently.'[46] There were also women at other stations, he said, 'who have had actual fire-fighting experience.[47]

Despite these examples, when the General Instruction on women's jobs was issued in October 1942 no mention was made of pump-operating, let alone fire-fighting, and by April 1943 the Home Office was able to claim: 'No whole-time women [are] ... employed as pump operators or members of pump crews.'[48]

Pay, Hours and Conditions

Despite the government's need for female labour it always sought to keep their pay at two-thirds that of men. At the start of the war AFS women were paid £2, while men received £3, and when the AFS and regular fire services were nationalised in August 1941 women's pay rose to £2 7s., and the men's to £3 10s.[49]

Although the majority of firewomen were doing different jobs to firemen, there were, of course, exceptions. Men were often to be found working in control rooms alongside firewomen or as drivers or dispatch riders, and there was also the small number of women pump-operators and fire-fighters. In all these circumstances, the same job was being done, but for different rates of pay.

While the Home Office was keen to extend the range of duties carried out by firewomen, it was most anxious to do so in a way that precluded equal pay claims. It was emphasised: 'No very close comparison can be made between firemen and firewomen for the purpose of settling the pay of the latter by reference to that of the former.'[50] It was even proposed to change the title of Leading Firewoman to Head Firewoman to avoid comparison with Leading Fireman.[51] Treasury policy for women doing work normally carried out by men was to pay women about £100 a year less than the men.[52]

Equal pay was a major claim of firewomen at the special FBU Women's National Conference held in London in March 1943,[53] and later in the year Annual Conference insisted on the inclusion of equal pay for equal work in the forthcoming pay claim.[54] One delegate, Mrs Stein, presented the issue in terms of men's best interests, rather than of a basic principle for women:

> ... after the war, when the men come back from the Forces and demand their jobs back, the employers will find that they can do very well with the women and only pay 60 per cent of the wages ... the men may only receive those wages and not the wages they used to get ... [55]

The Home Office rejected the union's claim, making it clear that 'there is no hope of getting this until the principle of equal pay for equal work is generally accepted by the government ... '[56]

It was the same for most women during the war. In January 1944 women in metalwork and engineering earned £3 10s, half the male rate.[57] The average weekly wage for women in manufacturing industries at that time was £3 3s 9d, and average hours were 45 a week.[58] It was only in transport that women received equal pay as a result of an industrial court award at the start of the war.[59]

From the summer of 1942 women were liable to be conscripted for civil defence and fire service duties, and women MPs had opposed this unless the principles of equal pay and equal compensation were accepted. They did not win equal pay, but they did force the government to concede the principle on compensation for injuries. Edith Summerskill highlighted the government's discriminatory policies. Even though a woman could be

> called upon to serve and perform the same duties as a man, her monetary value is assessed at four-fifths of her male colleague. If, in the course of her work, she is disabled and loses a limb or an eye, the loss is reckoned as being only four-fifths of that of a man. The government has never explained how a woman earning a living with her hands suffers less than a man through the loss of an arm.[60]

Herbert Morrison claimed that the government had simply followed pre-war practice, but, following a Select Committee report equal compensation for women injured by enemy action was conceded.[61]

There was widespread concern that some of the temporary fire-station accommodation was too poor, and the union continually pressed for thorough medicals for firewomen. Underground control rooms were used in some cases, and although these were thought to give greater protection from enemy bombing, the union believed that, combined with the long hours the women worked, they contributed to the high incidence of tuberculosis among firewomen.[62]

The union wanted the Home Office to appoint a medical adviser for each of the NFS Regions, with mobile nurses in each division, access to mass radiography units and periodical medical checks. Medical examinations had been introduced for women entering the service in 1942, though they were described as 'a most cursory affair'.[63] It was said that health problems often arose because of the shortage of bedding and blankets leading to an increase in the incidence of skin diseases such as scabies.[64] Joan Betteridge, for instance, caught dermatitis when her control was temporarily moved to the Bootle Cricket Club and she used someone else's blankets.[65]

The poor standard of medical checks made it harder for women who contracted tuberculosis to prove that it was related to their fire service work. This was important, as the Ministry of Pensions had accepted that such claims might be work-related. The union also called for better standards of lighting and ventilation in the control rooms, as well as 'a break for fresh air after a four-hour duty period, wherever possible'.[66] Sir Arthur Dixon at the Home Office accepted that the sickness rates among firewomen were unduly high and was sympathetic to the claims for medical examinations. He proposed even more medical advisers than the union was calling for![67]

At the 1943 Annual Conference Mrs McGrandle, a delegate from the North-West, criticised the executive for not having fought vigorously enough to resist the imposition of the 110-hour week. She highlighted the additional problems the longer hours could cause where firewomen had the sole responsibility for bringing up the children:

> ... they were looking after homes ... It has definitely got to be done. But you must realise that the married women have given up quite a lot when they came on to the 48/24 [110-hour week]. They cannot give their attention to the children, and the children need attention at the age of five up to fourteen, or else you are going to get a lot of children being brought before the courts, and the reason is that mothers are not being allowed to look after their children.[68]

Short leave and shopping time were also called for by firewomen.[69] Although women could ask for short leave to go shopping in lull periods, this was not automatically granted until the following year when the union's executive claimed success 'in obtaining shopping time of two hours per week for women on twelve-hour shifts ... '[70]

Leave was only allowed, however, if there were sufficient members of staff available to cover. Those who worked in administration recalled being able to get short leave, but the women in controls could not remember any special arrangements for shopping, and it seems likely that it was restricted in practice to administrative workers.

Women in the Fire Brigades Union

Women's trade union membership doubled during the war, increasing from less than 1 million in 1939 to 2.2 million in

1944, a quarter of all women workers.[71] Female membership of the FBU increased quite dramatically, from 1,000 in 1941 to 5,500 in 1942, reaching 8,200 by July 1943.[72] From this point on it declined and the FBU's Annual Report for 1944 claimed 'roughly 5,000' women members.[73] This figure continued to drop and by 1948 the union claimed only 500 women members.[74]

It is difficult to gauge exactly what this meant in terms of union density. If the peak figure of 8,200 women FBU members in 1943 is assumed to be composed of both whole- and part-timers, and since there were approximately 77,700 women in the NFS in 1943, 30,700 whole- and 47,000 part-timers, the level of union membership among firewomen was less than 10 per cent.[75] If, as was more likely, most of the 8,200 in the FBU were whole-timers, then women's membership level was more substantial at over 26 per cent.

While women joined the union they tended not to play a prominent part within it.[76] Marjorie Herd, from Richmond, was appointed in 1941 to recruit women into the union and look after their interests. She already had experience of both trade unionism and the fire service.[77] Two additional women's organisers were taken on during 1943, Betty Wallace and Betty Harrison,[78] but the decline in women's membership in 1944 led to a reduction in special organisation. Regional committees took over the job of organising and representing firewomen, with assistance from the women's officer at head office. There were, however, two special seats allocated for women on the National Council of the union.[79]

Although Pat Thompson and Masie Gillard served in the AFS/NFS in different parts of London, they had entirely opposite experiences of the FBU. Pat Thompson simply did not know there was a union. Her background in the Labour League of Youth would have made her responsive to any suggestion to join a union. She served at Tooting and could not recall even the regular firemen mentioning a union.[80] Ironically, Masie Gillard, a life-long Conservative supporter, knew about and joined the union. She was quick to point out how important the union was in the early days of the war. It was the old regulars who talked about the union and who persuaded her and a few others to join, but she saw it mainly as the men's union, only going to meetings that were held on her station. 'I could understand the pushing for uniforms and things, when you think a man's putting his life on the line.' The union was strongly identified with the battle to get the proper protective clothing and equipment, she remembered; she also knew about the left-wing views of many officials.[81]

In Worthing Mary Robinson thought that all the women had joined the union around the time of nationalisation, although none played much part in it. Mary appreciated what the union could do when her husband, Fred Wells, an ex-regular with the Worthing Fire Brigade, was badly injured during a hook-ladder drill. While hospitalised he was twice taken off the payroll, and only union pressure kept him on it and secured him a pension when he was eventually discharged.[82]

Alice Flurer collected the union subscriptions for a while after joining the union in Barking, East London.[83] Again, the men had suggested the women join, and most did, but Alice never went to meetings and did not think that the union placed much store by its women members.[84] None of the AFS/NFS women interviewed from the Liverpool area could recall any mention at all of the union.[85]

There were probably two factors that determined the pattern of women joining the union. All the women interviewed who had been members of the union during the war joined because of encouragement from ex-regular firemen. Pat Thompson always served at sub-stations in South London, and never saw much of the London Fire Brigade ex-regulars. The second factor was the hostility that many ex-regulars felt towards the AFS in the first place, especially their membership of the union.[86] This suggests that the role of the regular firemen in recruiting women unionists was an important one.

The lack of women's membership in Liverpool is probably explained by the fact that, under the Police Act of 1919, trade union membership had been illegal in the city's police fire brigade before the war. The union tended to make slow progress in these brigades, even when the prohibitions were lifted once the service was nationalised.[87] If there was no ex-regular membership at all it is hardly surprising that the women never heard of the Fire Brigades Union.

At the end of the war women's membership of the NFS collapsed more sharply than men's. In March 1945 there were 15,000 wholetime and 136,000 part-time firewomen; by September of that year they were down to 5,500 and 47,600 respectively.[88]

Yet women were not completely excluded from the peacetime brigades. They continued to be employed in many of the control rooms, though the London Fire Brigade quickly reverted to its pre-war practice of men only.[89] As the need for dispatch riders and car drivers disappeared the service again became a predominantly male enclave.

Post-war

The control rooms were where most of the women were employed after the war; and, of course, the policy of *un*equal pay was part of the reason. In spite of the union's efforts equal pay never was conceded during wartime, and in fact was not achieved until 1972 for women in control rooms.

James Chuter Ede, Home Secretary in the 1945–51 Labour government, supported women's employment in the fire service, though he was careful to avoid specifying which jobs they should do.[90] The government had the anticipated shortage of able-bodied men in mind when it gave such encouragement, and this was also used by the union to justify its support.[91]

This pattern of female employment in the fire service continued until the 1980s when, as a direct result of the Greater London Council's equal opportunity policies, the question of women firefighters was forced back onto the agenda.[92] Senior officers in the London Fire Brigade had no wish to change the traditional white male recruitment base, but were obliged to conform to the council's determination to extend the numbers of women and members of ethnic minorities it employed. There were strong parallels with the situation when the AFS was set up; the idea of women firefighters was bitterly resented by both officers and rank-and-file firefighters.

It has been a very slow process – there were just 34 women firefighters in the London Fire Brigade in March 1990 – and progress has been much slower outside the capital. The London brigade has run special pre-entry courses for young women and ethnic minority members in what to expect in the fire brigade. Women have found the technical and physical education sections of these courses especially helpful in preparing them for the entry tests. But once again there has been deep resentment from men who believed that women were getting preferential treatment in order to achieve what have been seen as political objectives.

Once in the service, women firefighters have found they need to work hard to gain acceptance from their male colleagues. One estimated that it took her two years to settle in, but thought that activity in the union had helped to break down a lot of the distrust.[93] A common complaint from the women is that because senior officers will often single them out for special attention the male firefighters worry that any complaint the women may have will go straight to the top, making them even more unsure of the women.

Well publicised cases of sexual harassment involving women firefighters and male colleagues have certainly tested the union's commitment to equal opportunities. Initially there was a reluctance to rock the boat as far as male members were concerned. The men accused in these cases were given legal assistance and representation at disciplinary hearings by the union, resulting in some instances in the FBU providing representation to both sides in the dispute! In consequence there is now discretion to withhold representation if Regional Committees so decide.

It was these cases that led to resolutions at the union's 1985 Annual Conference, calling for the extension of equal opportunity within the fire service.[94] There is now a

Standing Committee of the Executive Council on Equal Opportunities, and in London the union has set up a Women's Advisory Committee to provide a channel specifically for women's issues and help counter the isolation that women firefighters still feel.

But the union and the service are changing. While it is still predominantly a men's union, the majority of female FBU members in the control rooms, together with the women firefighters, are increasingly assertive on women's issues and demanding more of both the union and management.

Conclusion

Although women were members of the union in the war years, evidence suggests that their membership was patchy, with very few part-timers included. They seem not to have played a large part within the FBU, which remained a fire*men*'s union throughout the period. The same could not be said of the service in general; women were often highly visible and active in jobs that they would not have been considered for before the war. The fire service establishment nevertheless ensured that there was no challenge to existing sexual roles, and there is little doubt that in this they had the support of many firemen.

The expansion and reorganisation of the service that followed nationalisation in 1941 led to increased opportunities and promotion for many AFS women. Even so, they often regretted the shift away from the locally based AFS to the centralised and impersonal NFS. Discipline became stricter, people were drafted in from other parts of the country, often as officers, and the scale of the nationalised service made individuals feel less significant and involved.

Since the war, while women have become firmly established in control rooms, the more recent initiative to recruit women firefighters is still untested in most brigades, and remains controversial with many male members of the union. Although many barriers remain to equal opportunities for women, in most cases where recruitment has taken place it has been successful, and accepted by the men. The wartime experience shows that the union cannot afford to take a passive role on this issue, otherwise there is a danger that what little progress has been made will disappear altogether.

Notes

1. Terry Segars, 'The Fire Service: The Social History of a Uniformed Working-Class Occupation', Ph.D. Thesis, Essex University, 1989, p. 185.
2. *Firefighter*, June 1940, pp. 34-6.
3. Masie Gillard, taped interview, 17 July 1989.
4. Neil Wallington, *Firemen at War*, London 1981, p. 24.
5. *Fire*, May 1939. I am grateful to John Horner for bringing this article to my attention.
6. Segars, 'The Fire Service', pp. 221-5.
7. Mary Robinson and Frederick Wells, taped interview, 26 February 1990; Ivy O'Byrne, taped interview, 26 February 1990. All names of interviewees are those they were known by during wartime.
8. Alice Flurer and Gwen Kemp, taped interview, 26 September 1989.
9. Adelaide McCormick, taped interview, 30 January 1990.
10. Alice Flurer and Gwen Kemp, interview.
11. Adelaide McCormick, interview.
12. Masie Gillard, interview.
13. Anne Oakes and Hilda Clark, taped interviews, 30 January 1990 and 1 February 1990 respectively.
14. Masie Gillard, interview. See also Wallington, *Firemen*, p. 23: 'From their inception, both the men's and women's branches of the AFS had their own officer structure, with people from a suitable 'background' (usually the professional classes) being appointed officers ... '
15. Pat Thompson, correspondence, 6 December 1989.
16. Mary Robinson, interview.
17. Central Statistical Office, *Statistical Digest of the War*, London 1951, Table 16.
18. Gail Braybon and Dorothy Summerfield, *Out of the Cage*, London 1987, p. 155.
19. *Digest*, Table 16.
20. Ibid.
21. PRO, HO187/395, 29 July 1941, R. Hewison, Draft Memo, 'Women in the National Fire Service – rates of pay'.
22. Margaret Goldsmith, *Women at War* (No place or date of publication given) p. 128.
23. PRO, HO187/1365, 14 January 1942, 'Meeting on the recruitment of women for the National Fire Service'.
24. Ibid.
25. Frederick H. Radford, *Fetch the Engine*, London 1951, p. 157.
26. Sid Withers, taped interview, 12 August 1985.

27. Terence H. O'Brien, *History of the Second World War: Civil Defence*, London 1955, p. 501.
28. Pat Thompson, taped interview, 2 September 1987.
29. Masie Gillard, interview.
30. Pat Thompson, interview.
31. Agnes Shacklady, taped interview, 31 January 1990.
32. Hilda Clark, interview.
33. Noreen Pope, correspondence, 14 November 1985.
34. Imperial War Museum, ref.87/14/1, Elsie Warren recollections: manuscript entitled, 'Fires of the Forties'.
35. Ibid.
36. PRO, HO187/445, 16 February 1942.
37. Ibid.
38. Ibid.
39. Peter Pain, *The Struggle of the AFS*, London 1941, p. 27; PRO, HO187/445, 5 March 1942.
40. PRO, HO187/445, 5 March 1942.
41. Ibid., 29 July 1942.
42. Ibid.
43. Mary Robinson and Fred Wells, interview.
44. PRO, HO187/416, 29 July 1942.
45. Ibid.
46. Ibid.
47. Ibid.
48. Ministry of Labour Circular, 159/15, 26 October 1942: PRO, HO187/445, 7 April 1943, Detailed statement on Medical Arrangements for WFNS.
49. Fire Brigade Circular, N.4/1939, 23 March 1939; National Fire Service (General) Regulations 1941, p. 21.
50. PRO, HO187/395, Women in the National Fire Service – rates of pay, 29 July 1941.
51. Ibid.
52. Ibid., 18 September 1941.
53. *Firefighter*, March 1943. This short report is the only account I have been able to find of this conference. Other issues dealt with were: station facilities for women; medical examinations; time off for shopping; the Second Front and Communist Party affiliation to the Labour Party. For a report of the FBU deputation to the Home Office on issues raised at the conference, see FBU, *Proceedings*, 1943, p. 24.
54. FBU, *Proceedings*, 1943, p. 29.
55. Ibid., p. 31.
56. FBU, *Annual Report*, June 1944, p. 9; *Royal Commission on Equal Pay*, Cmnd 6937, HMSO, London, 1944-46. For a brief discussion on the Commission and its findings, see Denise Riley, 'Some Peculiarities of Social Policy concerning Women' in Sonya Michel and Margaret Collins Weitz (eds.), *Behind the Lines*, New Haven and London 1987, pp. 264-5.
57. Angus Calder, *The People's War*, London 1971, p. 465.
58. *Digest*, p. 204.
59. Braybon and Summerfield, pp. 180-1.
60. Sarah Boston, *Women Workers and the Trade Union Movement*, London 1980, p. 194.

61. Ibid., p. 195.
62. FBU, *Proceedings*, 1943, p. 13.
63. Ibid., p. 26.
64. Ibid., p. 27.
65. Joan Betteridge, taped interview, 31 January 1990.
66. FBU, *Report*, 1943, p. 15.
67. Ibid.
68. FBU, *Proceedings*, 1943, pp. 60-1.
69. *Firefighter*, March 1943.
70. FBU, *Report*, 1944, p. 33; General Fire Force Instruction 13/1943.
71. Braybon and Summerfield, p. 180.
72. TUC, *Annual Reports*, 1941, p. 51, and 1942, p. 375; FBU, *Proceedings*, 1943, p. 42.
73. FBU, *Report*, 1944, p. 20.
74. TUC, *Annual Report*, 1948, p. 37.
75. *Digest*, p. 14.
76. Peter Pain, *The Struggle of the AFS*, London 1941, p. 26.
77. Ibid., p. 27.
78. FBU, *Proceedings*, 1943, p. 42. John Horner also pays tribute to the work done by Connie Tudor-Hart as chair of the union's Women's Advisory Committee. She was the first woman on the executive council elected to represent both men and women: correspondence, 25 January 1990.
79. FBU, *Report*, 1944, p. 20.
80. Pat Thompson, interview.
81. Masie Gillard, interview.
82. Mary Robinson and Fred Wells, interview.
83. Alice Flurer, interview.
84. Ibid.
85. Hilda Clark, interview.
86. I am grateful for Pat Thompson's assistance in developing this point.
87. For more information on the police-fire brigades and former police-firemen joining the union, see Segars, 'The Fire Service', pp. 173-85 and p. 251.
88. *Digest*, p. 14.
89. Frank Eyre and E.C.R. Hadfield, *The Fire Service Today*, Oxford 1953, p. 39.
90. FBU, *Proceedings*, 1946, pp. 119-20.
91. Ibid., pp. 121-2.
92. I am indebted to Ghada Razuki and Greg Bluestone for their assistance with the section on the 1980s.
93. Ghada Razuki, correspondence, 22 November 1990.
94. FBU, *Proceedings*, 1985, pp. 95-110.

4 The 'Spit and Polish' Demonstrations

Victor Bailey

'The Fire Brigades Union was founded in 1918. I suggest to you that it became a reality in 1951.'[1] This was vice-president Arthur Coupe's verdict on the impact of the 'spit and polish' demonstrations of 19-20 November 1951 when firemen throughout the country boycotted non-essential duties for 48 hours. As a critical part of the union's post-war battle to regain pay parity with policemen all fire calls and all other calls for assistance were answered, but training, domestic chores and 'brass-bashing' were banned. The fire authorities responded vindictively; firemen were sacked, others demoted, hundreds fined and thousands put on disciplinary charges. For a good few months the fire service was convulsed. As Coupe correctly implied, and as we shall illustrate in this chapter, the 'spit and polish' dispute was an important watershed in the FBU's history. For the first time firemen took industrial action on a national scale. They successfully combated the ensuing wave of employer victimisation by mobilising the support of the wider trade union and labour movement. In the heat of that battle, moreover, firemen developed a stronger industrial and political consciousness.

For the origins of the 'Spit and Polish' dispute we must return to April 1948 when the Home Office handed the fire service back to the local authorities. It was soon evident that the union was faced with a difficult set of employers in the county boroughs, whose ideas of the fire brigades were rooted in the pre-war years; in the county councils, which had no experience of administering fire brigades; and in the London County Council, where, according to John Horner, 'the ghost of Herbert Morrison still walks the corridors ...'[2] According to these local authorities, whose representatives constituted the employers' side of the National Joint Council, the fire brigades were far too costly. Too many wholetime firemen were employed at too high a wage. This was particularly the view of those authorities which had formerly maintained police-fire brigades with a government grant of 50 per cent towards the pay of the firemen-constables; under the Fire Services Act, 1947, the government grant had sunk to 25 per cent. The employers' aim, therefore, was to effect economies; to take the fire brigades back to pre-war conditions of service. There seems little doubt, too, that the fire authorities were out to clip the wings of a union which had significantly increased its power and influence during the war. For the next three years, in consequence, a running battle raged between the union and the employers on pay, personnel and duty systems. The battle was fought out on the National Joint Council, and before the Ministry of Labour's Industrial Court, until in late 1951 the firemen turned to a unique and unusual form of direct action.

Police Parity

At the core of the dispute was the union's determination to maintain police pay parity. The FBU rested its case on four main arguments.[3] The first was historical: that since about 1888 the pay of the two services had been closely equated, if not identical. This was especially true of the interwar years. One-third of wholetime firemen were employed in the London Fire Brigade, with the same basic pay as that of the Metropolitan Police. Another third, particularly in the North of England, were employed in police-fire brigades and paid police rates. The remaining third were either in brigades whose rates of pay were related to the LFB, or in brigades which were on the Middlebrook scale of pay, which was roughly equivalent to police pay. In successive Industrial Court awards in the 1920s and 30s, moreover, parity was adopted, and challenged neither by the employers nor by firemen. Nor had the Second World War disturbed the general acceptance of the parity principle. At the end of the war the Home Office's recruiting leaflet promised prospective applicants police pay and conditions, one of the principal attractions to the 10,000 new recruits who flocked into the service at that time. As late as December 1946, finally, the Industrial Court had decided that pay and allowances in the two forces were to be the same.[4] For fifty years, then, the fire brigades and the police forces had marched in step with regard to rates of pay. The FBU could imagine no new circumstance which would justify a departure from this broad trend of history.

To this historical argument the union added that the duties performed by firemen were as arduous as, and often more hazardous than, those performed by policemen. This was true both of work on fires and of special service work (such as rescuing trapped persons or those overcome by noxious gases), which had increased considerably since 1938. Indeed, the fire service was well on its way to becoming the maid of all work.

The third plank of the union's case was that, broadly speaking, regulations for the two services, concerning uniform allowance, holidays, promotions, discipline and pensions were similar. Where they varied, notably in relation to hours of work, the regulations were favourable to the police. Policemen performed a 48-hour tour of duty per week. Firemen performed a regular 60-hour week duty, but in many of the larger brigades, owing to shortage of personnel, 80 hours per week were worked, without overtime pay. Large fires, moreover, could add considerably to the hours worked.

The final argument deployed by the union was that the problems of recruiting and retaining personnel were as serious in the fire service as in the police service, and that while police pay had exceeded the increase in the government's cost of living index firemen's pay had failed to keep pace with it.

The employers, in contrast, could not accept the proposition that, as a matter of principle, there should be automatic parity with the police. Police pay was, they argued, only one of the factors to be taken into account in assessing firemen's pay on the basis of the rate for the job. Within a few weeks of taking over responsibility for the new brigades, therefore, the local authorities challenged policy parity by demanding the abolition of the rent allowance and supplementary allowances paid to firemen. The union was compelled to refer the dispute forced upon it by the new employers to the Industrial Court. Fortunately, the court found in favour of the firemen in May 1948. Alas, the award also included the statement.

> It is not to be assumed that future increases or decreases of police pay and allowances should automatically apply to fire brigade personnel and the Court take the view that the National Joint Council when considering fire brigade remuneration should consider the advisability of consolidating pay and allowances.[5]

The employers took the hint. In January 1949 they recommended the consolidation of rent allowances and basic pay, on a level which would place the consolidated pay substantially below the level of police pay.[6]

The union's initial response was to postpone discussion of a consolidated wage rate until the appearance of Lord Oaksey's Committee on Police Conditions of Service. Oaksey recommended increases in police pay, which came into effect on 1 July 1949. The union therefore countered the employers' consolidation proposal with a request for police parity. It was now the turn of the employers' side of the NJC to drag its feet. The employers refused to consider the union's claim for wage increases on a par with those granted the police until their consolidation proposals had been disposed of on the NJC. Months of delay took place, with the employers' side periodically walking out of the Joint Council. The continuation of this deadlock eventually provoked the

London district committee of the FBU to organise a march from County Hall over Westminster Bridge to Caxton Hall. In September 1949 over 600 firemen from London and the Home Counties took part in the march and the subsequent mass meeting, a demonstration of firemen's determination to get the stalled pay talks going, and to win police parity.[7]

At last, in December, the Industrial Court was asked to adjudicate. While the employers pressed for consolidation of pay and allowances, firemen counterclaimed for parity with the increased police pay. In the course of the hearing John Horner discovered that the amount the employers initially said they were prepared to pay to implement consolidation (£885,775) was *more* than the cost of funding the Oaksey scales, or police parity (£722,000). The employers had inadvertently over-estimated the cost of consolidation by some £450,000! Remarkably, this discovery did nothing to prejudice the employers' case in the eyes of the Industrial Court. In January 1950 the court found against the firemen, deciding that pay and allowances should be consolidated, and at the figure proposed by the employers. In short, the award consolidated pay and allowances, without conceding a general increase in pay. For many new recruits paying high post-war rents the award aggravated the pressure of higher living costs.[8]

The long-standing parity in pay between the fire brigades and the police forces was destroyed by the Industrial Court. The award dealt a severe blow to the union, constituting the first departure from the principle of parity. The union was confounded. Police parity had gone, and gone for good. Yet the only comparable group of public servants still remained the men in the police forces. There was no alternative, therefore, to demanding *comparability* with policemen in gross earnings. In late 1950 a claim for a 15 shillings increase sought to achieve this equality. In April 1951 firemen obtained only a 7s. 6d. increase, bringing starting pay to £6 18s. 6d. weekly; maximum pay to £7 19s. 6d. In August 1951, however, the police received another substantial increase, following recommendations contained in the Trustam Eve report, bringing starting pay for a constable to

£7 13s. 10d. weekly; maximum pay to £9 14s. 2d. exclusive of rent allowance. In all, the disparity between the weekly pay of a fireman and of a police constable on appointment was of the order of 35 shillings. The policeman's lot was the happier one.[9]

Abolition of parity was not, however, the union's only anxiety. 'No matter where you put the testing rod,' Horner told Annual Conference in June 1951, 'it is clear that over these last two or three years we have seen not only the end of the development of the service ... but there is now the danger that the standards of our service still will decline.'[10] Numerous obstacles threatened the standards of service efficiency: the persistence of the 24/24 hour duty system, the spread of the 'day-manning' duty system (an insidious form of continuous duty), the parlous condition of many fire stations and the stultification of the work of the Central Fire Brigades Advisory Council. The executive council of the union decided to undertake, therefore, a thorough review of the fire service. Entitled 'In Defence of Britain's Fire Brigades', the review set out the post-war decline in the standards and status of the service. It also appealed for fair consideration of the union's wage claim – and, significantly, for a reversal of the government's wage freeze policy, which the FBU had consistently opposed, and which overshadowed the entire discussions on pay parity.

Wage Freeze

The negotiations on policy parity were carried out, as the union's 'Blue Book' put it, 'against a background of the ever-deepening economic difficulties which have continued to face the government and the country'.[11] The post-war Labour government faced profound economic difficulties as early as 1947.[12] A bitterly cold winter, followed by a severe coal shortage, held up industrial production, and cost the country heavily in lost exports. More significantly, a balance of payments crisis, caused by a low level of commodity exports, a greatly diminished volume of 'invisible' exports and excessive imports of US food, fuel and raw materials led to a severe drain on the Bank of England's dollar reserves. Under these circumstances the US loan, negotiated in December 1945 to help Britain become self-supporting, would be spent far too rapidly. A difficult year became a disastrous one when, in July, the free convertibility of the pound, a condition of the American loan, took effect, leading to a flight from sterling and a further drain on the dollar reserves. Practically every country with sterling earnings hurried to convert them into dollars. To avoid bankruptcy a new economic policy was imposed, the main architect of which was the new Chancellor of the Exchequer, Sir Stafford Cripps.

Between late 1947 and mid-1950, the Chancellor sought to reduce dollar imports by food rationing and general austerity, to boost exports (with the help of Marshall Aid, available in the summer of 1948) and to control wages and prices. No attempt was made to reduce military expenditure overseas, which contributed to the balance of payments difficulties, or to reduce the number of men in the armed services (still almost one million in 1948) who could have been better used on productive work. For present purposes, however, the most significant step was the government's White Paper, *Statement on Personal Incomes, Costs and Prices*, known in the trade union movement as the 'Wage-Freezing Document'.

The White Paper demanded a total standstill of profits and rents, and a qualified limitation of wage increases. These were to be granted only where, for example, they were required to attract labour to undermanned occupations. Wages Councils and similar negotiating bodies were alerted to the government's views on wage restraint. At a special conference of trade union executives in March, and at the annual conference of the TUC later in the year, the demand for wage restraint was endorsed. Only a few unions, and mainly those with Communist officials – the ETU, the AEU, USDAW and the FBU – attacked the White Paper for seeking to freeze wages at a time when both the share of profits and the cost of living continued to rise. In practice, moreover, unions observed wage restraint.[13]

The 'Spit and Polish' Demonstrations

The policy of wage restraint held in 1949, despite the rise in living costs due to the heavy devaluation of the pound (from $4.03 to $2.80) in September; and it held for most of 1950. Only the increased inflation produced by the Korean War turned the balance of TUC opinion. In September 1950 the TUC voted down the wage freeze. But the freeze had held for three years during which the FBU had had the devil's own problem in wage negotiations. The White Paper's publication in February 1948 coincided, as the FBU was wont to point out, with the transfer of the fire brigades to the local councils and the first attempt to reduce the pay of firemen. The FBU always argued, furthermore, that the decision to break away from police pay parity in January 1950 was based on the government's wage freeze policy and its endorsement by the TUC. In the face of the government's attitude to wage increases neither employers nor the Industrial Court were prepared to accept a case for pay parity with policemen. Moreover, devaluation and the Chancellor's announcement of cuts in public expenditure had, the 'Blue Book' argued, 'a very direct effect on the Fire Service and on the Fire Brigades Union'.[14]

'Unofficial' Action

When the Executive Council met on 13 September 1951 it had before it letters from many areas and districts protesting at the decline in firemen's conditions and calling upon the union to apply for a substantial increase in pay. The EC also learnt of a mass meeting being arranged by the London district committee for 3 October. Almost 1,000 officers and men of the London and Home Counties' brigades, some with their wives, packed Beaver Hall, London. The speakers made it clear that it was time the gloves came off. Tom Goodrick (from South-West London) thought this was the last chance to regain police parity, and so asked the EC to tell the employers that it was parity, or else 'we seek the traditional methods of solving our dispute'. John Fildes, a fraternal delegate from Glasgow, urged the general secretary to warn the employers that 'unless they come across with police parity every fireman in Glasgow will be on the streets ...'[15] A resolution was then carried without dissent, requiring the EC to table a demand for equal pay with the police, and committing the membership of the London district to set up rank and file 'action committees', composed of station delegates, to consider the steps to be taken should the employers' side of the NJC reject this demand.[16]

At the NJC meeting on 11 October the employers were as intransigent as ever. The claim for the restoration of comparability, to take the form of an increase of 35 shillings a week, was referred to a further meeting of the Joint Council. With as little grace the employers threw out the union's requests to tell all local authorities to grant full pay while sick to firemen and officers (a few authorities remaining recalcitrant in this regard), and to allow brigades on the 24/24 hour system of duty to introduce improvements which fell short of the 60-hour week. This display of employer attitudes set the seal on militant trade union action.[17]

The rank-and-file Action Committee called for a 48-hour 'fires only' demonstration on 16 and 17 October. A press statement emphasised that while the ban on all 'spit and polish' duties was an *unofficial* action, it was an attempt to help the union's official wage negotiations.[18] In fact, there is evidence to suggest that the leadership, notably those in the Communist Party, preferred at this stage an unofficial demonstration to official industrial action. We can only speculate that union officials feared the government would intervene legally and militarily against an official dispute. Officials may also have been uncertain how members would respond to a call for action, at a time when some regions were critical of the Communist complexion of the executive council.[19]

Tom Harris of the Soho fire station in Shaftesbury Avenue was secretary of the Action Committee. He had joined the AFS in 1939 and fought fires throughout the London blitz. Following service as an RAF pilot he had returned to the London Fire Brigade in September 1946. He remembered

Tuesday 16 October, he told me, 'as if it were yesterday'. At 9 a.m., 'after roll had been called and riding positions allocated,' he continued, 'I as Branch Secretary of A5 Soho, stepped out of the ranks and informed the Station Officer that, in accordance with the Action Committee's instructions, members would only perform fire fighting or special service duties for the next two days.'[20] In London and Home Counties, the turn-out was solid.

That might have been the full extent of the demonstration had not the chief officer of the Southend brigade suspended three union activists from duty. Other brigades around the country – Liverpool, Manchester, Birmingham, Glasgow – came out in solidarity with the Southend men. By the end of the week, something like 70 per cent of the entire service had staged 'spit and polish' demonstrations. BBC news bulletins featured the dispute, as did the national press, bringing public attention to the firemen's case for pay equality. At the end of the London action the LCC put out a press statement acknowledging that over the 48-hour period, all emergency calls had been responded to within thirty seconds. On 19 October, as the wave of 'spit and polish' demonstrations rolled on, the EC met again. It congratulated members on the action taken, but asked for no further demonstrations until after the NJC meeting on 30 October.[21] The unofficial action had, it hoped, done enough to change employer attitudes on pay equality.

The Official 'Spit and Polish' Demonstration

On 30 October the employers announced that, while they rejected the principle of pay equality between the fire brigades and the police, they were willing to enter into wage negotiations 'in a new spirit' when discussions resumed on 13 November. They also made it clear that they would advise fire authorities to abstain from using the discipline code in the recent 'labour matter', for which, they rightly believed, the code was inappropriate. As a result no disciplinary charges were pressed. The union prepared carefully for 13

November. A delegate conference was called for the day prior to the NJC meeting and a march organised for the same day. National delegates walked in the pouring rain from Euston fire station to Hyde Park in a further attempt to bring the union's claim to public and parliamentary attention. It was all in vain, since on the 13th the employers countered the union's 35 shilling wage claim with an offer of 15 shillings. So much for the 'new spirit' in which employers were to approach the wages problem! The delegate conference rejected this offer, and called a 'fire and emergency calls only' demonstration to involve the entire fire service for 19-20 November.[22]

The former action committees stood by, although the demonstration was now under official union auspices. That was not the only change from the first 'standstill'. A Conservative ministry, led by Winston Churchill, had recently replaced Attlee's Labour government. The impact was soon felt. The new government evidently wished to signal a new insistence on labour discipline. On 15 November the Home Secretary, Sir David Maxwell Fyfe, declared that the imminent work stoppage 'would be clearly a serious breach of the regulations'. The discipline code was now seen as an appropriate response to a 'labour matter'.

The Home Secretary's backing emboldened the employers. The County Councils' Association advised chief officers to charge under the discipline code any fireman refusing to carry out normal duties. Any fireman attempting 'to prevent any other member of the Brigade from carrying out his duties' was to be suspended from duty. If the suspended man failed to leave the station the local police were to be called to eject him. Quite recklessly, the Home Office and local authorities were prepared to see men suspended, appliances taken off the run and fire cover reduced in order to break the demonstration. The documents containing this advice fell into the union's hands at the eleventh hour. Branch secretaries would have to be informed of this development, so documents were hectically duplicated and distributed in the 24 hours before the demonstration began.[23] The battle lines were clearly drawn.

The 'Spit and Polish' Demonstrations

The first engagement was not long in coming. At 10.30 a.m. all 31 firemen at Manchester Square fire station in London's Marylebone were suspended by the chief officer. They displayed a notice telling the London public that they would continue to provide fire cover. Later in the day, however, as the men prepared to leave the station to answer a fire call, a senior officer stood in front of the machines and ordered them to halt. In Nottingham, Plymouth, Exeter and Cambridge police were called in to evict suspended firemen from the stations. Only as the demonstration neared its end was the Home Secretary pressured by parliament into declaring that police help should not be sought simply to remove men suspended from duty. In Manchester, finally, sixteen suspended firemen voluntarily went to fight a blaze in a rag waste mill. Their help was declined by the chief officer, and they were ordered off the returning fire engines. They had no choice but to trudge back to their station on foot in full fire kit. Again, the national and local press gave maximum coverage to the dispute. While few newspapers endorsed the 48-hour station work 'strike', many condemned the authorities for irresponsibly preventing firemen from fighting fires.[24]

On the final day of the demonstration, Henry Brooke, the Conservative leader of the London County Council, provocatively described the ban on routine duties as 'a Communist-inspired mutiny'. The *Daily Mail* took up the issue, condemning the extent of Communist influence among firemen.[25] Dragging in the red bogey came as no great surprise to the union; it was not the first time it had suffered a smear campaign in the press. Since 1949 the FBU had attracted public attention as it struggled to maintain unity in the face of calls from branches in Southampton, Tilbury, Stretford and Hull to withhold contributions and quit the union until all Communists had been removed from office.[26] In the 'red scare' climate of 1949-51, moreover, it was *de rigueur* to ascribe any organisation demanding a wage increase, or taking industrial action to secure one, as the tool of Communist agitators. Critics of Labour's policy of wage restraint, of which the FBU was one, had invariably aroused government accusations of Communist infiltration. Unofficial strikes were always described as Communist-fomented, part of a master plan to intensify Labour's economic difficulties.[27] It was to be expected, then, that the Conservatives would play the same red card.

But the depth of Communist influence among firemen was greatly exaggerated. While national and district officials were largely CP-inclined, the head and body of the union were not in close alignment. Few among the rank and file were Communist. Frank Cannon, a 39-year-old sub-officer at Manchester Square fire station, suspended for refusing to obey orders on 19 November, strongly denied that the 'spit and polish' demonstration was Communist-inspired, and added for effect: 'You can take it from me there is not one Red in this station.'[28]

Victimisation

There was, nevertheless, little love lost between the union and the local authorities, as the sequel to the work stoppage made abundantly clear. No sooner had agreement been reached with the Chief Industrial Officer of the Ministry of Labour for the union to put its case before a special Board of Arbitration than the union learnt that Nottingham City Council had reduced five junior officers in rank and fined 55 firemen amounts ranging from £6 10s. to £13. Kent county fire brigade committee quickly followed suit, and charge sheets were issued against 1,578 firemen in London alone. When the wave of victimisation subsided nearly 70 fire authorities had dismissed, broken in rank and fined large numbers of firemen and some firewomen for participating in an official trade union dispute.[29]

To resist this victimisation the membership combined in mass meetings, and in the distribution of information to trade unions, trades councils, co-operative bodies and the Labour Party. The EC also organised a special delegate conference for 20 December to consider what further action should be taken. A number of delegates called for direct action, but the EC won agreement for putting the wage claim before a board of inquiry, for contesting every single discipline charge and for calling on the labour movement to force town halls and fire brigade committees to withdraw all charges. The union then launched an energetic nationwide campaign. Large meetings were held in London and Birmingham. MPs were lobbied; church leaders appealed to. The General Council of the TUC and the Executive Committee of the Labour Party both lent their support. By Christmas 1951 the local fire authorities had lost control of the contest and found themselves on the rack of press and public opinion.[30]

Escape came in the tragic shape of an enormous fire in a railway goods depot in Broad Street, London. A collapsing wall crushed to death three firemen, all of whom had taken part in the 'strike' and were due to appear before a disciplinary committee. The LCC used the tragedy to save face, withdrawing all charges against London firemen. Provincial authorities followed the LCC's lead and capitulated – all except the Tory-controlled Nottingham City Council. Not until Labour gained leadership of the council (with the help of the FBU's influential leaflet, 'Britain's Firemen Say Vote Labour'), did the FBU's campaign of protest meetings and marches, orchestrated by the assistant general secretary, Jack Grahl, finally succeed. In August 1952 Nottingham's fire brigade committee voted to revoke all penalties, repay all fines, and reinstate with full seniority all men who were demoted.[31]

The Ross Award

By August 1952, however, the union had met final defeat on the wages front. In January of that year a special board of arbitration, chaired by Sir David Ross, had for three days examined the union's wage claim. The union's case was presented by Sir Frank Soskice, QC, MP, and Attorney General in the previous Labour government, with Peter Pain as junior counsel. In a unanimous decision the board rejected the principle of automatic pay parity between firemen and policemen. As for the level at which firemen's pay ought, therefore, to be fixed, the board could not agree. So Ross took the individual decision to award an increase of 16s. 6d., or 1s. 6d. more than the employers' offer. With this award the last vestiges of police parity were destroyed.[32]

For a few months after the Ross Award a feeling of dispiritedness infected the union. In general, members regarded the award as a defeat, and union membership declined temporarily.[33] Long-time opponents of the FBU took advantage of this low point in the union's fortunes. With the collusion of a number of chief officers, Mr Reader Harris, Conservative MP and general secretary of the National Association of Fire Officers, sponsored a breakaway organisation from the FBU, to be known as the Junior Fire Officers' Association, for sub-officers and leading firemen. Harris also renewed his attempts to establish a separate NJC for officer ranks. Finally, chief officers asked the local authorities' associations to get the Home Secretary to form a Fire Service Federation, along the lines of the Police Federation, in place of the FBU. It all had the foul smell of a government-backed conspiracy to rid the fire service of independent trade unionism.[34]

The conspiracy was doomed to failure, however, for the FBU was revitalised by the 'spit and polish' dispute in a number of important ways. For a start, the union had fashioned an effective form of militant action, yet one well suited to a service essential to the protection of life and property. For many of the post-war recruits to the service, moreover, the demonstrations had been a baptism in the principles and practices of trade unionism. A wealth of experience had been gained during the two-day stoppages and the subsequent fight against victimisation, which improved immeasurably the quality of leadership at all levels of the organisation. The demonstrations, finally, buried the idea that firemen, as members of a disciplined, semi-military social service, were somehow different from the mainstream of working people. FBU president, John Burns encapsulated this significant development in his address to Annual Conference in 1952:

> For the first time firemen on a national scale have played their part in a real working-class manner. They have been caught up, as it were, in the broad stream of the working class movement ... The growing awareness of the membership to the economics of the present situation, plus the ever-growing political consciousness means that a new FBU is in the process of being formed ... For in those momentous and dynamic days of the demonstrations our membership received an education in working-class solidarity that all the books, discussions and summer schools could never have produced (*applause*).
>
> From all sides, trades councils, Labour parties, trade unions both at national and local level, the support came pouring in in ever-growing volume and unstinted measure. Members came to feel that they were part of a far greater movement than they had ever visualised. That there was another world outside the four walls of their stations, and that they were not some peculiar animal with no connection with the rest of the workers (*hear, hear*).[35]

Aftermath

Sir David Ross's unilateral decision on the rate of pay of firemen was unceremoniously rejected by the FBU; 'it could never be conceived by our Union', Horner told Annual Conference, 'as a settlement of the wages dispute.'[36] The union did accept, however, the board's unanimous recommendation that no longer should a fireman's pay be related to police remuneration but determined on the merits of a fireman's job. Consequently, the union was now committed to obtaining the employers' agreement to a comprehensive review of the fireman's job, and of the position firemen should occupy in the league of industrial earnings. This task would pre-occupy the FBU for the next 25 years, and would culminate in the first national strike of firemen.

Notes

1. *Report of the 33rd Annual Conference*, 1952, p. 18.
2. *Report of the 29th Annual Conference*, 1948, p. 21. In December 1949 there were 135 fire brigades in England and Wales: 50 county brigades, 75

county borough brigades and ten joint area brigades. The total number personnel in the fire service under local authority control was 18,258 (13,579 of whom were firemen).

3. The following account of the FBU's case on police pay parity is drawn from Minutes of Proceedings before a Board of Arbitration appointed by the Minister of Labour and National Service under the Industrial Courts Act 1919 (in library at FBU headquarters, Bradley House, London); *Report of a Board of Arbitration to the Right Honourable, the Minister of Labour and National Service*, London 1952, published by the FBU. And cf. David Englander, Ch. 2 above, pp. 129-30.

4. Industrial Court, Award No.2076, 18 December 1946.

5. Industrial Court, Award No.2156, 24 May 1948. See also *Report of the 29th Annual Conference*, 1948, pp. 42-7.

6. *Report of the 31st Annual Conference*, 1950, p. 110.

7. *Firefighter*, September 1949, pp. 13-14.

8. Ibid., February-March 1950, pp. 4-5; Industrial Court, Award No. 2249, 31 January 1950.

9. Ibid., January 1951, p. 3; October 1951, p. 3.

10. *Report of the 32nd Annual Conference*, 1951, p. 121. See also *Firefighter*, March 1951, pp. 8-9.

11. *Our Wages Fight – The Next Step*, Discussion Statement prepared by the EC of the Fire Brigades Union for Annual Conference, July 1950, p. 367. This document was known in FBU circles as the 'Blue Book'.

12. The following account of the Labour government's economic difficulties rests upon: S. Pollard, *The Development of the British Economy, 1914-1980*, London 1983, Ch. 6; K.O. Morgan, *Labour in Power 1945-1951* Oxford 1985, Chs. 8-9; K.O. Morgan, *Labour People*, Oxford 1987, pp. 162-75; D. Marquand, 'Sir Stafford Cripps' in M. Sissons and P. French (eds.), *Age of Austerity*, Oxford 1986, pp. 157-75.

13. See *Firefighter*, October 1948, p. 7; *Report of the 31st Annual Conference*, 1950, pp. 16-17.

14. *Our Wages Fight*, p. 370. See also Executive Council's Report, 1951, pp. 220-1.

15. *Firefighter*, November 1951, pp. 7-8. See also Executive Council's report on 'The Wages Campaign (1951-52)' in *Report of the 33rd Annual Conference*, 1952, pp. 4-5; Minutes of EC meeting, 13 September 1951, para. 121.

16. Minutes of EC meeting, 10 October 1951, para. 140.

17. 'The Wages Campaign (1951-52)', p. 5.

18. Ibid., p. 6; London and Home Counties Fire Brigades Action Committee, press statement, 14 October 1951.

19. See Terry Segars, 'The Fire Service: The Social History of a Uniformed Working-Class Occupation', unpublished PhD thesis, Essex University 1989, pp. 347-8.

20. Tom Harris, personal communication, October 1987. See also *Firefighter*, December 1952, p. 11. The chairman of the Action Committee was 'Shiner' Wright of Lambeth.

21. See 'The Wages Campaign (1951-52)', pp. 6-7; *News Chronicle*, 17 October 1951; Action Committee, Bulletin, 17 October 1951. The Southend firemen were quickly reinstated.

22. See ibid., pp. 8-9. For the march to Hyde Park, see Enoch Humphries,

Ch. 11 below, pp. 369-70.
23. Ibid., pp. 9-10.
24. See ibid., pp. 11-12; *Daily Mirror*, 20 November 1951; *Daily Graphic*, 21 November 1951.
25. *Daily Mail*, 21 November 1951.
26. For the internal debates on Communist influence, see *Report of the 30th Annual Conference*, 1949, pp. 143-9; Minutes of EC meeting, 14-15 September 1950; Executive Council's Report, 1951, pp. 269-75; Executive Council's Report, 1952, para. 206; interview with H.V. Birkwood, 13 May 1987. And cf. Segars, 'The Fire Service', p. 354.
27. See K.O. Morgan, *Labour in Power*, pp. 371-8.
28. Cutting, 23 November 1951, in Norman Greenfield's collection. Cf. Saville on the union and the Communist Party, Ch. 7 below, pp. 225-8.
29. See 'The Wages Campaign (1951-52)', pp. 12-13.
30. Ibid., pp. 14-15.
31. See ibid., p. 15; *Firefighter*, May 1952, p. 3; October 1952, p. 3; Labour Party Archives, GS/FBU/10i-10v; GS/FBU/11.
32. See ibid., p. 16. See also references in note [3] above.
33. See Minutes of EC meeting, 17 September 1952.
34. See Labour Party Archives, GS/FBU/5i-5ii; GS/FBU/14; GS/FBU/15i; Executive Council's Report, 1952, para. 103; Minutes of EC meeting, 8-9 November 1950.
35. *Report of the 33rd Annual Conference*, 1952, pp. 13-14. See also Bob Bagley, personal communication, October 1987; Jim Raphael, personal communication, July 1987.
36. Ibid., p. 108.

5 Firemen's Trade Unionism in Northern Ireland

Kenneth Brown

Fire-fighting provision in nineteenth-century Ireland was entrusted to a wide variety of institutions, ranging from brigades maintained by insurance companies and the larger military garrisons to the numerous volunteer forces.* If fires proved too serious for such limited local resources call could usually be made on the services of the few full-time brigades which existed. Effectively this meant Belfast or Dublin, although by 1914 some smaller towns were also employing firemen. Only the island's two major cities, however, had professional fire brigade establishments of any size. In 1904 the Belfast Brigade had 64 men and drivers, seven engineers and two officers.[1] Dublin was somewhat smaller with an official complement in 1905 of six officers, two foremen and 40 men.[2]

In general Victorian Ireland was unpromising ground for trade union development. A predominantly agricultural economy, small scale industry and the suspicions of a powerfully entrenched clergy all combined to confine the spread of working-class consciousness and organisation to the major cities. Thus at the turn of the century almost two-fifths of the 13,000 or so members of Irish-based trade unions worked in Dublin. They included the men of the city's fire brigade who had been unionised since 1892.[3] At 19,000, trade union membership in Belfast was greater than in any other Irish city in 1900, but the pattern of trade unionism in the northern part of the country tended to reflect the region's strong economic links with mainland Britain. Quite a high proportion, therefore, belonged to British-based unions while certain sectors of the labour force, including firemen, remained, as in Britain, unorganised.[4] The lack of unionisation among the Belfast firemen before 1910, therefore, was a reflection of the comparable weakness of contemporary British firemen. Furthermore, most men who joined the fire brigade tended to come from occupational backgrounds which in Ireland did not have much tradition of organisation. A surviving staff return for 1912 shows that over three-quarters of Belfast's current force had previously been general labourers, seamen, soldiers, self-employed or in personal service.[5]

Union development among firemen generally was inhibited by the highly disciplined nature of the service. When Belfast first organised a professional brigade in the 1840s operational command was the responsibility of the local police superintendent. Although the two offices were separated in 1859, political control remained in the hands of the Council Police Committee which continued to exercise strict oversight of the workforce. The arrival of a new chief officer from Bootle in 1892 heralded a particularly strict regime. In the next six years 126 men left the brigade, 68 of them being dismissed for disciplinary offences.[6] Organisation was further hampered by other, though more positive, features of the fireman's working life. Firstly, the job was relatively secure. Although labour turnover was high among those who could not cope with the discipline or the physical demands, the mean period of service of men on the staff in 1912 was over eleven and a half years.[7] Secondly, the pay was relatively good. In the years before 1914 the average unskilled male worker in Belfast earned between 15 and 18 shillings a week. In 1907 skilled male workers averaged in excess of £2 and sometimes earned up to £3 a week.[8] In 1912 a First Class fireman had a basic weekly wage of between 30 and 34 shillings. With the addition of various bonuses and allowances this rose to over £2 a week, placing firemen into the same earnings bracket as skilled men, although hours were much longer.[9] These figures seem to confirm the internal evidence of the 1912 staff return that the Fire Brigade, like the Council and the Police Committee to which it was ultimately responsible, was predominantly Protestant at this time; at least, they give an annual wage of about £104, exactly the average amount, it was alleged, earned by the council's Protestant employees.[10] Finally, the fact that the Belfast Fire Brigade was among the most modern in Britain may also have reduced any potential for discontent and thus for unionisation. New central headquarters built in the 1890s included recreational facilities far in advance of those available to the men of most other forces, and the city also possessed very modern fire-fighting equipment, being completely motorised by 1914. This generosity of provision was, moreover, in marked contrast to the parsimony which usually characterised Belfast's local government.

Firemen's Trade Unionism, 1910-1939

The first signs of co-ordinated activity among Ulster firemen came in January 1910 when the Belfast Police Committee received a memorandum from members of the brigade asking for a pay increase and changes in conditions. Two years later a further request was submitted, this time from the Scottish district secretary of the Municipal Employees' Association on behalf of 'the Fire Brigade Staff who are members of the Association'.[11] Soon the MEA claimed to represent over two-thirds of total brigade strength.[12] This rapid development of trade unionism within the Belfast Fire Brigade has to be seen in the wider context of the general contemporary upsurge of organisation among Britain's municipal workers, including firemen. It is tempting, too, to see it as part of the legacy of increased union awareness left in the city by the activities of James Larkin. Every one of the men recruited to the Belfast Brigade between 1907 and 1912 was either a seaman or a labourer, the very types of worker most galvanised by the Larkin-inspired strikes of 1907.[13]

Firemen's Trade Unionism in Northern Ireland

The political unrest accompanying the establishment of the new Northern Ireland state in 1922 meant that development on the two sides of the Irish Sea subsequently tended to diverge. Ulster firemen were not considered by the Middlebrook Committee in 1920 or by the Royal Commission of the following year. Nor did the foundation of the Firemen's Trade Union in 1918 have much impact in the province. It was still the MEA and, subsequently, the National Union of General and Municipal Workers, which represented the Belfast firemen. By 1924 this union was also acting for Londonderry's very small wholetime force. In the years of industrial militancy which followed the Armistice Belfast and Londonderry firemen, like most municipal employees, pressed for pay increases to keep up with other grades of workers. In this, they appear to have been relatively successful, maintaining comparatively generous pay scales throughout the interwar period. A survey of wages in 29 other comparably sized British fire brigades, which was undertaken by the Londonderry Corporation in 1938, concluded that local men were favourably treated.[14] Similarly, in Belfast, wages, superannuation, housing and boot allowances were all more generous by 1938 than in most fire-fighting forces. The Belfast men's sick pay entitlement of six months was twice the period typically granted in Britain, for example. No deductions for superannuation were made from their wages which ran on a scale from £3 10s. to a maximum of £4 13s. after ten years' service. In British brigades remuneration frequently began at much lower minima (the lowest was £2 10s. according to information laid before the Belfast Police Committee in 1938) and in some cases did not reach its highest levels (slightly over £4 13s. until after as long as 22 years' service.[15] Belfast wages also compared very favourably with those payable to local skilled workers, as indeed did the underlying security of the fireman's job in a region noted for heavy unemployment during the interwar depression.[16]

There is little evidence that this level of wages owed much to union activity, and it was still achieved only at the cost of very long working hours. After an initial flurry of activity in the years of the postwar boom the NUGMW made periodic representations to the council about wages, but rarely pressed matters very vigorously. Indeed, most improvements seem to have represented a continuation of the Belfast City Council's enlightened pre-war attitude and any inclination to follow English local authorities by applying the Geddes Axe to firemen was doubtless discouraged by the enhanced dangers of fire risk arising from the political troubles of the early 1920s. The NUGMW was also lukewarm in its efforts to improve other aspects of firemen's working lives, despite the fact that the local organiser, John Malcolm, was a council member for a part of the interwar period. Little was achieved on either of two issues mainly responsible for discontent in the fire service, pensions and rotary leave.

Under the terms of an Act of 1911 the council could grant discretionary pensions to its employees of two-thirds salary after 25 years' service. The firemen's wish that this be made mandatory was included in a list of demands presented to the Police Committee by the MEA in 1919. It was rejected and although the issue simmered on throughout the interwar period the union's representations were so feeble that in the early 1930s the council actually reduced employees' pension entitlements as part of an economy package. Nor was the slight upward revision made in 1937 caused by union action. It owed its provenance to a general improvement in council finances.

The MEA's 1919 list also included the demand that firemen's rotary leave be granted at the rate of one day in six, but the Police Committee granted only one in eight. This remained the entitlement for several years, the NUGMW again failing to exert any effective pressure on behalf of the disgruntled firemen. Indeed, when the union resurrected the matter in 1930 it was two years before the Police Committee deigned even to discuss it. A further union approach in 1937 was also ignored. In 1938 the committee told a union deputation seeking one day in five that while rotary leave arrangements were not as generous as in the rest of Britain, pay and pension arrangements were both superior and if the men would accept UK wage scales then the request could be granted. Not surprisingly, this offer was refused. A few months later rotary leave was increased to one day in five but the NUGMW made no protest about the sting in the tail. To provide adequate manpower for the new leave arrangements, six extra men were to be recruited – but these men started at a lower rate and would take longer to reach the top of the pay scale than firemen already serving.

This was a fairly typical act on the part of the council which had always adopted a very disdainful attitude towards the NUGMW and its predecessor. Even in the early 1920s, when labour's bargaining position had been at its strongest, union meetings could be held in fire stations only with the express permission of the Police Committee. Behind this attitude was an underlying desire on the part of both the committee and the city council to preserve what was perceived as managerial prerogative, a policy which became easier to implement in the less favourable labour markets of the 1930s. In 1932 Belfast firemen's wages were reduced as part of the national economy measures then being implemented. Three years later the cuts were partially restored, but the NUGMW apparently made no protest when the officers received 50 per cent of the original deduction, the rank and file just over 40 per cent. In the same year the Police Committee decided to abolish the firemen's boot allowance, and though this decision was quickly rescinded by the full council, it was initially taken without consulting the men's representatives in any way. By early 1938 this abrasive management style had generated so much cumulative rank-and-file resentment, particularly over the leave issue, that strike action was threatened. The Police Committee responded by empowering the chief officer to replace any men who refused to obey orders. Its hand was greatly strengthened by the knowledge that the NUGMW had already advised the firemen against taking industrial action. Faced with this lack of official support the men had little alternative but to back down.

Given the difficulties which all trade unions experienced in the economic depression of the 1930s, it is perhaps unfair to criticise the NUGMW unduly for failing to achieve more for the firemen of Northern Ireland. In terms of pay, perhaps, the men seem to have done quite well without much positive union intervention. It may be, too, that the union's own weakness sprang from a lack of support within the brigade. But in the absence of any internal documentation about the extent of union membership among firemen this must remain speculative and it is still difficult to avoid the conclusion that firemen were not well represented by the NUGMW. Not until 1938 is there even any evidence that the union was taking a co-ordinated approach towards conditions in Belfast and Londonderry, while no initiatives at all were taken on behalf of retained men. It is also worth noting the comments of one later union activist that the NUGMW was an employers' union.[17] Certainly, the Belfast City Council, the Londonderry Corporation and their respective fire brigades were all overwhelmingly and disproportionately Protestant, which must have further weakened the development of trade union consciousness, particularly in the heightened sectarian atmosphere of the interwar years.[18] But whatever its causes, the failures of the NUGMW before the Second World War and the resulting legacy of rank-and-file discontent paved the way for the subsequent establishment and success of the FBU in Northern Ireland.

The Fight for Pay Parity: Belfast

As elsewhere in the United Kingdom, the fire services of Northern Ireland were strengthened just prior to the Second World War by the recruitment of auxiliary firemen. In the capital 282 were in post by April 1939 with a further 200 undergoing training.[19] Along with an increased staff of regulars they became part of the National Fire Service in 1941. Although the province was not subjected to frequent air attacks, very thin air cover combined with the fact that German bombers contrived in the main to hit heavily populated residential areas rather than the Belfast shipyards meant that the main raids, in April and May 1941, proved to be among the most devastating of the entire war. In these circumstances local fire-fighting resources proved less than adequate and had to be reinforced. English and Scottish brigades sent 50 pumps and crews by sea, while neutral Eire dispatched assistance from Dundalk, Drogheda and Dublin, a gesture which might easily have been misunderstood when the southern appliances roared through the blackout with blazing headlights.

The war over, the NFS was formally disbanded in 1947. In the subsequent reorganisation of fire-fighting, responsibility for Ulster was divided between Belfast and three regional brigades. This was accompanied by a considerable increase in the number of professional firemen, although they were still stationed mainly in Belfast and Londonderry. Belfast's initial establishment was 170, a figure which rose to 190 by 1959. By 1954 the whole-time strength of the Northern Ireland Fire Authority, set up in 1950 to replace the three short-lived regional authorities, was 64 firemen and 24 officers.[20]

This expansion, and the circumstances of war and reconstruction which had brought it about, combined with the poor prewar record of the NUGMW to provide a very fertile ground for the FBU's post-war recruitment drive. In Britain the contemporary reorganisation of the fire service saw the establishment of the National Joint Council as a forum in which conditions, pay scales and other fire service matters could be discussed. None of the Northern Ireland fire authorities joined this new body, however, fearing both the loss of their independence in dealing with employees and also the likely financial implications of wage agreements determined by reference to the state of the mainland labour market. As a result men in the province soon found that many of their pre-war advantages no longer existed. Furthermore, individuals like Louis Reford, who joined the Belfast brigade during the war and then stayed on afterwards, were dismayed to find that contemporaries who had been in the pre-war force received more favourable remuneration. By 1950 this anomalous situation meant that while rent and mess allowances were equal, pre-war employees could earn a maximum of 2s. 3d. a week more than Belfast regulars appointed after 1 January 1939, and 16s. 9d. more than former members of the National Fire Service and new entrants whose weekly maximum was £6 2s. There was also considerable resentment at the way in which relative newcomers, both during and immediately after the war, entered the service and were then rapidly promoted over the heads of the longer-serving regulars. Jimmy Mackey recalled that 'There were clerks, commercial travellers, shop assistants ... joining and not knowing anything about the job ordering men who in many cases had up to twenty years' service how to carry out their duties.'[21] Such grounds for discontent enabled the FBU to establish a presence in Northern Ireland. The union's earliest years in the province are undocumented, but by 1947 Leading Fireman Harry Gunning was a member of the national executive and telling the annual conference that Ulster firemen were now 'poor orphans' as far as pay and working conditions were concerned.[22] A part-time local organiser was appointed the following year but he resigned in 1949, perhaps, said Gunning, because of 'the magnitude of the job'.[23] By 1950 a Northern Ireland District Committee had appeared and two Area Committees, one each for Belfast and the NIFA region, followed in due course, but it was, as Gunning had implied, an uphill struggle to establish the union in the province.

For one thing, while the FBU had successfully recruited virtually all the former members of the National Fire Service, most of the pre-war regulars still belonged to the NUGMW. An added complication was that two other unions were also trying to attract the firemen. The Ulster Public Officers Association had some limited success in organising various officer grades, while the Ulster Transport and Allied Workers won the support of some of the Belfast rank and file.[24] In the years after 1948 all four of these unions pressed for pay parity with Great Britain, but the employers were able to play off one against the other. Thus Louis Reford recalls at least one occasion when he presented an FBU wage demand to the Belfast Police Committee, only to be told that the NUGMW representatives had already agreed to accept a lower offer, and similar disagreements continued to hamper the FBU's progress.[25] In 1948 the union rejected a deal for the Belfast men which had already been accepted by the other unions, forcing the dispute to arbitration. The arbitrators recommended only a reduction of hours to 72 a week, and a weekly pay increase of 5 shillings. Two years later the FBU reluctantly accepted another pay offer which left the Belfast men still below British rates. The union was, however, successful in its opposition to an offer already agreed by the NUGMW which would have given the men less than the old Belfast fire service rate. Yet this comparatively militant line, coupled with the regular appearance of national FBU officials, most notably Jack Grahl, before the Belfast Police Committee, clearly impressed firemen when the NUGMW generally deployed only local or district organisers on their behalf. Similarly, neither the UTAW nor the UPOA could call upon such support, being nothing more than small local unions. Furthermore, the FBU represented only firemen, in marked contrast to the three rival unions, all of which recruited more widely. It was perhaps this which led the NUGMW in September 1952 to accept a proposal that firemen's wages in Belfast should be linked to awards made to labourers by the Joint Industrial Council for the Northern Ireland Electricity Service. It was a fatal error. Not only did it threaten to deprive firemen of independent wage bargaining, thus undermining their attempt to establish parity with British rates, but it also seemed to imply that they were unskilled workers. This inference was difficult to sustain in view of the growing technical and scientific complexity of fire fighting. These were points which the FBU was quick to emphasise when it rejected the proposed link, a stand which finally killed off the NUGMW's already diminishing support in the Belfast fire service. By October 1953 the FBU was claiming to represent 138 out of 146 rank-and-file firemen in the city.[26] Thus strengthened, the union was confident enough to step up the parity campaign, threatening early in 1954 to impose first a 60-hour and then a 48-hour working week in the city if mainland pay rates were not granted. Initially the Police Committee prevaricated but its repeated failure to spell out the basis of its resistance to the demand – which was purely financial – considerably weakened its standing in the eyes of a public whose attention had been drawn to the firemen's case by a clever publicity campaign. The union lobbied every single council member, elicited the support of most local trade unions and organised street demonstrations in the city centre. It was at this point that the few remaining members of the NUGMW quit to join the FBU. At the same time, and to the complete astonishment of FBU officials, the general secretary of the UPOA urged his men to follow suit and join the FBU.[27] This they did, thereby adding the threat that officers too would join the threatened action. With a push or two from sympathetic councillors such as Sir Cecil McKee, Unionist alderman for St Anne's Ward, and Cronan Hughes, sometime local FBU treasurer, who had won the Falls Ward for the Northern Ireland Labour Party in 1952, the Police Committee caved in. Assistant general secretary Grahl said subsequently that he had never known 'such determination to win, such unity and such a militant fighting mood'.[28]Even at this point, however, victory was not quite secure. In 1955 the committee first deferred and then rejected the FBU's request that the most recent National Joint Council award be applied in Northern Ireland. It did so on the grounds that a similar request to the NIFA had been rejected, and, after arbitration, had produced an agreement which left NIFA pay scales lower than those current in Britain. This somewhat undermined the FBU case and it was able to secure the *principle* of British parity only on condition that it agreed to regard the existing 72-hour working week as normal. But from August 1955 British levels of pay were automatically applied in Belfast.

The Fight for Pay Parity: The NIFA Region

Exactly the same process happened in the areas covered by the Northern Ireland Fire Authority. Here the FBU had to contend not only with the problems caused by overlapping unions, but also with two other difficulties. Firstly there was the problem of the authority's composition. Of the sixteen members, four were nominated by the Ministry of Home Affairs, six by the Rural District Councils Association, five by town and city councils and one by the County Borough of Londonderry. Many of these representatives were temperamentally suspicious of trade unionism and they were also concerned to keep down the cost of local rates from which the fire authority was partly financed. They were only too keen, therefore, to accept a proposal from the NUGMW that firemen's wages be geared to the awards made by the Joint Council for the Northern Ireland Building and Civil Engineering Industry. By 1954, however, wholetime NIFA firemen were so dissatisfied with the NUGMW's pay policy and so spurred on by the success of the FBU in Belfast that they quit their union *en masse* in favour of the FBU. Soon the NUGMW was compelled to cancel its agreement with NIFA. 'It may now be regarded as having fallen into disuse by reason of the fact that the personnel of the Fire Force have ceased membership of the Union.'[29] As negotiations between the FBU and the NIFA proceeded the men started to work a 48-hour week while retained men answered only fire calls. Faced with this resolve the NIFA accepted the union's proposal for arbitration. When both this and a second arbitration board found against the union claim there was little alternative but to accept the arbitrators' recommendations. These left NIFA firemen 7 shillings and leading firemen 7s. 6d. worse off than their Belfast counterparts. After ten years a wholetime NIFA fireman received 15 shillings a week less than a mainland colleague with comparable experience. Thereafter, while NIFA granted increases in line with those awarded in Britain, these differentials remained in place, NIFA officials taking the view that 'If Belfast decided to make a mistake and put Belfast on the English rates, they did not see why they should make the same mistake.'[30] It should be remembered, too, that these men were still working a 72-hour week, while 56 hours was then current in Britain. This was a useful bargaining counter, however, and in July 1961 the union agreed not to raise the question of hours for two more years in return for a NIFA commitment to phase out the pay differentials completely by April 1962. Once more this was a gain which owed much to the support given by national officers, in this case, Tom Harris.

The other difficulty which the FBU faced in the areas protected by NIFA was that the fire service consisted mainly of retained men who had sometimes been used by the employers against the whole-time component, and whose primary loyalties were frequently local and communal, rather than to the trade union. Historically, recruitment had been hampered by the precarious state of the FBU's finances. Costs could often be met only from the officials' own pockets. Both Louis Reford and Ken Kernoghan paid tribute to the selfless activities of Cronan Hughes, the union's area treasurer, who covered hundreds of miles on his motor bike in the quest to organise the retained sections in widely scattered rural fire stations.[31] On the other hand, the FBU's task was perhaps made somewhat easier by the fact that the rival unions had shown no interest at all in the retained firemen, even though their remuneration was also very much lower than that paid to their counterparts in Britain. The annual retaining fee, for example, was £20 in 1952 and that in Britain £30. Once more the FBU pursued this issue in a resolute fashion, at the end of 1952 backing the three-month action of retained men in refusing to do anything but answer fire calls. Similarly resolute action was taken in 1954 in conjunction with the whole-time men and NIFA's resistance gradually crumbled. By 1956 retained men in the province were receiving turn-out and attendance money at British rates, and a higher hourly rate. The differential in the annual retainer remained, but it was now a mere £2.

Given the success of the campaigns for pay parity both in Belfast and Northern Ireland and the withdrawal of the NUGMW, it was hardly surprising that when formal negotiating machinery was established for Ulster firemen in December 1958 the FBU was granted the exclusive right of representation for men and officers. The granting of proper negotiating procedures was itself a major victory for the union. Previously no formal mechanisms existed whereby men's grievances could be communicated to management, there was no automatic right of access to the Chief Fire Officer and union officers could merely *request* that the employers receive deputations. Leading union officials at that time, some of them relatively new to trade union work, sought advice from English colleagues and drew up a suitable scheme for Belfast. The major stumbling block, however, lay in the hostile attitude of some council members and full-time officials who dealt with personnel matters and resented this threat to their domain. A sufficient number of councillors were won over, however, by a clever campaign of personal lobbying in which the union contacted them all individually at home with details of the scheme. This effectively bypassed the obstructionists on the Police Committee, although even there the union had now some supporters, most notably Sir Cecil McKee. In the next few years the new machinery was utilised to negotiate numerous concessions on matters such as holiday pay and leave, disciplinary codes and mess allowances. More significantly, minimum physical and educational qualifications for employment and proper procedures of recruitment and promotion were also established. These latter were defined in close co-operation with Chief Officer Taylor, whose brief period of office between 1960 and 1962 was characterised by a determination to produce an efficient force. The resulting agreements did much to undermine the old, questionable processes of recruitment which had often depended as much on an individual's ability to nobble a local councillor as on any potential or actual merits he may have had as a fireman. This was certainly the intention of the leading provincial officials who were united not only by their dislike of such practices, which tended to foster sectarianism, but also by their involvement in the Northern Ireland Labour Party.[32]

The Working Week

Having secured pay parity and formal negotiating machinery, the union next turned its attention to the hours of work, for, as the *Belfast Telegraph* noted in 1959, Belfast firemen 'agree that conditions are vastly improved since pre-1948 days, when they worked a 120-hour week, but they are still conscious of the fact that English firemen are on a 56-hour week'.[33] Early in 1961, therefore, the union informed the Belfast Police Committee that it no longer regarded itself bound by its earlier commitment to the 72-hour week. The Chief Officer was opposed to the implementation of a 56-hour week, arguing both that his men would attend fewer fires, thereby diminishing their efficiency, and that it would cost £43,000 a year to employ the necessary extra manpower. Nor were firemen themselves unanimously enthusiastic about shorter working hours. The shifts for the 72-hour week had been organised in such a way that men could take on secondary employments which they were naturally reluctant to sacrifice. Only by threatening to resign did the local officials secure the necessary backing.[34] Their case rested on the argument that shorter hours would increase the efficiency and professionalism of the brigade and this appeared to convince the Police Committee, although the swift concession of the 56 hours was perhaps influenced by the fact that in Britain consideration was currently being given to a 48-hour week. It was also indicative, however, of just how the balance of power had shifted between employer and employed, and in 1966 the Belfast authorities granted a 48-hour week with relatively little discussion. In any case, by then better working conditions were perhaps seen as a higher priority since Belfast, like mainland British fire authorities, was finding it increasingly difficult to recruit and retain firemen. In October 1965, for example, Chief Officer Mitchell reported that he had had 'some difficulty ... in obtaining suitable recruits ... the number of firemen leaving the service to obtain employment elsewhere had increased considerably over the past year'.[35]

Given these developments in Belfast it could have come as no surprise to NIFA that the FBU asked for discussions about the length of its working week just before the agreed time period expired in the spring of 1962. The authority found itself in some difficulty. Any reduction of hours would entail the employment of more men. Yet it would be difficult to recoup the extra costs of this because NIFA's finances depended partly on local rates and partly on an exchequer grant which could only be changed by Act of Parliament. By 1963, however, the NIFA's financial resources had been restructured, facilitating a more positive response to the demand for reduced hours. The outcome was a 60-hour week. Once more this was indicative, not only of the easing of the NIFA's financial position but also of the FBU's enhanced bargaining position and, following further union representations, a further reduction of four hours was made in December 1965.

By the mid-1960s, therefore, NIFA men still had a somewhat longer working week than their Belfast and British colleagues, although the differential was much less than it had been in 1950. In 1967 NIFA agreed to observe all the conditions of service laid down by the National Joint Council, the culmination of a long, steady campaign masterminded by Archie McArdle, Northern Ireland representative on the national executive since 1954. To all intents and purposes, therefore, British conditions and hours had been conceded to the Ulster firemen. Accordingly, when in 1968 the Wilson government negotiated away its own policy of national pay restraint by allowing firemen to work longer hours Belfast firemen reverted to a 56-hour week. Locally, longer hours were perhaps acceptable also in face of the pressures placed upon the fire service by the progressive deterioration of law and order in the city. The FBU won further recognition of these pressures in 1971, negotiating a special call-out allowance of £104 a year. Two years later a similar arrangement was made for NIFA employees.

Reorganisation and the Troubles

In 1974 the province's fire services were again reorganised. The merger of the Belfast and NIFA forces created one of the largest brigades in the United Kingdom with about 500 whole-timers and 650 retained men under the sole control of the new Fire Authority for Northern Ireland. The origins of this amalgamation lay in the 1971 recommendations of the Review Body on Local Government in Northern Ireland, but a contributory consideration was probably the stressful circumstances of the continuing terrorist campaigns. These not only helped to swell the province's fire damage bill to over £40 million in the early 1970s but also took a toll of firemen's lives. In Londonderry Fireman McArtney died in a hotel fire, caused, it was widely believed locally, by a firebomb. In Belfast Brian Douglas was shot dead while engaged on fire-fighting duties. On numerous occasions Belfast had been so stretched that NIFA units had been summoned for assistance and as early as 1970, before the troubles reached their height, brigades controlled by the NIFA had on their own account to deal with an average of over two calls a week arising from civil disturbances. In such circumstances there was much to recommend the establishment of a united force which would also, by eliminating unnecessary duplication, be more economic. These at least were the arguments which FBU officers advanced in support of the proposed changes.[36]

The first Chief Officer of the new force was the former NIFA commander, George Morrison. Interviewed in retirement about his experiences, he suggested that by the 1970s the FBU was trying to assume many of the roles of management.[37] Whatever the truth of his observation – not surprisingly it was hotly disputed by some former FBU members – it is perhaps a fitting comment on the success of the union in changing the status and bargaining position of Northern Ireland firemen. Historically, they had always been better treated than the majority of their British colleagues, although this had owed little to trade union activity. But in the years after 1945 major restructuring and reforms in Britain left the Ulstermen's pay and conditions way behind. It was only the commitment and perseverance of FBU activists, both local and national, which enabled Belfast and NIFA firemen to win equal pay and hours, fringe benefits, and formal negotiating machinery. These were impressive achievements, gained over a relatively short space of some twenty years in a province not traditionally associated with trade union militancy and which was already beginning another of its periodic descents into the abyss of sectarianism.

Notes

* I am indebted to Dave Higgs and to the following present and past members of the Northern Ireland Fire Service whose help enabled me to write this piece: Charlie Bell, G. Broadhurst, J.G. Devenny, Ken Kernoghan, George Morrison, Louis Reford and Harry Walsh.

1. *Belfast Directory*, Belfast 1904, p. 104.
2. S. Redmond, *The Irish Municipal Employees Trade Union, 1883-1983*, Dublin 1983, p. 77.
3. The early history of the Dublin firemen's union is recounted in ibid., pp. 69-77.
4. I. Budge and C. O'Leary, *Belfast: Approach to Crisis*, London 1973, p. 125.
5. Belfast Fire Brigade, Return of Staff, 1912.
6. Belfast Police Committee, Minutes, 17 October 1898.
7. Belfast Fire Brigade, Return of Staff, 1912.
8. Wage details are drawn from J. Gray, *City in Revolt. James Larkin and the Belfast Dock Strike of 1907*, Belfast 1985, pp. 5-6.
9. Belfast Fire Brigade, Return of Staff, 1912. In London wages were lower, reaching 35 shillings only after ten years. It has been calculated that firemen's wages in 1912 were 20 per cent below the national average. See F.H. Radford, *Fetch the Engine. The Official History of the Fire Brigades Union*, London 1951, p. 42. It should also be noted that skilled wages were generally higher in Northern Ireland than in the rest of Britain.
10. The average wage of Catholics, who made up a quarter of the corporation workforce, was much lower at £60 a year. These figures are from A.C. Hepburn, 'Catholics in the North of Ireland, 1850-1921: the Urbanisation of a Minority' in A.C. Hepburn (ed.), *Minorities in History*, London 1978, p. 88.
11. Belfast Police Committee, Minutes, 1 February 1912. The MEA was formed in 1894 as an outgrowth of the London County Council employees' organisation. Its development is traced in H.A. Clegg, *General Union*, Oxford 1954, and B. Dix and S. Williams, *Serving the Public. Building the Union. A History of NUPE, 1889-1928*, London 1987. In Belfast the union had an early success which perhaps helps to explain its pre-war growth. In March 1912 the Police Committee awarded long service gratuities to a number of men, excluding a number whose disciplinary records had been unsatisfactory over the previous ten years. MEA representations to the full council got this exclusion period reduced to seven years, thus greatly increasing the number of men qualifying for the gratuity. It was shortly afterwards that the MEA claimed to represent

two-thirds of the entire Belfast brigade. These early developments of trade unionism are more fully explored in my forthcoming article, 'The Belfast Fire Brigade, 1880-1914'.
12. Ibid., 6 February 1913.
13. Belfast Fire Brigade, Return of Staff, 1912. James Larkin, of course, is one of the great heroes of Irish labour history in that he is often thought to have come nearest to breaking the sectarian mould of Ulster's working class. See particularly, Gray, *City in Revolt*; E. Larkin, *James Larkin. Irish Labour Leader, 1876-1947*, London 1965; H. Patterson, *Class Conflict and Sectarianism: The Belfast Working Class and the Belfast Labour Movement, 1868-1920*, Belfast 1980.
14. Londonderry Corporation, *Report from Finance Committee*, 22 February 1938. In the immediate post-war years wages in Birkenhead, which 'leads as regards pay', started at 68s. 6d. a week. *Departmental Committee on the Hours, Pay and Conditions of Service of Firemen in Professional Fire Brigades, Minutes of Evidence*, PP 1920, XVI, Cmnd 876, p. 17. The same source gives a wide variety of weekly maxima in other British cities: 62s. in Southampton, 75s. in Edinburgh, 65s. in Newport, 72s. in Dundee and 37s. in Gloucester.
15. Belfast Police Committee, Minutes, 14 February 1938.
16. In 1936, for example, skilled wages in Ulster's engineering and shipbuilding industries ranged between 62s. and 69s. 9d. per week. Skilled wages tended to be higher in the province than in the rest of the United Kingdom. K.S. Isles and N. Cuthbert, *An Economic Survey of Northern Ireland*, Belfast 1957, p. 218.
17. Louis Reford interview, 17 September 1987.
18. It always remained the case that the majority of professional firemen in Northern Ireland were Protestant. In part this was due to the tradition of sons following fathers into the service, but see also note 32.
19. Belfast Police Committee, Chief Officer to the Chairman and Members, 20 April 1939.
20. These figures are from Belfast Police Committee, Minutes, 22 January 1948; NIFA, Minutes, 12 March 1954.
21. J. Mackey, 'The Veterans', *Nire Fire*, Autumn 1987, p. 21.
22. FBU, *Annual Conference Report* (1947), p. 147.
23. Ibid. (1950), p. 73.
24. For the Ulster Public Officers Association, see E. Donnelly, 'The History of the Northern Ireland Public Service Alliance', unpublished MA thesis, Queen's University, Belfast, 1985, pp. 61-79.
25. Louis Reford interview, 17 September 1987.
26. Belfast Police Committee Minutes, 15 October 1953.
27. FBU, *Annual Report* (1954), p. 45; Ken Kernoghan interview, 3 December 1987.
28. *Firefighter*, March 1954, p. 8. Cf. *Daily Worker*, 26 January 1954, p. 2.
29. NIFA, Minutes, 16 July 1954.
30. FBU, *Annual Report* (1958), p. 183.
31. Louis Reford interview, 17 September 1987; Ken Kernoghan interview, 3 December 1987.
32. This paragraph relies heavily on Ken Kernoghan interview, 3 December 1987. At the time of his death in 1973, for example, Archie McArdle, a long-time party activist, was chairman of the NILP. The

officials also took an active part in encouraging trade union contacts with fellow workers in the South. Despite the new procedures of recruitment and promotion, however, the Fair Employment Agency subsequently claimed, in a controversial report, that while the religious composition of the total population was accurately reflected in the number of fire service applicants, actual membership of the force in 1984 was over 80 per cent Protestant. Fair Employment Agency, *Report of An Investigation by the Fair Employment Agency for Northern Ireland into the Fire Authority for Northern Ireland*, Belfast 1984, p. 4. 'The major differences in the success rate of Protestant and Roman Catholic applicants appeared at the selection stages in which the marks awarded to candidates were dependent upon the subjective judgements of individuals.' Ibid., p. 37.
33. *Belfast Telegraph*, 2 April 1959.
34. Ken Kernoghan interview, 3 December 1987.
35. Belfast Police Committee, Minutes, 14 October 1965.
36. Ken Kernoghan interview, 3 December 1987.
37. George Morrison interview, 25 August 1987. Louis Reford, who was also a senior officer with NIFA, made an identical comment. Louis Reford interview, 17 September 1987.

6 The FBU, the TUC and the Labour Party

Graham Johnson

British trade unionists have often been accused of being self-absorbed, unconcerned with anything other than their own wages and conditions, and ignorant and uncaring when it comes to broader issues and international concerns. The FBU has for most of its history been far from parochial; over the years it has supported a wide range of working-class, radical, progressive and libertarian causes, and continues to do so. The attitude of many activists to these subjects was captured by John Horner speaking on peace at the 1951 FBU conference:

> Let there be no suggestion here this afternoon ... that the FBU should not participate in these matters, that we should confine ourselves to wages, uniforms, conditions of employment. We, as a union, must understand that our daily struggle to improve our conditions is, and must be, unbreakably linked with our daily struggle to preserve peace.[1]

FBU members and branches belonged to and worked for a variety of organisations as well as the FBU, and the union affiliated to an impressive number of bodies ranging from the Campaign for Nuclear Disarmament, the National Council for Civil Liberties, the Movement for Colonial Freedom and the Fabian Society, through to the Anti-Apartheid Movement, the Anti-Nazi League, the British Council for Peace in Vietnam and the League for Democracy in Greece.

The FBU, the TUC and the Labour Party

For much of its history the union has been considered a left-wing union. Since the early 1950s the union's rule book has contained in its foreword the following full-blooded commitment to socialism and the labour movement:

> The Fire Brigades Union recognises that workers, however employed, can only improve their lot by their own endeavours and organisation. A richer and a fuller life can be achieved only by similar means. To this end the Fire Brigades Union is part of the Working-Class Movement and, linking itself with the International Trade Union and Labour Movement, has as its ultimate aim the bringing about of the Socialist system of society.

For such a statement to be contained in the rule book tells us much about the nature of the union and the depths of its attachment to the wider movement. The purpose of this chapter is to consider the relationship of the FBU to that movement in Britain between 1919 and 1978, and there will be a brief consideration of the role of Communism in the union's history and how this has affected relations with the TUC and Labour Party.

The Issues

Between 1939 and 1956 the British Communist Party had a good deal of influence on FBU affairs. John Horner and Jack Grahl, the union's two leading officials, were both members, and at certain times a significant number of executive members also belonged to the party. This led to strife and divisions within the FBU and had an adverse effect on TUC and Labour Party relationships, particularly at the height of the Cold War in the late 1940s and early 50s when anti-Communist sentiment was rife. Communist members worked for party policies in the union during these years, often successfully, although letters attacking Communism were a regular feature of *Firefighter*, and the subject was a frequent topic of debate at union conferences, culminating in the 1951 decision that the FBU withdraw from the

Communist-backed British Peace Committee, the British-Soviet Friendship Society and other similar organisations.[2] In 1948 the Labour Party sent out a circular letter headed 'The Communists: We have been warned', to all affiliated trade unions which spoke of the threat to the government and the labour movement and called upon trade unionists to organise against it.[3] The following year the TUC issued two pamphlets on the subject, *Trade Unions and Communism* and *Democracy Defended*, and sent copies to each union. The response of the FBU leadership was that these publications had no relevance to the union and that such 'witch-hunting' could only weaken the working class.[4] The stigma of having Communists as permanent officials, and the animosity and suspicion that this gave rise to, was lifted from the union in 1956 when Horner and Grahl resigned from the party in the aftermath of the events in Hungary,[5] although the union was to remain identified with the left within both the TUC and the Labour Party.

The TUC Congress and the Labour Party conference are the two major policy-making bodies of the British labour movement. Since the Second World War the FBU has been an active participant in these annual events, unlike most other small unions, many of which have shown a notable lack of interest in policy making particularly within the Labour Party.[6] Before the war the union was a small organisation with limited representation within the larger institutions and contributing little to the proceedings. The war saw an increase in the size of the FBU, a growth in the number of delegates at conferences and a much more political stance being adopted by the union. Over the years the FBU concentrated its energies in three areas: fire service conditions particularly safety matters, incomes policies and peace and international affairs.

Although both platforms were used to raise fire service issues, the TUC Congress was used more often. The issues included the recognition of officers raised in 1945, disputes with JFOA and NAFO in 1952, firewomen's pay in 1958 and 1959, the domestic cleaning of fire stations in 1964, a change in the regulations for working in compressed air in 1974 and the enforcement of the Fire Precautions Act in 1977. TUC-backed, Labour government incomes policies were attacked by FBU speakers at the 1948 TUC, and at both Labour Party and TUC conferences in the 1960s and mid-1970s. Broader political issues including peace and international affairs were a common preoccupation of FBU delegates from the 1940s. Calls for peace and the renunciation of nuclear weapons were vociferous and strong from FBU delegates and the union became particularly associated with the issue. Nuclear disarmament was first raised in the Labour Party nationally through an FBU resolution in 1958, and in the famous debate which resulted in the commitment of the Labour Party to unilateral nuclear disarmament in 1960 one of the two motions passed on the subject was seconded by John Horner. Speaking for the 1958 resolution Horner spoke of American H-bomb tests which were said to have produced the greatest power ever known. He denied that this was the case:

> ... for we believe there is a power in this world greater than the bomb. Even now that power remains in our hands. It is the desire and the will of millions of men and women all over the world who are looking to this Conference ... men and women who believe that even now, under Labour leadership Britain can save humanity, this generation and future generations.[7]

In the 1980s Ken Cameron continued this tradition, calling upon the Labour Party to consider the effects of a modern nuclear war and condemning the government's civil defence policies as 'a cruel public fraud of the most heartless kind'. The fire service, he told them, was not equipped to deal with the effects of a nuclear war, and even if it had been, he wondered if there would be room for the 42,000 FBU members in the Whitehall nuclear shelter. The FBU he emphasised was 'not going to be part of that confidence trick of pretending to the British people that there could be life after a nuclear holocaust'.[8] In the 1940s it was moved at the TUC that congratulations be sent to India and Pakistan on achieving dominion status, and during the Cold War friendship and trade with the Soviet Union was recommended and opposition voiced to the setting up of NATO and SEATO. In 1948 there was a call for the removal of British forces from Greece. An FBU resolution on the dangers of apartheid was passed by the Labour Party in 1963, and in 1966 Terry Parry moved a resolution calling for a cessation of the bombing of North Vietnam.[9] The FBU, then, used the Labour Party and TUC as platforms for the furtherance of their members interests, for criticisms of particular policies of Labour governments and the pursuance of progressive political concerns in the international sphere, especially peace and the elimination of nuclear weapons.

Firemen and the TUC

'It was at the TUC's 100th Congress', boasted the executive council in 1969, 'that the General Secretary, Bro. Parry, in the Union's 50th year, was elected to the General Council.' The entry of the FBU leader into the Mount Olympus of trade union leaders was a long drawn out process not without its setbacks and problems. That the FBU should ever have reached such heights is unusual indeed for so small a union, as seats on the General Council tend to go to the big unions with their large block votes.[10]

This journey began when the FBU affiliated to the TUC in 1923. By then the TUC was already well established and dominated by the bigger unions, and the FBU formed a relatively small and insignificant part of this conservative body, lampooned by the cartoonist David Low as a large plodding cart-horse. The union was to remain a small and weak part of the organised movement for many years. When the young John Horner and others raised the question of other unions recruiting firemen at the 1937 annual conference and asked if the TUC could help, Percy Kingdom's pessimistic reply was that the TUC 'lean ... towards the big battalions'.[11]

The war was to transform the size and nature of the FBU and this strengthened its relative position, though it was still in the shadow of the 'big battalions'. In the aftermath of the War, however, the atmosphere of Cold War was to weaken the FBU's standing in the ranks of the TUC. In the late 1940s it took 'persistent representations' from the executive committee to ensure two representatives on the TUC's Local Government Advisory Committee, and when the resignation of the member for the Local Government Group of the General Council meant that John Horner should have taken his place, the General Council changed the rules and asked the unions involved to nominate a successor. In spite of the fact that the Local Government Group of unions still nominated Horner, it was the COHSE representative who was eventually chosen to take the place on the General Council.[12] The weariness of members trying to obtain any kind of TUC position is captured in the failure of the president John Burns when standing for the TUC Canadian delegation. 'Experience at the TUC', the executive reported, 'goes to show that unless you are supported by one or two of the big unions, you require to be nominated for a position year after year before you have any prospects of being ultimately elected.'[13] When members did achieve positions they used their influence to the full. Burns and Horner used their places on the Local Government Advisory Committee to raise the demand for the reintroduction of protective legislation for their members recalled to the armed forces, and Burns was able to serve as part of a deputation from the committee to discuss the Pensions (Increase) Act of 1947 with the relevant minister, and later to meet Hugh Gaitskell as Chancellor of the Exchequer on the issue of pensions for those members who had retired between the wars.[14]

By the 1960s the FBU had become much more involved in the various decision-taking bodies of the TUC and the STUC, as well as taking an active part in various conferences under TUC auspices. In 1963 Enoch Humphries became a member of the executive committee of the Scottish Congress, a position he was to hold for some years, being elected President in 1968, the same year that Parry was elected to the TUC General Council. The union was represented at the TUC Conference of Non-Manual Workers and sent women members to the Conference of Women Workers. The FBU also affiliated to the National Federation of Professional Workers, and the assistant general secretary, Tom Harris, became a member of its executive.[15] Fraternal delegates from the TUC had been regular visitors to FBU conferences, and in 1968 it was the TUC general secretary, George Woodcock, who addressed them, the first in a series of TUC leaders to do so. By the 1970s the FBU had progressed from being a weak and relatively insignificant part of the organised trade union movement to the position of an important, though still small, section with elected officers in strategic positions in both the TUC and the STUC, and representatives on a range of influential committees and conferences.

The TUC itself has gone through many changes in its role and function since the FBU has been an affiliated union, and its strength has varied considerably at different periods in the twentieth century. At times of war and full employment in peacetime it has been a powerful force in the land; at times of high unemployment it has tended to become relatively weak and defensive. Such factors have had their effects upon the relationship between the two organisations, on the way the FBU has used the larger body, the extent to which the TUC has been able to be of assistance and the way TUC policy has at times run counter to the aims and desires of the FBU.

In the aftermath of the General Strike the TUC was a much weakened body in national political terms. Throughout the 1930s governments paid little heed to the views and policies of the trade union movement. The outbreak of war in 1939 transformed the situation; unions were seen as an important force for stability in an economy at war, and almost overnight trade union bargaining power and strength increased. The trade union movement now had direct access to the ears of those who governed, and the FBU was able to take advantage of this. This is not to say, however, that those in power would necessarily listen, even if the individuals concerned were themselves the products of the labour movement. Although the TUC general secretary, Walter

Citrine, initially advised Horner against organising auxiliary firemen when they began to be created in large numbers, it was a TUC delegation including Ernest Bevin which accompanied Horner on his visit to the Home Secretary to demand union recognition for auxiliary members.[16] TUC delegations on behalf of the FBU became a regular feature of the war and the immediate post-war years, and they were an important factor in preventing the setting up of a representative body or federation to replace the FBU and in gaining recognition for the Officers' Section.[17]

In the early 1950s during the 'Spit and Polish' demonstrations, with their resulting dismissals, demotions and discipline charges, the FBU had cause to be grateful to the TUC, notably for its intervention with the Home Secretary over the use of police to evacuate fire stations, and the provision of other help.[18] The TUC also helped to hinder NAFO's attempt to set up a separate negotiating body for officers, and in 1958 threatened Blackpool council that it would stage that year's Congress elsewhere if the council did not settle their dispute with the union.[19]

The TUC, in its advisory capacity to government departments, also took up fire service issues and tried to ensure that the FBU was consulted when its interests were clearly at stake. In 1965, for instance, the FBU sent a memorandum on fire safety to the General Council which then made representations to the government. When asked by governments for their opinion on particular pieces of legislation, the TUC consulted the union where its expertise was clearly of value, and also passed on all of the draft British Standards for fire service equipment for union approval.[20]

The FBU however had its differences with the TUC, usually coinciding with the TUC's compliance with the incomes policies of Labour governments. In 1950 the General Council approached the union to reconsider its wage claim for that year in the light of the government's wage freeze policy, and was strongly criticised by the FBU.[21] The pay policies of the 1960s were initially given qualified support by the FBU leadership, but when in 1966 the union decided to oppose pay restraint, the TUC refused support, limiting its assistance to the question of hours.[22] In 1966 FBU President Enoch Humphries spoke at the TUC Congress opposing the Prices and Incomes Act and calling for the ending of the wage freeze, but to no avail.[23] In the 1970s there was also initial but qualified support for TUC-backed pay restraint, but when the pay policy led to the 1977 strike the TUC remained committed to the government's policies and did little to help the firemen directly. The next FBU Conference condemned the General Council of the TUC 'in respect of their betrayal of the Union in its recent dispute', although at the TUC Congress FBU president, Wilf Barber, was careful to thank the affiliated unions which helped them as well as thanking Len Murray and David Basnett, the general secretary and president of the TUC, for putting their case to the Prime Minister.[24]

One of the major weaknesses of the TUC since its inception has been the periodic clashes between its component unions, each of which has a different basis of organisation and many of which claim the right to organise in the same sectors and the same industries. The FBU is what is known as an industrial union, it organises at all levels, but limits its recruitment to the fire service.[25] In theory this could lead the union into conflict with other unions organised along different lines. NUPE, COHSE and NALGO, for instance, compete with one another in the recruitment of public sector workers as does the GMB, and the other large general union, the TGWU, also organises extensively in the public sector; with the exception of COHSE, all could see fire service personnel as potential recruits. This kind of problem poses a major headache for the TUC which was founded on the principle of trade union unity and co-operation. Numerous methods have been devised to try to prevent competition between unions developing into open warfare. The most ambitious of these have been those calling for structural reorganisation of unions in the form of amalgamation and federation, and at times the FBU has been drawn into the debates.

Ever since the Firemen's Trade Union separated itself from the NUCW (the forerunner of NUPE) in 1919 there has been a proud sense of independence among its members and those of its successor, the FBU. Pride, however, did not mean that the union held itself aloof from other trade unions. At times there was resentment and minor conflicts, particularly when larger general unions attempted to recruit firemen into their ranks; but by and large relationships with TUC-affiliated unions were good, animosity tended to be reserved for minor offshoots and those organisations in direct competition for the recruitment of firemen and fire officers only, especially NAFO and JFOA. Organisational pride could at times lead to feelings of exclusiveness and a desire for separation, as with the initial unwillingness to recruit and accept auxiliary firemen in the early years of the war, but this sense of isolation became less strong as the union grew and began to broaden its base and extend its contact with the rest of the trade union movement, particularly during the war years and after.

Five years after the FBU had been formed the TUC sought to reduce the number of trade unions by means of amalgamation.[26] The idea of one large public sector union was mooted and the move back into the NUCW was briefly considered before being rejected, probably as a result of the residual animosity from the circumstances of the union's formation.[27] During the war years the FBU worked closely with other unions representing civil defence workers, taking an active part in the Joint Consultative Committee for Civil Defence along with the TGWU, NUGMW, NUPE and the NFBTO.[28] In the years immediately following the war there was a revival of the calls for structural reorganisation through amalgamation, federation and the reduction of inter-union competition.[29]

The TUC investigated the nature of its constituent organisations and made suggestions about closer working unity and possible amalgamation. Overall the long-term effects of these discussions and negotiations were negligible, but a motion seconded by the FBU and passed at the 1943 TUC Congress deepened the discussions within the FBU on the nature of its isolation and similarities and differences with other unions.[30] The TUC investigators noted that as public employees with a common financial basis, the membership of COHSE, NUPE and the FBU had a good deal in common.[31] The 1944 FBU conference decided to seek affiliation with its parent union NUPE. Following this decision the executive prepared a report on the benefits to the union of amalgamation with other unions. It was suggested that inter-union friction and overlap in the public sector were unlikely to be resolved by merging with the large general unions, the NUGMW and the TGWU, as their interests were not confined to the one industry. The executive memorandum agreed that NUPE was the most suitable candidate for amalgamation and the decision was further endorsed by the 1946 conference of the union, the general feeling being that while public servants remained in separate unions the employers could play them off against one another.[32]

However, this enthusiastic embrace of fusion with NUPE, like similar attempts at fusion elsewhere in the trade union movement, came to naught. A portent of failure had appeared in the aftermath of the winding up of the Joint Consultative Committee for Civil Defence the previous year. At the time the FBU asked the TUC to convene a conference consisting of the FBU, the TGWU, NUGMW and NUPE 'in order to consider how to apply in Local Government circles the proposals for closer working and unity which were agreed generally by the TUC Annual Congress some eighteen months ago'. This conference, the FBU executive reported later, 'unfortunately, was not productive of any real results', although they did manage to obtain an agreement from two of the unions that the FBU should be the only union recruiting in the fire service.[33]

The failures of the amalgamation attempts forced unions to adopt a more defensive posture. By 1948 members were complaining that NUPE had been accepting fire brigade members, and the general secretary told that year's conference that discussions had been held with the TGWU, NUPE and NUGMW at FBU headquarters and letters had been sent to the leaders of each union asking for written agreements that they would cease to enrol fire brigade members. The letters would seem to have had little impact judging by the later actions of the General and Municipal Workers' Union, which was a major source of problems for those members organising firemen in Northern Ireland.[34]

Inter-union relationships were considered again at the Margate conference of 1955 which instructed the executive council 'to bring about some form of cohesion between all the organisations representing employees in the local government service'; in spite of preliminary discussions, however, the executive had to advise the 1957 conference that the problems were seen differently by the large general unions, but they intended to continue with negotiations. At the same time the executive had to report difficulties with NUPE officials in Wales who were recruiting firemen, although Bryn Roberts, NUPE's general secretary, assured the FBU that his union had no desire to recruit in the fire service.[35]

In spite of the FBU's exclusiveness as a small union recruiting uniformed personnel, from the early 1950s the union became much more firmly established in the trade union movement. Firemen began to be recognised much more as a group of workers with problems similar to those of other trade unionists, and offered assistance themselves to other groups of workers in need. The support given to firemen during the demonstrations of 1951 was crucially important in this respect and the FBU went to great lengths to express its gratitude. A pamphlet was sent to all organisations which had offered assistance or given support and a double page spread in *Firefighter*, headed 'Solidarity', listed for the membership all those who had been of help.[36] An editorial in the following edition emphasised the importance of the help received but warned: 'Solidarity is not a one-way principle. We must see to it that in future firemen play an even bigger part in the Labour Movement.'[37]

In the 1950s the union increasingly found itself providing financial support to other groups of workers in need both at home and abroad.[38] When industrial conflict intensified in the mid-1950s assistance was given to workers in dispute in the motor-car and motor-cycle industries, as well as engineering and shipbuilding, and in the course of these disputes, the executive

> constantly sought to stress upon our membership the ever-present need to see the problems of other trade unionists as our problems, to understand that the workers in industry who have fought the bitter battles of the last eighteen months have indeed been fighting the battles for the Fire Brigades Union and for all other organised and unorganised workers.[39]

By the end of the 1950s the FBU had become much more firmly entrenched in the trade union movement, but one result of the stronger sense of belonging was a waning of enthusiasm for amalgamation. Instead, the demand for solidarity and unity with other unions was expressed in a call for improvements in the TUC machinery for co-operation among public sector workers.[40]

The 1960s saw a rising trend towards mergers among British trade unions, reaching a peak in the early 1970s.[41] The 1962 TUC decided that 'it is time the British trade union movement adapted its structure to modern conditions', and in response to TUC inquiries the FBU executive submitted a memorandum to the TUC General Council. This acknowledged the exclusiveness and insularity of the FBU. 'The uniformed fireman regards non-firemen as "civilians". Loyalty is felt primarily to the Firemen's Union.' In spite of their attempts to widen this loyalty, they felt 'that amalgamation with any other union is out of the question at the moment'. The absence of the large white-collar union NALGO from the TUC, and weakness and conflict among other local government unions were further factors militating against any proposed amalgamation. Instead it was suggested that a confederation of local government unions be established to provide a better machinery for consultation and co-operation, and that NALGO should be invited along.[42]

In spite of TUC attempts in 1963 to bring the unions together, and an informal amalgamation proposal from the TGWU, little came of these initiatives. The extent of enthusiasm within the FBU for amalgamation was made clear by the solitary two votes in favour of a proposed amalgamation with NUPE at the 1966 conference and the fact that a motion suggesting amalgamation with the TGWU in 1969 could not even find a seconder.[43] The final position reached with regard to the relationship with other unions was expressed well by Terry Parry at a conference of TUC-affiliated unions in 1969. If there could be a single local government union he said, the FBU would willingly join it. 'Under any other sort of circumstances then the firemen are far better off, in their own interests, where they are.'[44]

Firemen and the Labour Party

The relationship of the FBU with the Labour Party has throughout its existence been influenced by various factors, most notably the political stance adopted by the union and its leadership. Initially a ballot of the membership decided not to form a political fund, let alone affiliate to the Labour Party, but in 1921 a further ballot reversed this decision. At first the commitment to the Labour Party was relatively vague; it was decided that individual branches could affiliate to the party where they desired it, while the union nationally would remain outside.[45] The Labour Party was only beginning to establish itself as a major political force in these years and there was still a good deal of opposition to and distrust of it in the country at large. In 1924 the party took power for the first time as a minority government with Liberal support. Although short-lived, this experience of government did a lot to establish Labour as a respectable political party capable of governing the country in a responsible manner. With its support growing in the 1920s the FBU affiliated nationally in 1926.[46]

Despite its national affiliation it was the union's local contacts that were the most important; yet political differences and personality clashes within the Labour Party often led to difficulties at this level, particularly in the 1920s.

The union's main strength at the time was in the London area, and the major force in Labour politics in London was Herbert Morrison. Morrison, however, did not like Jim Bradley, the FBU's general secretary, considering him too left-wing and a troublemaker. Bradley was elected to the Bethnal Green borough council in the 1920s and was involved in the struggle usually associated with Poplar over the refusal to levy high rates on the London poor, and the controversy when Poplar, Bethnal Green and other councils decided on a minimum wage of £4 for council employees. The London Labour Party was deeply divided politically and Bradley remained committed to the left; as a result, his future candidacy in the borough was challenged by the leaders of the London Labour Party headed by Morrison, and the executive of the FBU was persuaded to withdraw its backing for Bradley.[47]

The Labour Party nationally took office again as a minority government in 1929. This period in office was to result in disaster for the Labour Party. In response to an economic crisis Ramsay MacDonald and his Chancellor of the Exchequer, Philip Snowden, decided that the only option available to them was to accept Treasury advice and make severe public expenditure cuts which were unacceptable to their Labour colleagues. The outcome was a National government headed by MacDonald, but the Labour Party abandoned him and in so doing abandoned any hope of governmental power for the rest of the 1930s. The FBU remained loyal to the Labour Party in these years of despair, despondency and depression.

One of the main values of affiliation to the Labour Party was the way that party members in positions of power could provide help and assistance to the FBU, and ordinary members and activists provide them with support in times of need. In the pre-war years appeals for assistance were mainly directed at local councils. The early problems in London with Morrison have been mentioned already. He was likewise of little value to the FBU in the 1930s when the union appealed to him as leader of the Labour-controlled London County Council on the question of a 48-hour week for firemen. Morrison was unsympathetic, suggesting that the fireman's lot was an easy one, with ample leisure time in which they played games and lounged around. Having appealed to him as a member of the Labour Party, the executive concluded that he appeared 'to make for a position of purity in municipal affairs which is unaffected by unholy party policy or prejudice'.[48]

The war years saw a strengthening of the Labour Party with Labour members in key positions in Churchill's War Cabinet. Unfortunately for the FBU, the man responsible for the new National Fire Service as Home Secretary was Herbert Morrison. Morrison initially considered setting up a Fire Service Federation along similar lines to the Police Federation as an alternative to the FBU. TUC pressure was brought to bear, and the scheme shelved, but Morrison assisted in setting up a separate organisation, the National Fire Service Officers Association (later National Association of Fire Officers) to represent fire officers. He further angered the FBU by forbidding the holding of union meetings in fire stations and retaining an enthusiasm for a form of negotiating machinery that would enable him to bypass the union.[49] The executive's report of 1944 summed up its feelings towards him: 'The Minister's attitude is similar to that of the big bankers, whom he once publicly castigated, who refused to deal with the democratic trade unions in the banking world and insist on dealing only with company unions fostered by themselves.'[50]

As the war drew to a close the Labour Party called a special meeting of trade union executives to discuss funds for the forthcoming general election. The FBU was informed that it had a lower percentage of members paying the political levy to Labour Party funds than almost any other union. 'It was clear from the reports', said the FBU executive, 'that this was partly due to a lack of enthusiasm for the Labour Party which sprang from very definite reasons amongst many of our members.' The executive committee promised the party that it would try to improve the situation and guarantee £1,000 to the election fund.[51] When the election came in 1945 *Firefighter* pointed out that during the war there had been many occasions when the FBU had been severely critical of Herbert Morrison, but it was conceded that: 'His actions must of necessity have been conditioned by serving in a government predominantly Tory in composition.' These criticisms, however, were not allowed to stand in the way of progress and they wholeheartedly supported the Labour Party. In an editorial entitled 'An Historic Opportunity', *Firefighter* wrote:

> Never before in history have the working people of this country been presented with such an opportunity to sweep away the old order of things – mass unemployment, malnutrition, slums, depressed areas and social insecurity. Let us seize this opportunity and move forward to the realisation of our Movement's dream for over a century – SOCIALISM.[52]

Labour was swept to power with a landslide victory.

Between 1945 and 1951 two factors dominated the union's attitude and relationship to the Labour Party. The first was the Cold War, which has already been considered. The second was the government's policy of austerity following its initial burst of reforms. The union was also critical of governmental policies in other areas, notably the use of British troops in Greece and the close relationship developing with America at the expense of Eastern Europe. In response to the economic problems of the late 1940s a wage freeze policy had been adopted. This was attacked strongly at FBU annual conferences and in its place a stricter control of prices was recommended, investigation into the distribution of consumer goods, a survey of the administrative costs of nationalised industries and the rigid limitation of profits.[53] In terms of assistance given to the FBU, the position was a little brighter after the war. On the surface, the difference between the union's relationship with Morrison and that of his successor, the post-war Labour Home Secretary, James Chuter Ede, could not have been more stark. When a Home Office official objected to Horner speaking on one occasion as if the Home Office and the FBU were co-partners, Chuter Ede said that he found nothing objectionable about such a notion. However, despite a much more friendly and fruitful relationship, the union still had problems and had to fight to get some things accepted. Chuter Ede, for instance, refused at first to recognise the Officers' Section of the FBU and the union had difficulty ensuring that there would not be a separate negotiating body for officers with NAFO as their sole representatives. The FBU was also dissatisfied with the lack of consultation over the appointment of Chief Officers and the rights given to NAFO to represent them.[54] The union's major fear once the National Fire Service had been disbanded, however, was that the post-war service would be starved of resources by Conservative councils, and members were reminded of the importance of working for a Labour victory in local elections.

In 1950 the Labour government was re-elected but its majority was severely reduced, and the FBU executive council spoke in its report of 'a Labour Movement bewildered and leaderless'.[55] A resolution was carried unanimously at that year's conference criticising Labour representatives both in parliament and local government for 'being used to act as spearheads in the current attack by our employers on our living standards', and it was further resolved that in future the union would be less generous to the Labour Party nationally, reserving its generosity instead for those divisions of the party recommended by District Committees of the FBU and which 'demonstrate progressive policies and practical support for the Fire Brigades Union'.[56]

The executive council argued that the Labour Party's abandonment of its socialist aims was at the root of its electoral problems, and the executive were well represented at the 'Victory for Socialism' conference of left-wing Labour supporters in 1951. This conference, although calling for a victory for Labour at the next general election, was critical of the current policies, particularly in the areas of foreign policy, peace, and rearmament. Peace was the central concern, and it was suggested by the FBU participants that 'Loyalty to socialist principles by the British Labour government (rather than subservience to uncontrolled capitalism in America), if applied in international affairs, would produce a new hope for the world.'[57]

In spite of receiving an increase in votes and achieving a slightly higher poll than the Conservatives in the 1951 election, the Labour Party had fewer seats in the House of Commons than the Conservatives and Labour was to remain in opposition for the next thirteen years. The FBU remained a critic of the Labour Party from the left during these years of change. In the year after the election the executive issued a Supplementary Report on Political Action for conference discussion in which the Labour Party was criticised for abandoning the policy laid down in the 1945 manifesto, 'Let Us Face the Future'.

During the 'Spit and Polish' demonstrations of the early 1950s the value of Labour Party membership and support was particularly evident. Parliamentary pressure from Labour MPs, linked with TUC delegations, resulted in the Home Secretary's guarantee that the police would not be used to remove people from fire stations.[58] In some areas local Labour Party members raised the issue at council meetings. In Dudley they did so but were initially defeated; in other areas they were more successful and pressure brought to bear on employers resulted in the early lifting of disciplinary charges. In Liverpool charges were dropped after the Labour group walked out of the council proceedings, and the threat of similar action in Middlesex had the same result. In some areas large meetings were called by the Labour Party and trades councils, and in Nottingham, which had been the first authority to punish firemen and was the last to withdraw charges, there was a lengthy campaign in which the 'whole trade union and Labour movement in the Nottingham area was mobilised behind the FBU. Members of parliament for Nottingham City were contacted, [and] Labour members of the Nottingham City Council maintained the campaign in the council chamber.'[59] The FBU's debt of gratitude at the time was made clear in the letters and printed leaflets of thanks they sent out. 'It was the Movement alone', said *Firefighter* afterwards, 'which prevented the employers' attack from penetrating our defences.' It was this help and their sense of gratitude that led to the call for Labour Party affiliation in as many constituencies as possible to 'deepen our roots in the great labour movement in which we ourselves are proud to have played no insignificant part.'[60]

Firemen made a significant contribution during the ensuing municipal elections of the early 1950s, and many within the FBU felt that this help cemented the relationship between the two organisations and guaranteed further help in times of need. When NAFO tried to obtain a separate negotiating body to deal with the pay and conditions of junior officers, Horner had meetings with the Labour members on various councils to obtain their assistance in opposing this move, and he pestered the party's officials to the point where their patience wore thin. The party's Local Government Assistant complained, 'On each and every occasion when Mr Horner has been in this Office he has referred to the grand work carried out by the firemen during the municipal elections in 1952 and for this reason seems to think the Labour Party has a debt to repay to his union.'[61]

The 1950s and early 1960s were a time of reflection and readjustment within the Labour Party very similar to the 1980s. The party was excluded from power and many of its leaders began to feel that it was the party's commitment to socialism and radical change that was the major reason; they felt that the old slogans and the old analyses were out of date. Britain was experiencing economic growth and stability, and it was felt that capitalism could no longer be regarded as an evil and necessarily unjust system. These Labour Party 'revisionists', led by Hugh Gaitskell and with Tony Crosland as their mentor, sought to adapt the party to the new conditions. The language of class was abandoned and socialism redefined to mean gradual reform in a mixed economy managed intelligently in the interests of the whole community. To those on the left these changes were seen as an abandonment of basic principles in an opportunistic striving for power. Horner told the FBU conference of 1954 that

> Those in our movement who talk now about having gone far enough, that we have got to call a halt, that the new mixed

> economy is quite satisfactory, deny the basic principle of the Labour Party and turn their backs on the fundamentals of the labour and trade union movement.[62]

In the aftermath of the general election defeat of 1959 this debate within the Labour Party intensified and the demand was made that Clause 4 of the party's constitution, which committed it to 'the common ownership of the means of production, distribution and exchange', should be abandoned as a part of its modernisation. This issue was raised in the FBU executive's political statement to the 1960 conference, which stated that 'The Executive Council stands for the *unqualified* retention of Clause 4 in the constitution of the Labour Party.' This statement, unanimously endorsed by conference, was also critical of the Labour Party's defence and foreign policies; it was becoming impossible, the union said, in the light of the commitment to a British H-Bomb and a NATO strategy based on nuclear weapons, to distinguish Labour from the Conservatives.[63]

Assistance from Labour councils was not always clear cut and support for the FBU was not always guaranteed. Fire Brigade committees, although Labour-controlled, were none the less employers of firemen, and relationships with Labour councillors as employers could occasionally prove problematic, as they did with the Labour-controlled London County Council in 1948, the Labour Council in Glasgow in 1953 and with the Labour members of Lanarkshire Council in 1960 in a dispute about the establishment of adequate negotiating machinery. The interesting point about the Lanarkshire episode was the way that the FBU could use the internal machinery of the Labour Party and the labour movement to win supporters to its side. The Labour Party's Scottish Secretary sent a private letter to Morgan Phillips, the party's general secretary:

> You should be warned that the FBU has been canvassing all the local Labour Parties in Lanarkshire; the Trades Council; the Lanarkshire MPs; the Scottish Council of the Labour Party and the STUC as well as yourself, and it is rather futile to pretend, as Mr Horner does ... that the FBU is not desirous

> of the Labour Party interfering in what appears to be purely an industrial matter.[64]

The re-election of the Labour government in 1966 meant that Labour was in power for the rest of the 1960s. The FBU found itself at odds with these Labour governments in three major areas: pay, industrial relations legislation and foreign policy. By 1964 an incomes policy had become a central feature of the Labour Party programme and, at first, the FBU leadership went along with the voluntary restraint this involved, although not without criticism within the union.[65] The 1966 wage freeze occurred at the wrong time for the FBU, however, coming as it did within a fortnight of a proposed 7.5 per cent wage increase for firemen. That year's conference carried a resolution opposing 'all forms of restrictive legislation on wage negotiations', though it is worth noting that in his speech Terry Parry qualified the executive's support on the grounds that it did not want to be seen as opposing the principle of a planned economy. The more limited policy of pay restraint, following the freeze, continued to be unpopular with the FBU. Already having had its pay award held up for eleven months, the union was told that the new award was expected to last for two years. Further, an important part of many pay increases at this time was productivity and bonus schemes. As little could be done to incorporate these into fire service pay bargaining, their pay was further held in check, as others benefited from what was referred to at the time as 'wage drift'.[66] As Terry Parry put it in 1968, 'We do not sit around a table discussing whether we would get another 1s. 6d. if we went up the ladder two rungs at a time.'[67]

The Labour government came into conflict not only with the FBU but the whole trade union movement when it issued its White Paper on trade union reform. Entitled *In Place of Strife*, it proposed a radical overhaul of industrial relations and recommended severe restrictions on the powers and established practices of trade unions. On foreign policy the government came under attack on a range of issues, most notably its refusal to distance itself from American involvement in Vietnam. The FBU president, Enoch Humphries, voiced a common sentiment when he said at the end of the 1960s that since 1966 'our government have taken on more and more the role of proxy for the International Monetary Fund, and less and less the role they were elected to perform as agents of the working people who put them into office'. On what he called the 'litmus test issues', such as unemployment, the health service and social services, the Labour government ran 'for cover into the bosom of the orthodox Treasury'; too often, he said, 'our government went in red and came out blue.'[68]

The point about Treasury orthodoxy is an apt one, and one that could be applied with added piquancy to the position of the Labour government which followed the brief but eventful period of Conservative rule between 1970 and 1974. Labour governments are invariably confronted with the problem of how to manage a capitalist economy, and what steps to take when confronted with crises that can only be resolved at the expense of the working people they have been elected into power to represent. In the 1950s John Horner had attended a conference of union executives, and found himself siding with a group of people who were criticising the Labour Chancellor of the time, Sir Stafford Cripps, when '... a bloke got up and said that we ought not to criticise Sir Stafford. He said, "Tell me where there is a Chancellor of the Exchequer who could have led us so brilliantly from one crisis to another as Sir Stafford Cripps has done."'[69] Such a sentiment could well stand as an epitaph to every Labour government this century: leading brilliantly from one crisis to the next.

In one sense, the situation of the Labour governments in the 1970s was very similar to that of 1931. Faced with a crisis, they were informed by their advisors that the only way to maintain economic stability was to cut expenditure and carry out a range of policies that would weaken the organised trade union movement and lead to an increase in unemployment. Faced with a choice between accepting Treasury advice or adopting an alternative approach, they found themselves wanting; they did not have an alternative which could be presented as forcefully or as coherently as that of their Treasury officials. In the 1930s the result had been fragmentation of the Labour Party and Labour's exclusion from power for the next fourteen years. In the 1970s the party remained intact, but was similarly devastated and forced into a lengthy period of opposition, unable to square the circle by pleasing both the labour movement and the International Monetary Fund.

The most important factor from the FBU's standpoint in these years was the government's pay policy which eventually led to the strike of 1977. The strength of feeling towards the Labour Party in the build-up to the strike is captured by a conference delegate moving a motion in 1977 opposing cuts in public expenditure:

> We had an original resolution that the Fire Brigades Union withdraw their support from the Labour government. That was our original resolution – frustration, bitterness, anger ... We have to change that message now to read the Fire Brigades Union withdraws its support for the present policies of the Labour government.[70]

Following the strike some of that frustration, bitterness and anger took more concrete forms. 'Since our strike', said the president in his opening address to the 1978 conference, 'we have had a considerable number of members requesting to opt out of paying the political levy.'[71]

In the light of all these difficulties, problems and policy differences, what is it that has kept the FBU a hard-working, active and loyal affiliate to the Labour Party? The obvious answer lies in a commitment to the ideals and aspirations of the labour movement and to working-class unity, but there was also the value of having access to those in government circles with power and influence even when in opposition. Despite the criticisms and attacks, the nature and extent of FBU support for Labour is clear from the financial aid to the party both locally and nationally, even though at times the generosity has been equivocal. This ambiguity is captured well in an advertisement in the front pages of the Labour Party's *Annual Report* for 1975. These advertisements placed by organisations sympathetic to the party usually take the form of congratulations, calls for unity and uplifting slogans. The FBU's advertisement read: 'Fire Brigades' Union supports a Labour government but at the same time, expresses concern at rising unemployment and the forecasts of even less jobs in the public service. The FBU would oppose any proposals which meant a reduction in standards of protection from fire.' Money was forthcoming, though, often in large amounts. The union provided lump sums at times of general elections as it had in 1945. In earlier decades they had supported particular candidates in local elections. In the early 1950s, when accusations of Communist association were at their height, it was particularly important to the leadership of the union not only to support the Labour Party financially, but to be seen supporting it. For the 1952 municipal elections 250,000 copies of a leaflet 'Britain's firemen say vote Labour this time' were produced nationally for local distribution, and 750,000 of 'Vote Labour' the following year.[72] In 1952 a further leaflet specifically aimed at the London County Council elections was also produced, which was effective enough to generate an attack in the *Daily Telegraph*, though in true FBU tradition, as well as warning of the dangers of a Tory victory, it stated that it had 'had many quarrels with the Labour LCC ... and we shall have them, no doubt, in the future'.[73] The union also financed local MPs, at first making donations to the constituency parties of particularly helpful MPs, and eventually in 1964 sponsoring its own candidate, John Horner.

Conclusion

In the years between 1919 and 1978 the FBU grew from a small London-centred organisation into a national union, still small by the standards of the wider labour movement, but an important, respected and at times influential affiliate of both the TUC and Labour Party. For most of these years the union inhabited a position on the left of each of these organisations; between 1939 and 1956 it was at times heavily influenced by its Communist Party members, although the problems this posed were illustrated by the decision of the 1951 FBU Conference to distance itself from Communist-supported organisations. At national conferences of both the TUC and the Labour Party the FBU adopted a high profile from the 1940s onwards, raising issues that directly concerned its members at work, as well as criticising government policies that affected firemen adversely and highlighting a number of progressive political concerns, notably opposition to nuclear weapons.

As an affiliate to the TUC, the union was able to call upon its assistance at various times of trouble, particularly when the TUC itself was in a position of influence during the war and during periods of Labour government, though the union often came into conflict with the General Council over wages policy. The FBU involved itself in the periodic discussions within the TUC on trade union structure, and for a time was keen on the idea of amalgamation with NUPE. The enthusiasm for amalgamation ebbed as the union grew in stature and confidence, and by the end of the 1960s the FBU had reverted to a proud sense of its own identity, willing only to consider abandoning this individuality if all of the other local government unions would do likewise.

The FBU's involvement with the Labour Party was initially rather vague and at times ambiguous. In the war years and the immediate post-war period there were problems over Communist membership and government policies, but from the early 1950s support for the party became much stronger, particularly at the local level, and was to increase towards a high point in the mid-1960s when John Horner became the union's sponsored MP. Commitment to the party remained strong in spite of the wide range of policy differences, particularly over pay in the 1960s and 70s, although the relationship reached its lowest point in the immediate aftermath of the 1977-78 strike. The FBU nonetheless remained an active if somewhat critical affiliate to the Labour Party, and continued to be an important and active participant in the wider British labour movement, preserving a proud sense of its own independence, but unlike many other unions of a similar size, maintaining a progressive and critical position towards a traditional and often defensively conservative national leadership.

Notes

1. FBU, *Annual Conference Report*, 1951, p. 43.
2. Ibid., pp. 195-9. For CP influence during the Second World War, see Victor Bailey, Ch. 1, above.
3. FBU, *Executive Council Report*, 1948, pp. 317–8.
4. FBU, *Executive Council Report*, 1949, p. 265.
5. Henry Pelling, *The British Communist Party*, London 1958, p. 174. See also John Saville, Ch. 7 below, pp. 225-8.
6. Martin Harrison, *Trade Unions and the Labour Party Since 1945*, London 1960, p. 204; Lewis Minkin, *The Labour Party Conference*, London 1978, p. 39.
7. Labour Party, *Annual Report*, 1958, p. 193.
8. Labour Party, *Annual Report*, 1983, pp. 156-7.
9. The above assessment of FBU involvement in TUC and Labour Party conferences is based on TUC *Reports* and Labour Party *Annual Reports*, 1918-1978.
10. It is interesting to note that the example of Terry Parry is used by Coates and Topham to illustrate the point that seats do not always go to the big unions. Ken Coates and Tony Topham, *Trade Unions in Britain*, Nottingham 1980, p. 113.
11. FBU, *Annual Conference Report*, 1937, p. 14.
12. FBU, *Executive Council Report*, 1949, p. 265.
13. FBU, *Executive Council Report*, 1950, p. 331.
14. FBU, *Executive Council Report*, 1951, pp. 296-7; FBU, *Executive Council Report*, 1952, para. 139 (no pagination).
15. FBU, *Executive Council Report*, 1967, p. 93.
16. FBU, *Fifty Years Service, 1918-1968*, London 1968. See also John Horner, Ch. 10 below, p. 321.
17. PRO, HO 187/450/1082; 'Recognition of Officer's Section', leaflet dated 14 June 1944 and addressed 'To all Members', copy in TUC Library.
18. FBU, *Executive Council Report*, 1952, para. 210.
19. FBU, *Executive Council Report*, 1953, pp. 299-306; FBU, *Executive Council Report*, 1958, p. 93; TUC, *Report*, 1957, p. 342.
20. FBU, *Annual Conference Report*, 1966, pp. 42-5; FBU, *Executive Council Report*, 1967, p. 91; FBU, *Executive Council Report*, 1975, pp. 121-3.
21. *Firefighter*, December 1949, pp. 4-7, February-March 1950, pp. 6-7, December 1950, p. 2; FBU, *Executive Council Report*, 1950, pp. 332-3.
22. FBU, *Annual Conference Report*, 1966, p. 75.
23. FBU, *Executive Council Report*, 1967, p. 91; TUC, *Report*, 1966, p. 480.
24. FBU, *Annual Conference Report*, 1978, p. 77; TUC, *Report*, 1978, p. 561. See also Victor Bailey, Ch. 8, below.

25. In other accounts it would be called a vertical union, in that it organised all groups in one industry, as opposed to a horizontal union which would organise across industrial barriers. For the categories of British unions and their different types, see Coates and Topham, *Trade Unions*, Ch. 2; H.A. Clegg, *The Changing System of Industrial Relations in Great Britain*, Oxford 1979, Ch. 5; W.E.J. McCarthy, *Trade Unions*, Harmondsworth 1985, Pt. 3.
26. Coates and Topham, *Trade Unions*, pp. 39-40.
27. FBU, *Annual Conference Report*, 1946, p. 98; Bernard Dix and Stephen Williams, *Serving the Public – Building the Union*, London 1987, pp. 174-9.
28. FBU, *Executive Council Report*, 1943, p. 2.
29. John Lovell and B.C. Roberts, *A Short History of the TUC*, London 1968, pp. 152-5.
30. FBU, *National Council Report*, 1944, p. 4; TUC, *Report*, 1943, pp. 171-2.
31. FBU Executive Council, *Memorandum on Amalgamation and Closer Unity*, copy in TUC Library; FBU, *Annual Conference Report*, 1946, pp. 93-4.
32. FBU, *Annual Conference Report*, 1946, pp. 93-107; *Firefighter*, April 1945, p. 3.
33. FBU, *Executive Council Report*, 1946, p. 183.
34. FBU, *Annual Conference Report*, 1948, p. 148; FBU, *Executive Council Report*, 1948, p. 295; FBU, *Annual Conference Report*, 1953, pp. 194-5. See also Kenneth Brown, Ch. 5 above.
35. FBU, *Executive Council Report*, 1957, pp. 107, and 111.
36. 'Firemen Thank the Labour Movement', leaflet, copy in TUC Library; *Firefighter*, February 1952, p. 9.
37. *Firefighter*, March 1952, p. 2.
38. FBU, *Executive Council Report*, 1951, p. 300; FBU, *Executive Council Report*, 1952, para. 154.
39. FBU, *Executive Council Report*, 1957, p. 112.
40. TUC, *Report*, 1958, pp. 319-20; TUC, *Report*, 1959, pp. 333-4.
41. Robert T. Buchanan, 'Mergers in British Trade Unions: 1949-79' in McCarthy, *Trade Unions*, pp. 138-56; Richard Hyman, 'Trade Unions: Structure, Policies, and Politics' in George Sayers Bain (ed.), *Industrial Relations in Britain*, Oxford 1983, pp. 35-41.
42. FBU, *Annual Conference Report*, 1963, pp. 175-80. The FBU was very keen to ensure NALGO participation in negotiations in the years before it affiliated to the TUC. FBU, *Executive Council Report*, 1958, pp. 94-5.
43. FBU, *Annual Conference Report*, 1964, pp. 66-9; FBU, *Annual Conference Report*, 1966, p. 70; FBU, *Annual Conference Report*, 1969, pp. 198-9.
44. TUC, *Collective Bargaining and Trade Union Development. Public Sector* (1969) p. 66.
45. Firemen's Trade Union, *Annual Report*, 1921, p. 9.
46. Labour Party, *Annual Report*, 1926, p. 105.
47. *Firefighter*, February 1954, p. 9; Frederick H. Radford, *Fetch the Engine*, London 1951, p. 98; Noreen Branson, *Poplarism 1919-1925*, London 1979.
48. FBU, *Annual Conference Report*, 1936, p. 75; see also Radford, *Fetch the Engine*, pp. 102-6.
49. PRO, HO 187/450/451/941.

50. FBU, *National Council Report*, 1944, p. 3.
51. Ibid., p. 5.
52. *Firefighter*, May-June 1945, p. 2.
53. FBU, *Annual Conference Report*, 1948, p. 148; FBU, *Annual Conference Report*, 1949, pp. 152-3; FBU, *Annual Conference Report*, 1950, pp. 109-18, 170-2.
54. FBU, *Executive Council Report*, 1948, pp. 253-7; 'National Joint Council for Local Authorities' Fire Brigades in England and Wales', Labour Party Correspondence, GS/FBU 5ii-vi; HO 187/1082/1176.
55. FBU, *Executive Council Report*, 1950, p. 373.
56. FBU, *Annual Conference Report*, 1950, pp. 174-7.
57. FBU, *Annual Conference Report*, 1951, p. 40; FBU, *Executive Council Report*, 1951, pp. 295-6.
58. FBU, *Executive Council Report*, 1952, para. 210.
59. FBU, *Executive Council Report*, 1952, para. 102; *Firefighter*, February 1952, pp. 8-9; Labour Party Correspondence, GS/FBU/10i-iv.
60. *Firefighter*, March 1952, p. 2. See also Victor Bailey, Ch. 4 above.
61. FBU, *Executive Council Report*, 1952, para. 140; 'Memorandum on conversation between Mr John Burns, President of the Fire Brigades Union, and Mr Gwilym Williams', Labour Party Correspondence, GS/FBU/15i-ii.
62. FBU, *Annual Conference Report*, 1954, p. 36.
63. FBU, *Annual Conference Report*, 1960, pp. 223-5.
64. Letter from W.G. Marshall to Morgan Phillips, 11 February 1960, Labour Party Correspondence, GS/FBU/48i; FBU, *Annual Conference Report*, 1953, pp. 62-4; FBU, 'London District Committee', leaflet, copy in TUC Library.
65. Ibid., pp.132-48; 152.
66. FBU, *Annual Conference Report*, 1966, pp. 63-70; FBU, *Executive Council Report*, 1968, p. 94; FBU, *Executive Council Report*, 1969, p. 104.
67. FBU, *Annual Conference Report*, 1968, p. 70.
68. FBU, *Annual Conference Report*, 1969, pp. 3-7.
69. FBU, *Annual Conference Report*, 1953, p. 43.
70. FBU, *Annual Conference Report*, 1977, p. 112.
71. FBU, *Annual Conference Report*, 1978, pp. 5-6. See also Victor Bailey, Ch. 8, below.
72. *Firefighter*, April 1952, p. 10, June 1953, p. 1.
73. FBU, *Executive Council Report*, 1953, p. 415; *Firefighter*, May 1952, p. 5.

7 The Communist Party and the FBU

John Saville

The Communist Party was founded in 1920, and during the first decade of its existence the policy towards the established trade unions was erratic.* It was only during the years of the united front and popular front – from about 1934 on – that Communist activity in the building of trade unions and organising those not in trade unions became of increasing importance; and by the beginning of the Second World War the number, and quality, of the rank-and-file activists was impressive. During the war years, and especially after the German invasion of Russia in the summer of 1941, the influence of the Communist Party at the factory level grew rapidly and the number of full-time officials increased accordingly.

John Horner, the outstanding personality of the Fire Brigades Union when it began seriously to establish itself as the representative voice of the fire service, belonged to the Labour Party during the years of war although he became increasingly influenced by the dynamic leadership of the Communist Party and the self-sacrifice of its rank and file; and he joined the party during the first year of peace. It was a time, it must be remembered, when large sections of the British people had become politically radicalised. Six years of war against the fascist powers had imbued in many a determination never to go back to the days of unemployment and the Means Test but, to the surprise of many in Britain, and to the astonishment of the rest of the world, the British people rejected Winston Churchill and the Conservative Party and voted the Labour Party into power in July 1945 with a very large majority. The Labour government, under Clement Attlee, then proceeded to introduce the domestic policies on which the general election had been fought, and these included the nationalisation of certain basic industries and above all the introduction of a comprehensive system of social security and the National Health Service. The foreign policy of the Labour government, with Ernest Bevin as Foreign Secretary, was a much more controversial issue, but that is not a matter for discussion here.

To be a Communist trade unionist in the early days of peace was acceptable to most in the broader movement, and within the Fire Brigades Union the excellence of the leadership in general united Labour and Communist in their common endeavours. It is, however, likely that there were few unions where the Communists were so prominent in the leadership as in the FBU. John Horner's open membership of the Communist Party undoubtedly encouraged recruitment of many among the rank and file, reinforcing those CP veterans of the wartime NFS who had remained in the service. In accordance with Communist practice, CP 'fractions' operated at different levels within the FBU, linking party members in a network which sought to influence the policy of the union in keeping with the current political line of the party. Most of the controversial issues related to foreign policy. Thus, in all the great, and at times bitter, disagreements which dominated and divided the British labour movement in the years of the Cold War, the FBU was certain to be found on the left of the divide: issues such as the American loan, the wage freeze which followed and the resultant American influence over both domestic and foreign policies in Britain; German rearmament and British policy over nuclear weapons; the Korean War and Britain's own rearmament programme which cut into Labour's social security plans and led to the resignation of Aneurin Bevan and Harold Wilson from the Cabinet. In all these arguments and disputes the FBU ranged itself alongside the Bevanite group of MPs. As the Cold War intensified – the Korean War period was the nadir – the position of Communists in trade unions became ever more difficult. The right-wing leaders of the Transport and General Workers' Union, for example, banned all Communist Party members from holding office; and the TUC followed by effectively blocking the election of any Communist to the General Council. In close partnership with the American Federation of Labor – which operated as a branch of the American State Department – the British TUC played a major role in the break-up of the World Federation of Trade Unions in 1949. The anti-Communism of the McCarthy years in America was never as virulent in Britain, but it was more pervasive than is often appreciated, and the governments of Britain, of whatever political colour, have always been more secretive than those in the United States.

Membership of the Communist Party disqualified any trade unionist from being a delegate from his own union to the Labour Party Conference. Such disadvantages as the FBU might have suffered as a result of the ban were offset by the respect which the top leaders of the FBU had for each other, regardless of political affiliation. John Burns, president throughout this period, was an honourable man and greatly admired by his Labour Party colleagues. At Labour Party conferences, when the Cold War was in deepest freeze, he fiercely defended his Communist officials against attacks, from whatever quarter they came. At FBU annual conferences, as a devout Catholic, he would gather together each morning the Catholic delegates for early morning mass before he opened the day's session.

In the early months of 1956 the revelations of Nikita Khrushchev at the 20th Congress of the Communist Party of the Soviet Union shocked Communist Parties all over the world, and many fell into disarray. What Khrushchev did was to reveal in secret session many of the crimes of Stalin in the years immediately before the Second World War and in the years which followed. The doubts and debates within the British Communist Party grew rapidly from the early summer of 1956, and a strong movement of dissent and criticism developed which reached crisis point when the Soviet Army invaded Hungary at just the same time as Britain, France and Israel embroiled themselves in the Suez disaster. Within the British Communist Party the massive disquiet was common to intellectuals as well as to blue- and white-collar workers, and some 8,000 members left during this year; a political haemorrhage from which the Communist Party never recovered. Inevitably, among the FBU as elsewhere the bitter political arguments became coloured by individual differences and personal recriminations. Jack Grahl, assistant general secretary, and a prominent Communist in his own right, who during his period of office had shown outstanding organisational abilities, resigned from the union. Among the leading personalities who resigned from the Communist Party but continued to play a major role in the union were John Horner, Terry Parry and Enoch Humphries. There were many others. Grahl's place was taken by Tom Harris, a senior Labour councillor in London; at the same time of his election Harris had been London regional secretary of the union and had led the London Brigade membership during the Spit and Polish demonstrations a few years earlier.

When, in the following year, John Horner, as a FBU delegate to the Labour Party conference, walked to the rostrum to move the FBU's resolution on local government finance he was met with a discreet round of applause.

* This piece was written with the benefit of discussions with John Horner.

8 The First National Strike

Victor Bailey

I don't know who will ever write the history of that strike or whose version will ever be accepted as the true record, but I want to make it quite clear that no one person or groupings of people can take credit for anything which may have been achieved. It was a collective decision of Conference, collectively pursued, and eventually Conference collectively accepted the advice to return to work. Let no man take away the credit from those members on the picket lines for the disciplined way in which they conducted themselves.

It is natural that there were to be inquests, that there was to be criticism and that people took stances on who was right and who was wrong; but surely, Comrades, the Fire Brigades Union has come through its baptism of fire, and instead of flagellating and dividing ourselves let us make it clear that we are stronger and more unified than ever before, and we will continue to grow stronger if the spirit and determination of the strike is to be translated into our trade union activities.[1]

The first official strike in the Fire Brigades Union's 59-year history began on 14 November 1977, and ended, after nine weeks, on 16 January 1978.* If one image encapsulates the strike, it must surely be that of firemen on picket duty, huddled round braziers outside closed fire stations, acknowledging the signs of public support in the form of financial donations and tooting car horns. To go on strike had been a profoundly difficult step for people who saw themselves as uniformed servants of the community, providing an essential service that only they had been trained to provide. It must mean, Neil Kinnock told the House of Commons on the second day of the strike, 'that they were provoked to do so arising from a long-standing cause'.[2] That cause was low pay, as statistical and personal evidence make abundantly clear.

The national average wage of all adult male workers in 1977 was £78.60 for a basic 42-hour week. The weekly wage of firemen ranged from £52.53 on appointment at the age of nineteen to £65.70 for a qualified fireman with four years' training. The majority of firemen, some 20,000 of the 33,000 wholetime firemen were in the latter category. Their weekly pay was thus £12.90 below average weekly earnings. For a married man with two children under eleven years of age this meant, after tax and pension deductions, a take home pay of £46.71 – and this for a 48-hour week of fifteen-hour night shifts and nine-hour day shifts.[3] Firemen received no overtime and no extra payment for shifts or weekend work. Their low wage was increasingly subsidised by part-time 'moonlighting', by wives' wages and by state hand-outs.

These desiccated facts and figures lay behind the deep-rooted anger and frustration of enormous numbers of individual firemen. Threading all the *cris de coeur* of firemen in the final countdown to the strike was anger and exasperation at having been forced to take strike action to secure a living wage. Terry Bennett, aged 30, left the Devon county brigade three weeks before the strike started, citing low pay as the reason: 'How can a man live today on a £45 take home pay with no overtime, rent or housing allowances?' Increasing numbers of firemen were reluctant recipients of welfare benefits. A fireman with three children, an FBU member but 'not a militant', complained of having 'to skulk into the local education office to claim free school meals for two of my children'. He also received a rates rebate. John Law, 33 and married with two children, sitting at the mess table in Liverpool's Hatton Garden station a few days before the strike declared: 'This isn't bloody-mindedness. It's need and pride. We've been driven to it. We've waited too long for too little.' Another Liverpool fireman, Ronald Sherbern, expressed the feelings of perhaps 90 per cent of firemen: 'We don't want to strike. It makes us sick to do it, but what other choice have we got?'[4]

What, then, were firemen asking for? For a pay formula that would make the qualified fireman's rate equivalent to the national average wage of £78, plus 10 per cent to take account of the hazards faced and special skills required by firemen. In all, an increase of about 30 per cent or £20 per week on the qualified fireman's rate, which then stood at £65.70 per week. The stumbling block, as we shall see, was the Labour government's determination to restrict all pay increases to 10 per cent, which would have put only between £5.50 and £6.60 into firemen's pay packets. Firemen, to a man, considered this amount derisory. 'Surely,' union spokesmen maintained, 'a fireman is worth the national average plus 10 per cent for his skills, long hours, shift working and the hazards he faces.'[5]

If the strike was the result of need, not greed, it was also based on neglect. Firemen had been the subject of favourable reports by government-instigated enquiries, all recommending pay improvements; they were the subject of acceptable pay awards via the National Joint Council yet the object of so many refusals. Over the previous eighteen years, Neil Kinnock informed the Commons, firemen 'have achieved a number of pay settlements and recommendations only to have them taken away at the eleventh hour, or in some cases even later, because of the incomes policies practised by successive governments'. Former fireman and Labour MP James Sillars put it more vividly: '... on wage policy after wage policy the guillotine came down on the firemen more often than it ever came down on any other group'. More expressively still, serving Liverpool fireman, Ronald Sherbern, declared: 'Promises, promises. We've had promises every year since 1966 and we've got nothing.'[6]

Incomes Policy, Low Pay and a New Pay Formula

This longer view of the issue merits close attention if we are to understand why by 1977 firemen felt the last ditch had been reached in the battle for an enduringly fair wage. Throughout the 1960s and 70s industrial relations were overshadowed by government incomes policies. Indeed, incomes or wages policies pretty much replaced unfettered collective bargaining, the latter increasingly considered to be incompatible with the post-1945 goals of both political parties: stable prices, full employment and an expanding economy. The theory of incomes policy was disarmingly simple: if workers would accept lower money wages, prices would rise more slowly, permitting faster economic growth, as a result of which real wages (or what could actually be bought in the shops), and thus living standards, would rise faster than they would under conditions of free collective bargaining. In practice, however, incomes policies simply kept a lid on wages while price inflation continued to rip (giving the lie to the belief that inflation was solely wage-induced). Living standards actually declined in 1966-67, for the first time in the post-war era.[7]

This was the context in which the Fire Brigades Union sought to make a reality of its new charter, *A Service for the Sixties*, an integral part of which were pay scales commensurate with the skilled nature of modern fire-fighting.[8] A public campaign on behalf of firemen in 1962 led to a wage increase which gave them a 7s. 6d. lead over male average weekly earnings. By 1966, however, firemen had slipped back to a point where they were £2. 8s. 4d. behind average weekly earnings. Negotiations that year led to an employers' offer to increase firemen's pay by 7.5 per cent, considerably more than the norm of 3.5 per cent laid down in the Labour government's White Paper on prices and incomes. The two sides were close to agreement when on 20 July the Prime Minister, Harold Wilson, announced a pay standstill. The Home Secretary, Roy Jenkins, had to inform an utterly dismayed general secretary, Terry Parry, and president, Enoch Humphries, that the fire service pay claim would not be exempt from the freeze, despite the late stage of negotiations, but would instead be referred to the National Board for Prices and Incomes (NBPI) under Aubrey Jones.[9] Not for the last time, this appeared to the union to be a case of one step forward, two steps back.

Undeterred, the union set about convincing the NBPI that

to staunch the serious drain of trained firemen from the service, and to recruit in the right numbers and quality, required a substantial pay increase. This increase, the FBU felt, should recognise that firemen were not just physically strong water-squirters, but skilled craftsmen facing new and dangerous hazards, acting increasingly as an emergency service in relation to road accidents and other disasters (requiring knowledge and skills additional to fire fighting), and administering fire prevention and fire safety legislation.[10] Here, in embryo, was the union's central strategy, which it was to deploy for the next ten years. It looked to a new and detailed assessment of firemen's duties as the key that would turn the lock on the manacle of low pay and long hours. The NBPI, however, had more immediate concerns.

In May 1967 the Board recommended a 7.5 per cent pay increase from 1 July, to last for two years, coupled with a pensionable bonus of £170 a year for firemen willing to increase their working week from 48 to 56 hours.[11] If the pay rise was conceded, it was, in effect, deferred for almost a year, and was to be staged over two years. Additionally, the union's effective post-war campaign for a shorter working week was thrown into reverse, for the carrot of a pensionable bonus was understandably taken by the great majority of firemen (the main exception being Glasgow firemen, of whom more later). Within a year, 90 per cent of the service was on the 56-hour duty system.[12]

The NBPI did at least acknowledge what the FBU had long maintained, that 'wage drift' masked the true disparity between firemen's and industrial workers' earnings. In the fire service nationally determined wage rates accounted for a high proportion of total earnings; in manufacturing industry, by contrast, nationally agreed rates were considerably supplemented by allowances and bonuses gained through local workplace bargaining. As a result, incomes policies, which apply to wage rates not earnings, severely penalised groups like firemen who could not circumvent the full impact of pay control by the expedient of wage drift. As Terry Parry declared in 1969, 'We get a pay rise, but every three years or so we find we've fallen behind again. What we need is a built-in factor to keep us up with the wage drift in other industries.' For firemen, however, incomes policies would continue to add to the injury of nullified and delayed pay settlements, the insult of terms that were more economically restrictive than what private sector workers achieved.[13]

At this point, rank-and-file firemen entered the bargaining picture. In October 1969 dissatisfaction with low pay, low status and the negotiating machinery came to a head in the dangerously under-manned London brigade, where firemen threatened to strike unless the Greater London Council improved its pay offer. The men were demanding improved travel and rent allowances totalling around £5 a week. In July 1970 the Essex brigade began 'emergency calls only' working in protest at the employers' introduction of two rates of pay across the brigade. When in September the employers sent 86 men off duty without pay it was only with difficulty that the executive council averted a mass walk-out of Essex firemen. Both events testified to a heightened union consciousness among firemen in London and parts of the Home Counties, to growing discontent with the union's national leadership (which the London committee considered too conciliatory) and to an inchoate commitment to strike action as a last resort, which the paramilitary ethos of the service could not now quell.[14]

In the early 1970s the union's strategy of securing an evaluation of the many-sided job of a modern fireman, with a pay scale to match, met with a modicum of success. The report of the Departmental Committee on the Fire Service (appointed by Roy Jenkins in 1967 and chaired by Sir Ronald Holroyd of ICI) appeared in May 1970. While dealing primarily with the organisation of the fire service, the report made a significant statement on pay. It considered that in view of the unique combination of required skills – physical, technical and educational – 'The earnings of fully trained men with all-round operational experience should be comparable with the national average earnings of skilled craftsmen.'[15] To secure the most effective recruitment and use of manpower, moreover, the report endorsed *A Service for the Sixties* with regard to the abandonment of station cleaning chores and their replacement by fire prevention duties.[16]

More significant still, in 1971 an independent inquiry under the chairmanship of Sir Charles Cunningham was given the task of evaluating the fireman's job. In its evidence to the inquiry the FBU stressed that firemen were frustrated at the employers' reluctance to negotiate a fair valuation of the job, and 'to introduce a formula which would give that valuation some degree of permanence'.[17] Cunningham's contribution was, first, to equate the fireman's job with 'a band of jobs stretching from the top "semi-skilled" occupations in industry and merging into the bottom half of the skilled manual occupations' and secondly, since the character of the fireman's job was changing rapidly, to recommend a revaluation within two years.[18] Thus pressure was put on the employers to take a positive attitude towards assessing the value of the modern fireman and towards devising a pay formula to lend permanence to the valuation.

Conservative Pay Policy

As for actual pay deals, the union was again the victim of government interference, even though no statutory wages policy existed in the early 1970s. In December 1970 Reginald Maudling, Home Secretary in Edward Heath's Conservative government, called upon the fire service employers to withdraw their offer of a £130 a year increase and substitute a 10 per cent pay increase. The union reluctantly accepted the 10 per cent offer, on condition that the Cunningham Inquiry was appointed. The latter proposed a rate of pay for qualified firemen working a 56-hour week of £35.58 (an increase of about £5). This was accepted by both sides of the NJC in December 1971, which put firemen at a position on the pay ladder £2.58 above average male earnings.[19] From then onwards, however, the pay position of firemen relative to the average industrial worker worsened relentlessly due to the rigid application, especially to public sector workers, of a further set of government incomes policies.

On 6 November 1972 the Heath government enacted a statutory pay policy. Until February 1974 a stage of total freeze was followed by two more stages of rigid limits to pay increases. The Trades Union Congress opposed this legal interference with wage settlements, particularly as escalating food prices and the introduction of value added tax took the annual inflation rate to 13 per cent by early 1974. Firemen likewise contested the Conservative controls. At the FBU's Annual Conference in May 1973 Bro. Totterdell (Bristol) impressed upon the executive council that 'the so-called £1 plus 4 per cent', stage two of the three-stage controls, 'does not, nor will not suffice the membership of this union'. 'When one relates our pay', he continued, 'a measly 63p [an hour] for a qualified fireman – and you equate this against a comparable industrial rate of 75p or even £1, they make our wages look small.'[20] Pressure began to build within the union for a firmer line of action to stem the decline in firemen's living standards.

The Glasgow Strike

This pressure temporarily cracked the unity of the FBU in October 1973. Glasgow firemen had never accepted the eight-hours bonus shift, introduced in 1967, preferring the flexibility of working casual overtime. In a brigade that was seriously under-strength such overtime was readily available. Unlike the bonus shift, however, overtime earnings were not pensionable, an anomaly that rankled. And as incomes policies again reduced the effectiveness of national bargaining the Glasgow men decided to supplement their earnings by negotiating a local 'plus' payment of £5 a week. When Glasgow Corporation conceded only £2.48 local union officials held a ballot on strike action. As both the 'plus' payment and the ballot were contrary to union policy, the executive council suspended brigade officials. A national delegate conference, moreover, overwhelmingly declined to make the Glasgow strike official and instructed a return to work.

The First National Strike

A ten-day strike none the less took place, the first full-scale withdrawal of labour in the union's history, albeit unofficial and regionally limited. Firemen in other cities voted to respond to emergency calls only. In the capital the Regional Committee organised an unofficial work-to-rule in the cause of an improved London weighting allowance. Troops were deployed in Glasgow, ostensibly to protect life, in truth to break a strike that lacked union and TUC backing. On 5 November Glasgow firemen agreed to call off the strike and return to the fold.[21] If a divisive piece of trade unionism, the Glasgow strike doubtless strengthened the hand of union leaders. On 16 November the NJC were allowed to ignore stage 2 (£1 plus 4 per cent), and use instead the 'unsocial hours' provision of stage 3 to give firemen up to £7.80 a week more. The new pay deal was coupled with an agreement to introduce the 48-hour week as the standard duty system in twelve months' time.[22]

The FBU thus succeeded in evading the full rigidities of Tory wages policy, without, however, securing any improvement in the position of firemen relative to the average industrial worker. A few months later a minority Labour government came to office; in October 1974 it was re-elected with a slender majority. Firemen would surely fare better from the political wing of the labour movement, despite the unpromising experience with a previous Wilson government.

Labour's Social Contract

Labour came bearing gifts: the so-called Social Contract. For two years a Labour Party-TUC Liaison Committee, representing the industrial, political and parliamentary wings of the labour movement, had been drafting this contract. In return for favourable economic and social policies (on prices, rents and pensions), the trade unions agreed voluntarily to moderate their wage demands. Wage increases in the first year of the Social Contract were to be pegged to the cost of living. Unfortunately, price inflation had soared to 27 per cent by June 1975; average earnings had increased by 26.6 per cent. This was not what the government had in mind.

In a White Paper entitled *The Attack on Inflation* the government, therefore, set out a voluntary incomes policy, based on proposals to develop the social contract in a recent TUC document. Phase one of this policy enforced a £6 limit on pay settlements. A year later, in August 1976, came phase two: a limit of 5 per cent, with a £4 maximum, again with TUC agreement. A less stringent pay limit of 10 per cent was proposed for phase three, starting in August 1977. This time the TUC neither approved the pay limit nor actively opposed it. Phase three was the straw that broke the firemen's back.[23]

What impact did Labour's incomes policy have on firemen? In November 1974 union delegates accepted a pay adjustment in line with social contract guidelines. In addition, however, they pressed the NJC working party to get on with the evaluation study of a fireman's job, in the expectation that a productivity payment for extra duties, like fire prevention, would at last result. They also called for a reduction in the fireman's working week from 48 hours, now reintroduced in the fire service, to 40 hours. Delegates finally voted for a ban on shift overtime, to ensure that the 48-hour week would not again be undermined by the employers. The unfortunate side-effect of this laudable proposal on overtime was to deprive firemen of the only real way of adding to their basic pay and withdraw what little scope firemen had for wage drift. Banning overtime left members exposed to the full blast of the icy wind of pay restraint.[24]

Lack of progress in negotiations on this programme of action, and on an interim cost-of-living increase, provoked Conference to introduce 'emergency calls only' working for three months in May 1975, as phase one of the voluntary incomes policy came into view. At the end of that period, by which date the Secretary of State for Employment, Michael Foot, had incensed the FBU by his decision that any productivity bonus would count towards the £6 pay limit under phase one, the executive council decided to escalate the work-to-rule. The attempt by the Strathclyde and Merseyside brigades to have a strike ballot on the pay and hours claim was, it should be noted, rejected by the Recalled Annual Conference in July.[25] But the work-to-rule got the union nowhere. General secretary Parry, though a consistent critic of phase one, was obliged to settle within it.

The immediate consequences of Labour's new incomes policy for the FBU were twofold. Firstly, the claim for a 40-hour week was derailed as it entailed increased expenditure on manpower. The issue was shunted into a Home Office siding for a feasibility study with which the union refused to co-operate. The worst effect of phase one, however, was that the interim report on job evaluation, which had emerged from the NJC working party in April and still awaited full NJC endorsement, was shelved. This meant that the union's main strategy of winning extra pay for new skills and wider involvement in fire prevention was well and truly foiled by the social contract.

By the time of the next Annual Conference Harold Wilson had resigned as Prime Minister and been succeeded by James Callaghan. The change of leadership led to no alteration either in government pay policy or in TUC support for it. FBU delegates had before them, therefore, the TUC's 1976 pay guidelines. The executive council had already voted by the narrow margin of eight votes to seven to recommend that Conference support the TUC policy. Enoch Humphries had argued on the executive against the guidelines, and now took the decision to present no presidential address to Conference, an unprecedented step that reflected the increasing split within the union over the social contract. In contrast, general secretary Parry, a member of the General Council of the TUC, accepted the pay guidelines and had the task of convincing Conference to do likewise.[26]

In an uncompromising speech Parry asked delegates to put economic recovery and counter-inflation policy above the sectional interests of firemen. He accepted the need to press government to adopt the complementary parts of the

TUC's economic programme, notably industrial investment and import controls. And he emphasised that the claims for the 40-hour week and the evaluation study of firemen's work, if again invalidated by the guidelines, would remain on the agenda. But Parry's conclusion returned to the main theme: 'We are not propping up capitalism but seeking the preservation of the economy of Britain on behalf of the working men and women on a much wider view than the Fire Service.'[27]

Conference endorsed the executive's recommendations and so in November firemen's wages rose in line with phase two's 5 per cent guidelines. The latter related to 'total earnings', not just basic pay, but the continued overtime ban in the fire service meant that, for firemen, they were practically one and the same. Yet again, pay policy hit firemen much harder than those workers who cashed in on wage drift. Relative to other occupational groups, indeed, firemen experienced a greater decline in real earnings in the first three years of the Social Contract. According to one estimate, the real earnings of firemen declined by over 15 per cent between 1974 and 1977.[28] The combination of declining living standards and a union leadership that seemed, to some firemen, more concerned with the management of the economy than with fighting for a realistic living wage now served to ignite the embers of unofficial militancy, still smouldering in places like Glasgow and Merseyside.

Unofficial Militancy

It is difficult to put an accurate figure on the number of local disputes in the eighteen months prior to the national strike. A generational factor possibly accounts, in part, for this heightened industrial action. A younger generation of firemen had gradually replaced the war and immediate post-war firemen, the former less reluctant perhaps to kick over the traces.[29] The brush caught fire in many places, extinguished each time by executive intervention. In March

1976 the executive disciplined officials of the South Yorkshire brigade for disregarding the union ban on overtime. In June industrial action in the London brigade ended only when the FBU and the GLC agreed to refer the issue of industrial relations in the brigade to the Advisory Conciliation and Arbitration Service. In October the executive secured a return to work in Northern Ireland by taking over from a 'local action committee' the ultimately successful campaign for an extra responsibility allowance.[30] 1977 brought no respite for the leadership.

In February Essex firemen began a work-to-rule campaign over the county council's plan to cut brigade expenditure. An attempt to get a mandate for a strike was suspended when the executive offered assistance with local negotiations. On Merseyside an unofficial action committee led an 'emergency calls only' demonstration to reinforce the brigade's resolution on pay at the impending Annual Conference.[31] Just prior to Conference, finally, the publication *National Rank and File Fireman* put out by an unofficial body with which four FBU officials were associated and which had links with the revolutionary Socialist Workers Party, appeared demanding a £15 a week minimum pay rise.[32] With union leaders under growing rank-and-file pressure the stage was set for a stormy Conference discussion of the government's campaign for a third round of pay restraint.

But the storm held off. On behalf of the executive the general secretary asked Conference for authority to use the NJC Working Party report, entitled 'The Qualified Fireman's Job' and recently endorsed by the full NJC, as the weapon with which to negotiate a pay agreement. Evaluation, said Parry, had been shelved in 1975, but was back on the table and remained central to the union's entire strategy. To ensure that it was not again nullified by pay policy, however, the executive recommended that the union oppose a third phase. Finally, Parry announced that no decision on pay would be taken without again consulting delegates.[33]

All this was endorsed by Conference and, to all intents and

purposes, by the Home Secretary. In his address to Conference Merlyn Rees accepted that the composite job description of a fireman's work

> is bound to be of inestimable value in the discussion which have [*sic*] to take place in what has got to be in the next stage of greater flexibility and a move back to the sort of collective bargaining where the constraints which have been necessary in the last two years are of a different kind.

But the Home Secretary unwittingly misled delegates into believing that union negotiators would have greater latitude to remove the anomalies that two years, of what he himself called 'rough justice', had created. In fact the Treasury wanted a rigid 10 per cent earnings target, and the Prime Minister concurred.[34]

The 10 Per Cent Limit

In July 1977 the Chancellor of the Exchequer, Denis Healey, informed the House of Commons of the 10 per cent limit. An anxious FBU executive urged the Home Secretary to use his influence to ensure that the findings of the evaluation study would not be strangled by this policy. The NJC then set about translating the valuation of a fireman's job into pay terms by appointing a working group under the independent chairmanship of Lord McCarthy. The McCarthy Report recommended that the most appropriate comparison for the purpose of assessing a fireman's value was with 'the generality of jobs in the community'.[35] The union's pay formula was based on this proposal to bring firemen's wages in line with adult male earnings (£78 a week) plus 10 per cent to take account of the range of skills of qualified firemen and the physical dangers involved, or 30 per cent in all. Negotiations on the NJC began in the autumn, with the two sides an ocean apart.

Between 25 October and 3 November the NJC met on three separate occasions. At each meeting the position reached was essentially the same: the employers offered to increase earnings by 10 per cent, in line with the government's guidelines, with continued talks on both a future pay formula and a reduction in the working week from 48 hours to 42. The Home Secretary endorsed these terms, and in fact had initiated discussion on a negotiated reduction of hours in line with the Home Office feasibility study which had appeared in September. Yet he also emphasised that the government would not accept a pay settlement outside the 10 per cent guidelines, and that with the future pay formula, 'The phasing of any further pay increase will have to be considered in the light of circumstances prevailing at the time.' For its part the union refused to moderate its claim, even though the Police Federation had in the meantime accepted an offer of 10 per cent plus an independent inquiry on pay. Instead, the executive decided that the time had come to report back to a Recall Delegate Conference.[36]

Tension had mounted in the fire service during the autumn. In September firemen marched through Manchester and Birmingham in support of their claim; in October it was the turn of demonstrating Liverpool firemen. Strike threats had come from Birmingham, Manchester, Strathclyde and Staffordshire – even from the so-called 'soft underbelly of the South'. Executive council members from some of these regions argued for strike action.[37] Terry Parry, however, continued to argue that a strike represented the will of a militant minority, not that of the membership. His view prevailed. In Eastbourne on 7 November the EC asked the Recall Conference of 300 delegates to approve the continuation of negotiations on pay and hours for a few more weeks, subject to their being reported back to a further delegate conference.

Eastbourne

The executive's motion was challenged by two other motions: one calling for a strike ballot of the wholetime membership, moved by London, and another for a strike to begin on 14 November, moved by Strathclyde. Merseyside threw its support behind the last motion, though initially wanting an immediate strike. Participants confirm that the mood of the Conference was decidedly hostile to the executive's resolution.[38] Many delegates seemingly felt that the general secretary and the new president, Wilf Barber, were out of touch with feelings at the grass roots and too reluctant to challenge a Labour government. If Terry Parry believed he could defuse the strike call by an impassioned address, he must have been stunned by the outcome.

Fewer than twenty hands were raised in support of the executive's proposal. The motion calling for a strike ballot was also rejected, on a card vote, by 21,982 to 17,830. The strike resolution was then moved by Ronnie Scott (Strathclyde), seconded by Terry Fields (Merseyside):

> The Conference agrees to commence strike action as from day-shift Monday, 14 November 1977 in support of a wage claim based on male average earnings plus 10 per cent ... This strike action to be terminated upon the attainment of this claim or the decision of a Recall Conference.

By 25,874 votes to 13,752, a two-to-one majority, the resolution carried.[39] Only one factor, a genuine and widespread sense of grievance, can explain the outcome. London voted against the resolution, but a day later the regional secretary declared that London's 6,000 firemen would give full support to the strike. The executive council offered a dispensation to Northern Ireland, but the province's 500 wholetime firemen decided to join the strike in spite of a threat of an incendiary campaign by the Provisional IRA.[40] No one on the executive could have been left in any doubt about the will of the membership.

The vote was a severe personal blow for the general secretary. He had made no secret of his apprehension of what a strike would mean for the fire service; he had asked for more time to negotiate. But Conference rejected his lead, and then tied the executive's hands tight on the claim for a 30 per cent pay rise. His immediate response, impolitic if, under the circumstances, understandable, was publicly to deplore the strike decision and to recount what had taken place behind the closed doors of the conference. 'We opposed the strike resolution with everything we had,' Parry was quoted as saying by the *Evening Standard*. 'We are not in charge of the situation, I am sorry to say.' He also reported that when he had asked delegates, 'Are you going to let old people's homes burn down, and children's homes, and are you going to let houses burn down and city centres burn down?' he had been greeted with shouts of 'Yes' from the floor. Parry also stated, however, that while against the strike, '... I am general secretary and it is my job to carry it out.'[41] This he did, once the intervening days failed to bring a settlement.

The government was also taken aback by the strike decision. The Cabinet had taken a tough line towards the public sector in the knowledge that it tended to act as pace-setter in pay settlements. If firemen breached the government's defences, council manual workers, power workers and the rest would pour through the gap, or so it was thought. The Prime Minister was taking comfort from the fact that, 'Although the activists had forced the pace at some of the union conferences, not all their leaders were happy that they were following the right path.'[42] Yet here was the FBU throwing down the gauntlet.

Contingency plans had been made but for stoppages in areas where firemen were most militant rather than a nationwide strike. The government reacted quickly by announcing that 9,000 troops and 850 'Green Goddess' appliances, built in the 1950s as part of the civil defence service, would be standing by to take over from the firemen. On the eve of the strike the Home Secretary played the conscience card in a special ministerial broadcast on television and radio. Echoing Terry Parry's words, he said: 'I cannot believe that anyone would allow children's, or old people's homes to burn down around their occupants.' Sub-officer Michael Brown, in charge of Windsor fire station, came up with one of the most quoted retorts: 'We will not turn out even if the Queen is trapped in Windsor Castle.'[43] And so the national ordeal by fire began.

It should be evident from this extended prologue that the firemen's strike was long in the making and that its roots stretched deep into the post-war period. For over ten years the FBU campaigned for a pay scale commensurate with the enlarged skills and duties of the modern firefighter. To this end the union sought NJC endorsement of an evaluation of firemen's work as the basis of a formula for defining future wage settlements that would give firemen a guaranteed position in the wages league. Alas, this strategy fell foul of successive government incomes policies. Time and again the union was informed that any extra payment for new skills and duties would have to fit the Procrustean bed of pay guidelines. The centralised bargaining procedures of the fire service, moreover, contributed to a rigid application of the pay norms of these years. Not for firemen the gratuity of local supplements or wage drift. And the union's ban on overtime, in defence of a shorter working week, unintentionally aggravated this inequity.

Tired of hopes constantly deferred and faced with declining real living standards firemen began to consider an alternative strategy to evaluation studies and pay formulas. The 1973 Glasgow dispute broke the myth that firemen would never put lives and property at risk for money. Since 1973 groups of younger firemen, particularly some associated with the 'rank and file' politics of the far left in the large metropolitan brigades, canvassed the strike as an appropriate weapon of wage bargaining. This strategy gained the day at the Recall Conference because it most defiantly voiced the repressed anger and frustration of ordinary firemen. Yet many, perhaps most, of the delegates knew they had voted for the strike in the hope that the threat alone would suffice to put more money on the table. 'We never believed that firemen would ever strike,' said Bro. Ross (Essex) a year later.

> Even when building our huts and fires we still told ourselves that the government – a Labour government – would bend or give in. We told ourselves that they couldn't seriously weigh the lives of people against an economic policy which had been rigidly applied to the working class while they had done

> nothing to stop prices rising or speculators creating havoc with the pound.

A fireman from Poplar fire station put it more feelingly: 'Even on the night before, I think I said a little prayer that it wouldn't happen. Because we're putting our own families on the line as well.'[44]

The Firemen's Strike

The first national strike of firemen began on Monday 14 November 1977. How the union membership would respond became the question of the day. Firemen had no established traditions of industrial action to draw upon, nor would they receive strike pay. The London branch was sufficiently unsure of its members' response to invoke the closed-shop agreement with the GLC: strike-breaking would lead to loss of union card and hence to loss of job. In fact, the esprit de corps and camaraderie of firemen carried over to the picket lines. Entire watches, men and officers, took up position outside the stations, as formerly they had assembled in the station mess. By nightfall on the first day 98 per cent of the membership were on strike: practically all wholetime firemen, and most control room and retained members.[45] Moreover, the level of support for the strike remained remarkably constant for the next nine weeks, despite financial hardship, the lure of Christmas, bitter winter weather and tugs of conscience. Firemen surprised both union officers and the government, and perhaps themselves, by the enormous solidarity they demonstrated.

The Home Secretary and his colleagues in the firm belief that firemen would find it impossible to remain faithful to a strike that threatened death and destruction, expected the strike to last for days rather than weeks. However much ministers would deny it, their initial strategy was to wait for a couple of well publicised tragedies to shame firemen back to work by public obloquy. Support for this strategy appeared in the shape of Basil Hume, Archbishop of Westminster, who described the FBU's action as

> an intolerable threat to the whole community ... Christians believe that human life has an incalculable value and so are dismayed that the lives of innocent individuals are put at risk in what is seen as a struggle for economic benefits ... It poses acute moral problems for the Christian conscience.[46]

Firemen were certainly defensive, not to say fearful, about the public mood. 'I reckon the public will turn against us once it starts,' one fireman predicted, 'if there's a major fire, if someone gets killed. It could be pretty bad, if there's a backlash.'[47] Firemen would soon be torn, the government estimated, between loyalty to the strike and loyalty to the job.

There was considerable public support, moreover, for holding the line on incomes, particularly as the rate of price inflation fell. 'There is a national revulsion,' proclaimed the *Sunday Times*, 'at the idea that any particular group should benefit from the sacrifices of the last two years, and so jeopardise the possibility of killing inflation.'[48] There was, in addition, a rare political consensus on government policy. In the emergency debate on the strike on 15 November both sides of the House of Commons were critical of the government's 'Maginot line mentality', in James Sillars' phrase, and called on it to be more flexible in its superintendence of the 10 per cent limit. Yet the House backed the Government's stand towards the firemen, with only 58, mainly left-wing Labour MPs voting against. Conservative and Liberal MPs abstained, the latter warning that they would break the Lib-Lab pact if the firemen breached phase three.[49]

The firemen were not without their champions. Gordon Honeycombe, well known as a newsreader with Independent Television News and author of *Red Watch*, a hymn of praise to the fire service, wrote an article in the *Daily Mail* in support of the firemen's claim. He was suspended from broadcasting duties until the end of the strike, but two days later, wishing to speak freely on the issue, he resigned from ITN. A few local authorities – East Sussex and South Yorkshire County Councils and Belfast City Council – called on the government to make firemen a better offer. And the IRA, a dubious ally, resisted the temptation to launch a fire-bombing campaign, which would have put pressure on the strikers to return to work because of its support for the firemen.[50] This somewhat ill-assorted group of supporters, however, hardly seemed likely to deflect the government from its strategy of defeating a small and supposedly faint-hearted union as an example to all other public sector workers.

The Government Miscalculates

A week into the strike, however, it was evident that the government's strategy had misfired. For a start, each new fire demonstrated that the troops, while intrepid and courageous, were desperately inexperienced and ill equipped. Servicemen received only four hours of training in elementary fire-fighting, confined to running out lines of hose and coping with jet reaction. As for equipment, the 'Green Goddess' fire engines were sluggish pumpers and their 30-foot ladders reached only the second storey of most buildings. The government would not allow the troops to use the equipment standing idle behind picket lines at fire stations, partly so not to antagonise strikers (who threatened to black forever any fire engines used during the strike); partly because inadequately trained troops could not handle the more sophisticated appliances; and partly, one suspects, because the government had no power to requisition the equipment without an emergency proclamation, under the Emergency Powers Act (1920), for which parliamentary approval would have been needed. Inevitably, the main technique of the substitute crews was literally to flood buildings with water. When the doors of a large building full of plastics products were opened, according to a fire officer assisting the troops, 'So much water came out one expected Noah's Ark as well.'[51]

Mercifully, fire calls in most parts of the country were far fewer than usual, but indications quickly appeared of the consequences of a shortage of expertise and equipment. On the third day of the strike a fire that burnt out of control all day closed the £70 million Tilbury B power station for nine months. In Newcastle city centre soldiers succeeded in stopping a blaze in a furniture warehouse from spreading to a warehouse of inflammable liquids, but only by borrowing Rentokil's turntable ladder, used normally for spraying pigeon repellant on the roofs of office blocks. In Glasgow troops took eleven long hours to bring a burning warehouse in the Gorbals under control. Forty antiquated appliances and 480 soldiers had replaced the 2,000 full-time firemen in the Strathclyde region, containing Glasgow, whose tall Victorian tenements earned the city the title 'the tinderbox of Scotland'. In Birmingham frightened families living in tower block flats began to abandon their homes and move in with relatives. After only four days, therefore, amid mounting criticism of the emergency service, the government had to send 33 two-man RAF fire teams, with breathing apparatus and metal-cutting equipment, to thirteen cities. Yet the view prevailed, as a fireman's placard stated, outside a Cardiff school the Prime Minister was visiting: 'Merlyn fiddles while Britain burns'.[52]

Secondly, the government badly miscalculated public reaction to the strike. Whether due to fear of the consequences of a prolonged strike, or to sympathy towards the men's low wages, or, most likely, to action of firemen who left picket lines and drove in their own cars to offer help when lives were in danger, public opinion began to move behind the strikers. In the first 24 hours pickets outside Poplar fire station helped fight a fire at St Andrew's Hospital, Bow, during which 90 patients were evacuated; Battersea firemen helped troops fight a blaze on the eighth floor of a block of flats at Clapham Junction. The next day pedestrians and motorists passing the picket lines gave generously to the strike fund. As strikers shed their fear of a public backlash, picket lines that had looked like campfires before a battle took on the appearance of street parties on the pavement.[53]

Two weeks into the strike an opinion poll commissioned by the *Daily Mail* found that 63 per cent of those questioned thought firemen should be treated as a special case and get a rise above the 10 per cent limit. A Gallup poll found a still higher level of approval. Increasing public support for the firemen began to alarm the Cabinet, particularly as the political consensus cracked. Labour Party chairman, Joan Lestor, described the firemen's pay claim as 'a moderate one', and warned the government:

> If, as we are told, we are relying on public opinion to support us, we may be in for a shock. Until the firemen came out on strike most people had absolutely no idea of their work conditions, nor their pay, nor the hazards – mental and physical – associated with the work.[54]

For the Opposition Tory leader Margaret Thatcher said on BBC radio that the government should pay firemen a bit more, while her mentor, Sir Keith Joseph, Shadow Industry Secretary, attacked the policy of holding down pay for 'an undermanned and underpaid essential service'.[55]

Thirdly, the FBU grew more determined and the rank and file more militant as the strike went on. The union authorised members to picket peacefully anyone who attempted to do a fireman's job, but not to interfere with troops brought in to provide fire cover. By the end of the first week, however, Ken Cameron, West Midlands member of the national executive, warned that firemen might soon consider ways of cutting off supplies to the troops by involving other unions. 'There is no such thing as a nice strike,' he declared. Ten days later, in fact, firemen picketed a new army billet in Bootle to stop workmen improving the quarters. Senior officials of the FBU, concerned not to alienate public support for the firemen's case, moved quickly to dissuade the Merseyside strike committee from obstructing the troops.[56] The incident, however, revealed how strikers were beginning to dig in for a long fight.

A more alarming sign of the hardening mood of strikers were the wide rifts which opened between firemen and their officers (at least those who were members of the National Association of Fire Officers), and between wholetime and part-time firemen. Before the strike started NAFO, with 4,000 members, ranging in rank from station officer to assistant chief fire officer, announced that it would adopt a neutral stance towards the strike: its members should not cross picket lines and should act only in advisory capacities to the troops. In practice, NAFO officers played a vital role helping train troops in fire-fighting and accompanying them to fires to give advice on the spot. Some unquestionably assisted with fire-fighting. Firemen were angry at the role played by NAFO officers, and so moved against them by picketing army depots. Relations only worsened when NAFO voted not to go on strike in support of the firemen. A seasonal greeting in a Birmingham fire station window said it all: 'NAFO needs PAXO'.[57]

There was a similar breach in relationships between the FBU and the part-time section of the service. Many of the 16,000 part-timers, 9,500 of whom were members of the FBU and 5,000 of whom belonged to the recently formed rival union, the Retained Fire Fighters' Union, crossed picket lines at fire stations and fires. By mid-December 'flying pickets', operating out of London (particularly Battersea station), Merseyside and Strathclyde, organised by local militant FBU members, were violently confronting part-time strike-breakers in Epping, High Wycombe, and Reigate. Many more wholetime firemen vowed never again to work with the part-timers.[58] Relationships essential to an effective fire brigade were thus damaged, some feared irreparably. Against all government expectations, loyalty to the service, not loyalty to the union, crumbled first.

On all counts, then, the government's strategy was found wanting. Yet for all that, the government held obdurately to its strategy. When the employers met the firemen's leaders on 18 November there was no new pay offer to discuss; the employers simply indicated that an agreement could probably be reached on a future pay formula, if it formed the basis for ending the strike. The union had to make it clear that the strike was about more money now, not future improvements. When later that afternoon the executive council went to see the Home Secretary, he reiterated the government's determination to stick to its pay guidelines. Not even a 'mini-formula' of reducing the working week to

42 hours, with overtime pay for the six hours' difference between 42 and 48 hours, was acceptable to government. In desperation, the union leaders asked for, and were granted, an urgent meeting with the Prime Minister.[59]

Prime Minister Callaghan

In all outward respects James Callaghan was the Prime Minister with whom a firemen's union would most wish to deal. The son of a seaman, Callaghan had served in the navy during the war and was the first trade union official to become Prime Minister. But as Ian Waller of the *Sunday Telegraph* rightly reported,

> the Prime Minister is now so personally committed to battling out the firemen's strike, as a symbol of the government's determination to contain wage increases, that he cannot give in without suffering a damaging blow to his authority.[60]

Callaghan's personal commitment to a reduction in the level of inflation did not bode well for the 29 November meeting.

On 26 November around 10,000 firemen, with their wives and children, marched through London to a rally at Hyde Park, addressed by Joan Lestor and Frank Allaun, chairman and vice-chairman respectively of the Labour Party. During the course of the march a petition of half a million signatures in support of the firemen's action was handed in to Downing Street.[61] Three days' later the full FBU executive returned to Downing Street. It was the first time that Callaghan had intervened in a national strike. At a tense 90-minute session, possibly best described as a confrontation, the premier made it brutally clear that, in order to avoid the knock-on effect of a large firemen's pay settlement, the government could not allow local authorities to depart from the pay guidelines. In what Lou Lewis and Dave Challoner of London region subsequently denounced as a 'God-like' lecture, Callaghan bluntly told the executive: 'Your strike will not win. You cannot be allowed to succeed.'[62]

The only new move was a willingness to consider how a

future pay formula, agreed between the union and employers, could be underwritten by government, 'so that it was not thwarted by some unforeseen adverse change in our economic circumstances'. This did not form the basis on which to recall a delegate conference for the purpose of recommending a return to work.[63] There was nothing left but to seek the help of the TUC in a concerted campaign to break the 10 per cent guidelines and their application as though they had the force of law. It is now clear that this was the decisive issue of the strike. With the considerable public support the firemen enjoyed, and with TUC backing, the FBU was in a position to wreck the government's pay policy; but if the trade union movement did not respond the firemen would be visibly isolated and the strike would almost inevitably collapse.

The TUC

On 2 December the union executive met the Finance and General Purposes Committee, the TUC's 'inner cabinet'. Terry Parry invited the committee to mount a campaign against government inflexibility on pay, in line with TUC policy, which called for 'an orderly return to free collective bargaining'. After five hours spent talking with the firemen Len Murray, general secretary of the TUC, announced the committee's unanimous decision to reject the demand for a campaign against the pay policy. The statement also advised the FBU, in view of the fact that 'the government is not likely to be deflected from its present course of action', to go back and talk to the employers about a reduction in working hours and about the Prime Minister's 'unprecedented offer to underwrite a pay formula which will be sustained even in the event of unforeseen economic difficulties', a phrase lifted from the Downing Street statement.[64]

The TUC line embittered the firemen. 'It was treacherous,' said Lou Lewis. 'We know where we stand now,' said Dave Challoner, 'we are fighting the government and the TUC.' The decision angered other union leaders. Ray Buckton (ASLEF), Ken Gill (AUEW-TASS), Gerry Gilman (SCPS) and George Guy (sheetmetal workers) accused the

TUC of giving tacit support to the government's incomes policy, and indicated their intention of getting the decision rescinded.[65] In fact, the FBU had already decided to challenge the decision at the next meeting of the full TUC General Council on 21 December. But the writing was on the wall. TUC leaders, including those of the biggest unions – Jack Jones (TGWU), Hugh Scanlon (AUEW) and David Basnett (GMWU) – had backed away from a confrontation with the Labour government and left striking firemen to battle on alone for a pay rise in breach of pay policy. Suddenly the odds seemed heavily stacked against the FBU.

After nearly four weeks of strike action the government's resolve to hold to the pay policy seemed firmer than ever. The TUC had snubbed the firemen. Public support was waning: almost 70 per cent now believed that firemen should settle for 10 per cent. Public sympathy began to transfer itself to the soldiers, most of whom earned even less than firemen. The army fire-fighters were proving to be more adept at putting out fires than anticipated; no conflagration had swept through a city, though one suspects that this was due more to luck than management. NAFO officers decided not to strike in support of their pay claim, and strikers faced their first real anxieties about money, since their last cheques (at the end of November) gave them only thirteen days' pay.[66]

The Cabinet Offer

At this critical time for firemen the Cabinet launched a new initiative. The Home Secretary told the NJC on 8 December that if it could agree upon a pay formula the government would be prepared to implement the agreement in two stages, in November 1978 and November 1979, and would guarantee that the phasing-in would not be thwarted by any adverse economic changes, including incomes policy. This was, of course, a slightly refined version of the Prime Minister's earlier suggestion. A day later the employers proposed that firemen's pay be linked, once and for all, to the average weekly earnings of skilled workers, or 'the adult male manual upper quartile figure.' Firemen were offered, in effect, a secure place in the national wages league table. Implementation of the agreement was contingent upon a resumption of normal working and there being no victimisation of strike-breakers. Along with a reduction in working hours, the government considered that this was 'an honourable basis for settling the present damaging dispute'.[67]

The FBU executive had now to decide if the offer was a basis for starting moves to end the strike. That always seemed unlikely. An immediate rise of only 10 per cent would hardly find favour with the men who did not feel that they had been on strike for 'bread today, jam tomorrow'. The proposed pay structure would take two years to come fully into effect. No one could guarantee that the Conservatives would honour the agreement, if and when they took office. Some of the conditions attached to the pay document were seen as particularly objectionable, especially the no-recriminations clause (which threatened the union's right to impose discipline, not to mention the closed shop), and the one requiring immediate working of the full range of duties, including fire prevention, which the union felt was still subject to separate negotiation. 'It's a damn insult', said Dick Foggie, assistant general secretary, 'to ask us to do more work now when we are not going to be paid for it, while we have to wait two years to get what's our due.'[68]

Opinion within the executive was, therefore, strongly in favour of rejecting the offer. After a five-hour discussion, however, it was agreed to let firemen have their say, to circulate branches with details of the employers' pay proposal and to await reports from the union's regional councils.[69] There is little doubt that the executive expected firemen overwhelmingly to reject the offer, and they were not disappointed. A few cracks appeared in the united front of striking firemen; in Leicester firemen voted by 340 to eleven to accept the offer, and acceptance votes came in from several rural areas, including Surrey, Hertfordshire and Bedfordshire. But in Scotland and the major urban and industrial areas of England firemen poured cold water on the deal. Encouraged by the shift in the government's position on future pay, strikers looked forward to the government giving way on the 10 per cent limit.[70]

On 14 December reports from executive council members on their region's response to the pay document, indicated that the majority view of the membership was that the offer did not justify recalling Conference. Thereupon, the executive endorsed this view by ten votes to two, with four abstentions. However, regional councils had not turned down the principle of pay parity with industry, allowing executive moderates to argue for renewing talks with the employers. By thirteen to three the executive voted to seek exploratory talks on the phasing-in of the pay formula, on the 'back-to-work' conditions, and on the possibility of more than 10 per cent immediately.[71]

It could be argued, however, that the firemen were foolish to reject the government's offer, which looked generous in the long term. Certainly, senior trade union figures – Len Murray, Moss Evans (general secretary-elect of the TGWU) – advised the strikers to accept the offer, because of its long-term advantages. Indeed, Moss Evans hailed the formula as a possible basis for pay settlements throughout the public sector.[72] It is also clear that some members of the executive, and numbers of ordinary firemen, now believed they had no chance of breaking through the government's 10 per cent ceiling. The rumour was abroad that any accommodation with the employers, however long the strike, would have to incorporate the three points of their pay document: an immediate 10 per cent, reduced working hours and a pay formula. But firemen on take-home pay of less than £50 could hardly be expected to live in the long term; they wanted something tangible to show for a month of hardship. November 1979, when parity with skilled manual workers would be a fact, was a speck on the horizon; final demands from the gas and electricity boards were as large as life. Hope remained too, of overturning the TUC's refusal to mount a general offensive against the wage guidelines.

On 21 December, in what amounted to a state of siege outside Congress House with 800 striking firemen held back by a five-deep line of policemen, the General Council of the TUC decided by twenty votes to seventeen not to approve a public campaign against the 10 per cent limit. The majority was unexpectedly small, reflecting the dissatisfaction felt by many union leaders with the government's over-rigid pay strategy and with the TUC's inaction. But this was cold comfort for the picketing firemen who reacted angrily to news of the vote. Hoping to hear of TUC support for what would have amounted to a general mobilisation against the government's incomes policy, they found themselves more isolated than ever. The fight went out of a lot of firemen on that day.[73]

Backs Against the Wall

Surrounding events only compounded the FBU's difficulties. Unions representing a million 'dirty-jobs' council workers, originally demanding 30 per cent or more, settled for pay rises within the 10 per cent guidelines. A 're-opener' clause enabled the unions to go back for more if the councils, who also employed the firemen, made pay deals elsewhere above the 10 per cent. The settlement gave a decided boost to the government's effort to hold the line on pay and undermined the firemen's attempt to mobilise support among public sector unions to fight the pay policy.[74] Then suddenly the Department of Health and Social Security clamped down on supplementary benefit payments to strikers' families. A circular advised social security staff to deduct tax refunds from benefit payments, whether or not firemen had received their refunds, and to apply rigidly the rules on 'urgent need' supplements.[75] Divisions in the union also became sharper.

Uncertain how best to pursue the dispute, the executive council agreed to seek again the views of its 30,000 members and to reconvene on 29 December. Firemen braced themselves for a bleak Christmas on the picket lines.[76] In the run up to the 29th a split developed in the strikers' ranks and on the executive council. Terry Fields, executive member for

Merseyside and Cheshire, later told how the failure to get TUC support was a blow

> to those on the executive who were holding the line and arguing that the strike should go on because the big battalions were about to come over the hill ... After the TUC decision we were really laughed out of court on the executive. But we still believed that the grass roots would do something about it.[77]

In keeping with this rank-and-file persuasion, Merseyside firemen planned an inter-union conference in Liverpool to marshall support for one-day stoppages on 16 January, when a mass lobby of parliament was to be held. In contrast, the union's traditionally moderate South-Eastern region mandated its executive member, David Shephard, to press for a recall conference, without which the strike could not end. Firemen were already drifting back to work in Surrey, and Shephard forecast that if his region's demand was not met many more of his 3,000 members could follow their example, for which comment he received the opprobrium of more militant executive members.[78]

On the 29th, however, the executive's backbone was as firm as ever. The proposal to recall the delegate conference was trounced by fifteen votes to one, the latter being that of the South-East area leader. Yet the executive did agree unanimously to seek early tripartite talks with the employers and the government, with a view to ending the dispute.[79]

As these talks got underway in the New Year, the union ran into more flak. In an intemperate outburst, Martin Brannan, chief negotiator for the overwhelmingly Conservative-controlled local authorities, said they were 'fed up to the teeth with the firemen', who for years had wielded the strike threat to get all kinds of benefits. The strike had revealed, he said, that the country could manage with half the present number of firemen. William Whitelaw, Shadow Home Secretary, muddied the waters by declining to commit a future Conservative government to any agreement with firemen which guaranteed immunity from incomes policies. The vultures started to circle: Woodrow Wyatt, newspaper columnist, former Labour MP and champagne socialist, insisted firemen be paid not another penny, since 'their skills are simple and learned in a few weeks', their duties 'arduous only very occasionally'.[80]

In the tripartite talks, firemen's leaders made no headway in attempts to win pay increases above a tenth, and fell back to secure ancillary improvements in the 'non-pay' paragraphs of the employers' offer. Having gained amendment to the 'no victimisation' clause, among others, the executive voted by thirteen votes to three to recall Conference, and to recommend acceptance of the employers' offer, the three 'hold-outs' being Lewis and Challoner of London and Fields of Liverpool. The membership was urged to vote for this recommendation on the grounds that the index-linked pay formula was a substantial and permanent improvement in future pay prospects, and that the strike had forced the government to guarantee this formula against any incomes policy.[81]

Bridlington

It looked as if the firemen's vote on the return-to-work recommendation would be close. Militant firemen from the metropolitan brigades (London, Merseyside and Strathclyde) were mandating their delegates to reject the offer; moderate firemen from the shire county brigades (Norfolk, Leicestershire, Warwickshire) and the South-East desired an end to the strike.[82] In the event, the outcome was less close than expected. At the Bridlington conference on 12 January the 180 delegates from 63 brigades voted 28,729 to 11,795 – a majority of nearly three to one – to call off the strike. Firemen from the militant regions mounted a bitter and violent demonstration outside the conference hall. Terry Parry was barracked and knocked to the ground on his way in; Willie Miller, executive member for Scotland, was punched, kicked and accused of treachery by Scottish firemen as delegates left. The militants, however, had no monopoly on disappointment. 'None of the men', said Dick

Foggie on the eve of the return-to-work, 'is going back thinking he has won a victory ...'[83] Firemen had apparently little tangible to show for nine weeks of industrial action.

As the all-night braziers and the picket huts were removed from station forecourts and 30,000 firemen reported for duty, the first concern for both union and employers was the inevitable backlash against those deemed to have 'blacklegged'. Firemen work in crews; they have to feel they can depend on each other for their lives. The reaction to firemen and officers who had undermined the strike was, therefore, always likely to be more violent than among, say, factory workers. Firemen's anger was intensified when they learnt that those who worked through the strike would get the 10 per cent rise backdated to November 7 – 'a scabs' bonus', as the *News Line* called it. The union had agreed, of course, 'to use their best endeavours' to achieve a smooth return to work, but the phrase was open to more than one interpretation.[84]

In many areas retained firemen, wholetime 'rebels' and NAFO officers were socially ostracised, and in a few places, firemen refused to work with non-strikers before a grudging compromise was worked out. Union officials were still determined, moreover, to institute disciplinary procedures against members who defied strike instructions. In all, 340 wholetime, 1,396 retained and 88 Control members were recommended for expulsion, although an internal disciplinary sub-committee ultimately deprived fewer than 200 members of their union cards. Petty discrimination against NAFO officers persisted in some areas long after the strike; the seven Rhyl strike-breakers were driven out of the fire service by their unforgiving colleagues. But given the bitterness engendered by the dispute, the return-to-work went fairly smoothly, thanks to a desire on the part of most firemen to get on with the job after nine long weeks.[85]

Assessment

Looking back, what were the problems in the FBU's campaign to secure an immediate 30 per cent increase? The activities of the senior officers in advising the military fire-fighters was a major factor in weakening the strike's impact, as was the contribution of those part-time firemen who continued working, 6,000 of whom were not FBU members and 1,000 of whom and more who were. They made it possible for the government to ride out the firemen's strike, since the difference between the civilian and emergency services was not great enough to force the government to give in.

In addition, the union paid the price of spearheading the attack on the government's phase three wage ceiling. Firemen mounted the only sustained and large-scale challenge to a pay policy which was inflexible with regard to the public sector; private sector settlements (notably at Ford, ICI and Midland Lorries) drove a coach and horses through the 10 per cent limit, by way of self-financing productivity deals, some of which were less than genuine.[86]

Firemen also failed to make their dispute the business of the entire labour movement. Having struck a militant posture, the TUC backed down when the firemen called its bluff. The General Council of the TUC betrayed the union by lending considerable tacit support to the very wage limit that Annual Congress had rejected. Moreover, the twelve-month rule (which Congress did accept) compounded the FBU's isolation by delaying many major pay claims into the spring and summer of 1978, by which time firemen had thrown in the towel.[87]

What, finally, of the contentious view, advanced by the more militant firemen and executive members, many of whom were sympathetic to the rank-and-file politics of the Socialist Workers Party and the Workers Revolutionary Party, that the union leadership lacked commitment to a strike the membership had forced upon it. Still smarting from defeat at the Eastbourne delegate conference, the FBU leaders, and Terry Parry in particular, did not, according to this view, act like men conducting an official strike. Rather, in Ronnie Scott's judgement, the executive 'axed [the strike] when we could have won'.[88] By mobilising rank-and-file industrial support it was believed that the union could have defeated the 10 per cent policy. Our reading of the strike leads us to suggest that this view not only does less than justice to Parry's and the executive's unswerving loyalty to the collective decision to strike but also ignores political reality.

Incomes policies laying down pay curbs that seemed to permit no exceptions did tend, at least for a time, to be accepted by the majority of trade unionists and their leaders. Why else were so few groups willing to challenge the 10 per cent limit in the 1977-78 pay round? When firemen decided to confront the government, therefore, they found it difficult to win broader support, and were increasingly isolated. The strike lasted for over two months due to the remarkable solidarity and determination of the firemen. There is little evidence, except in the optimistic bluster of the revolutionary press, to suggest that had firemen held out for just a few days, weeks, months longer, the Labour government would have conceded defeat. It is more likely that a decision to stay on strike would have accelerated the drift back to work in the less militant regions, leading to disunity, demoralisation and a complete loss of industrial influence. The majority on the executive doubtless wished to avoid this denouement. They also recognised that the strike had secured an important advance in the industrial status and pay of firemen.

While the militants viewed the strike's collapse as a sickening defeat, and the mass of firemen returned to work disappointed with the short-term results of the settlement, the FBU leadership, and Terry Parry in particular, knew that the strike had delivered what they had long campaigned for: a formula that permanently linked firemen's pay to that of skilled manual workers.[89] This formula, moreover, calculated firemen's wages in relation to the increase in manual workers' *earnings*, thus allowing firemen to benefit vicariously from wage drift. This new relationship to the pay of skilled workers was the crucial victory of the strike; it allowed firemen to emerge with honour from the traumatic episode of the first national strike in their union's history. The long-term benefits of this index-linked pay agreement have been so pronounced, moreover, that one of the FBU's main tasks since 1979 has been to protect the 'upper quartile' against the Conservative government's attempts to cut the cord that connects firemen to it.

Notes

* I am grateful to Ken Cameron, Dave Higgs, John Saville, Terry Segars and David Shephard for help with this chapter.

1. FBU President, Wilf Barber, *Report of the 55th Annual Conference*, 1978, pp. 4-5.
2. *Hansard*, Vol.939, 15 November 1977, col.325.
3. FBU, *The Fireman's Case*, Modern Records Centre, MSS 21/1045; *Financial Times*, 31 October 1977; *Sunday Times*, 13 November 1977.
4. See *Daily Mail*, 24 October and 11 November 1977; *Daily Telegraph*, 9 November 1977; *Observer*, 13 November 1977.
5. *Daily Mail*, 24 October 1977.
6. *Hansard*, Vol.939, 15 November 1977, col.325 (Kinnock), col.290 (Sillars); *Daily Telegraph*, 9 November 1977.
7. See Richard Hyman, *Strikes*, London 1984, 3rd ed., pp. 200-1; Peter Jenkins, *Mrs Thatcher's Revolution*, Cambridge, Mass. 1988, Ch.1.
8. See FBU, *A Service for the Sixties*: A programme of development for Britain's fire brigades determined by the annual conference of the Fire Brigades Union, Rothesay, 1960. For John Horner's Statement on *A Service for the Sixties*, see Appendix I below.
9. *Hansard*, Vol.939, 15 November 1977, col.326 (Kinnock); FBU, *Branch Officials' Handbook*, introduction, p. 8. See also Graham Johnson, Ch.6 of this volume, p. 217. For Enoch Humphries's own account of this set back, see his 'Reminiscences' below, pp. 376-7. 23 sponsored MPs, including John Horner, signed a motion protesting at the Incomes Policy Bill: W.D. Muller, *The 'Kept Men'? The First Century of Trade Union Representation in the British House of Commons, 1874-1975*, Hassocks 1977, p. 178.
10. FBU, *By What Yardstick*, submission by the FBU to the National Board for Prices and Incomes, 1967, pp. 5-20.
11. National Board for Prices and Incomes, Report No. 32, *Fire Service Pay* (Cmnd. 3287, HMSO, London, 1967) chs.4 & 5. See also, H.A. Clegg, *The System of Industrial Relations in Great Britain*, Oxford 1970, p. 431.
12. See D.M. Shephard, 'Fire Service Pay and Government Pay Policies', Diploma in Labour Studies, Polytechnic of Central London, 1984, p. 13; FBU, *The Fire Brigade Union's Fifty Years of Service, 1918-1968* (1968), introd. by Terry Parry.
13. Parry was quoted in Jeremy Bugler, 'Fire; Ambulance; Pay', *New Society*, 30 October 1969, p. 688. See also, NBPI, *Fire Service Pay*, p. 10; Edward Gregor Murray, 'Trade Unions and Incomes Policies: British Unions and the Social Contract in the 1970s', Ph.D. thesis, Warwick University, 1985, pp. 250-2.

14. *Fixing a Price*, the FBU's Submission to the Committee of Inquiry into the valuation of a fireman's job (Cunningham Committee), pp. 24-7.
15. *Report of the Departmental Committee on the Fire Service* (Cmnd. 4371, HMSO, London, 1970) p. 148. See also FBU, *Backing Britain's Fire Service*, London 1968.
16. Ibid., pp. 150-52.
17. FBU, *Fixing a Price*, passim; *Report of the Cunningham Inquiry into the Work of the Fire Service* (Cmnd. 4807, HMSO, London, 1971) p. 42. The January 1970 pay settlement had included an agreement to continue with the NJC Working Party on the question of the valuation of a fireman's job, in relation to comparable service in outside industry, but no meeting of the working party took place in 1970. The FBU's nominee on the Cunningham inquiry was retired general secretary of the miners, Will Paynter.
18. *Report of the Cunningham Inquiry*, p. 66.
19. *Branch Officials' Handbook*, pp. 10-11.
20. *Report of the 51st Annual Conference*, 1973, p. 87; Jenkins, *Revolution*, p. 14.
21. See Gordon Honeycombe, *Red Watch*, London 1976, pp. 16-17 and 24; Peter Hain, *Political Strikes*, New York 1986, p. 153; Murray, 'Trade Unions and Incomes Policies', pp. 255-56; *National Rank and File Fireman*, 20 July 1977; Advisory Conciliation and Arbitration Service, Report no. 8, *Industrial Relations in the London Fire Service*, 1977, p. 87. For a detailed account of the Glasgow strike by Jim Flockhart, chairman of the Glasgow area executive, and strike leader, see Ch. 12 below. Flockhart's account underlines the antagonism between the Glasgow area executive (indeed, the entire Glasgow membership) and the Executive Council, concerning direct action.
22. *Branch Officials' Handbook*, p. 14.
23. See Jenkins, *Revolution*, pp. 15-17; Hain, *Political*, p. 268; Hyman, *Strikes*, p. 201.
24. Murray, 'Trade Unions and Incomes Policies', pp. 256 & 260.
25. See *Report of the 52nd Annual Conference*, 1975, p. 19, Executive Council's Report, pp. 18-22; FBU, 'Proposed Programme of Action', pp. 1-8. The executive temporarily expelled nine members of the Strathclyde Brigade Committee from the union in 1975 for failing to comply with the decision of Annual Conference: Ronnie Scott, 'The Lessons of the Firemen's Strike', *News Line*, p. 13; Murray, 'Trade Unions and Incomes Policies', pp. 451-52.
26. *Report of the 53rd Annual Conference*, 1976, pp. 6-7 and 32. For Enoch Humphries's decision to present no Presidential Address, see Ch. 11 below, p. 380.
27. Ibid., p. 37.
28. *Firefighter*, February 1978; Murray, 'Trade Unions and Incomes Policies', pp. 555 and 651.
29. See Margaret Thomas, *The Fire Service and its Personnel*, Government Social Survey, SS 417/B (HMSO, London, 1969) pp. 14-18 and 24-29. And cf. David Englander, Ch. 2 above, pp. 108-9.
30. ACAS, *Industrial Relations*, pp. 89-90; Murray, 'Trade Unions and Incomes Policies', pp. 557-59.
31. See Bob Roxburgh's strike memoir in Ch. 13 below.

32. See *Report of the 55th Annual Conference*, 1978, Executive Council's Report, pp. 99-101; *National Rank and File Fireman*, May and July 1977; Executive Council Minutes, 20 July 1977. Both Ronnie Robertson (Strathclyde) and Terry Segars (Essex) were temporarily suspended from office within the union for their association with the rank and file movement, an organisation outside the fire service.
33. *Report of the 54th Annual Conference*, 1977, pp. 27-31. See also *The Qualified Fireman's Job*, as prepared by the National Joint Council Working Party on Job Evaluation, May 1977.
34. Ibid., p. 51; Bernard Donoughue, *Prime Minister. The Conduct of Policy under Harold Wilson and James Callaghan*, London 1987, p. 139.
35. See *Report of the 55th Annual Conference*, 1978, EC Report, pp. 4-5; *Branch Officials' Handbook*, p. 16; *Firefighter*, February 1978, p. 6.
36. See *Fire*: Special Bulletin, 26 November 1977, p. 2; *Guardian* 1 November 1977; Minutes of Executive Council meetings, 31 October, 1 November, 2 November 1977.
37. *Financial Times*, 31 October 1977; *Guardian*, 3 November 1977; personal communication from D.M. Shephard, EC member, South-East Region FBU.
38. See Bill Craig's strike memoir below, p. 424.
39. See Minutes of Executive Council meetings, 6 and 7 November; *Guardian*, 8 November 1977; *National Rank and File Fireman*, 9 November 1977.
40. *Evening Standard*, 8 November 1977; *Sunday Times*, 13 November 1977.
41. Ibid.; *Daily Telegraph*, 8 and 10 November 1977. Peter Rockley, an EC member during the strike, believed Parry to be an effective strike leader: see below, p. 418. In contrast, Spence, an Aberdeen fireman, felt Parry and the EC acted 'like a drag anchor': see below, p. 428.
42. James Callaghan, *Time and Chance*, London 1987, p. 469.
43. See *Sunday Times*, 13 November 1977; *Times*, 11 and 12 November 1977; *Daily Telegraph*, 8 and 14 November 1977; *Guardian*, 14 November 1977. See also *Hansard*, Vol.938, 9 November 1977, col.673.
44. *Report of the 55th Annual Conference*, 1978, p. 76; *Sunday Times*, 20 November 1977. Many firemen could not believe the government would allow a strike to take place: see Paul Kleinman's strike memoir below, pp. 405-6.
45. *Times*, 15 November 1977; *Hansard*, Vol.941, 15 December 1977, col. 349. 35 per cent of the union's 33,000 full-time firemen were covered by closed shop agreements in London, the West Midlands, West and South Yorkshire.
46. *Times*, 16 November 1977. One immediate and tragic consequence of the strike was that, because of the absence of the King's Troop, the Royal Horse Artillery, on fire-fighting duties, the birth of Princess Anne's baby received only one 41-gun salute, instead of the customary two!
47. *Sunday Telegraph*, 13 and 20 November 1977.
48. *Sunday Times*, 13 November 1977 (editorial). See also *Guardian*, 14 November 1977; *Daily Telegraph*, 13 November 1977; *Observer*, 13 November 1977.
49. *Hansard*, Vol. 939, 15 November 1977, cols. 289-354, at col. 292 (Sillars); *Daily Telegraph*, 16 November 1977.

50. *Daily Mail*, 14 November 1977; *Guardian*, 17 and 21 November 1977; *Times*, 17 November 1977; *Fire*, 26 November 1977, p. 7.
51. See Hain, *Political*, pp. 154-55; Keith Jeffery and Peter Hennessy, *States of Emergency. British Governments and Strikebreaking since 1919*, London 1983, p. 242; *Daily Telegraph*, 18 November 1977.
52. See *Sunday Times*, 20 and 27 November 1977; *Daily Telegraph*, 12 and 18 November 1977; *Birmingham Mail*, 11 November 1977; *Daily Express*, 19 November 1977.
53. *Daily Telegraph*, 16 November 1977; *Times*, 16 November 1977. There were a few lighter moments: at Abingdon FBU pickets helped soldiers to extinguish a fire at their local pub, opposite the fire station! Two firemen collecting for the strike fund in a North London pub were on hand to help a stripper doing a fire dance, whose G-string caught fire. We owe this tit-bit to the intrepid journalism of the *Sun*, 21 November 1977.
54. *Daily Mirror*, 19 November 1977; *Daily Telegraph*, 24 November 1977.
55. *Daily Telegraph*, 19 November 1977; *Daily Mail*, 21 November 1977.
56. See Minutes of EC meeting, 9 November 1977; *Birmingham Evening Mail*, 19 November 1977; *Birmingham Post*, 21 November 1977; *Daily Mail*, 1 December 1977; *Times*, 1 December 1977; Terry Fields, 'Lessons', *News Line*, p. 19. *News Line* was put out by the All Trades Unions Alliance, the industrial section of the Workers Revolutionary Party.
57. See Minutes of EC meeting, 8 November 1977; *Birmingham Post*, 21 November 1977; *Times*, 18 and 19 November 1977; *Guardian*, 19 November 1977; *Sunday Times*, 20 November 1977. For the anger aroused by NAFO officers, see James Alexander's strike memoir below, p. 435. It should be emphasised that officers who were members of the FBU, as opposed to NAFO, came out on strike. For a discussion of the conflict between the FBU and NAFO, see A.I.R. Swabe and P. Price, 'Multiunionism in the Fire Service: A Burning Issue?', *Research Working Paper*, no. 18 (Central London Polytechnic, 1982), pp. 4-7. Individual fire chiefs could be supportive. Peter Darby, London's fire chief, visited picket lines frequently, and openly admitted that his sympathies were with his men: *Daily Mail*, 31 December 1977.
58. See *Guardian*, 17 November 1977; *Economist*, 19 November 1977, p. 110; *Sunday Telegraph*, 18 December 1977; *Daily Strike News* (National Rank & File Fireman), 15 November 1977; *Guardian*, 14 and 19 December 1977. See also R.G. Puffitt, 'The Fire Service', *Local Government Studies*, Vol. 5, March-April 1979, p. 118. For a wider discussion of the attitude of the Retained Firefighters' Union to the strike, see Swabe and Price, 'Multiunionism', pp. 9-10.
59. Minutes of EC meetings, 17, 18 and 28 November 1977; *Hansard*, Vol. 939, 21 November 1977, cols. 1100-1101 and 1108; *Economist*, 19 November 1977, p. 110.
60. *Sunday Telegraph*, 27 November 1977. See also Jenkins, *Revolution*, pp. 24-6.
61. *Sunday Times*, 27 November 1977; *Firefighter*, February 1978, p. 11. The FBU also placed advertisements in the national press on November 23 and produced a 4-page leaflet entitled *The Fireman's Case* in support of its claim.
62. *Times*, 29 and 30 November 1977; *News Line*, 29 and 30 November 1977. Cf. Pete Rockley's strike memoir below, pp. 419-20, which confirms

Callaghan's steely resolve to enforce the pay guidelines.
63. Minutes of EC meeting, 29 November 1977; *Times*, 30 November 1977; *Daily Mail*, 30 November 1977.
64. Minutes of EC meeting, 2 December 1977; *News Line*, 3 December 1977; *Times*, 3 December 1977; *Daily Mail*, 3 December 1977.
65. *Daily Telegraph*, 3 December 1977; *Sunday Telegraph*, 4 December 1977; *Times*, 14 December 1977.
66. See *Times*, 6 December 1977; *Daily Mail*, 6 and 7 December 1977; *Economist*, 10 December 1977, p. 86.
67. See Minutes of EC meeting, 8 December 1977; *Hansard*, Vol. 940, 8 December 1977, cols. 1651-52 (Rees); *Daily Express*, 9 December 1977; *Daily Mirror*, 9 December 1977; *Guardian*, 10 December 1977; *Daily Telegraph*, 10 December 1977.
68. *Hansard*, Vol. 940, 8 December 1977, col. 1657 (Kinnock); *Birmingham Post*, 9 December 1977; *Sunday Times*, 11 December 1977.
69. Minutes of EC meeting, 9 December 1977; *Times* 10 December 1977; *Observer*, 11 December 1977.
70. See *Guardian*, 13 December 1977; *Daily Telegraph*, 13 and 14 December 1977; *Birmingham Post*, 14 December 1977; *Daily Express*, 14 December 1977; *Times*, 12 and 14 December 1977.
71. Minutes of EC meeting, 14 December 1977; *Guardian*, 15 December 1977; *Sunday Times*, 18 December 1977.
72. *Guardian*, 13 December 1977.
73. *Daily Telegraph*, 22 December 1977; *Daily Mail*, 22 December 1977. See Paul Kleinman below, p. 413, for the sense of having being betrayed by the General Council of the TUC.
74. *Daily Mirror*, 20 December 1977; *Daily Mail*, 20 December 1977.
75. *Daily Telegraph*, 19 and 20 December 1977. On 20 December the Social Security Minister, Stan Orme, admitted that his department had been wrong to delay benefit payments to firemen's families: *Daily Telegraph*, 21 December 1977. Some firemen preferred resignation from the fire service (particularly men with ten years' service or more) rather than accept another unsatisfactory pay offer. Nearly 1,000 had resigned during the seven-week strike: *Daily Telegraph*, 24 December 1977.
76. Minutes of EC meetings, 19 and 20 December 1977; *Times*, 21 December 1977. Conservative MP, Mr Winston Churchill, launched a Christmas appeal for servicemen on fire-fighting duty, an act of humanity he never thought fit to extend to firemen on duty on subsequent Christmases.
77. Terry Fields, 'Lessons', *News Line*.
78. Minutes of EC meeting, 20 December 1977; *Evening Standard*, 29 December 1977; *Times*, 29 December 1977; *Daily Mail*, 29 December 1977.
79. Minutes of EC meeting, 29 December 1977; *Morning Star*, 30 December 1977; *Guardian*, 30 December 1977.
80. *News Line*, 3 January 1978; *Daily Telegraph*, 3 and 4 January 1978; *Sunday Mirror*, 1 and 8 January 1978. Whitelaw argued throughout the strike that firemen, like policemen and the armed forces, should relinquish the right to strike, in return for an agreed position in the earnings table: *Daily Telegraph*, 24 November 1977; *Times*, 10 December 1977.
81. Minutes of EC meeting, 5 January 1978; *News Line*, 6 January 1978;

Guardian, 6 January 1978; *Financial Times*, 6 January 1978.
82. See *Times*, 7, 9 and 11 January 1978; *Sunday Times*, 8 January 1978; *Guardian*, 7, 10 and 11 January 1978; *Daily Express*, 10 January 1978.
83. *Times*, 13 January 1978; *Guardian*, 13 and 16 January 1978; *Daily Telegraph*, 13 January 1978. Pete Rockley describes the intense disappointment felt by many firemen at the Bridlington decision: see below, p. 422.
84. *News Line*, 9 January 1978; *Sunday Times*, 15 January 1978.
85. See *Daily Telegraph*, 14 and 16 January 1978; *Daily Mail*, 20 and 23 November 1978; R.G. Puffitt, 'The Fire Service', p. 119; FBU, 'Internal Discipline Sub-Committee Report', supplied by D.M. Shephard. Kleinman suggests that the threatened backlash against the scabs never materialised: see below, p. 414.
86. David Coates, *Labour in Power? A Study of the Labour Government 1974-1979*, London 1980, pp. 76-7. Firemen felt so shabbily treated by the government that many, particularly in Durham and Yorkshire, stopped paying the political levy to the Labour Party: Minutes of E.C. meeting, 20 December 1977; *Daily Telegraph*, 16 January 1978.
87. Ibid., p. 75; *Report of the 55th Annual Conference*, 1978, pp. 77-9.
88. Scott, 'Lessons', *News Line*, p. 15.
89. For other judgments on the effects of the strike, see below, p. 384 (Humphries), p. 436 (Alexander), and p. 415 (Kleinman).

9 Terry Parry: A Profile

John Saville

Terence Parry – always known as Terry – was born in Coniston in the Lake District, in 1921. The family was poor, and at the age of fifteen he joined the Blue Funnel line sailing out of Liverpool. During the Second World War he served in the Royal Navy in the Pacific and in the seas around Burma. Immediately on demobilisation he joined the fire service at Sutton Park, near Birmingham. This was in February 1946 and very soon he became district secretary of No. 7 region. In 1949 he was elected executive committee member for No. 7 region, and ten years later he became president of the union. When John Horner retired in 1964 (in order to enter the House of Commons), Terry Parry stood successfully for the position of general secretary and he held this position until his own retirement in September 1980.

He was a big man physically, possessed of a considerable speaking style and a characteristically dry wit. His jokes, good and bad, reverberated around the FBU, retold both at union conferences and in fire stations. One of the most quoted was the story of the cross-eyed javelin thrower who didn't win many medals but who kept the crowd on its toes. It is not wholly clear when Parry became political, but it must have been during his early years in the union when John Horner was rebuilding the organisation after the very rapid decline in membership when the war ended. At the time that Parry joined the FBU the union was losing its wartime auxiliaries at a weekly rate of thousands, and scores of branch secretaries and regional officials were leaving. The job market after 1945 was booming, and while many of the newly demobilised came into the FBU, larger numbers soon left for what they hoped were better prospects. The disciplinary stupidities and the daily chores not connected with fire-fighting repelled many, and it was this background that provided the opportunities for Terry Parry's rapid promotion within the FBU. He was highly intelligent, of course, and very shrewd, but as he himself said at the 1981 Conference which gave him such a splendid send-off into retirement, he had never thought of being a trade union official at any level when he first joined, but you only had to open your mouth wide once, and you were branch secretary. He continued:

> It was a rough old time in fire service conditions. We have a long history of these struggles, with marches, protests, rallies, and we never did them on a fine day, at least not one that I can remember. I bought a new bespoke overcoat – that is to say I got it on tick – I turned out with these Tommy Farr shoulders, you know, on the march in 1950 from Hyde Park Corner to Trafalgar Square, and it bloody well poured down every inch of the way. I gave the overcoat away shortly after that because it was just impossible, and every march has been the same. But we have come a long way. We issue standard kit now – oilskins, sou'westers and wellies – so we are all right.

Parry joined the Communist Party in the early 1950s, and left it at the same time as John Horner, in 1956.

During the 1950s Terry Parry became a passionate advocate of nuclear disarmament, and it was in his first presidential address to the union in 1960 that he spoke eloquently of his opposition to nuclear weapons. 'I don't want Britain to own nuclear weapons,' he said. 'I don't want Britain to be a party to the building up of NATO nuclear weapons. I don't want American nuclear weapons in Britain at all.'[1] It was at this same conference that John Horner introduced *A Service for the Sixties* in a brilliant speech which summarised the ideas and proposals which were to make such a qualitative change in the long run to the working conditions within a highly technical fire service.[2]

Terry Parry had become the obvious candidate for the position of general secretary when John Horner announced his retirement in 1964. Horner was a very big man to follow – in all respects – and it could not have been easy in the early days for Parry. But his abilities shone through and he quickly established a respected position in the wider trade union movement. He had been attending the annual conferences of the TUC since 1950, and five years after he became general secretary of the FBU in 1969 he was elected a member of the General Council of the TUC. The FBU was a small union, and for a representative of the unions at the smaller end of the scale to be elected was a remarkable tribute to the recognised qualities of the man. His record of service on the General Council was impressive. He served on all the major committees of the TUC, including the Finance and General Purposes Committee, the Economic Committee and the International Committee. He chaired the TUC Social Insurance Committee for eight years, his especial interests being child benefits and the 1974 Act which established the Health and Safety Commission on which Parry served from its inception.[3]

Life for the national officials of the FBU in the 1960s and 70s was not easy. The previous chapter examined the mounting discontent within the fire service over wages and conditions which culminated in the 1973 strike in Glasgow. The strike remained unofficial and unrecognised by the national executive, but the support it received undoubtedly strengthened the hands of Parry and his colleagues in the next round of negotiations. Difficulties continued, however, and the years leading up to the 1977 strike were increasingly troubled. Parry himself supported the TUC's acceptance of the Social Contract, but there was a growing number of local and regional disputes between FBU branches and management. In July 1977 Denis Healey, the Chancellor of the Exchequer, announced a rigid 10 per cent earnings target; and this was the maximum for the employers. It made the current negotiations in which the FBU were involved impossible, and the FBU executive came under very strong pressure from the rank and file. Terry Parry himself continued to believe, right up to the decision to take strike action, that firemen would never take industrial action on a national basis, of the kind that would leave the country without a professional fire service. He argued to the last that a national strike did not represent the will of the majority of the membership but was the policy of a minority of militants of the left. He was wrong. On 7 November 1977 Terry Parry delivered an impassioned speech at Eastbourne, in favour of an executive committee resolution which called for the continuation of negotiations on pay and hours of work. It was, without question, the most traumatic episode in the whole of his trade union life, as the EC resolution was overwhelmingly defeated on a show of hands. A strike ballot was rejected on a card vote of a not very large majority; but a resolution calling for an immediate national strike was carried by a two-to-one majority.

Parry must have been devastated, for the possibilities of catastrophe in some major incident were always in his mind. But as everyone recognised, if not at the time then later, once the decision was taken Parry then worked within the resolution which Conference adopted. Throughout the strike he acted as a trade union leader should, and he used his considerable capacities to support the strike, to keep the union together and to continue to press for negotiations which would satisfy his members. The government remained obdurate, the TUC refused to back the firemen and the deadlock was broken, or begun to be broken, by Merlyn Rees, the Home Secretary. Merlyn Rees came down hard on the employers in the matter of a new pay formula whereby a fireman's wage would be linked with the upper quartile of the male manual workers' wage. The agreement was to be spread over two years and certain of the conditions for the return to work were only agreed after further discussion, often of a markedly hostile kind.

Parry remained desperately conscious of the effect on public opinion of any major fire incidents, although the disciplined and principled behaviour of the firemen during the strike suggested that in a really critical situation help would have been forthcoming. At the time of the return to work, agreed to by the Recall Conference, he was bitterly attacked – on one occasion physically assaulted – for what was regarded as a 'sell-out' by the militant sections of the membership. At the time it can be agreed that there were many problems which had to be worked through at ground level, and it was only in the medium and the long term that the pay formula has come to be appreciated as the bedrock upon which the status, and the stature, of working firemen has been preserved, leaving more opportunities for negotiations on issues such as working conditions and the like.

Parry went on until the autumn of 1980 before he retired with the warm gratitude of his members for his very long service. He had been a member of the Fire Service National Joint Council since 1950 and a member of the Central Fire Brigades Advisory Council since 1952. He represented the TUC at the International Labour Organisation (ILO) on a number of occasions, and he had been involved at many points with the international trade union movement. A year before the national strike he was awarded the CBE, and in his last year as general secretary of the FBU he was also chairman of the 1980 TUC. He was a good chairman, said Len Murray: 'He kept that Congress moving.'

The 1981 conference of the FBU was the occasion for a number of presentations to be made to Terry Parry, including life membership of the union. Parry himself made a reply, and one statement summed up his philosophy:

> I am proud of the way in which in the FBU we have played our part in the post-war politics. We never did duck post-war politics. We have had all kinds of things hurled at us. 'Tools of Moscow' ... 'Reds under the beds' and all those things, but we have fought our part in this fire service in the broader political field, this union, as well as fighting also in the interests of firemen. We have been against racialism, against fascism, anti-nuclear weapons, against aggression, against exploitation, against unemployment; we have been very, very strict and must remain so on all these issues, on the neutrality of the fire service in civil disturbances – we are not being used on that score. Also, and I am not saying anything that is not union policy, we must see that we are very careful the way we are brought in at any time when there is incendiary, in civil

> disturbances, wherever – in Northern Ireland, Brixton or anywhere else – that the firemen are protected. We are not sticking our blokes in for a good hiding and to be maimed. Indeed, in those situations it is a neutral role, along with these other things we have fought, and may we always do this.

And then in typical Terry Parry style, he followed this solemn and serious statement with this:

> After leaving the fire service and becoming the general secretary I used to have a particular nightmare which got me up a few times in a bit of a cold sweat. That was that the bells had gone on [for an alarm] and I did not know where my fire kit was, which was not an unusual situation, actually! However, that was my nightmare and I am very pleased to say that I do not have it any more; I just wake up now believing I am at an Executive Council meeting.

Like so many trade union officials, full tribute was very properly paid, by Parry himself, and by his colleagues, to his wife Doris. He had married during the war. 'We have two children, both married, and she brought them up almost on her own. She has suffered more for this union than I have.'

The wives (and children) of active trade unionists are often forgotten: the women are the unsung heroines of the labour movement. It was the same with John Horner who together with Parry shared just over forty years as general secretary. With Horner, who also married during the war, his wife Pat was a constant source of love and support and shrewd advice throughout his industrial and political life. Doris Parry likewise provided Terry with the spiritual sustenance – although she would not have recognised it as that – which provided succour and encouragement in the dark hours which come to any and every working-class leader.

Terry Parry is a man to be remembered, and not only by his own union, but certainly and above all by the firemen of Britain whose interests he served so devotedly and for so many years. He lived only a short time in retirement, bearing an illness which caused him at times great pain with good humour and courage. He died on 15 April 1982, and he deserves to be remembered in the words of his favourite quotation:

> Then let us pray that come it may
> As come it will for all that,
> That Sense and Worth, o'er all the Earth
> May be agreed, and all that,
> For all that, and all that,
> It's coming yet for all that,
> That man to man, the world o'er
> Shall brothers be for all that.

Notes

1. *Firefighter,* July 1960, p. 5.
2. See Appendix I below for John Horner's Statement, *A Service for the Sixties.*
3. See obituary in *Times,* 16 April 1982.

III Memoirs

10 Recollections of a General Secretary

John Horner

I locked the door and walked down to where I had left my bike at the foot of the stairs. I then rode home to my wife and our new baby. The room, shut for weeks, had been stuffy and dirty, for the Shoreditch end of the City Road before the war was a grotty place. Most of the space in the office had been taken up by a large table, on one side of which there used to sit the general secretary facing the assistant secretary behind the union's single typewriter. There was no filing cabinet and I guessed that the untidy pile of papers on the table comprised years of correspondence. A small safe stood in one corner; four chairs were lined up against one wall.

The day before I had driven Holloway's pump back from a damping down job, to be met by the station officer saying that a Mr Willis had tried to ring me. When I had spoken to this gentleman I was to report to him. I did so. I told him that I had been elected general secretary of the Fire Brigades Union. He replied that headquarters had already been so informed by Mr Willis and that their instructions were that I was to be relieved from duty 'for the time being'. I was to have my dinner and then 'get away home'.

When I saw Mr Robert Willis at the offices of the London Trades Council next day, he handed me the key and advised me to keep away from the Reds.

I never really wanted to be general secretary. I had come back to England in 1933 to sit for my second mate's ticket.

Successful, I was qualified to act as second officer on any deep-sea going British ship. Unfortunately there were no ships. I had returned to a Britain sunk in the depths of the world economic depression, with three and a half million unemployed, a cruel and lasting slump in shipping and the Means Test. Without a job and means tested at 9s. 6d. (45p), rising six foot at fourteen stone and with a horse's appetite, I was determined not to live off my navvy father's meagre and uncertain earnings. Someone told me that service in the Royal Navy was a recommendation for a job in the London Fire Brigade. My qualifications might not be 'RN', but I would put them to the test. Thus, I joined what to me seemed a dry land branch of the Navy. Of the intake of my training school, I was the sole recruit who was not an ex-matelot.[1] The maximum age of recruitment long fixed at 31 years was designed to dovetail in with the periods of naval service. Thus, a naval rating starting his twelve year term of man's service at eighteen was ripe for entry into the brigade at the age of 30. At 21 I was the baby of my drill class, the 'sprog' in naval parlance – 'young Johnnie'.

The Deputy Chief Officer by whom I was interviewed went by the splendidly apposite name of Commander Sir Aylmer Firebrace, RN, hero of Jutland, gunnery officer on *Centurion* during that battle. For many years it had been the practice for London to engage commissioned officers from the armed forces for the post of 'Principal' officer. No fireman could rise beyond the rank of superintendent. These 'principals' were frequently drawn from the Navy and some years before I joined, the job of Chief Officer had actually gone to a retiring admiral!

When I passed out of the training school Firebrace sent for me. I loved examinations, I was a great show-off and I had registered 100 per cent in all subjects. He told me I was to be attached to headquarters, and in due course, after passing the sub-officers' examination I would be placed in the 'zone' of accelerated promotion. He had heard that I had a propensity for sky-larking; he warned me against it. He would be receiving regular reports on my progress. My parents were thrilled.

I earned the sobriquet of 'big-headed bugger', when it was discovered that my brass helmet was too small. In fact, there was no helmet in store of my size and in despair the workshop tinsmith inserted a gussett in my helmet and hid the ugly seams under the crossed axes of the frontal badge. My heart sank when I tried the object on. Its elongation had made it look like an inverted, misshapen coal scuttle. It was a joke, but it was to be mine for all my years of service. Unless ... principal officers had silver helmets – made to measure. As I removed that ugly abortion from my head ambition stirred.

How was it, then, that after only six years my fire service career was coming to an abrupt end; that from being a blue-eyed big-head at HQ I had found myself second line pump driver at a station 'out in the sticks' reserved for old timers?

It was an odd story. The FBU was an odd union. The London Fire Brigade was an odd outfit. I suppose I was a bit of an oddity myself.

* * *

In reality the FBU was but one third of a union. Two thousand of its members were employed by the London County Council which refused to recognise it. Indeed, union recognition was not conceded by the LCC until 1948. The other thousand members were scattered over a dozen and a half 'professional' brigades in London's suburbs with a residue spread thinly over a handful of small provincial brigades. There was little scope for further recruitment since almost all major fire brigades were then adjuncts of police forces, and as police constables, 'fire bobbies', were prohibited by law from joining a trade union. The strike of the Metropolitan Police in 1918 had led to the destruction of the National Union of Police and Prison Officers, the dismissal of its leaders and the forcing upon policemen of a toothless Federation in place of their militant union.

London firemen had been caught up in those upheavals. Many had joined a union to form a branch of the National

Union of Corporation Workers (NUCW). Led by their park-keeper branch secretary, Jim Bradley, they had then broken away from the NUCW (later NUPE), to form a separate Firemen's Trade Union. Like the Metropolitan Police, London's firemen were seething with discontent. Their wages, too, had been slashed by wartime inflation. They demanded pay increases and a relaxation of their oppressive continuous duty system; they got police pay and a 72-hour week. But when Bradley sought recognition for his FTU the government appointed a commission to adjudicate on his claim. Instead of recognition, Sir George Askwith, the commission's chairman, with the Police Federation as his model, awarded London's firemen a 'Representative Body'. The 'RB', as it came to be known, was 'prohibited absolutely from engaging in any kind of industrial action or from inducing its members to withhold any of their duties or from interfering in any way with methods of management or discipline or Brigade Regulations, but to concern itself solely with conditions of service and the welfare of the brigade'.[2] Only firemen and sub-officers could be members of this body. However, if it were so desired the 'RB' might choose a 'Spokesman' who need not be a serving fireman.

Jim Bradley got himself appointed 'Spokesman', and then saw to it that the committee of the RB doubled up as the London branch committee of the FTU. Everyone in fact proceeded to wear two hats. The London firemen continued their membership of the union (contribution four pence per week), while the RB conducted its own affairs without interference from the union. I was to be the last 'Spokesman of the London Fire Brigade'.

Few London members of the union took any interest in the affairs of 'outside' brigades since nothing that could happen in any other brigade could possibly influence them in London. There was no union journal, no link to bind the branches together. In Birmingham, the largest of the non-police brigades, the union could make no headway against the Conservative council's anti-trade union policies. So, five years before I joined, to show the union flag the FBU annual conference was held in that city. It consisted of eleven delegates, four of whom came from the LFB. With the Executive Council members and officials, the total attendance was nineteen. The annual report of the Executive makes no mention of the London Branch (not even its membership figure is given), and no specific reference to London was made throughout Conference, which concluded at 3 o'clock in the afternoon. The union flag flew limp in Birmingham.

In my early days of membership the FBU as such was no more than a strange, alien element within the life of the LFB. If later, as Spokesman, I were inadvertently to address a letter to the Chief Officer on union notepaper, it would be returned with a polite request that it would need to be retyped on RB notepaper before it could be received.

The autonomy of the RB in its own affairs was never challenged. Equally London never sought to dominate the collection of small branches which made up the rest of the union – that is until 1939, when enough members in London decided that it was I who should unlock that dusty room in City Road.

It was an insular, disjointed, lop-sided and deeply divided union which I had been elected to lead.

* * *

Orphaned, my father was brought to London from their Essex village by his elder brothers, all seeking work. So at the age of thirteen he started a life of hard manual labour. He was to remain an illiterate navvy until, his strength failing him and no longer able to work, he simply died. I remember him as a powerful, muscular man, constantly in search of work, honest and shy. We had little to say to each other. He had married my mother when she was 'in service'. With her I could talk, and she would talk to me. She brought up three hefty sons and a daughter in a tiny two-up two-down cottage in a back street in Walthamstow. She lived in that house for 53 years.

The baby of the family, and bright at the elementary school, I won a scholarship to an ancient grammar school.

Navvying was poorly paid and with spells of unemployment my parents were hard put to keep a large and rapidly growing youth at what they thought was a 'posh' school. Conscious that there would be no money to see me through university, the headmaster proposed to ease the burden on my parents by instituting cramming sessions for me so that I might squeeze into a single academic year the curricula of my last two scheduled years at school. It was a horrible grind and a miserable way to end my school days. But I matriculated as the headmaster said I would. He then set about to find me a job.

I left school with romantic ideas of becoming a journalist, of travelling the world as a foreign correspondent. The headmaster's efforts on my behalf landed me not in Fleet Street – my Street of Adventure – but in Brompton Road, Knightsbridge, to become a junior trainee buyer for Harrods, then as now the most famous store in the world, the most opulent, the most expensive, the most snobbish. Only the 'best people' shopped at Harrods. The proficiency I had displayed in Spanish would lead me to being seconded to the buying house of Harrods BA, the subsidiary in Buenos Aires, then the Paris of the Southern hemisphere. It was a prize appointment – the gateway to a prime career in commerce. My mother was thrilled. My headmaster congratulated me (and I think himself).

My new colleagues were friendly and helpful, the senior buyer under whose direction I was to start my career in trade the kindest of men. After a week or two in which I was free to wander around the opulent store in Knightsbridge in the wake of various morning-coated shopwalkers 'just to get the feel' of the place, my principal took me to Manchester to watch the making of expensive poplins he was commissioning for the shirts of well-to-do Argentinian gentlemen. I, who had never spent a night away from home alone, was a guest in a hotel at the firm's expense. My mother was overwhelmed.

My salary was generous and of actual work I had little to do. In the evenings I attended a local Quaker educational centre where I argued with my fellow students about what was wrong with the world and how we should set it right. Ever since the defeat of the General Strike in 1926 I had been filling my head with ill digested ideas of radical socialism. At Friends' Hall I found young Christian pacifists, members of the Independent Labour Party and a sprinkling of Communists. The blend of youthful idealism thus produced went ill with the luxury and ostentatious display at Harrods, and the prospect of a career of buying silk and poplin shirtings for Argentine millionaires began to revolt me. To the dismay of my mother and to the puzzlement of my buyer I resigned. I had stuck it for just a year.

At Harrods I must have been an awkward self-opinionated young man, yet when nearly thirty years later I left the Communist Party in a blaze of abusive hostility from the tabloid press, Mr White, the buyer under whom I started my brief career in commerce, sent me a kind letter of encouragement. He had remembered his young and voluble 'bolshie' junior.

I went away to sea in tramp steamers, and of those years I have written elsewhere.[3]

* * *

It was a year or two before I realised how conservative, how rooted in the past, was the London Fire Brigade. In the nation's fire service (such as it was) we Londoners were derisively dubbed 'Round Threads', for while any brigade of substance employed, as standard equipment, the instantaneous hose coupling introduced fifty years earlier, stubbornly the LFB would have none of this simple easy device. Instead we clung to the slower, age-old screw coupling ('round threaded' to protect the edges of the threads from rough usage). The blinding revelation that in the event of war reinforcing brigades working in London would not be able to join their hoses to ours required the miles of emergency hose supplied by the Home Office, already in store at our stations, to be returned to the manufacturers. 'Round Thread' has continued for many years to denote a member of the pre-1939 LFB. I am one of the last of that dwindling band.

In 1866 Sir Eyre Massey Shaw, London's infamous Chief Officer, had written: 'Seamen are the best material from which to make firemen. They are already trained to instant obedience, they are used to working at heights, and to handling ropes and such like tackle and, above all, are accustomed to shipboard life with its long hours of duty and its isolation.'

Docile material indeed, to serve in the closed, confined community life of a fire station with their families, and only free from the tyranny of the bell on every fifteenth day of duty. But hardly the stuff from which to build a trade union.

We still wore the quaint round hats of the mid-Victorian navy, and a recent suggestion that this headgear might be replaced by a peaked cap had been rejected by the lower deck. With its brass buttons, its long wide-skirted tunics and a man's brigade number set out in brass and enclosed by a yellow circle in his left breast, the uniform derived directly from the Thames Watermen of the late seventeenth century, after the Great Fire London's first organised firefighters. In the words of command, the design of our appliances, in the watch system, the canvas hammock – like 'trestles' – which we used for 'resting', the sea chests for our kit, in the lingo of the 'Andrew' as they called the Navy, generations of recruits had been accustomed to perpetuating the tradition of the disciplined uniformed service they had just left in the enclave of the disciplined, uniformed LFB.

The headquarters in which I now served was an old rambling, up-and-down range of buildings adapted from an ancient workhouse. When forming his brigade in 1865 Massey Shaw had lighted upon this grim place in dingy Southwark Bridge Road, strategically close to three of the Thames bridges. The living space of the paupers was converted to accommodate firemen and their families, and their burial ground into a drill yard. Long after, if the old cobblestones of the yard were dug up to repair a gas main or a drain, a pauper's bones might be disturbed. Even today, when what remains of the old place is in use as a recruiting centre, the left-hand desk just inside the door of the main office hides a trap in the floor which on being lifted reveals the tablet on the grave of a workhouse master who wished to be buried with his wards – a last, most un-Dickensian wish – so many years ago. I frequently did patrol duty in the vestibule, along the passage from that grave, where all visitors to HQ were required to register. On the wall above my head the visitor would be confronted by a large stuffed dog in a glass case, its tablet reading:

Stop me not, but onward let me jog,
For I am Chance, the London firemen's dog.

Chance, who would run alongside the horses of the leading steamer, barking all the way to the fire, was fatally injured by a falling wall in 1892.

But it was the brass helmet which for me epitomised the hidebound traditions of the LFB. Polished every day and after every fire, the crown might become worn dangerously thin by generations of elbow grease, since a helmet could have previously served more than one fireman throughout his entire service. Heavy and cumbersome, awkward in confined spaces, it provided little protection. Since the dawning of the age of electricity the high crest with its splendid embossed dragon, had been a constant danger to the wearer. This handsome object, to all Londoners the noble symbol of their gallant firemen, embodied for me all that was innately conservative about the brigade. Our insularity was safeguarded by refusing to recruit any fireman or officer serving in another brigade. There was a unique flavour about the LFB. We were special – distinctive – not to be diluted. It was old Chance who persuaded me that apart from being out of date, there was also something faintly comic about the LFB.

Its naval ethos had suffered a rude, if temporary, shock when the Brigade was swept up in the turmoil and industrial unrest at the end of the First World War. Then, with millions of men demobilised from the armed forces and demanding jobs, the LCC introduced the 72-hour week. Government policy obliged the council to recruit the additional men needed from *all* the services. Among the young men then engaged, the 'Hungry Thousand' as the old-timers called them, were war-scarred survivors of the blood-drenched fields of Flanders. True, the traditional policy of going to the navy for recruits was resumed and when I joined, the brigade was still an enclosed, seemingly, at times, an almost cloistered community, deeply conservative in every way. But the Hungry Thousand had stirred up undercurrents of change, and when Firebrace finally became Chief Officer and began to prepare for the Second World War those currents were still flowing.

By now, I too had begun to conceive of changes and it was among the veterans from France that I was to find my staunchest supporters when the time came to try to introduce them into the brigade and the union.

* * *

I enjoyed the LFB. After months of unemployment I had landed a permanent job on police pay and was, at last, able to help out at home. After tramp-steamers the work (so called) was easy. Theoretical instruction in school was minimal. There were no manuals, no handbooks, no technical guides. Everything a recruit needed to know was contained in his personal copy of the 'Question and Answer Book', the revered 'Q and A'. In examinations the closer one's answer to the actual text, the higher the marks. In the examination for second mate, the 26 closely printed pages of the International Rules for the Prevention of Collision at Sea had to be learnt by heart. I had therefore had ample practice of absorbing and regurgitating official prose and the 'Q and A' I took in my stride, word perfect.

The physical aspects of those four months of training I found exhilarating. Every day, up to the fifth floor with a hook ladder; three times a week racing over the top of the 85-foot tower using escape, first floor ladder and then two-hook ladders; twice a week jumping out of the second floor window into a canvas sheet held out by your mates on the cobblestones below. (Before you stepped off the window sill you called out 'Taut Sheet' and hoped that they would pull the sheet tight.) You carried a man off the roof down the 50-foot escape, then reversing the drill he carried you across his shoulders, and no matter how many times you performed this 'pas de deux', you shut your eyes as he stepped off the parapet and sought a foothold on the rounds. No safety devices were ever used (or contemplated) and those cobbles always looked a long way off. (They were.) Each week we showed off our skills in a public display (ticket holders only) – another relic from the days of Massey Shaw.

Years at sea had put muscle on the frame I had inherited from my father. A show-off in the class room, I was also an exhibitionist in the drill yard. And always there was the element of rivalry, for I had to show the matelots that the merchant navy (the 'working navy' as they not ungenerously called it) was equal to their RN. In an unofficial contest to see who could extend the old-fashioned heavy wooden 55-foot escape to its limit with one hand I beat the rest of the field. Only at squad drill was I at the bottom of the class. One of the least pugnacious of individuals and averse to all forms of organised sport, I could yet be persuaded to allow my fourteen stone to be employed as a punch bag by our aspiring boxers. Sir Aylmer's rebuke of my propensity for sky-larking sprang from the incident on my training school record. In a friendly rough-house in the ablutions block, I had thrown my opponent through a hardboard partition, the resulting damage leading to my appearance, on report, before the school commandant.

Throughout these months we all worked together – as members of a crew. We were learning to become so expert with our tools, our gear and equipment that we could unhesitatingly employ them in the densest smoke, on the darkest night. You knew that there might come a time when your life would depend on that ability. Or the life of a fellow crew member. You relied on him. He knew he could rely on you. The essence of firemanship is to work as a team – self-reliant but interdependent – as comrades. Ex-matelots moving straight across from the navy to the LFB might not be thought of as the most promising of trade union material. But I came to realise that the strong bond of mutual reliance which characterised 'the job', could be a powerful element in forging a special kind of trade union for a special kind of service.

My new station HQ, of course, had the largest complement of men and of various special appliances in the brigade. There was a small number of uniformed administrative staff, half a dozen inspectors of theatres and cinemas and of petrol installations, a pool of cars with their drivers for principal officers, and workshops with friendly mechanics, craftsmen and their mates. The contacts and the friendships I made at HQ were to stand me and the union in good stead in the troubled days to come.

Our weekly hours of duty were 72, fifteen per night – nine per day. The change from days to nights required a 22-hour shift every other Sunday. Every eighth tour of duty was free so that this process allowed a 'long' weekend from 6 o'clock Friday evening to 6 o'clock Monday evening – every fourteen weeks. Twelve days annual leave 'subject to the exigencies of the service' were allowed. Bank holidays and overtime pay were not recognised. Exactly half a fireman's life was thus spent on duty.

In the warren of our quarters amenities were spartan. After eleven at night we were allowed to 'rest' on canvas trestles, a version of the naval hammock. Each man was issued with a large, rough, board-stiff blanket. According to brigade orders the escape's crew was required to rest top booted – tunic buttoned and girdled with the canvas and leather hook belt with its nine-inch steel hook. There were no dormitories and at night these trestle hammocks would litter locker rooms and alley ways. With no central heating we kept a well banked fire in the mess. There was, of course, a supply of domestic hot water, but no showers, and only two tub baths. Navy style, each watch elected from its number a cook and an assistant. (I was frequently stand-in assistant cook.) The only facility provided in the kitchen was the gas stove. Beef and suet duff was our standard fare. As in the navy, groups of four or five men would club together to launch a 'tea boat', putting a shilling or so each week into a kitty to provide tea and biscuits throughout their duty periods. Tea boats were pushed out after every shout and at stand easy. Tea boat chums became special friends. I had to wait a while before I was asked to join a boat. Doubtless, I was being weighed up by my new comrades. Then four of the Hungry Thousand invited me into their boat, one a submariner, another a regular hussar, an artilleryman and a foot-slogger from France. They became dear friends and I think of them now with deep affection. They advised me, watched over me, to them I was 'Young Johnnie', and long after should I meet one of the old tea boat, he would still call me 'Young Johnnie' which would please me much. When Pat and I got married their handsome wedding gift clock graced our mantlepiece.

It was on the Monday morning of my first day shift that things took an odd turn. The apartments for principal officers, Silver Helmets, were at the rear of HQ. Monday morning work detail showed me as having to report to one of these houses. I rang the bell, to be met by the fireman batman (authorised by the LCC), who at once took me down to the kitchen and introduced me to the cook. Cook looked me over and remarked that I must be new to HQ. Puzzled, I acknowledged that this was so. 'Very well,' said Cook. 'You can start in the nursery – scrub the floor, then wash along the passage outside and by that time I shall have finished in the kitchen and you can clear up after me and then scrub this floor. Then we shall all have a cup of tea and see what's left to do.' With that, she motioned to a bucket and some cleaning rags. I stuttered that there must be some mistake. The cook sought to reassure me, commenting again on my recent attachment to headquarters. I said something about getting further instructions and retreated back across the yard to the station office.

In answer to the Station Officer's demand as to what I was doing there, I said that I had met a cook in her kitchen who wanted me to scrub her back stairs and clean a nursery and other things. 'That's right,' said the officer, 'What's wrong?' I mumbled something about being a fireman. My association with Station Officer Charters was to last many years, and when he became one of Her Majesty's Inspectors at the

Home Office we joined forces in seeking to enhance the efficiency of our country's fire service. But on that Monday morning he was genuinely puzzled. I sought to explain. Accepting orders from a cook and scrubbing a nursery floor did not, in my view, fall within a fireman's duties. Charters became sympathetic. This job which I might find distasteful would, in due course, be taken over by the next junior recruit. I was not to be persuaded. I said that if I were ordered to scrub a nursery floor, I would carry out the order and I would then seek advice since I did not consider that the London County Council paid me to skivvy for a nurse maid. Charters kept a firm control of himself. Changing his tack he took the 'young Johnnie' line. To no avail and I was abruptly dismissed. Every other Monday on the day shift for a week or two, he and I played out our farce, he telling me off to report to the cook, I politely asking, 'Is that an order sir?' then to be taken into the office. There, Charters would fume for a moment and then close the business with more admonitions about 'keeping one's nose clean', 'not stirring things up', 'being young enough to go all the way'.

From such modest beginnings as a nursery floor did my reputation as a 'bolshie' become so soon established. 'Bolshie' was a term much used by my mess-mates, deep set as they were in that special brand of jingoism of the Senior Service. Most of the post-war entrants had had little experience of civilian life and 'bolshie' was an omnibus word to describe even the most modest form of independent behaviour outside the accepted norm of the lower deck. My stand over the nursery incident puzzled them. But their patriotism had proved no defence against the economic depression which was gripping their country. In the training school I had discovered a number of recruits who had joined in the Invergordon Mutiny of 1931, when the crews of the Atlantic Fleet anchored in Scapa Flow had 'struck' against savage pay cuts. They were proud of their part in the mutiny, although confessing to me that perhaps they had been a 'bit bolshie'. A 'bit bolshie' was a moderate way indeed to describe the action of thousands of rebellious sailors which, in the greatest mutiny since Spithead, had immobilised half of Britain's navy and so terrified Whitehall that the cuts were restored in a week. At that time the London Fire Brigade, along with the police, had suffered a 10 per cent cut in pay. For millions of unemployed there was a reduction in their miserable dole and the barbarities of the Means Test.

There was no television then to help pass the tedious hours of stand-by on night duty, only a single wireless set, fixed over the fireplace in the mess. Around that fireplace the yarns were spun, the friendly gossip flowed. At sea I had been an omnivorous reader and if the gossip and the stories became too noisy, I would take my book down to a former stables, where, in a quiet corner stood a large, comfortable bench. On that bench single firemen in the days of continuous duty had entertained their girl-friends. There, my cavalry tea-boat chum told me the girls were introduced to the horse with the blue tail. I had begun to tackle Marx and to take the monthly volumes of the newly launched Left Book Club. I was taking the *Daily Worker* and leaving my copy on the mess table, to be glanced at, sometimes even to be read, until some outraged patriot would put it to humbler uses. I was going to meetings of the Communist Party and helping to barrack black-shirted speakers at fascist ones. I was in search of explanations of what I had so recently witnessed at first hand.

For I had seen the collapse of world capitalism. I had seen the unwanted wheat of the prairies of America mixed with tar to fuel dockside locomotives, while starving jobless immigrants wandered the quays and begged for scraps from the hogswill in our galley's shit-bucket. From a ship's bridge I had seen the low hills along the Brazilian coast aflame as the worthless coffee plantations were fired, their produce without value in the markets of a bankrupt world. I had come home to pay off in Newcastle. Along the Tyne I had seen no fewer than a hundred large sea-going vessels crewless, laid up, rusting. I had seen the finest shipbuilding yards in the world, their slipways empty and silent. I had come back to be assessed by the Means Test tribunal as being worth to society, 9s. 6d. a week. And I had seen the sinister swastika flag begin to replace the old republican ensign at the stern of German ships and had wondered at its portent.

When I came up from the stable for supper and the fireside forum was in full session, I would be greeted with demands to know what book was under my arm, questions clearly designed to start an argument. I was ready to argue. They would bait me. I took the bait willingly.

These unruly disputes which frequently sunk my impromptu dissertations in a wave of good humour took a more immediate slant when Labour first gained control of the LCC. Under Herbert Morrison's leadership Labour in London had struggled up from the depths into which it had been plunged by the catastrophe of 1931, when Prime Minister Ramsay MacDonald almost destroyed his party by joining the Tories under Baldwin. Labour's plans for London's housing, transport, health and education marked a turning point in British politics. It was to be expected that in our mess we should begin to ask what plans Labour had for London's firemen. We learnt that in place of our dingy former workhouse we were promised a magnificent new headquarters on the Embankment. Labour would launch an expensive programme to re-equip the brigade with a fleet of modern appliances of advanced design. And Firebrace (Aylmer the Innovator) would be our new Chief Officer. But for us firemen? Nothing.

Someone remembered that when the RB won the 72-hour week its original claim had been for a 48-hour week on three shifts, but that in accepting pay on police parity the RB had undertaken to shelve the claim for four years. Since then nothing had happened. So a claim for a 48-hour week was now fourteen years overdue. To call it an 'agitation' would be too strong a word, but the swell of interest that spread across the brigade from our mess, was strong enough to bring us a visitor.

In this way I met Sam Randall, a driver at Red Cross Street, secretary of the RB committee. Sam had come to tell us to pipe down and to invite us to a general meeting where our Spokesman, Percy Kingdom, FBU general secretary, would listen to anything we had to say. Sam impressed upon us that if the RB was to move on hours then that move should be properly organised and should be a united one.

And as he spoke, he impressed himself upon me. He was giving me my first lesson in practical trade unionism. One of the Hungry Thousand from France, his clear speech shone with intelligence. From then on I became a Randall man. I had joined the RB immediately I took duty at Southwark, paying my fourpence. At my surprise on being handed in return an FBU membership card, I was told, 'Don't worry, it's all the same.' Sam Randall made it all plain to me.

The small hall (which I was to come to know so very well) was half empty – with perhaps forty of us from the entire brigade. We had come straight from a fifteen-hour tour of night duty and since we would report again at six that evening, few of us would get home for a meal and a decent rest. Of the meeting itself I remember little. Spokesman Percy agreed to renew the twenty-year-old claim. I, the most junior of those present, wisely said not a word. But Sam took me up and introduced me to Kingdom. On the death of Jim Bradley, six years before, Kingdom, already retired from the brigade which he had joined just before the Boer War, had been acting as assistant secretary and was thus ready to step into deadman's shoes. As I listened to Kingdom's gruff voice he struck me as a dour, tough fighter, but he had little to say to me as I stood alongside Sam.

Our application for the 48-hour week was turned down flat. There then followed a long, acrimonious dispute between Kingdom and Herbert Morrison which later was to cloud my own relationship with Herbert. Finally Labour promised that, if returned for a second term of office, a cut in our hours of duty would be considered.

My growing involvement in RB business did not deflect me from my own career. Station Officer Charters (nursery floors no longer an issue between us), took every opportunity to detail me as 'runner' to one or other of the principal officers. Principal Officers attended only the more serious fires or emergencies, and with no walkie-talkie or personal radio, a 'runner' was kept busy carrying messages between his officer, the fire control centre and the operational superintendent in charge. As a 'runner' I was thus able to expand my fire experience and to establish a personal contact with the higher echelon of the brigade, a contact which was to prove most useful to the union, when later the Silver Helmets all took senior posts in the National Fire Service. As deputy to Sir Aylmer, Major Jackson enjoyed a respect, bordering on affection, among the lower deck, 'Gentleman' Jackson as they called him. I looked forward to attending upon his heels at a fire. I got to know him and like him, and I think he liked me. When the war came and he took charge of the London Brigade we forged a useful but very private alliance.

* * *

The education papers for the examination to sub-officer could be taken at any time and were prepared by the Education Department at County Hall. I tackled them at the first opportunity. They were the usual subjects – simple mathematics, general knowledge and an essay of at least a thousand words for which there was set a choice of subjects. I chose 'London's Parks'. Ever the show-off, I launched into a rhapsodic description of the beauties of Hyde Park, of St James's Park with its pelicans on the lovely lake between the Palace and Whitehall, the charms of Green Park abutting the clubs of Piccadilly, all in a purple, plagiaristic prose. Then I wrote of the streets I knew in Stepney, of the drab desert of the square miles between Commercial and Bethnal Green Roads, bare of a blade of grass or a single tree. There, that torrid summer, children were condemned to play on the hot pavements of dangerous streets. I concluded my essay – London's parks were truly beautiful. They suffered one defect. They were in the wrong place. They epitomised the evils of our unjust society. They should be moved eastwards. It was all an undisguised pastiche of William Morris, a hero for me then – and now.

When the result of the exam was published, I was ordered to see Major Jackson. With him was a stranger, introduced to me as the chairman of the LCC Education Committee. Officials at County Hall had drawn his attention to this effusion of mine and he had decided to seek out the author.

With Major Jackson looking smiling on, the visitor and I chatted about my various interests outside the brigade. When I left the room I thought that at this rate I might need another gusset in my brass helmet. I was to be surprised.

* * *

In 1935 Hitler formally repudiated the Versailles Treaty and promulgated the Nuremberg 'Laws' which were to lead to the deaths of six million Jews. In that year Mussolini launched his poison gas upon Abyssinian tribesmen. In that year shocked Londoners witnessed the largest Hunger March of the Depression to their city, and Sir John Boyd-Orr's commission published the shameful facts of malnutrition (starvation) among the children of the long-term unemployed.[4] In that year British people were called upon to join in the Day of National Thanksgiving to mark the Silver Jubilee of King George V (our ex-matelots being delighted to learn that the celebrations would include a review by His Majesty of the Atlantic and Home Fleets at Spithead). A magnificent religious service would be held at St Paul's where, at the altar, the monarch and the archbishop would offer up prayers of gratitude to the Almighty for the blessings He had bestowed upon us throughout that glorious reign in which a million men had died in war and the country had been plunged into the worst slump in history.

A smiling Charters broke the news to me that I had been selected to be among the small band of young firemen who would be on fire duty at various points around the cathedral during the service. My post would be at the transept itself, in full view of the altar and the royal family. Sir Aylmer and Lady Firebrace would be among the congregation and they would see me. I was shattered. For days I had been supplying the mess-table with the special anti-Jubilee editions of the *Daily Worker* and with vitriolic pamphlets from left-wing organisations protesting at the jingoism and cynical monumental waste of millions on the celebrations. I begged Charters to find a substitute – it was the nursery floor all over again. This time, he raged, I would have to provide him with very powerful arguments before he would excuse me from a task which clearly fell within the range of my fireman's duties. I gave him two. I was an atheist, and my religious (or rather non-religious) feelings would suffer outrage by the mumbo-jumbo at the altar. And I was a republican. I claimed that due regard should be paid to these deep-seated and genuinely held objections. And so we argued about my atheistic republicanism or my republican atheism until Charters began to waiver. I was excused St Paul's, but he insisted that I should be among the LFB Guard of Honour to stand outside Cannon Street Fire Station as the royal procession passed on its way to the cathedral. What Sir Aylmer would say, he dared not think.

The story spread through the brigade reinforcing the reputation I seemed to be gaining as that 'queer bolshie bloke at HQ'. And it brought Sam Randall to see me. Ever outspoken, Sam did not mince his words. I had been stupid. If Charters had reported me for insubordination, Sam doubted whether the RB could have assisted me. If I was to work with him in the union, there were many things I had to start to learn. As a beginning, I should attend the forthcoming (1935) annual conference of the FBU. He would nominate me as a delegate.

So in a room in a pub in Southampton I joined the other four members of the LFB delegation. Single delegates came from seven outer London brigades. Bradford, Southampton and Gellygaer (a mining village in South Wales) were also represented. With EC officials and clerk we totalled 24. I found the whole occasion depressing and quite properly remained mute. Kingdom was his usual gruff self. He said nothing about London's claim for the 48-hour week, for that was RB business. I remember little of the short proceedings.

It is the journey back to Waterloo that I remember. I had been unable to hide from Sam my disappointment at the sad shadow of a trade union conference I had just attended, and I think he knew that the talk on the journey back to London would lift my spirits. There were four of us in the compartment. I knew Jim Bradley by repute, but since he was in the opposite watch at Euston, I had yet to meet him.

One of the Hungry Thousand, Jim had followed his grandfather into the Brigade, 'Young Jim' to the old hands who had known and worked with his father, the founder of the union. Jim was a man of quiet dignity with a contempt for authority, from whatever quarter it came. When I got to know him, I realised that this readiness to challenge authority came not only from his father's radical teaching, it was rooted in the bloody shambles in France. Bradley had little use for officers of any sort, for he had seen too many of his comrades die through their blundering incompetence. I was thrilled that afternoon to listen to someone who could remember listening with his father to men like Keir Hardie, John Burns and Tom Mann speaking on Tower Hill. Jim and I were to become close friends. He and his wife were childless and when our first baby was born, he made her a charming mobile toy, for he was a deft worker in wood. Last in our quartet was a surprising person to be found in the fire service. With receding hairline and noble forehead, a beautiful cultivated voice and never without a book under his arm, Harry Short had the air of an academic. Born on Merseyside, his intellect was nurtured by the Independent Labour Party and the National Council of Labour Colleges. When jobless his socialist friends had found him employment with the Labour-controlled Borough of East Ham where he had been allowed to carve out for himself a quiet niche in their local brigade. I never heard Harry discuss actual fire-fighting in which his interest seemed but minimal, but he was deeply read in the Marxist classics and I was accordingly impressed. To the semi-dormant conference after lunch he had spoken of his recent visit to Scandinavia as a guest of the Swedish Social Democrats. At Waterloo we promised to meet again.

Later, those four men in the railway carriage would determine the fate of the FBU.

The conference at Cardiff two years later in 1937 did nothing to inspire me. Our delegate from Gellygaer had been recruiting in the valleys and delegates came from Ebbw Vale and Pontypridd. Once again, the union was to fly its flag in new territory. The Cardiff City Police Brigade ignored our modest presence in their city, for there too the FBU flag flew but limply.

Supporting Randall and Bradley, I was among the group continuing to press for a 48-hour week. Jim's dad had ensured that from its birth his baby trade union was affiliated to the TUC and the Labour Party. So with our union hats on we three went to meetings of the London Trades Council and the London Labour Party to drum up support and it was there that I found that I could speak in public. By these appearances we infuriated Morrison, who charged us with going behind the back of the Labour group at County Hall. But it was poor Percy Kingdom who bore the full brunt of Herbert's displeasure. Herbert poured scorn on our claim that we 'worked' 72 hours a week, announcing publicly that we actually slept at nights – on beds – with blankets supplied by the LCC! Although at odds with some of our tactics, Percy stoutly defended himself against Herbert's attacks. Now I confess to a belated sympathy for Percy. A founder of the union, old enough to be my father, he was being asked to listen to someone with less than four years' service, a Johnny-Come-Lately who happened to have the gift of the gab. Slow in his movements, with drooping eyelids and a heavy jowl, Kingdom's speeches were blunt and free from any niceties. At the general meetings I would sit in the front row, but askew from the speaker's table so that when I was called I could properly address the chair and yet face the main body. Once when I sat down after criticising his handling of affairs, Kingdom sat grimly silent, his eyes hooded. I heard the chairman urge him to reply, whispering 'You'll have to say something, Percy,' and the old man's response – 'Fuck him' – spoken scarcely under his breath. He remained seated and silent. Only in later years did I come to understand how he must have felt.

* * *

When the Spanish Civil War broke out Pat and I decided it was time to marry before the big one was upon us. Two rooms with a kitchen were falling vacant at West Hampstead station. Headquarters agreed to reserve them till my next weekend leave when we moved in, a happy couple – newly wed. Hampstead in the 1930s was a thrilling place for two young left-wingers. A haven for Jewish, intellectual and political refugees from Nazi Germany, the place throbbed with social and political activity. It was the time of the Popular Front, and in Hampstead the Communists and the Labour Party found common cause in their support for Republican Spain and the International Brigade. Duty shifts limited my local activities, but when I was on nights Pat remained heavily involved. In my absence our tiny flat above the station's mess-room was often the venue for strange young people with their pamphlets and their papers. The sub-officer's wife once had to struggle over copies of the *Daily Worker* littering the stairs when his pile fell from under the arm of a young man. Meeting Pat on the landing she commented 'You do a lot of social work, don't you, Mrs Horner?' There was no side entrance, and access from the street to the flats was across the appliance room and past the watch room. Our callers were therefore always the subject of scrutiny and the station officer had been seen to shake his head sadly.

Labour's first term of office in London was ending and elections were pending. Our Labour candidate had little chance in well-to-do Hampstead, but he was active in all our campaigns and the Popular Front was behind him. One night Pat was keeping watch for the police while I daubed a well-placed wall with a 'Vote Labour' slogan in large whitewashed letters. She thought that in my conversation with a well-dressed gentleman who had interrupted my whitewashing I was canvassing his support. My interrupter was, in fact, a plain clothes police inspector. Foolishly, I gave him the street number of the fire station as my address. Some days later a policeman dropped in at the watchroom for help in finding No. 325 West End Lane. 327 was the greengrocers, 323 was the bakers. Where, asked the policeman was 325? 'Right here,' replied the duty man and so the summons was delivered with full publicity. When today every vacant yard of accessible wall-space in London is a palimpsest of graffiti, it is difficult to recall how seriously the court regarded my modest offence. But while political slogans might then be suffered in London's East End, nothing of that kind would be tolerated in bourgeois Hampstead. I was fined 30 shillings and ordered to pay 10 shillings towards the cost of removing the whitewash from the wall. It was more than half my week's pay. We were short for weeks. The novelty of a London fireman in court on such a charge at such a time made good copy for the evening papers, and I was brought before the Senior Superintendent to explain my conduct, since for a member of the brigade to appear on a charge in a police court was itself a potential offence against good discipline and must needs be investigated. The old superintendent was less at ease than I. Clearly HQ was not sure of its ground. I explained how important a Labour victory would be to the brigade, how if we won there would be a 48-hour week, brigade manpower would be increased, promotions would ensue, morale would be raised.

I gave the union case – pat. I added that I would accept no restriction on my democratic rights as a citizen which I would exercise, off duty, how I pleased. He should have run me in for impertinence. Instead he enquired anxiously, 'And do you really think Mr Morrison will get back?' I assured him nothing was more certain and he closed the interview with, 'Oh very well, laddie, but use your loaf – use your loaf.' The story got round the brigade, reinforcing my growing reputation as a 'Red'.

With Labour returned, Sam said the place for me was with him and Bradley on the committee of the Representative Body. I was elected, despite, perhaps because of, the whitewash. Things began to happen to me. My ex-cavalry chum casually asked whether I had packed my bag? 'You're moving out,' he said. I protested that I was awaiting the results of the technical papers of the sub-officer's examination, and that I would then enter the zone for promotion. With a world-weary smile, my chum exclaimed 'You've gone and got yourself on the RB committee. They don't have committee men at HQ, so get ready to move.'

Thus began my peregrination around the brigade – three stations in the next three years. Worse still, I failed the sub-officer's by one mark. 'Surprised?' asked Bradley when I told him.

I was really out of the boat. But that was my problem.

* * *

A problem the like of which no union had yet to meet was facing us all in the tiny FBU. Hitler and Mussolini had joined forces. Hitler was forcing the Anschluss on Austria and threatening Czechoslovakia. In March 1938 the first volunteer in London's part-time Auxiliary Fire Service reported for training – the beginning of a flood. Six months later there were 18,000 invaders occupying our stations.

It is impossible now adequately to explain the violence of the regular firemen's resentment at this mass intrusion into their traditional privacy. At once we declared our quarters to be strictly out of bounds to these 'civvies', and any volunteer venturing into these areas was in danger of being rudely evicted. After Munich the invasion became a mass occupation. The slow delivery of AFS pumps was outstripped by the influx of volunteers, so our regular appliances were commandeered for their practice and drill. For thrills and to gain experience some AFS men even demanded to be allowed to ride to fires with us. Our machines, their brass work polished with such care, their red and gold enamel mirror-bright, each piece of manifold equipment neatly stowed in its right place, in its proper locker, so that it might be found without hesitation – these splendid creations, the darlings of their drivers, were now violated by over-enthusiastic strangers – clerks and shop-assistants – playing at firemen, dressed in dungarees and steel helmets. At evenings and weekends our station yards were taken over by noisy, eager amateurs. Now for us there was no football on Saturday afternoons, no quiet evenings in which to stroll and chat. Our monastery walls were crumbling, our secrets revealed to inquisitive outsiders, the mystique of the 'job' becoming public property. The presence of women on the station was an intrusion not to be tolerated. The close chumminess of the century-old male enclave which had been the London Fire Brigade had gone.

And over all there hung the cloud of unarticulated fear at the outcome of this assault on their professional standards and livelihoods. Still the union refrained from any comment, issued not a single word of guidance. To concern itself with the organisation of the AFS would be to go against the union's long-standing policy of non-involvement in 'methods of management'. Inevitably, with no lead to follow, those men who did succumb to the offered bonus in pay and undertook to act as instructors to the AFS were the sole link between them and the regulars. Such men were the least staunch supporters of the union. For the rest it was enough to arouse suspicion merely to be heard bidding an AFS man a polite 'Good evening', let alone to be seen actually talking to him.

I was now convinced that war would come and that if the AFS was mobilised before the FBU had found a constructive relationship with it the union would be swamped out of existence. And time was running out. So I took the risk of meeting with small groups of AFS men. I was now serving at Clerkenwell, the HQ of B District, where I found two young men, both holding responsible posts in the City, who were eager to learn about the union and the problems their presence had created for us regulars.

No one knew what form the wartime organisation of the fire service would take, or what would be the employment conditions of the AFS, matters on which the union had made no representations and sought no consultation. The 1938 Fire Brigades Act required some sixteen hundred separate local authorities to organise a fire brigade by April 1939, each with its own separate AFS. Sixteen hundred fire brigades – sixteen hundred auxiliary fire services! It promised chaos.

As the year 1939 opened out, I began to win support for my attempts to convince my fellow LFB men that among the AFS we could find allies rather than enemies, that to continue to ignore them was the worst of all policies. So in the evenings after their drill periods I set up a number of casual gatherings in Clerkenwell's appliance room. Bradley and Randall pledged their help and occasionally dropped in. My two City friends, innocent of any political ideas, spread our message of goodwill among their colleagues.

* * *

In due course Kingdom was invited to County Hall to receive the council's offer of a 60-hour week. Foolishly, I had not sought re-election to the RB committee, impatient at the trivia of its usual agendas, and so I did not hear Percy recommend acceptance of the offer. Later it seemed that either he had omitted to make plain, or in their eagerness to report progress, the committee failed fully to appreciate that the offer depended upon our surrendering a number of long-standing privileges. Taken separately, some of the changes were modest enough – smoking would be banned, except in our own quarters; the 'cease work' at 1 o'clock on the day shift would be abolished; 'wet' canteens would go, in other words no alcohol would be sold or drunk on station, a survival from the days of continuous duty; men reaching the age of 47 would be subject to annual medical examinations – and so on.

When he sat down at the general meeting called to hear our Spokesman's report, I knew that Percy had failed. He had seemed insensitive to our irritation at the contingent clauses and unhappy in his replies to interjections and questions. He had seemed to justify them until a suspicion grew among his listeners that he had already committed himself with County Hall. One of the last speakers from the floor, I said that the conditions were irrelevancies. We should throw them out. If at some time in the future the LCC wished to raise any of these matters, we might then consent to hear what they had to say. This attempt to impose them now was an abuse of negotiating procedures and if they were insisted upon we should reject the offer absolutely. In any case, it went only half way to meet our claim. The meeting was with me, and Kingdom was told to take our answer to County Hall.

A 'Silver Helmet' commenting on this incident wrote,

'Horner's attack on Kingdom's handling of the issues was blistering.' I did not think so, but what none of us understood was how bitterly Percy took his defeat.

Time passed with little progress at County Hall, and still AFS volunteers continued to stream into our stations, and still the silence of the executive council remained unbroken. Perhaps, some argued, war would be avoided after all and the AFS would never be mobilised. The union rules which provided for annual elections for the general secretary and the assistants had always been treated as formalities, those in office remaining unchallenged. It was Jim Bradley who mooted the idea that, properly handled, these rules could be used to ventilate the AFS problem. If I, accepted as the protaganist of bridge-building, were to stand for election, we would have a national platform from which to argue our case. No one would assume that it was a serious threat to Percy, but it would provide a chance to canvass our ideas about the AFS. Sam Randall, who had been critical of my defection from the RB Committee, was doubtful, thinking that such a move would deepen the divisions in the union. Harry Short was for tackling Kingdom. As always I took my worries to Pat. With the baby on the way, we had moved out of our tiny, but very cheap fire station flat and, set on promotion, I had just taken the sub-officers' exam again. If by a fluke I were to win the ballot, I could hardly declare that it had all been a ploy to advance a hitherto unpopular policy, and that I would rather stay in a safe job than risk my livelihood in a chancy annual election. Kingdom had his brigade pension – I had a young family. But with Pat confessing that she had never imagined I would spend my life in the brigade I allowed my name to go forward.

When the list of nominations was presented to the executive council, it contained a single name – mine. Kingdom then informed the EC that he was resigning forthwith, but before doing so, he wished to nominate as his successor assistant secretary Harold Gibbs (Mr Gibbs, who had not formerly been a fireman, was head office typist and general administrator). Percy went on to remind the EC that, with regard to the only nomination on the paper, under the rules it had to satisfy itself that the nominee possessed the qualifications necessary to discharge the duties of General Secretary. Percy recommended that Horner's nomination should be disallowed on the ground of his lack, both of years and of experience in union affairs, and because it was well known that he propagated political views that were not shared by the main body of union members.

The executive disallowed my nomination. Percy Kingdom was never seen in the office again.

The circular informing the union of these unexpected changes was signed by the new general secretary, Mr Gibbs, who thoughtfully sent me a copy for my personal use. What little I knew of Mr Gibbs convinced me he would prove a disaster. A pleasant enough man, he was completely dominated by Kingdom's powerful personality and had seldom been allowed to speak in public. There was no evidence that he had ever expressed an independent point of view.

There could be no going back for me now. For the next week or so I saw little of Pat and the baby, as on my bike I visited stations around London until enough protests had been registered with the new general secretary to convince him that, unelected, he would have to face a deeply divided membership and a lasting and bitter opposition. He bowed to the whirlwind, called another meeting of the executive, resigned as general secretary and recommended that fresh nominations be invited. Meanwhile he would wish to resume his duties as assistant secretary until elected to succeed Kingdom. A docile executive agreed.

This time, my nomination met no opposition. There was one additional issue. Paid officials were fully entitled to vote at meetings and to nominate each other for office. The London branch tabled an amendment to rules for the forthcoming annual conference designed to strip them of this privilege. Gibbs and his colleague, the other assistant secretary, responded by declaring that if the amendment were carried they would regard it as a vote of no confidence and would be obliged to consider their positions. No one knew what they meant, and they refused further comment.

At the end of May the 1939 annual conference was held in London with a record number of delegates, their interest aroused by all this controversy. The election for general secretary was under way. Towards the end of the morning session, conference agreed to the proposed rule change. The two officials then left the platform and, bidding the president goodbye, walked out of the building to play no further part in the union's affairs. President Augustus Odlin, a West Ham member, deemed it appropriate to adjourn for lunch. To Mr Robert Willis, secretary of the London Trades Council, who was to have been the union's luncheon guest, it proved difficult to explain how any union half way through its annual conference could succeed in losing all its officials. He had never known anything like it.

At half-past five that morning, I had driven Clerkenwell's pump to Hyde Park for the final rehearsal of that day's annual display of the London Fire Brigade, then a popular event in London's calendar, and which this year would be combined with a grand review of the AFS by royalty. Repeatedly I had driven round and round the Royal Carriage Drive, while my timing had been meticulously checked. It was from these wearisome preparations that I had come directly to the conference hall where the union was almost dissolving in angry disarray, whilst a couple of miles up the road, their Royal Highnesses, the Duke and Duchess of Kent, were reviewing more than 20,000 AFS men and women.

The Lambeth meeting, the disappearance of Percy, the deadlock in our discussions at County Hall, the fiasco of conference with the desertion of the remaining officials and the threat of those 20,000 in Hyde Park led to such confusion and uncertainty among our members that talk was heard of the union having 'had it'.

With the office now closed, Bob Willis undertook to run the election, and so it was he who gave me the keys and the advice about the 'Reds'. I had not the slightest idea what to do. There was no filing cabinet to examine. The office had a single typewriter, but I couldn't type. The cash box contained a few pounds and some silver but I had never been in a bank or handled a cheque. Next day I cycled round to Sam Randall's station, then over to East Ham to Harry Short. Harry took me to his neighbouring brigade, West Ham, and to President Augustus Odlin, who in turn undertook to convene the Executive at which they agreed to my request to be allowed to engage a typist but stipulated that no woman should be employed. They agreed to my insistence that the union's accounts be professionally audited. I knew nothing about current accounts, deposit accounts, how to prepare a cash statement, or to read a balance sheet. (Hitherto, head office accounts had been audited by the fireman canteen manager at Lambeth.) Heads shook, first a typist – now an auditor! All this would cost money. A few months before he disappeared, Kingdom had had an increase in salary, bringing his pay to approximately that of a sub-officer. For my first year of office the executive decided that I should be placed upon the earlier, lower rate of pay. If I was still general secretary after one year, consideration would be given to applying the improved scale.

All in all it was an unpropitious start.

* * *

I handed in my top boots, helmet, and belt-axe and spanner. The rest of my gear I was allowed to keep. The tweed-lined melton cloth fire tunics I gave to an old sea-going chum, who later put them to good use on the Atlantic convoys. I kept my brigade overcoat.

To my delight, Harry Short agreed to stand for election to the vacant post of assistant general secretary. Harry proved a great comfort to me. His reputation with our few provincial brigades, coupled with my standing in London, could be the basis of a real national leadership. His wider knowledge of and experience in the labour movement offset my immaturity.

Although Hitler's threats against Poland daily became ever more menacing, Pat and I, in the joy of our lovely child, left unspoken our fears of the war which was coming ever closer. What we could not hide from ourselves was the fact that Pat was gravely ill. At Bart's the doctors insisted that she should then and there remain in hospital in readiness for immediate surgery, a proposal which Pat, with a seven-month-old baby at home, flatly rejected. When she had made arrangements for the baby, then would be the time for operations. Bart's reluctantly agreed, but urged speed. A day or so later the Soviet-Nazi Non-Aggression Pact was announced and at Bart's all admissions were cancelled, the wards being cleared for war casualties. Their letter advised us that Pat must lead a quiet life, undertake no exertion of any kind, uninterrupted rest and freedom from worry being essential. Hitler then went on to invade Poland and to bomb Warsaw. On the Friday afternoon in the week we had heard from Bart's the BBC broadcast an appeal for AFS volunteers to report to their stations, bringing blankets and enough food for two days. The evacuation of London's children was well under way. Harry and I could learn nothing from Whitehall or Lambeth. In officialdom's scheme of things, as they were unfolding, the FBU had no place. Harry was not married and we agreed that he should man the office, while I tried to find a refuge out of London for Pat, the baby and Pat's mother. By Saturday evening she was, for the time being, in the home of Quaker friends in the country. On Sunday I drove in a hired car down to deepest Dorset to a farm where we had once spent my annual leave. I thus missed Chamberlain's broadcast declaring war. Our farmer and his wife welcomed me with every kindness, and I knew that if Pat lived she and our baby would be safe in their hands.

Back in blacked-out London that evening I paid off the car, called in at Clerkenwell for my first wartime fire service supper, got cheered up by my old mates (for I was, by then, in desperate need of cheer) and walked down to Kings Cross to try to get a night train to York in order to be at Bridlington next morning for the 1939 Trades Union Congress.

* * *

My time would have been better spent in London. Excited delegates had been gathering in Bridlington throughout the weekend. I was a late-comer. The first wartime Congress proved the shortest. A long statement from Walter Citrine, the general secretary, on how perfidious had been Russia's conduct, a short session for immediate business and an address from the president, which he concluded by hoping that 'when we meet again, the skies will be less dark and we can continue in time of peace our constructive work'. (When we tried to meet again, Hitler had swallowed up most of Europe, Britain was threatened with invasion and the fire service was losing the battle of the London docks.) With the agenda cancelled, Citrine dismissed us with the words 'No doubt you all have much to do.' The 1939 TUC Report disclosed that the FBU had an affiliated membership of 3,150 and had paid its fees for that year in the sum of £17 7s. 6d.

Arrived back in London the next morning, I held my first council of war with Harry. He had spent much time trying to discover what was happening throughout the service and the whereabouts of our EC members. London, it was thought, remained in danger of imminent attack from German bombers. All leave had been cancelled, shift systems were in suspense. The Admiralty had mobilised the Royal Fleet Reserve, the LFB alone thereby losing nearly 400 of its younger men, the very group upon which I had most relied, matelots again for the duration. Harry himself was tired out. The union seemed to be disintegrating.

We thereupon decided to organise the AFS.

* * *

Were we mad? Certainly the general secretary of the TUC thought we were. Sir Walter Citrine to whom we had gone for advice was a precise, pedantic speaker and his acerbic description of the AFS is sharp in my memory – 'a heterogeneous collection of transients'. No basis existed for trade union organisation among such diverse groups whose links with our profession must be purely temporary. We should concentrate on holding onto our present membership and, by providing a more personal service to them in their wartime difficulties, hope to sit out the war. It would be foolish to risk our slender funds and over-stretch our resources on the dangerous venture we were proposing. There might be legal objections to the use of funds for purposes unspecified in our rules and in the absence of any decision of our annual conference.

Since, with all leave cancelled, there was no chance of convening the executive council, Harry and I satisfied ourselves with consulting those EC members in and around London and sending reply-paid telegrams to the others. We won strong support from Bradley and Randall, and a reluctant 'go ahead' from Gus Odlin, our president. It was all very irregular, but we hoped for ratification at the next annual conference – supposing there would be another annual conference.

There were now no less than 90,000 AFS in makeshift stations, men, women and boys. We proposed that as union members men should contribute 3d., women 2d. and messenger boys under eighteen 1d. to our funds, which then stood at £2,000.

To Harry and me £2,000 in the bank seemed a great deal of money so, with advice from our newly engaged male clerk, we bought the union its first duplicator – hand operated.

Then the storm broke.

Hope of the 60-hour week vanished with the war. For this the newly-elected Spokesman of the LFB could not be blamed. What could not be forgiven him was his crazy idea of inviting the AFS into the union! With their stations flooded by these amateur newcomers, with the proud identity of their brigade dissolving before their eyes, 'the job' as they knew it had gone, and the man they had so recently chosen as their champion was proposing that these intruders (any other union would have called them 'dilutees'), should be given a brotherly welcome into their one remaining stronghold – their union. 'Traitor', 'bloody sell out' they wrote in the letters sent to us with torn-up union cards.

There was nothing for it but to bike round as many stations as I could while Harry held the fort in the office. I would meet the critics face to face. One of my AFS City friends insisted that I abandon my bike and borrow his spanking Wolsey car. To my detractors, the fact that I was coming round in a posh

Firemen attending a blaze in Manchester, October 1960

Station Officer Colin Townsley's funeral procession passing Kings Cross station, 27 November 1987

Firefighters and other emergency personnel working in the wreckage of the Clapham rail crash, December 1988

Firemen fighting a blaze in Oldham, April 1961

Fireboat *Phoenix* on the River Thames following the *Marchioness* disaster, August 1989

An exhausted firefighter wearing breathing apparatus at the Kings Cross tragedy, November 1987

car belonging to one of the AFS was further proof of my subjection to them.

Further help came from an unexpected quarter. Firebrace had been seconded to Whitehall and Major Jackson given charge of London. He asked to see me. A strange meeting – he, saddled with the largest command of the entire service, I, his erstwhile junior 'runner'. We talked of the problems of welding the two discordant sections of that command into a cohesive unit. He welcomed our efforts to enrol the AFS as a possible unifying factor, and promised me every facility, leave for serving union representatives, for station meetings and freedom of entry to all stations. He himself would be accessible to me at all times.

Jackson was as good as his word. Later, when by Home Office direction FBU meetings on stations were banned (with our members on a 48/24 duty system, a deliberate wrecking move), Jackson coolly ignored the order. After the great raids he paid tribute to the FBU and told Londoners that he doubted whether his service could have 'come through', as he put it, without the co-operation of the union. When Morrison retired him from active service, he received no honours, no knighthood, but 'Gentleman Jackson' deserves honourable mention in this history.

* * *

Suddenly Pat had a letter from Bart's. With no casualties from France, an emergency surgical unit which the hospital had set up far away from London was standing idle. If I could manage, somehow, to get Pat there, the operation would be performed without delay. I turned my AFS friend's car into an ambulance. Weeks later in the limousine ambulance I was taking Pat, miraculously restored as they had promised, back to her cottage, her mother and her baby. By now I thought I had earned a week's leave with this wife who had come back to me. I had brought a portable typewriter and was teaching myself to type. I was contemplating a pamphlet.

Before the war the government had covered each AFS volunteer with a personal insurance against accidental death in training, up to a limit of £1,000. This scheme had lapsed at the outbreak of war to be replaced by one which was so complex and unclear that AFS now injured or falling ill were without sick pay at all. They were being sent to the Unemployment Assistance Board and means-tested. After two weeks they were sacked. We were getting reports of accidents involving both regulars and auxiliaries. In the same hospital the regulars were on indefinite full pay, the injured AFS men sacked after a fortnight. It was all beyond belief and I attacked the scheme root and branch.

'AFS – Your Rights to Compensation' was sold among all branches of Air Raid Precautions. The press took up the story and our mass protest meeting in the Kingsway Hall overflowed. The pamphlet was debated in parliament, supported by MPs from all parties. A government rebuttal of my pamphlet was posted up in all ARP depots and fire stations, a nationwide advertisement for the FBU which brought us a tidal wave of new members. 'AFS – Your Right to Compensation' became a best seller, and at a penny a copy actually brought in a profit for our funds.

Stage by stage we forced concessions from the government. At the point where we had won thirteen weeks' pay before discharge Brother Bill Errington, the only AFS man to win the George Cross (the civilian VC) was still in hospital when his own thirteen weeks expired. Bill was sacked on the same day he received the citation from Buckingham Palace and a letter from the King.

* * *

As I remember Jim Bradley's story, his father, disgusted at what he regarded as the betrayal of the General Strike, left the Labour Party in 1926, joining some breakaway 'militant' organisation. In the following year he persuaded the union's EC to nominate him as a candidate in the LCC elections, a decision which brought down upon their heads the wrath of official Labour and a visit from the London Labour Party Secretary who threatened the union with disaffiliation unless it withdrew its support for Bradley. His nomination was accordingly withdrawn. The surrender clouded the remaining two years of Bradley's life.

The visitor had been Herbert Morrison. Morrison was to earn for himself a reputation as the scourge of the left – Labour's Great Inquisitor. The *Daily Mirror* once wrote of him that he had inherited his intolerance from his father, a London policeman, adding that 'the truncheon in the hall remains his mace'. As wartime Home Secretary he once threatened to close the paper down. When I first clashed with him the war was only a few months old.

I was leading my first deputation. The Representative Body was claiming compensation for the 48-on and 24-off duty system, imposed under Emergency Powers without notice or consultation with the RB. They had been promised a 60-hour week; they now worked 112 hours. True, the AFS were on the same system, but they had volunteered.

We had taken our claim to County Hall where Morrison now reigned supreme. All the normal council committees were suspended for the duration and plenary powers vested in an emergency committee of which he was a chairman. To that committee I put our case. In his reply Morrison compared us to a branch of the armed forces. Though the British troops in France had still seen no action, in that winter, the coldest for years, which they had endured in the field, their misery and suffering had been dire. Herbert contrasted the hardships of the army with the not too uncomfortable existence of fire station life and the opportunity, every third night, to sleep in one's own bed. 'When you make such claims for compensation as these,' he told my deputation, 'you should think of these men and the sacrifices they are making.'

During the First World War Morrison, if he had wished, could have sheltered behind his already weakening eyes and have avoided call-up. Instead, he had courageously supported the cause of conscientious objection and had done alternative war service in agriculture. I was facing him, supported by former gunner Randall, and other members of the Hungry Thousand. One such veteran of the Western Front, incensed by Herbert's lecture, could contain himself no longer. His cockney voice burst out: 'Don't you tell us what it's like in France. We know. We were *there*! Where were you! Fucking cherry picking in Kent.' It was an awful moment. Morrison quietly said that his committee would consider our arguments and bade us good day. We got a weekly bonus of 10 shillings (50p), a payment of just under 1d. per hour. We claimed it a victory.

By now Harry Short and I were desperately looking for help in the field. In 1917 the chairman of the RB had been torpedoed in a North Atlantic winter and lost some toe joints from frost bite following his exposure in an open boat, an injury which in no way impeded his agility as a fireman. He now began to complain that his loss of toes was troubling him. He further declared that he felt giddy at the head of a ladder. Flat feet might be endured, but vertigo could prove fatal, yet despite examination by LCC doctors, no physical cause of his recurring giddiness could be diagnosed.

On the sick list 'Chick' Merrells was an invaluable reinforcement to us. The mysterious vertigo persisted, and with twenty years of service Chick was discharged on an ill health pension to become our full-time organising secretary. He stayed with us throughout the war, a rock upon which I often leant. His calm, good sense and earthy criticisms of some of the more flighty of our propositions were invaluable to me. When Harry Short, his health broken by the strain of war and overwork, was compelled to leave us, Chick took his place as assistant general secretary.

Peace with its fresh round of problems of demobilisation and reorganisation, persuaded Merrells that it was time for him too, to retire with honour. Incidentally, in all my association with him, I never witnessed a giddy fit, but then vertigo, I was told, is very difficult to diagnose.

Chick was the first of our wartime band of brothers. In the urgency of the times the executive boldly gave me a free hand in choosing my helpers. For the moment, since nationalisation of the service was then far off, we needed men with local government experience. In Edinburgh the union had a branch of regulars who had been making headway in Glasgow, Scotland's largest brigade. In England

Bradford remained our provincial stronghold. We sought the help of our members in each of these branches in finding two men who would take on the job of organiser. Each recommended an ally who had supported them in local disputes with their respective councils. The two men could not have been more unlike. Councillor Thomas Murray, a left-wing socialist, had fought in the International Brigade in Spain. He was a perpetual thorn in the side of the ultra-respectable Labour group on the Edinburgh City Council. Reared in the strictest conventions of Scottish Calvinism, he abhorred smoking and drinking. When I first met him on the recommendation of the Edinburgh branch he was earning his living as organiser for the Scottish Temperance League.

Bradford put forward Councillor John McHugh, older than Tom, a mill worker and a leading member of his union. He told me his father had been one of the union delegates at the conference held in Bradford which created the Independent Labour Party. He had trade unionism in his blood. To Murray's annoyance, he smoked the strongest of tobacco in a pipe, which to me always seemed in need of cleaning. The cautious, dour, middle-of-the-road Yorkshire mill worker was a perfect foil to the mercurial left-wing Scotsman. Both men took a little time to accustom themselves to working with a general secretary so junior to them, both in years and experience, but when they did they taught me much.

The government, in readiness for invasion, had divided Britain into fourteen regions, each under the control of a Regional Commissioner who, among other manifold duties, had to oversee the general administration of civil defence and the AFS. By the time our own war organisation had been completed, the union was maintaining a regional office in each one of these fourteen regions, and the structure we set up then remains the basic organisation of the union today. Never before or since has any union been able to draw upon so wide and diverse a field of recruitment for its organisers. Like the armed forces, the AFS was drawn from all walks of life, and all walks of life came to be represented among our regional organisers and leading union members. In Wales a former miner. In the North-East a retired policeman. In the South, a music hall comedian. A businessman whose timber trade with the Baltic had collapsed with war. A plumber. A Jewish commercial traveller from London's 'rag trade', cultivated, witty and a brilliant linguist. Lawyers from the Inns of Court (there was an AFS station in the Middle Temple), among them Fred Willey, a Blackstone Scholar, later to become the Home Secretary's PPS in Attlee's post-war government and a minister under Harold Wilson. Gordon Sandison with a beautiful actor's voice, who on demob left us to lead Actors' Equity as its general secretary, and young Peter Pain, now Sir Peter, Judge of the High Court. A jazz saxophonist. And our three women organisers – Betty Harrison who had worked with Barbara Castle and Vic Feather (later general secretary of the TUC), along with our own John McHugh in Bradford's labour movement and who, in 1945, left us to become assistant secretary of the Tobacco Workers Union. Brilliant, volatile Betty Wallace, widow of Captain Wallace killed at Dunkirk, the son of Edgar Wallace, best-selling crime writer of the 1920s. And prim, competent Mrs Herd, church-going Scot, picked from the Women's Auxiliary Fire Service Officers, whose motherly good sense held the balance between the two Bettys.

And our foremost part-time officials, those still serving in the AFS and who gave their spare time to the FBU. Among them, Tom Murray's right-hand man in Scotland was to become Professor of Music at St Andrew's University. A senior executive of the Oxford University Press, who regretfully resigned from our executive council when the Home office asked him to assist in editing the first volumes of the Manual of Firemanship. Jack Dash, the dockers leader, and his mate, Ted Dickens, who were to be among the 'Dockers' Seven', the striking dockers later sent to prison by Labour's Attorney General, Sir Hartley Shawcross. Reg Underhill, area secretary in London's blitzed East End. He later became Labour Party national organiser, and finally a life peer. We even had a real lord, Faringdon of Buscot. The man from Lloyds who drafted the first scheme of the union's benefit fund and got it underwritten.

Among our rank and filers were Sir Jocelyn Lucas, Bt., Tory MP for Portsmouth; Leonard Cassini, concert pianist; the poet, Stephen Spender, and the novelist Henry Green (who in their post-war writings were not always good humoured when they mocked my old friends, the regular pre-war 'Round-Threads'). And above all, that host of working-class men and women, many of them equipped with a wealth of trade union experience, which riches they readily set at our disposal. But overwhelmingly, most of our members were new to trade unionism. There was among all these people a ferment of ideas and a fresh enthusiasm which gave to the wartime FBU a style and a place unique among working-class organisations. Citrine had called them a 'heterogeneous collection of transients'. Heterogeneous they might have been, transient they were. But while the war lasted these men and women were united in their determination to make it 'a people's war', and the organisation they created in the Fire Brigades Union was their means to achieve that end. The debt I owe to those wartime comrades I can never redeem. I write of them not only out of an old man's nostalgia. In the Britain of the 1990s the idealism we shared, the fellowship of our socialist convictions and our hopes for a Britain after the war whose people would be united in their efforts to win for themselves a nation free from poverty and unemployment are now derided as idealistic and impracticable, as 'wet'. When I observe my country today it is not nostalgia which moves me to recall the spirit and ideals of those men and women with whom I shared so much. Those days were dark indeed. It is in remembering my comrades of those years that my own hopes are strengthened in this still dark world.

* * *

When Percy Kingdom had urged rejection of my nomination he rightly emphasised my lack of experience. It was a useful deficiency, for only someone totally bereft of experience would have embarked upon the foolhardly venture against which Citrine had pronounced so dire a warning. How fortunate was I then in these new colleagues and friends who advised and encouraged me. Perhaps none has more right to my gratitude than Harry Thompson, solicitor. In the First World War W.H. Thompson had been in prison as a conscientious objector, and on his release had devoted himself to working for other COs and their families, work that was well known to the Quakers and pacifists at Walthamstow's Friends' Hall, which Pat and I attended before we married. His name was therefore familiar to me, and it was to him I turned for advice. When his firm and the union were both bombed out of Chancery Lane he took over spare rooms in our new head office. The great nationwide legal organisation, which serves the British trade union movement today, has been built up by Robin and Brian Thompson on the foundations laid by their father when he was a tenant of the FBU. In those days I was then the most privileged of union secretaries, for in the room just over my head I had the sharpest of intellects, the most liberal of minds and the possessor of the widest experience in trade union law. He taught me procedures, constitutions and rules. He drafted the amendments necessary to launch our AFS section. A founder of the National Council of Civil Liberties, he had written 'Let us take care that the totalitarian state is not introduced while we sleep.' If my self-confidence wavered or I was overwhelmed with doubt in the dark days of the war, a nip upstairs for a chat with W.H. Thompson could be a real stiffener for me. When he died, the cause of democracy and trade unions lost a staunch champion. I lost a good friend. The firm he founded has now served Britain's firemen well for over half a century.[5]

Most Chief Officers around London followed Jackson's lead and gave us the freedom of their AFS stations. Elsewhere, particularly in those areas controlled by chief constables, we found the going hard. In Cardiff and Swansea I was tailed by plain-clothes men, and policemen took shorthand notes of the proceedings of the meetings we held in Cardiff Trades Hall. Government departments were unresponsive to our approaches and our letters to the Home Office, when not ignored, were treated with delay and indifference.

ARP rescue squads were made up of skilled building workers, still members of their peace-time unions. NUPE discovered that its ambulance staffs were working alongside volunteers whose pay and conditions were determined by the Home Office. So we formed the Joint Trade Union Civil Defence Committee and asked Arthur Deakin, assistant general secretary of the TGWU, to serve as our chairman. His request for governmental recognition getting nowhere, Deakin decided to ask his general secretary, Ernest Bevin, to intervene.

By now the war was entering a new phase. The Germans had occupied Norway, assisted by a fifth column of pro-Nazis organised by the fascist Vidkun Quisling. It was in an atmosphere of mounting crisis that, led by Bevin, we waited upon the Home Secretary, Sir John Anderson. Anderson had earned a sinister reputation with unions as author of the Baldwin government's revenge measures against the Trades Union Congress following the General Strike, and I looked forward to the encounter. But that afternoon Sir John was busy elsewhere. We would have to make do with the Deputy Under Secretary who conveyed Sir John's apologies. These were grave times, the secretary put to a disgruntled Bevin, and he hoped that we would understand. Mollified, Ernie put our case for recognition. In his reply the civil servant emphasised Sir John's misgivings. If recognition were granted to trade union officials, not all of whom might be full-time, these individuals would seek access to ARP depots, report centres, fire stations and so on. In times of war no Home Secretary could be expected to lightly agree that such sensitive establishments should be open to all and sundry, particularly trade union officers whose political affiliations might be 'widely spread'. Mr Bevin was asked to take note of the recent occupation of Norway by the Nazis. That country's administration had been easily taken over by the enemy since it had already been undermined by Quisling groups in public administration. In the Home Secretary's view these matters were relevant to Mr Bevin's request. At the mention of Quisling I saw Bevin's great neck redden and as the civil servant expanded on this theme Bevin exploded.

'Don't dare mention Quislings and trade unionists in the same breath when you talk to me,' he growled, 'Tell Sir John that it wasn't our lot that sold Norway to the Nazis. Tell him ...' he went on '... that it was *his* lot – just as they would dig the ground from under our feet in this country and sell it abroad if they could get two and a half per cent profit.'

'And tell him this, too,' he added, 'Tell him to tell his friend Chamberlain that if he wants to win this war, he will only do it with the help of the trades unions. So he had better make up his mind.'

And hefting his great bulk from his chair, he turned with 'Let's get out, I won't sit here and be insulted anymore.'

A week or so later I saw Bevin again. As Minister of Labour in Churchill's War Cabinet, he was addressing a gathering of trade union executives and telling his hushed audience that it was doubtful whether the British Expeditionary Force, fast retreating to the French coast, could be rescued. He appealed to his comrades in the unions for an all-out effort to help equip a new army and to be ready for invasion. Even as he was speaking London's fireboat, the *Massey-Shaw*, with a mixed crew of regulars and AFS, was ferrying troops from the beaches to the larger vessels standing offshore. She was to be the last of the little boats to get out of Dunkirk's burning harbour.

* * *

As a curtain-raiser for the 1940 winter blitz, the Nazis had attacked naval fuel installations around the coast. At Pembroke Dock Cardiff's reinforcements were trapped by a flashover from burning oil tanks and a whole pump's crew was incinerated. A few days later the great tank farms at Thames Haven in Essex, thirty miles down river from London were in flames. The local volunteer fire chief asked London for help and 50 pumps went hurtling down the Southend Road. Embarrassed by the size of the reinforcements, the officer sent all but five back. Towards evening, and with the fires still raging, he told the London officer that he must go home since he had his business to attend to on the morrow. With his disappearance the London man asked Lambeth for 40 pumps back. On the phone he was treated to a lecture on the Fire Brigades Act 1938 under which calls for help could be accepted only from the senior officer of the *local* brigade, whose authority must in no way be usurped by those reinforcing him. The London man explained that no one locally seemed to be in charge. Commander Fordham was despatched to report. On arrival he immediately called for 50 pumps and three fireboats, but he was told that local authorisation was first required. Only those who knew Fordham personally could imagine his reaction. He threatened to ring Whitehall, the Home Secretary, the Prime Minister himself if need be. He was told to be patient, that efforts were being made to contact Sir William Spens, the Regional Commissioner for the Eastern Counties, whose headquarters were at Cambridge. Later Fordham had to be told that Sir William, Master of King's College, had retired for the night and that his staff was reluctant to wake him. However, an official had left Cambridge and was on his way to Thames Haven.

John Hampden Fordham was among the younger of the 'Silver Helmets', and, on his appointment had undertaken the full recruits' course at the training school. He claimed that the Hampden in his name stemmed from 'Ship Money' John Hampden of Civil War fame. With his red hair, progressive views and with such an ancestor, I was always pleased to be detailed as his runner. In turn he seemed to welcome me as a merchant navy man and in quiet spells at fires we often talked of matters maritime. Fordham's account of the 'young fellow in a sports jacket' who got out of a small car that night at Thames Haven and introduced himself as 'from Cambridge City Surveyor's Department' went into fire service folk lore. What the 'young fellow' saw before him obliged him to confess that he knew nothing about fighting oil fires and, as representative of the sleeping Sir William, to authorise Commander Fordham to take over. The 50 pumps and the fire boats Fordham then recalled had the fires under control by noon the following day. I believe that the idea of a *national* fire service was born in Fordham's mind that night at Thames Haven. He became a propagandist for reform and between us we maintained an uneasy contingent alliance for years.

* * *

The story of the blitz has long been chronicled. These random anecdotes are but some of my own memories of the times.

It all began at the end of the first week in September. By then Pat had surrendered her refuge in the country to our Quaker friends for members of their own family, fleeing from France before the sweep of the Nazi occupation forces, so now we were renting a house in Chingford. Gus Odlin, our president, was spending a rare weekend's leave with his son at nearby Edmonton and was coming to supper on Saturday evening with Mrs Odlin to meet Pat and see our baby. Supper was disturbed when the bombers which had been over in the afternoon returned to devastate London's dockland. When the raid finally eased I took Gus and his distressed and exhausted wife back to Edmonton but not before he and I had stood on top of Chingford Mount with London stretching below us, dark now with the searchlights dimmed, as the bombers flew homeward. A few miles to the east of us the very firmament was alive with flame and smoke. The loom of the fires in the docks was seen at Bedford and beyond. Helpless and frustrated, president and general secretary, we stood together, witnessing the first terrible round of a battle which our members were to fight without respite for the next 57 nights.

After I had found Pat and the baby a fresh haven in Oxfordshire I felt free to plunge back into the life of the service, toying with the idea of rejoining the brigade as a part-time volunteer, an idea ridiculed by my comrades and frowned upon by Major Jackson – I would have enough on my hands as general secretary without any such adolescent adventures. In the event my role acquired a degree of ambivalence when Jackson sent a despatch rider to head office with an LFB tin hat and a service respirator for my use. As we moved into another freezing winter the brigade overcoat I had retained was recommissioned. All in all, so rigged I was wearing an appropriate war time garb for the LFB Spokesman, in a way, symbolic of the unity of the brigade and the FBU, for in the months which followed an identity was forged between the union and the service which was to prove invulnerable to all attempts to divide us.

Firms were taking their business and staff out of London and office rentals plummeted, so we were able to get a cheap lease for a whole floor of the Chancery Lane Safe Deposit building. Harry Short and I each had a room, we had a committee chamber and ample space for our ever-growing staff. My self-importance swelled and I had my photograph taken for the *Firefighter*, now a regular monthly, behind my nice large desk in all my glory.

The glory was to be short-lived.

Although I had promised to spend the night with the lads in Millwall after an evening meeting in Whitechapel, I was tempted to put off my later engagement, for it had been a tough day. There was little point in driving home to Chingford (no home without Pat and the baby), and I was keeping a comfortable easy chair and rugs in my cosy office. Breakfast was always available in the all-night printers' cafés in Fleet Street. But the evening's raid warmed up and I was soon left alone in Whitechapel's messroom as the remaining appliances turned out. So I kept to my schedule and drove down to the East India Dock and the Isle of Dogs. I was fortunate to have resisted the solitary comfort of my easy chair, for when I drove back after an unquiet night on a trestle I found Fleet Street impassable with unexploded bombs, and half of Chancery Lane gone – our half. A crater spread across what had been our new head office. Nothing could be saved. All had to be begun afresh. For some time we worked from three addresses – Chick's house in Barking, ours in Chingford and Sam Randall's in Merton. When the flying bomb and the V2 hit us three years later we were better prepared. Ten years were to pass before demolition workers found the remains of a safe which the City Corporation identified as ours, for in it were two heat-blackened 'medals' engraved 'FTU 1918'. The 'medals' were the remains of the union's handsome gilt and engraved badges of office worn by the first president and vice-president of the union. Now restored and each with its silken ribbon, they adorn the present holders of those offices as they take their places at annual conference. Few delegates know of their ten-year interment in Chancery Lane.

At times Harry Short would join me in my nightly excursions. It was he who saved us from disaster. After calling at Bishopsgate Fire Station I had sought to avoid blocked-off streets by crossing into Curtain Road by way of little known Primrose Street. There was a lot of stuff falling and it was all very noisy. Primrose Street was no more than the approach to the narrow iron road bridge across the maze of railway tracks behind Liverpool Street Station. As I drove across in the pitch darkness of the black-out it was Harry who spotted, just in time, that half the bridge was missing. The 'incident' had been so recent that no one had yet shut off Primrose Street.

After Primrose Street I took my bike for my nightly rounds of our members. Vision was better and a bike could be humped over rubble, thus avoiding wearisome detours. Peter Pain, our newly appointed aide, joined me on these evening runs to meet our members at work. A young barrister, he had shortly before the war bravely fought a hopeless by-election for the Labour Party. Today Sir Peter Pain has been heard to say of those nights when we biked around bombed and burning London that I had once observed to him, 'There is one good thing about these raids, Peter, they keep our members' minds off their grumbles.'

Peter was a member of Lincoln's Inn in Chancery Lane, and before the great raids we occasionally snatched a half-hour at lunch when he would take me through the Benchers' ancient garden, across to Lincoln's Inn Fields. The Fields were the scene of my earliest victories on behalf of our newly recruited women members. The fine building of the

Royal College of Surgeons in the Square had been vacated and the most precious of the contents of its world-famous Hunterian Museum sent to safety. The AFS had taken some of the empty rooms as a sub-station, parking their appliances in the Fields. Earlier, the aged gorilla at the zoo, Mog, whose antics had made him a favourite with visitors had passed away. In the spirit of scientific fraternity the Zoological Society presented Mog to the Royal College for the study of comparative anatomy. There had been no room for Mog in the removal vans when the College was evacuated and he was left behind in one of the corridors, supine with arms above his head, in a tank of formaldehyde. Unfortunately, the makeshift dormitory of the WAFS lay at the end of this corridor. I was asked, as general secretary of the only union which these women ever joined, to arrange for the disposal of this sad spectacle, and I remembered to mention it at my next Lambeth meeting. Response was speedy. I cannot remember what happened to poor Mog. The next year a direct hit sliced off one wing of the College. In cataloguing their losses after that night's destruction, the Surgeons noted the disappearance of Captain Cook's kangaroo and, they said, of the skeleton of the first gorilla ever brought from Africa to England. But of that floating token of my earliest success in support of our womens' section of the union, they made no mention. Mog had disappeared.

Neither Harry Short nor Peter Pain was with me when, during one noisy evening, I was driving up Charing Cross Road and was caught in a shower of incendiaries – small slim cylinders weighing no more than a couple of kilos. Most of the shower were proving to be dud and were spluttering harmlessly in the roadway. But hesitating and scared, I turned for shelter into the narrow street which led into St Martin's Lane, and in which then stood a Metropolitan Police Section House, accommodation for unmarried policemen. It was for no more than a moment. I knew from the scream of its fall and noise of the explosion that the bomb had fallen but a few hundred yards to the west of me. I drove out into Cambridge Circus. Towards Piccadilly there was a small fire burning, but the left-hand side of Shaftesbury Avenue was a cloud of smoke and dust. I walked through the cloud and over the rubble. The bomb had taken a great slice off the top floor of Soho Fire station. Its ceiling collapsed, the appliance room was a shambles. Already the men who had survived were digging into heaped debris, soon to be joined by old mates of mine from Clerkenwell. Girls in the control room were badly injured and three LFB men who had been in the mess were dead. In the tally of that night's horrors the bomb on Soho got brief mention. The report that the Spokesman had been seen working with the crews rescuing his own trapped and injured members merely confirmed for the brigade the deepening affinity between the service and the union.

The brigade never wholly restored Soho station. After the war, with the damage squared off, the station presented a much truncated frontage to Shaftesbury Avenue for years until it was replaced by the present station, bigger and busier than ever. The old station was still there in 1977 at the time of the firemen's strike. On a cold afternoon I was walking down Shaftesbury Avenue, when a lone fireman stood warming himself over his brazier, a clipboard in his hand, soliciting signatures from passers-by in support of the union. I signed the sheet and moved inside. My name meant nothing to him. I said absently, yet hoping to strike up a conversation, 'I don't think I have been in this appliance room since the night the bomb fell.'

He looked at me. 'What bomb?' he asked. He was very young. And I knew then I was getting very old.

* * *

Still reeling from the catastrophe of Chancery Lane we suffered an even more serious blow – a breakaway. At the moment of our greatest vulnerability the man whom I had recommended as national chairman of our AFS section led some thousands of our members out of the FBU into his secretly planned National Union of Auxiliary Firemen.

In the earliest days of the blitz tensions between the AFS rank and file and the regulars which had long been smouldering flared up again. Many old-timers had been given temporary ranks and responsibilities for which they were untrained and ill-equipped, and they were easy targets for the resentment of the younger and, in many cases, better-educated volunteers under them. In this atmosphere anyone bent on disruption among us had an easy task. It was heart-breaking. We had worked hard to persuade the regulars to accept the AFS into the union. Now we had to persuade the AFS not to desert the regulars. The breakaway cluttered our feet for many months, an irritating diversion and a tragic waste of time, energy and spirit. True, after its first flush of membership which we proceeded to erode (at one time it claimed 12,000 members), it ceased to be a real threat, but its existence remained an embarrassment and gave the Home Office, and Morrison in particular (when it suited his purpose), the opportunity to challenge the FBU's claim for sole recognition.

I had met the man responsible early in the war. With a silver tongue he had claimed the acquaintance of Ellen Wilkinson MP, Morrison's Minister of State, since, he said, they were both at Manchester University. He was a most successful recruiting agent for our AFS Section and I recommended his co-option onto the executive council. There he heard me many times presenting to still doubtful regulars the advantages to them of bringing the AFS into the union and, in his propaganda for his breakaway he quoted my words, cunningly presenting them as proof that Horner's objective was solely to safeguard the privileged position of the regular firemen.

In this upheaval Major Jackson sent word that I should see him. When we met, he started by saying, 'I gather you are having a little trouble.' I acknowledged my difficulties. 'So am I,' he said. He asked that I would treat what he had to say in absolute confidence. I gave him that assurance.

It was a strange story. Churchill had been shifting some of his ministers around. Arthur Greenwood, an elder statesman of the Labour Party, had been made Minister without Portfolio. As a result of a bureaucratic mix-up along the corridors of Whitehall some papers had been deposited on his desk which seemed to have little to do with his current responsibilities. Among them were reports dealing with the conduct and efficiency of the senior command of the London Fire Brigade and of the behaviour of certain individual officers under fire. There were also reports on the attitude of the AFS to these officers. Examples were given of alleged failure of leadership, even of downright cowardice. To me much of it seemed commonplace tittle-tattle. Jackson explained. John Wilmot MP (later Lord Wilmot), who had been given a junior ministerial post by Churchill, was an old friend of Greenwood's and until the outbreak of the war had been chairman of the London Fire Brigade Committee. Greenwood, knowing of Wilmot's continued interest in the fire service, innocently passed over these reports to him. Wilmot, loyal to Jackson, had in turn passed them down.

Their author was the leader of the breakaway. Jackson said he thought I 'ought to know'. He confessed to be at a loss as to his own course of action. 'That's easy,' I retorted, 'Sack him.' Jackson gave me his wry smile, 'I would,' he added, 'but the police won't let me.'

I kept my word to Jackson. It was a useful piece of information to have.

* * *

For much of the war my relations with Morrison were prickly and suspicious, when not downright hostile. With his predecessor at the Home Office, Sir John Anderson, I had no relationship at all. My letters were, after delays, perfunctorily dealt with by an assistant secretary. My pamphlet *AFS – Your Rights to Compensation*, had sealed off any hope of closer association. Then, in the first weeks of the London blitz, homeless, bombed-out and panic-stricken East Enders by sheer weight of numbers forced open the barred-up concrete, fortress-like warehouses of the rail depots at Aldgate, there to shelter 'unofficially', without light, water or sanitation. Only once did I visit Aldgate. It was something out of Dante. Then the Home Office stupidly ordered the underground stations to be shut against the flood tide of raid-wracked Londoners. The subsequent outcry forced Churchill to move Anderson to make way for cockney Morrison – the Londoner's 'Erbert. Until then, such contact as I had made with the Home Office had, perforce, been through Arthur Deakin of the TGWU, Chairman of the Trade Union Joint Civil Defence Committee, now being recognised by officialdom, a slow and unproductive channel, as were my approaches to Sir Arthur Dixon, Anderson's Assistant Under Secretary in charge of the Fire Service Department. When the blitz hit the London AFS my requests for a meeting with him brought nothing but the usual evasive delays. I therefore had no compunction in exposing to the press the shortcomings of his department's policies and the avoidable strain and suffering they imposed upon our members as night after night they fought the fires of London.

When Jackson rang me and asked me to come to Lambeth for 'a private chat', I was surprised to be told to wait in his secretary's office. Time passed. Then Jackson came out and said, 'Here's someone who wants to meet you.' There, in the Major's easy chair was Sir Arthur Dixon. He did not get up. We did not shake hands. Jackson said, 'No doubt you two have a lot to talk about,' and left us.

I did not know what to say and was relieved when Dixon opened up. He said that he understood that I wished to put various matters to him. I should understand that our discussion must be regarded as purely unofficial and should not be taken as in anyway conditioning the policy or attitude of the Home Office towards the Fire Brigades Union. Clearly, I thought, Jackson had gone to great lengths to fix this meeting. I must take advantage of it. I think I started on pumps. I said that the lightweight mobile pumps towed by taxis had proved a great success. Sir Arthur allowed himself a thin smile. I said that Firebrace's London reinforcement scheme was running smoothly. I added that at times we had as many as 15,000 men in the inner London area alone. Another smile. I said that we had four mobile fire service canteens for the whole of London. Men cut off from help had been known to drink water from the Thames. We had no commissariat; no emergency rations; the few cooks we had in the stations were at home during the night. Men came back to their makeshift depots, sodden, tired out and filthy, with no means of drying their only uniform and liable to be called out again. True, a week or two earlier the government had relieved injured men in hospital of their liability to contribute towards the cost of their medical treatment, but I told him that discharging injured men from the service after three weeks, and sending them to seek help from the Assistance Board was doing more to destroy the morale of the AFS than any bombing. This I told him, and much more. Sir Arthur sat silent, his fine intellectual features grim. In all his questioning of me he made no reference to the union or to its public campaign against his department. He acknowledged nothing and promised nothing, but I felt that my account had gone home. I had told him what it meant to be an AFS fireman with only one pair of uniform trousers. That certainly hit the mark. Jackson told me later that before Dixon left, he had reached agreement with the Post Master General's office for 30,000 pairs of trousers to be made over to the AFS from GPO stores. In those days postmen had a red stripe down their trousers and striped trousers in the AFS became known as 'union issue'.

In the days which followed there were further changes. A funeral grant of £7 10s. was allowed to the families of men killed. I had told Dixon of the LCC van which had gone round delivering to their widows dead firemen, each encased in the sacking shroud used by the Heavy Rescue teams. An issue of second uniforms was authorised. (They took a long time coming.) We were making progress. Herbert had taken over.

Long after, when I saw Humphrey Jennings' *Fires were Started*, the most honest of semi-documentary films of the war, I laughed out loud where the AFS man retorts to the regular LFB sub-officer: 'Now I know why you have three pairs of trousers to our one. You sit on your arse so much!'

* * *

In November, breaking my journey from Bristol, I had snatched a night off with Pat in Oxfordshire. With others I stood in the village street listening to the throbbing as waves of bombers swept overhead – their target Coventry. By morning I was in that city, its heart ripped out, factories flattened, its glorious cathedral an empty shell, a thousand people dead. I found our branch secretary, George Dipper, with his crew in what was left of the Warwick Road. Men from reinforcing brigades were all over the town and George was released to accompany me on my tours of the stricken city, visiting them at work, spreading the union gospel. In the city there was neither gas nor electricity and precious little water. The main fire station had been badly damaged and while I stayed in Coventry I slept in the nearby blitzed but rain-proof tram depot at the back of HQ. The water shortage impeded fire-fighting but the local brewery had escaped and for the firemen there seemed to be a limitless supply of free beer.

We had lost 26 of our members and a service was arranged for all the city's dead in a safe corner of the ruined cathedral to which George and I were invited. I excused myself, for I was planning to go over to Birmingham. The stories I had heard and the things I had seen had begun to make me feel tired and depressed. Privately, I promised myself a quiet night in a good bed. Much of my stay in Coventry remains hazy in my mind. My last memory is of George in his filthy uniform walking up towards the ruins of the three spires of the cathedral in the gloom of the drizzling November afternoon.

In Birmingham I had just sat down to the evening meal when a raid began and the diners were ushered to the hotel's shelter. So this was to be my quiet night. I put on my tin hat and overcoat for the night was cold, and walked out into Corporation Street. Already there were fires all around.

Conservative-controlled since the days of Joseph Chamberlain the city council had for long resolutely refused to accept a trade union for their firemen. A few FBU stalwarts, led by George Dipper's friend, Oswald Morgan ('our Ossy') had refused to surrender. More than once I had visited this nucleus of a branch, being smuggled into Ossy's flat in the married quarters at HQ, for the continuous duty system prevented any meeting outside. Finally, the leader of the Labour group on the council persuaded the Chief Officer to meet me and to listen to my exposition to allay his genuine fears of what the FBU might do to his command in Birmingham. Chief Officer Tozer was the 'godfather' of the current family of Tozers in the British fire service. A Tozer had been in charge of the engines at the destruction of the Houses of Parliament in 1834. A Tozer commanded the Fire Protection Companies at the port of Sebastopol during the Crimean War. There were Tozers in Newcastle and on Merseyside. A Tozer was chief of the Finchley brigade. The Deputy Chief in Birmingham was Chief Officer Tozer's son.

My Tozer began our conversation by telling me that he was well aware of my surreptitious visits to Ossy's flat. In future if I wished to come onto the premises, I must first seek his permission. Failure to do so would be to risk eviction, if necessary by the police. The hoped-for informal chat in which I would expound the merits and mutual advantage of proper industrial relations in a disciplined service never got under way. After a few minutes he got up from his chair to indicate that the interview must end. He said he had promised certain city councillors that he would listen to what I had to say. He had heard me. Then he added, 'Industrial relations? I will tell you what my industrial relations are. If a man steps over the line in this brigade, I can get rid of him – like that,' and he snapped his finger and thumb. 'That's the only industrial relations I need.' I was shown the door.

The raid was a bad one. By midnight I thought that the Luftwaffe might be doing to Birmingham what it had just done to Coventry, for as far as I could gather there was no main fire zone. The whole city seemed to be ablaze. I had been exploring, making the union's presence known among the crews, occasionally lending a hand with a length of hose. Many fires were completely unattended. At others single-pump crews of AFS men were trying to tackle whole blazing warehouses, while some streets were blocked with pumps wasting precious water on ruins spread over what was nothing but a smouldering devastation. There seemed to be a complete lack of co-ordination or direction. Tozer's refusal to allow his cadre of regular men and officers to integrate with the AFS (for whom he always appeared to accept little responsibility) meant that in this night's ordeal most of Birmingham's fire crews were leaderless.

The raid eased off after midnight and in the early hours I made my way to headquarters. Surely, I thought, Tozer's prohibitions would not be enforced tonight? I walked through the arch and into the yard and ran slap into Dusty Miller, Firebrace's driver from Lambeth. Through him I heard the story. Firebrace and his Chief of Staff had come up with Sir Arthur Dixon. Two Silver Helmets were also in the city.

Before dawn broke Tozer and his son were removed from command. (It was said that throughout the night Tozer had never left the control room around which he had wandered in his carpet slippers murmuring – 'This thing can't go on – it must stop.') The Tozer dynasty had come to an end. Someone high up had snapped his finger and thumb.

It had been quite a night – quite a week in fact.

By the end of 1940 there had still been no respite from the raids and over Christmas Manchester suffered three nights of severe bombing. I was down in Oxfordshire with Pat and the baby and was determined to stay put. Only later was I called upon to commiserate with the reinforcing crews in Manchester who, they complained, were offered a single cold sausage for their Christmas dinner. On the night of 29 December the Nazis destroyed the City of London, and it was with our members in the smoking ruins around St Paul's that I welcomed in the New Year. It has been said that at the height of the raid Churchill had sent an order to Firebrace – 'Save St Paul's'. St Paul's had been saved and the photograph of the dome emerging from the clouds of smoke and flame, with the light of the burning City picking out the cross has featured in almost every popular history of the war. Today among the towering office blocks of dreary commercialism, which have condemned the rebuilt City to Europe's worst act of architectural vandalism, it is seldom possible to even glimpse the dome. Sometimes as I walk through the City, I feel we would have been better advised to let the whole place burn down. It would at least have made the job of the property sharks so much easier.

Of the many firemen who were killed that night, six died around St Paul's Churchyard. In 1990 annual office rentals there fetch £550 per square yard. The widows of our dead were each granted £7 10s. to bury them. In all the streets and squares of the new City of London there is at the time of writing no tablet recording that night's deaths, but the war memorial in the head office of the FBU carries the words of William Morris:

> There in the world new builded
> Shall our earthly deeds abide,
> Though our names be all forgotten
> And the tale of how we died.

* * *

The abrupt summons to appear before him came only a few weeks after Morrison had been appointed Minister of Home Security. I hadn't seen him since the 'cherry picking' episode at County Hall and by now I was well briefed on his coolness to trade union officials and on his reputed long memory. Some said that he bore grudges. His brilliance as an administrator had made him many admirers, but few friends. Ernest Bevin is said to have overheard someone say that Morrison was his own worst enemy. 'Not while I'm around, he aint,' grunted Ernie.'

He had required my attendance with the union's president, but it was not Gus Odlin who stood by my side that afternoon. Odlin's home had been destroyed in the bombing, and with a shocked and ailing wife Gus had asked to be relieved of union duties. The man who took up his task was a nominee of Harry Short, John Burns from Odlin's neighbouring brigade, East Ham. John was a former Royal Marine, tall, almost soldierly in bearing, a little younger than Gus and tougher. Dixon was standing behind Morrison, and as we sat down he spread before the Home Secretary issues of the *Firefighter*, copies of circular letters to our members and a sheaf of press cuttings. Herbert told us that he was worried about us.

'In normal times,' he said, 'all this', and he waved to the

papers on the table, 'all this might be good fun. But in war,' he went on, 'what might be regarded as legitimate criticism of a government, could, if persisted in, degenerate into defeatist propaganda.' The constant harping on weaknesses, unavoidable in wartime, could, if carried to unreasonable lengths, be construed as attempts to undermine morale and the nation's war effort.

'These have been examined by certain people,' he added, flicking over the pages before him, 'and I am under pressure to act. You must remember, as Minister of Home Security, I am charged with the nation's safety against subversion.' He felt, he said, that he should give us a 'friendly warning'. He was ready to make allowances for inexperience and for some over-enthusiasm (when speaking to John Burns over my head, he more than once referred to 'this young fellow'). He was anxious about some of the 'strange company' I was known to keep. We were only strengthening the hands of those who thought that a trade union had no place in a semi-military, conscripted organisation like the wartime fire service.

Recent emergency regulations had 'locked' our members who were volunteers into the service. No one could leave now. The same regulations had made it a criminal offence for a fireman to disobey a lawful order, punishable by one month's imprisonment. So we asked Herbert what sort of conscripted service it was which condemned men to live in the conditions our members endured, and when they fell ill took them off the payroll and sent them to the Assistance Board? What sort of army was it that dispatched hundreds of men across the country to reinforce local firefighters under attack and was unable properly to deploy them, let alone house and feed them when they got there? What sort of service was it that couldn't even provide its men with fire-fighting uniforms? Far from undermining morale, the union's activities were a major factor in sustaining it. Morrison had earlier talked about the 'need for a friendly chat'. John Burns took him at his word. With his Labour Party credentials, unsullied by links with Communists and left-wingers whom Morrison referred to as my 'strange company', Burns, to Herbert's annoyance, talked to him as one Labour Party member to another. A veteran of the battle of the London Docks and of the battered East End, his blunt account of what weaknesses of organisation could mean to the men on the branch in the inferno of the blitz fire-fighting, seized Morrison's attention, and Dixon began closing his folders.

Burns had been magnificent. (He was to be our president for the next eighteen years.)

We told Morrison of the ideas circulating among our members on service organisation. First, we should rid ourselves of the 1938 Fire Brigades Act. It had never worked and never could; it was a total disaster and should be scrapped. Herbert listened, but made no comment. This was ground he was not prepared to tread with us. He had not ordered us up to listen to our lecture on how to reshape the fire service. But when he did act he surprised us all with the scope and speed of his plans.

Herbert had recently interned an AEU shop steward on the Isle of Man for alleged industrial disruption. In the short chat before we left that afternoon he hinted that he had been advised that it might be difficult to intern a full-time trade union official on the island. I thought he was joking.

There would be further occasions when John Burns and I would be summoned to the headmaster's study. Once he had the whole executive council before him for a drubbing down.

Morrison took no more than thirteen weeks to nationalise the fire service. Sixteen hundred authorities, from the great London County Council down to the tiniest tinpot rural district council, had their brigade and AFS swept from under them. No more regulars. No more AFS. No more police brigades. One service. From Home Office downwards, one single chain of command. No longer when reinforcements were called for by a blitzed area would a town clerk, mayor or borough engineer demand to be consulted before their Council's fire engines might leave their district. All existing ranks were scrapped. All existing officers were re-assessed, shattering changes from which many an old-timer never recovered.

I gave the scheme the union's enthusiastic support when the BBC invited me to broadcast to the nation on the eve of the appointed day (while using this opportunity to advance the union's claims).

Before then Burns and I had once again been called to the Home Office. There Morrison reminded us that under nationalisation our members would no longer be employees of local government, for they would then be Crown servants and subject to all the wartime legislation covering all servants of the Crown. Indeed, in many ways they would be comparable with members of the armed forces. All this, he said, was throwing into question the role of the FBU. He thought that we should know that the government was giving consideration to the relevance of the post-General Strike, anti-trade union laws; to the functions and 'privileges' of the union. He reminded us of the earlier, but unheeded, warnings he had given us as to our behaviour and we went away duly chastened.

I lost no time in consulting W.H. Thompson. 'All bluff,' Harry said. Without an amendment to the Acts or an extension of his emergency powers, Herbert could do nothing. And in the existing political climate Thompson doubted whether he would seek either.

Armed with Thompson's opinion I told Citrine at the TUC of the Home Secretary's implied threats. Citrine looked grave and promised action. It was not long before Morrison was telling parliament that he was happy to inform the House that all doubts had been resolved and that the Trades Disputes Act, 1927, had no application to the newly created NFS.

We thought we had won hands down. But Herbert had not finished yet.

Dixon, then an up-and-coming civil servant in the Police Division, had been among the Home Office officials who after the Police Strike of 1919 had destroyed the National Union of Police and Prison Officers and created in its place the toothless Police Federation. He was now set to work planning a similar organisation for the NFS. A copy of the draft constitution was leaked to me. As in the Police Federation, no financial contributions would be called for from members since all expenses and facilities would be provided free of charge. There would be a National Representative Board with which the Home Secretary would deal. Similar boards would be set up at all levels of NFS administration. No association with 'outside bodies' would be permitted. Only serving members of the NFS would be allowed to participate in the affairs of the federation.

Such an organisation would be a formidable challenge to the union.

In parliament Herbert's Minister of State, Colonel Sir William Mabane, was hinting that something was afoot and telling MPs that the NFS was 'a highly disciplined body analogous to the fighting services'. Drawing upon his experiences as an army officer, he declared that he would have 'felt strongly' if someone not under his command, 'and not necessarily in the same surroundings and entourage as his men, came between him and them'. He added that, 'Without hostility to the FBU, these questions were exercising the minds of the Home Office and senior fire service officers.'

Back I went to the TUC, the senior committee of which demanded a meeting with Morrison. They took me along and for once I enjoyed an afternoon in Herbert's room. Heavyweights of Congress, I think they enjoyed the afternoon too. In his defence Morrison argued that as minister he had the duty to ensure that all NFS personnel had available to them the benefits and rights of collective representation, regardless of their attachment to any outside organisation. The FBU had never claimed 100 per cent membership. Unwisely he referred to the breakaway union, which still festered, as evidence of the weakness of the union's claim for sole recognition. With us was Ebby Edwards, president of the Mineworkers' Federation, a Yorkshire miner and one who had suffered from the breakaway union established by the coalowners among Nottinghamshire miners after the General Strike. Ebby knew about company unions. He was a little, wiry man, and I remember that he stood up to lean over the table to face Morrison as he said, 'You're opening a rival butcher's shop and we're not having it. So don't trouble to take the bloody shutters down.'

The federation was aborted. But Herbert had not given in. In an Order of the Day to 'commissioned' ranks he personally invited them to enrol in a new association (NAFO), whose president would be none other than Chief of Fire Staff, Sir Aylmer Firebrace. In the face of such sponsorship only the boldest of the recently appointed officers would throw in their lot with the union.

Firebrace relinquished his presidency after one year. An officer who later became a Conservative MP was appointed as secretary. The discord and disunity among the senior ranks was to plague the service for many years.

* * *

Nationalisation had brought in its train a personal message to all ranks from Herbert, floods of Home Office memoranda, a stiffer discipline code, a new hierarchy of 'commissioned' officers and the abolition of the London Fire Brigade. After a decent interval Jackson was relieved of his command and shunted sideways to a staff job. Other Silver Helmets were moved to new commands across the country. An Officers' Staff College was established with a Brigadier General as commandant, an appointment which heralded sporadic attempts to foster a quasi-military atmosphere in the new service.

Their proud brigade gone, their senior officers dispersed, many former 'Round Threads' were unhappy at all the changes swirling around them and depression had settled on the handful of my old comrades still serving at the ancient, and now much diminished Southwark Station. It was the last survivor of our former tea-boat crew who told me of the visit of their new Fire Force Commander, a former Assistant Chief Constable in the police fire brigade of a northern city, still happily unscathed by enemy bombers. Southwark's crews were mustered for his inspection and to receive his morale-boosting address.

The early months of 1942 were perhaps the darkest of the war. Among the ex-matelots left from the Hungry Thousand, pride in the Navy had suffered terrible blows when HMS *Hood*, the finest battleship ever built, was blown out of the water by the *Bismarck*. Singapore had then fallen to the

Japanese with Britain's two remaining great ships, *Repulse* and *Prince of Wales*, going to the bottom of the South China Sea. There were few survivors. To my old comrades, these sinkings were more than national disasters. They were personal tragedies bringing a deep and intimate loss.

The entire south side of the river from London Bridge to Blackfriars, a third of their station's fire ground, was now a blackened void. Facing them across the Thames was the City's own square mile of devastation, constant reminders of those terrible winter raids. And for most of these veterans this was their second war. Their morale certainly needed a boost. Standing at ease, they were inspecting their new Commander in his spanking new NFS uniform, a tall handsome man, young for his high rank, every inch an officer and sporting an unauthorised swagger stick. For the lower ranks, NFS uniforms were being issued in dribs and drabs, and some AFS men on parade were wearing makeshift army battle dress dyed blue. Former LFB men were still wearing their round sailors' hats. They were an ill-assorted assembly.

The Commander told the parade that having inspected their station, he had found it untidy and dirty. (By that stage of the war, station stores were well nigh exhausted.) He had examined the station's drill records and where they had not been actually falsified the drills themselves had been scamped. Gear was stowed in the appliances in an unorthodox manner and the general upkeep of the machines seemed slipshod. The Commander delivered a condemnation of all things sloppy and slovenly. He was, he said, aware that there were present long-serving members of the former LFB. He would remind them that London's days were over. No doubt the LFB had been entitled to its one-time reputation, but loyalty must now be to the new service – the NFS. Times had changed and he was determined to root out this happy-go-lucky way of running things. He intended to visit Southwark every month until he was satisfied that all round improvements were being achieved and maintained. Were there any questions? The swagger stick was tapping the thigh.

My old tea-boat chum paused in his tale. Did I remember Lofty Wothers? I did indeed – no friend of mine – a lanky ex-naval hand who always poured cold water on my enthusiasms and never failed to predict a miserable failure for our union activities, and to prophesy no end of trouble for me personally. He vented a morose, mordant wit in a doleful nasal drawl. I had cause to remember Lofty.

Lofty had mumbled, 'I've a question.'

'Two paces forward that man,' snapped the ex-copper.

'One two – one two. Name?'

'Wothers.'

'Say, Fireman Wothers, *Sir*,' barked the Commander.

'Fireman Wothers, *Sir*,' dutifully repeated Lofty.

'Straighten up man,' urged Swagger Stick.

Lofty drew himself up until his eyes met those of his Fire Force Commander.

'Well, what's your question Wothers?'

In that sibilant, nasal whine I disliked so much, Lofty asked, 'Why don't you piss off?'

Wisely, the Commander turned on his heel and stalked out to his car. I believe he never paid a return visit to Southwark.

By the time I had finished laughing at my old mate's tale I knew that Lofty's question had settled another which worried me. I knew then that they would never militarise the NFS.

* * *

To every company, column, division, fire force and region in the new service, the union had promptly and smoothly attached its corresponding committee and officials. A task further complicated as the insatiable demands of the forces for manpower took thousands of our younger men into the army. Their loss was made good by extending the unpopular 48/24 duty system – the 112-hour week – to the entire NFS. The resulting resentment deepened when it was realised that standardisation of pay would apply to 'commissioned' officers only. For the lower ranks, nothing would be done to remove the gross disparities of pay between the former AFS and regulars. We were to be an army with a dozen different pay scales. Most disappointing of all, there was to be no change in the miserly injury and sickness pay for the AFS.

So we launched the Firemen's Charter Campaign. Nothing quite like it had been seen in the trade union movement. Nothing quite like it has been seen since, until it was matched by the ambulance staffs in 1990. Our Regional Committees all over Britain competed with each other in the enthusiasm with which they spread the union's message. By the end of the campaign over some 400 public meetings had been held. At trade union branches, at dances, factory gates, film shows, boxing matches, classical concerts and rallies, the five points of the Firemen's Charter were expounded.

MPs of all parties, trade union leaders, parsons, mayors, actresses, all were eager to speak for the nation's firemen. The *Daily Mirror* ('the forces' paper', as it was known), presented our case in the cartoon reproduced opposite. Bernard Shaw, novelist J.B. Priestley and playwright Sean O'Casey wrote articles in our support. Our own comedian organiser enlisted his professional colleagues and Collin's Music Hall and the New Cross Empire, traditional homes of Cockney humour, each gave us a show. I was 'billed' at both. At Collin's, while in full flow in my interval speech, a note was handed to me from the wings. 'Your time is up. The artistes are waiting,' and open-mouthed I watched the curtain ring down before me. '*Artistes*,' indeed.

As the Charter Campaign rolled on thousands of our members with their appliances and equipment moved down from Scotland and the North into camps and depots in the South and South-West of England, their task to safeguard the mountains of stores, ammunition and fuel being stacked in readiness for D Day. Column by column, company by company, they moved off, each with their union organisation intact. From now on every aspect of the lives of the transferees, on or off duty, became the concern of the FBU. The war had, of course, dislocated the lives of millions, but any family wrenched apart was faced with added burdens to the complications of everyday life then endured by all British people.

Firemen cheerfully endured discomfort while the yet untested service tackled the logistics of these mass movements. In all this upheaval, the FBU speedily became the

The aim of the Firemen's Charter in *The Firefighter*, December 1941 summed up by Illingworth's cartoon

unofficial welfare branch for the exercise. Travel warrants for men returning home on leave, hardship allowances from the Ministry of Labour for families left behind, difficulties with landlords and lodging allowances for men billeted out of camp, legal problems, marital problems, nothing was beyond the union's range. When the Ministry of Food sought to impound our members' ration books, leaving them to scratch for themselves for food at home or off camp on leave, it was the union which fought and won the 'Battle of the Ration Book'. Food was then tight for everyone, we weren't greedy, but bureaucracy did stupid things. When official welfare officers were finally appointed, Fire Force Commanders in the reception areas accepted the union's nominees for the posts. Our national officer, Peter Pain, published a set of guides to the morass of official regulations emanating from the various Ministries of Food, Labour and Pensions as they affected our service. Each guide was a model of precision.

Later in life, Peter wrote the *Manual of Fire Service Law* which went through many editions and for years was the stand-by of every senior officer.

I was a frequent visitor to the camps. Once, lost on Dartmoor after midnight, I unavailingly sought help from a wandering American patrol. Newly arrived from Texas, the soldiers seemed unclear as to the exact country they were in, let alone the road to Ivybridge.

* * *

It was about this time that Herbert Morrison wrote to me. 'We are', he declared, 'now at a critical stage in the war, and in the vital part which the National Fire Service has to play, everything must be subordinated to the one paramount task of defeating the enemy. The Fire Brigades Union has a great opportunity to make a worthy contribution to our national effort. If you and your executive are prepared to co-operate with the Department in what should be the common aim of all of us, namely the building of a keen and efficient Service, you will not find any lack of co-operation on this side.'

As so it turned out to be.

Peter Pain and I, along with the Home Office officials, were invited to a conference with the War Office and Ministry of Pensions, charged with drawing up a scheme for our injured and sick, based upon the identical principles and practices obtaining for the army. Then a memorandum of agreement was jointly approved between the department and the union on collective representation in the NFS, relations with Fire Force Commanders, facilities for union work and for union meetings on fire stations.

In reporting to the TUC, I wrote – 'few, if any, unions enjoy the same comprehensive negotiating machinery as does the FBU'. In many Force Areas joint efficiency committees were set up between the union and the commanders. The discipline code was relaxed.

The Charter Campaign was succeeding.

By 1943 the FBU was 25 years old. We decided in this, our Jubilee Year, to dissolve the cranky arrangement of the two (now outdated) union sections – regular and AFS and to 'fuse' the union into a single whole. It was a complicated business, requiring three separate conferences in a single week, (two to be held simultaneously), with me as secretary of both sections and general secretary of the union, popping from one to the other. A difficult assignment, but W.H. Thompson had tutored me well. The 'fusion' complete and the new unified rules approved, the born-again FBU proceeded to its first annual conference.

It was a large conference, for although conscription into the army had reduced our numbers from a peak membership of 75,000 we now had branches from the Orkneys to the Scillies. Our contingent sent to India as the Japanese advanced through Burma kept up their membership and an intermittent contact with head office. They had sailed in two drafts. The first ship got no further than the Clyde where it collided and sank. The second was torpedoed off Freemantle, but they all got to India in the end and when they came safely home their claims against the War Office kept us busy for months.

To read the proceedings of that Jubilee Conference is to glimpse a little of the spirit which then moved ordinary British people and of their hopes for the Britain they wanted to build in the hard won peace. One woman delegate asked for a free issue of darning wool to the WNFS. Before conference was over that same woman was calling for the creation of mobile NFS columns of volunteers to support the Allied invasion forces when they landed in Europe. (When the Overseas Columns were formed later, each became an FBU branch, complete with its officials, and when American General 'Blood and Guts' Patton reviewed the NFS column attached to his army group in Germany ours must have been the only union branch committee he ever met.)

Sir William Beveridge, his bombshell of a report on a post-war welfare state just published, and himself at the storm centre of the debate which was sweeping the country, came to the Jubilee Conference and accepted the presidency of the League of Firemen that we were planning to help to resettle our members on demobilisation. The units of Canadian firemen who had crossed the Atlantic to serve with us sent fraternal delegates from their American Fire Fighters' International. Fernand Grenier, hero of the French underground resistance, recently arrived in London, thrilled delegates with his account of fighting with the Maquis. One resolution congratulated 'our comrades in the RAF on their thousand bomber raids' which were then plaster-bombing German cities. The resolution spoke of their 'loathsome, but necessary duty'. An amendment sought to delete the word 'loathsome'. We knew nothing at the time of the gas chambers of Auschwitz where productivity must have been reaching record levels, nor that a new kind of bomb was in the making which would mean that the post-war world would not be that to which conference was aspiring in its ringing declarations. (In 1947 I walked through the ruins of Berlin and Dresden examining the effects of those thousand bomber raids. I came home ill. I never went to Hiroshima. Since Coventry, the world had sunk deep into barbarism.)

We aimed to round off the week with a 'Jubilee Dinner'. Rationing would limit the meal to five shillings (25p) per head, a limitation which suited nicely our meagre funds – sausage tart and two veg, treacle pudding for afters and buy your own beer. Herbert indicated he would like to come, and brought his two knights, Sir Arthur and Sir Aylmer. Dixon (who had just spent a day with the union's National Women's Committee) surprised us all with his charm, and Sir Aylmer genuinely tried hard to unbend before a couple of hundred of his rank and file. Professor Harold Laski, Labour Party chairman, and Annie Loughlin, TUC president (the first woman in that post) represented the two wings of the movement. Beveridge dropped in. All our union friends came. The editor of the *Daily Mirror*, a valiant supporter of the Charter, had his picture taken with Morrison, earlier threats of closure forgotten for the evening. Hannen Swaffer, the doyen of Fleet Street and a speaker for the Charter, turned up. My own dinner companion was 'Red' Ellen Wilkinson, MP, leader of the Jarrow Hunger March, now Minister of State at the Home Office.

All had come to eat sausage tart with Britain's firemen and firewomen and to witness the public reconciliation between their union and the Home Secretary.

In a speech which touched lightly on the earlier difficulties, Morrison confessed his pride in sustaining trade unionism in 'Britain's Fourth Arm in time of war, to the surprise', he said, 'and perhaps no little concern of some in high places'. Initial misunderstandings had left their mark, but, 'we have learned from each other – both sides are still learning'. His reference to 'this young fella', to whom he had given so much advice which had been so persistently ignored, was no more than good humoured banter. He acknowledged the help his department was getting from the union and delivered a ministerial speech on 'our joint task in the testing time which lay ahead'. I, who by then could produce a speech at the drop of a hat, remained silent, wisely deciding to leave everything to John Burns, whose simple, dignified reply I could never have matched. Morrison's speech set the tone of the remainder of his period as wartime Home Secretary and cleared the way for co-operation with his successor, Chuter Ede, in the early years of Labour's post-war government.

What Harry Short, Sam Randall, Chick Merrells, Jim Bradley and I set out to save – the unity of the FBU – was now safe. We could face the upheavals and uncertainties which peace and demobilisation would bring. In a couple of years this monster wartime service would be dismantled and most of our members would return to factories and offices, to the building sites and docks. Our band of organisers would leave us, some to the Bar, some to posts in other trade unions proudly wearing their FBU badges as others wore their service ribbons. Rank-and-file and officials, good comrades all, they would leave a lasting mark on the political scene. In the inferno of the blitz, in the devastation of the flying bombs and rockets, by their readiness to 'lend a hand' in any crisis or public need (we organised NFS work gangs to weatherproof countless homes wrecked by flying bombs), by their co-operation with the forces in preparation for D-Day, they had won the nation's admiration and affection. And by their union work they had shown that even in the darkest days of the war a viable democracy fighting to destroy a fascism which had murdered trade unionism throughout Europe must needs preserve and nurture trade unionism at home. They really believed in a 'People's War'.

When the Nazi bombers turned eastwards to destroy Russian cities our members found themselves in a 'lull' period, condemned to endless drills and exercises. Tired of this inaction, they had broken through sceptical bureaucratic barriers and brought 'Productive Work' into the fire service. Herbert complained to the House of Commons that the 'FBU has entered the capitalist world and has drawn up contracts with industry using my electricity and my premises for which I pay rates, without any by your leave. After all, the service still belongs to the state. It hasn't yet been taken over by the Fire Brigades Union.' Not quite. Even while Herbert was speaking, no fewer than 40 branches in North London alone were already linked up with Plesseys Electronics and assembling radio equipment for Lancaster bombers, while still maintaining a state of instant readiness for action. That same spirit, welling up from below, had inspired the Overseas Columns, and when after VE Day they returned to be stood down in Regents Park I was at the saluting base with the 'caretaker' Home Secretary, Sir Donald Somervell, 'caretaker' because the Labour ministers had resigned from

Churchill's government in readiness for the general election. As the lads marched past they didn't know Sir Donald (Donald who?). They knew their general secretary.

* * *

With the war over, preparations began for the long deferred general election. I had refused nominations from constituencies and so did not join former FBU members in the new parliamentary Labour landslide victory. Instead I joined the Communist Party. On hearing of my apostasy, Herbert Morrison was reputed to have said, 'A pity.'

Ten years later, I left the Communist Party as the Soviet tanks rolled back into Hungary. By then I had come to agree with Morrison. It had been a pity.

Twenty more turbulent years in the union lay ahead before I would go to Westminster. To have become an MP in 1945 would have meant leaving a union once more plunging into deep crisis, for as the NFS was demobilised our membership plummeted, for a time, to below 12,000, threatening our very basic structure with collapse. It was a sadly shrunken service which in 1948 was handed over to local councils, already hard pressed by the problems of post-war reconstruction. Many a pinchbeck chairman of these new fire authorities would recall that when last he served on a fire brigade committee, labourers in the council yard had doubled up as part-time firemen with the town surveyor or borough engineer as captain. So what was all this talk of full-time firemen on police pay?

We were to be condemned to a chronic manpower shortage in which even the reconstructed London Brigade was for years 25 per cent below its strength. To make good such deficiencies the authorities were empowered to impose duty systems ranging from 60 hours a week to 84 – on the same scale of pay. Exploiting this undermanning, the county councils made no secret of their determination to return to retained duties as the norm, or at least to a combined system of wholetime retained duties. Their needs for men would thus be reduced to a bare minimum. All of our new employers were united in seeking to break our tenuous link with police pay.

So in November 1951, to draw public attention to our plight, and in defence of what was left of 'police parity', the union staged its first industrial action. It was a feeble enough gesture, but even so we gave the employers ample notice of our intentions. All calls would be responded to in the normal way, but for 48 hours no drills would be performed and in stations no windows would be cleaned, no floors scrubbed, no brass polished. We had launched our first 'Spit and Polish' demonstration. Our members everywhere responded to a man.

Councils up and down the country thereupon took leave of their senses. The London County Council publicly condemned the refusal to scrub and polish as 'sabotage' and placed nearly 1,700 of our members on disciplinary charges. We promised to defend every charge, a process which we calculated would take about ten years. Elsewhere men were suspended, fined, demoted and even sacked. In half a dozen brigades the police were called to eject our members from their stations. The union's pledge to maintain fire cover was sabotaged by this extraordinary display of panic, a panic exacerbated by the fact that the general secretary of the union, the leader of this mutiny, they were told, was a notorious Communist.

For the world was now deep in the Cold War. Indeed, while we fought for police pay for our members, some of them, army reservists on recall, were actually fighting in Korea where America was threatening to use the atomic bomb against the Chinese.

The employers had miscalculated. The victimisation and the reprisals against our members produced a sweeping wave of support for us from the labour movement and beyond. The General Council of the TUC demanded a meeting with the Minister of Labour. The executive of the Labour Party called upon the Home Secretary, Sir David Maxwell-Fyfe. Facing an outraged Opposition in the House he was compelled to plead with fire authorities for 'moderation'. The Dean of St Paul's and the Cardinal Archbishop of Westminster intervened on our behalf with the Tory government. The Dean in his

Christmas sermon asked his congregation to 'remember their firemen'.

The embarrassed disarray of the employers became plain for all to see. But the disciplinary procedures were under way, the demotions and sackings had been authorised and a public climb-down by the employers might have been seen as undermining their authority and that of their senior officers over their rebellious troop. No single fire authority would be the first to step out of line.

Then, three days before Christmas, three firemen were killed and a dozen injured in a fire in the City. Yesterday's 'saboteurs' became London's heroes. The LCC forthwith withdrew the 1,700 disciplinary charges (the dead men were on the list), in appreciation they said 'of the outstanding devotion to duty' shown that night by our members. Councils everywhere were keen to follow their lead. Fines were repaid, demotions rescinded, sacked men were reinstated. In the bitterness of the times I could not repress my feelings that the employers' ignominious retreat was, in part, a shabby cynical exploitation of the Christmas tragedy.

Not all charges were so easily withdrawn and by May the following year I was still appearing before fire brigade committees, but at the end every man sacked was back in the job.

The Ministry of Labour Arbitration Tribunal appointed to adjudicate on the dispute increased the employers' offer by eighteen pence (7½p). The hearing had taken three and a half days and at the end we had lost the last remnant of police parity.

When I was telephoned the result, for the first and only time in my life, I literally reeled.

* * *

After that every year seems to have been a campaign year. In the wake of any big fire or disaster which had commanded the headlines we would issue statements, hold press conferences, publish pamphlets, canvass MPs, lobby councils and public bodies. There was 'Don't Let Britain Burn' year, 'Whose Turn to Burn?' year, 'Don't Gamble with Lives' year. We campaigned for more men, more appliances, more powers of inspection, for fire regulations, for a truly modern fire protection service. We appeared before a Commons Select Committee. We met a series of Tory Home Secretaries. We fought every attempt to take the service back to continuous duty. And in retaliation against our direct action to thwart their plans for a brigade based upon a form of wholetime-retained duty, the Glamorgan County Council disciplined and sacked 42 of our members. So then we had a Glamorgan Campaign Year against continuous duty and for reinstatement of our victimised members. We won, on both counts.

Meanwhile the Cold War had been sliding into deep freeze. Britain had now tested its atom bombs in the Pacific and the government, as part of the war scare, was intent on creating a new AFS. But first our present members had to be trained in 'nuclear defence'. For that purpose an old RAF depot left over from the previous war was recommissioned as an Emergency Training Centre. Cracked and grass-grown runways would serve as drill areas, draughty wooden huts as living quarters, the old hangars as stores for the new government emergency tenders – 'Green Goddesses' we dubbed them. From the cold, windswept perimeter of Moreton-in-Marsh (RAF), these monsters were trundled along narrow Gloucestershire lanes and through idyllic Cotswold villages in a simulation of Britain in nuclear war. I regularly took advantage of the presence of a couple of hundred FBU members from brigades all over Britain, gathered together at the government's expense, to hold a miniature annual conference in the mess hall at Moreton and to expose the government's lying, cynical propaganda about the nature of nuclear war. At that time, in dealing with radioactive fall-out, rumours about which were beginning to worry people, the Ministry of Agriculture advised housewives that 'after a nuclear attack lettuces should be avoided' and that 'a hard hearted brassica would need to be well washed before cooking, whereas peas within the pod would be quite safe to eat'. The Ministry of Local Government was warning householders whose domestic hot water systems depended on solid fuel boilers 'to remember to draw the boiler fire in the event of a nuclear attack since if the water supply failed an explosion might occur'.

Chernobyl was then an unknown Ukrainian village.

When the delegates at the 1954 FBU Annual Conference marched against the A-Bomb along Southend front they were the first trade union demonstration against nuclear war. The FBU banner was carried on every Aldermaston March. In 1960 Frank Cousins, general secretary of the TGWU, and I successfully moved the unilateralist resolution at the Scarborough Labour Party Conference (and saw it overturned the following year, after Hugh Gaitskell's 'Fight, fight and fight again' speech).

Our opposition to the criminal waste of resources at Moreton was compounded by our conviction that the service *did* need a national training centre. The senior staff college at Dorking, housed in the charming home of the seventeenth-century diarist, John Evelyn, had become patently incapable of meeting the needs of the service. We argued that the funds so grossly mis-spent on Moreton should be used to create a purpose-built modern technical training establishment employing up-to-the-minute methods of instruction and of study, a centre of development and research open to all ranks, to carry forward our service into the next decade.

In 1958 John Burns retired from the service and from the presidency. He left the union deeply in his debt. Ours had been a good partnership spanning nearly twenty years. Sadly John Burns died a year or so after retirement.

I had recruited Terry Parry, just demobbed from the navy, into the union at the war's end when I spoke to the NFS recruits from the armed forces training in Sutton Park, Birmingham. As president, Terry was a man of ideas and was possessed by one particular aim – to rid the fire service of what he called its 'mop and bucket' mentality. Until that was rooted out, Terry argued, we would never be able to create the sort of modern fire service Britain needed. Station routine had changed little since I was in the job. Men still spent countless hours in unrelieved boredom scrubbing and polishing, in a demeaning round of household chores which dulled the spirit and satisfied only the station officer's obsession to present the shining face of his station to the visiting divisional officer, but had little to do with efficiency. We had long objected to the practice of the confidential report whereby a man's ability and conduct was the subject of a detailed and undisclosed annual report by his station officer to the senior command. At Terry's first Annual Conference as president, one delegate revealed that while cleaning the station office he had been able surreptitiously to glance at his own current report before it was dispatched to HQ. His officer had revealed to the Chief that when washing floors 'this man leaves puddles'.

Shortly before, Smithfield meat market in London had been swept by fire. The stench of roast meat from the thousands of incinerated carcasses hung around the City for a week. Two men from the first attendance from Clerkenwell had lost themselves in the market's network of underground tunnels. Their oxygen supply exhausted, they died in those smoke-filled catacombs. No one missed them. At the inquest it was disclosed to a shocked coroner's court that no plan of the tunnels had been available to the brigade, which indeed had no previous idea of their existence. For the market, a major fire risk, had never been visited let alone inspected by the brigade. No regulations existed in respect of its fire precautions. The brigade acknowledged it did not employ breathing apparatus control procedures, neither had it contemplated the need of such precautions. The outdated Siebe Gorman oxygen sets had no audible warning signal of cylinder content. The dying men had no means of calling for assistance or of denoting their whereabouts.

The acres of Smithfield meat market in which those death traps were set were less than five minutes from Clerkenwell Station at the top of Farringdon Road.

Then a large whisky bond warehouse blew up in Central Glasgow. Nineteen firefighters were killed, a score of others injured. The Procurator Fiscal's enquiry revealed that no fire precaution regulations existed for such establishments, the brigade had no powers of inspection and had never visited the building, had no knowledge of its layout, its storage system or of millions of gallons of volatile spirit which formed a veritable bomb, liable to explode at any time, and set in one of Glasgow's busiest commercial districts.

And yet the fire service which had to deal with such risks and with the consequences of in-built official negligence, still harboured a mentality which would report a fireman to his senior officer for 'leaving puddles'. So we launched the union on what was to be my last FBU campaign – 'A Service for the Sixties'.[7] Although I wrote it and presented it for acceptance to the 1960 Rothesay Conference, Terry Parry's was the enthusiasm and fresh thinking which did so much to inspire the campaign.

Half-way through the 1960s our crusade had been gaining public support and a growing official interest. By now I had completed more than thirty years of service and was approaching brigade retiring age. Sad at leaving, I was yet happy to place matters in Terry's hands as he succeeded me as general secretary. Another remarkably fruitful partnership blossomed when Enoch Humphries took Terry's place as president. Indeed, their joint talents and energy produced a dynamic leadership which carried the union along until Enoch's own retirement just before the national strike. Enoch and Terry were regular visitors to the House of Commons of which I now (1964) sat as a member of Harold Wilson's parliament. 'A Service for the Sixties' was set to become a reality when the Labour government appointed a high powered Committee of Enquiry into the Fire Service, under the Chairmanship of Sir Ronald Holroyd, Deputy Chairman of ICI. Their task was to examine and report on every aspect of the service, its function, organisation, administration, its legal powers (or lack of them), training, responsibility for fire prevention and inspection, employment conditions, all were subject to searching scrutiny. The committee toured our stations and visited Switzerland, Japan and the US in the most comprehensive look at 'the job' ever undertaken. My last formal service for the FBU was, from the vantage point of the House of Commons, to work with Terry and Enoch and the executive council to ensure that the Home Secretary received a report which vindicated 'A Service for the Sixties' up to the hilt. Terry said that

Holroyd's paragraphs on 'Station Cleaning and Fire Prevention' were 'music to my ears'.

The union had set the service on its new course.

* * *

In collating these random recollections I have had occasion to use the facilities of the splendid library and archives at Moreton-in-Marsh Fire Service Training College which caters for five hundred students of all ranks and is today universally considered the outstanding establishment of its kind in the world. I found the wind still blowing chill across the campus, beautifully landscaped from what was the old airfield. Walking from the dining hall to the library across Massey Shaw Avenue, I passed three students' halls of residence. They are called Firebrace House and Dixon House. The third is Horner House.

What would Sir Aylmer have said?

Notes

1. 'Matelot' was service slang for sailor, a lower deck rating in the British navy. In the pre-war London Fire brigade, according to Horner, the men were divided into three species: 'matelots' (Royal Navy), 'pongos' (Army) and 'civvies'. As a former Merchant Navy man, Horner always assumed he was an honorary 'matelot'.
2. Askwith Award, 18 September 1918.
3. This is a reference to the first volume of John Horner's unpublished autobiography.
4. John is probably thinking of the 1936 march, the last one to be organised by the National Unemployed Workers' Movement. For John Boyd Orr's findings, see his *Food, Health and Income* (1936).
5. See Appendix V for more on the contribution of W.H. Thompson.
6. This was not, perhaps, the only occasion on which Bevin made such a comment. Denis Healey claims that Bevin said the same of Aneurin Bevan at the time of the February 1951 defence debate in parliament: Healey, *The Time of My Life*, London 1990, p. 151.
7. See Appendix I for John Horner's statement on *A Service for the Sixties*.

11 Reminiscences of a President

Enoch Humphries

Enoch Humphries was born on 25 September 1922 in a two-room apartment at 33 Victoria Street, Rutherglen.[1] His mother had been made a widow from her first marriage, and she had four children; she married Enoch's father, who had been divorced, and had two children. The father was a driver who had served in the army during the First World War, and after Enoch was born the family moved from Rutherglen to Glasgow where the father worked for the main agent for the Rover car company.

Enoch went to school at St David's primary in the Townhead area of Glasgow, and at the age of eleven he went to Townhead Secondary. At this time his father died after a short illness, and his mother was left again a widow, with only Enoch at home. His mother took a job as a cook/housekeeper, and her wages were their only income. Enoch left school at the age of fourteen; worked in several jobs, beginning at 10 shillings per week, and his last job in 1939 was as a cellarman for a whisky firm. At the end of 1939 he joined the RAF, giving his age as eighteen, a year older than in fact he was. By 1940 he was in the Far East. He was in the transport department of the RAF and saw operational combat in Burma. He returned to the United Kingdom in 1944 and was demobilised in the early part of 1946. During his last months in the RAF he listened to representatives of various public services who were looking for recruits, and these included the prison service, the police and the fire service. He decided for this last and was accepted for the

National Fire Service in Glasgow. After six weeks' training which he describes as 'extremely elementary', he was sent to a pre-war fire station in Glasgow:

> Most of the time was spent polishing brass and cleaning while the main thought in young men's minds at that time was, in fact, the question and desire of attending fires. Now that may seem difficult to appreciate, but the degree of boredom that was centered around the duties in the fire station was quite extensive. There was a group of pre-war firemen who were also part of the mixture; most of those were pre-war tradesmen and, therefore, in the morning when you arrived on parade, all those who were pre-war tradesmen – painters, slaters, carpenters, electricians – were taken away from the normal crew and carried out whatever tradesman duties were required in the fire station ... the tradesman was a pre-war fireman most of whom already had houses which, in fact, were part of their conditions of service. He had a house in the fire station which he occupied rent and rates free, and although he was riding to fires along with myself, he nevertheless was involved in tradesman's work

The wage Enoch began with was £4 10s. a week, of which the 10 shillings was a rent allowance. It was a wage that compared reasonably with other workers, with the crucial difference that firemen worked 60 hours a week, and there was no overtime pay. Although he was not in any way political at the time he left the RAF – he read no newspapers nor did he read any literature or books during his wartime years – he joined the Fire Brigades Union as soon as he entered the service. Glasgow had been one of the few centres with some organisation before 1939; Enoch was approached by the dues collector on his own station and soon began to attend branch meetings. Enoch was clearly a natural political animal without knowing it, and he soon became a delegate from his own branch to the area committee, the Glasgow Western No. 1 area:

> I became extremely interested in what was taking place and availed myself of attending any form of continued courses, education courses, that were provided by the union ... induction courses I would put it, acquainting people with what the union was all about and why there was a need for a union and why, in fact, people should be thinking about political matters. We were in a period when rationing was still being continued, both in food and clothing; there was a great deal of discussion taking place about Cold War matters; there was discussion regarding trade with Eastern European countries; all those matters were the subjects of a variety of schools that were run by the union in the course of attracting new people like myself which was alongside many others in regard to membership of the union and playing a more active part in the union.

The structure of the fire service that Enoch entered in 1946 was not a great deal different from that of today. The National Fire Service continued until 1948 and the service then reverted to the control of local authorities. In Enoch's case his employer was the Glasgow corporation. Most of the pre-war firemen who were organised belonged to the General Workers' Union and not to the FBU, whereas after the war the new members almost to a man joined the FBU. There were a number of reasons for this. The pre-war firemen wanted to return to their pre-war conditions which had given them a tied house adjoining the fire-station but which also involved them in continuous duty; and they did not like the two-shift system which had been introduced in 1941 and which was in operation when Enoch joined the service. There was a further, and perhaps much more important reason why the FBU, although regarded as a 'red' union, was the choice for most of the new entrants after the war. There was one divisional organiser for Scotland, Tom Hasson, who had joined the Communist Party during the war and was a very capable person; quite unsectarian and an attractive man to his members. And around him he had a group of very active colleagues, left-Labour or Communist, some of whom had worked in the wartime fire service and who remained in the post-war years. It was also employment which, while serving a crucial social need, was beset with bureaucratic stupidity, and there were many small grievances which reminded the new recruits in the post-war years of the worst features of their time in the armed forces:

> There were a whole number of items, a great amount of them petty items that were imposed in the course of being in a fire station. I did mention to you earlier on about the cleaning of the stonework with carborundum. Obviously intelligent people who had been pilots in the RAF or sergeant-majors in the army and whatever they had been in the navy, resented very much this particular type of task. They resented the question of washing down a fire appliance every time it came back from a fire, whether it was two-o'clock in the morning or otherwise, cleaning pieces of nickel with Brasso, the question of doing, what seemed to us, like a lot of punishment duties; and the reason we were doing them, of course, was that there was not the understanding or the ability to deal with proper training and advancement of technology that should have been the order of the day.

During the period of his probation, the first two years, he had considerable experience of fire-fighting.

> There was a great deal of experience because Glasgow was a very fire-prone city, and most of the fire stations – there were sixteen in Glasgow – were extremely busy. There were docks and many different types of industry, and firemen in Glasgow had a great deal of experience ...
> I almost got sacked from the Glasgow fire service. It was just after my two years probation was completed, only two days after I think. I was on duty in the Central Fire Station in Ingram Street on a Saturday afternoon and we got a call to parade in the yard, a typical Central Fire Station cobblestone courtyard, and when we arrived we were told by the officer in charge that he wanted us to go and clean a

> pile of standpipes and brass equipment. Now, the normal routine was that on a Saturday afternoon you had a stand-down, that is, you were not required to do those types of chores unless they were of an emergency nature. Anyway, we were told to go and clean all this brass, and I registered with the officer in charge that this was not the normal arrangement, and I wanted to know why. He said: 'Get on with the job and that's all about it.' Anyway, on the Monday morning when I came on duty I learned that there was a letter awaiting me, and it told me to report to the Fire Master's office [The Fire Master was the name in Scotland for the Chief Fire Officer.] I had never met the Fire Master before. He was a huge man, a Geordie and he had become the Fire Master in Glasgow just before the war. He had been a police fireman in the North-East of England and I knew from the various reports I had from the area committee that he was very hostile towards the union. When I went in, there was the Fire Master, about six foot three, sitting in a huge chair which had several raised cushions on it, and he looked even larger. Around him were several senior officers whom I knew only by sight, and his Chief Administrative Officer. He said to me: 'So you are one of the persons who was working under protest?' And I said, 'Well, I did raise the question about us cleaning the brass on Saturday afternoon, and the officer told me that the ratepayers of Glasgow were not paying my wages or salary for me protesting.' I had done the duties as instructed, but the Fire Master said, 'I am sacking you. You are going to resign,' and he halted and looked at me and then repeated himself. 'I am sacking you. You are going to resign, aren't you?' I said, 'No, I'm not resigning,' and at that the Chief Administrator whispered something in his ear, almost certainly to the effect that my probation had expired and that he was therefore not able to dismiss me like that. He flew into a rage and told me to get out. 'Get out! Get out!'

There was considerable hostility to the union on the part of many senior officers as well as the Fire Master himself, and the local authority, which was a very right-wing Labour administration, was by no means unsympathetic to the ousting of reds and trouble-makers, the two no doubt being synonymous in many minds. Enoch himself, in talking about this episode, said that on the morning in question his thoughts 'were about my wife and my little son and what was going to happen to them'. But he was not fired, largely he thinks because the procedures laid down for dismissal by the city corporation would in fact have vindicated him.

Enoch lived for the first three years in a three-storey tenement building. He had married in 1946 a young woman whom he had met when she too was in the RAF, and they had two children, a son born in 1947 and a daughter in 1950. Enoch's wife had worked before the war in one of the mills in Glasgow and she was not a member of any union. Like Enoch she was not politically minded in those very early days, but Enoch discussed things with her as he himself expanded his own activities. Their living conditions were typical of so many of Glasgow's working people. They lived in one room and a kitchen; there was a black, cast-iron sink in the kitchen with a cold-water tap, and all water had to be heated on the kitchen range. There was a communal wash-house in the back court with a boiler for hot water. Each tenant took it in turns to use the facilities. They each provided their own wood and coal, and Enoch would take the wringer down for his wife. These tenements, Enoch said, were clean and free from cockroaches. There was a toilet on each landing for the use of the three families on the landing; toilet paper was cut-up pieces of newspaper.

Enoch was very quickly involved in union work. He was elected to attend the national conference at Rothesay in 1949, and in the early part of 1949 he became area secretary of Glasgow and almost immediately a member of the Scottish district committee:

> We didn't have a lot of resources, very little from the union in the way of assisting us; we got a little bit of money to hire a hall which we used every month and we were able to use a lot of the services of the fire stations for

communicating with each other and, therefore, when you were on duty you could make contact with the direct line to consult your colleagues about the various activities that were taking place. There was still only one full-time organiser for Scotland who worked from his home because there was no office in Scotland. Altogether there were eleven areas in Scotland, directed by the Scottish district committee. Now at the district committee we had two members of the executive council of the union for Scotland, and we would get a great deal of information as to what was happening through the executive council report, and also from the reports of the district officials. We had a secretary of the district, a chairman and a treasurer. They were all lay members.

I met John Horner some time around 1947, quite early on. I heard him at one of the gatherings, and he was talking about the new intakes, and he immediately made me realise that he wasn't speaking to a group of people that was referred to as 'recruits', he was speaking to people who he recognised as being mature individuals who had come into the fire brigade. I was extremely impressed by Horner, the way in which he was able to explain what the FBU was aiming at, and why. The matters he was speaking on were extremely topical, of course. At that time I got the same pay as a policeman, and rent allowance, and when the National Joint Council for Local Authority Fire Brigades was established, we ran into difficulties with the employers aiming to remove our rent allowances. All these matters of wages and conditions Horner was talking about, and I used to discuss with my wife what had been said at the meetings, and she was as interested as I was to preserve some of the conditions that were going to allow us to buy our new utility table or chair or a wireless set.

By 1947 Enoch was a very different sort of person from when he first joined the service from the RAF. He obviously had very considerable potential which simply hadn't been realised, but by 1947, that potential was beginning to develop very quickly.

> I was experiencing a variety of problems as to how to handle matters, and there wasn't as there is today, access to officials and people with a great deal of expertise. We were pretty well on our own. There were two officials in the Glasgow area who were very good colleagues and very helpful. Both were pre-war firemen in Glasgow and always very active in the FBU. One was Angus Beats who was a member of the union's executive, and the other was John Fildes. Both were members of the Communist Party, and I myself joined in 1948. There were one or two others who also joined and there was a little coffee shop in Glasgow called the Good Companions, and we used to go there once a week and talk about union affairs and politics generally. I started to read, and of course I took the *Daily Worker*. We also had national meetings of members who were party members when we would discuss topical questions, like German re-armament, the Cold War, the World Federation of Trade Unions. John was often at these meetings and also Jack Grahl, the assistant general secretary. Jack was an extremely good speaker, and very knowledgeable, so we always had people of substance. And because of my closer involvement with the union at the Scottish level I started meeting other people like Abe Moffat who had just become president of the miners' union in Scotland. And then from 1949 I attended every annual conference of our union.

Enoch, however, because of his close involvement in militant industrial politics inside the Fire Brigades Union, was becoming increasingly singled out by the top brass in Glasgow, and in 1949 he applied for a transfer out of the Glasgow fire brigade:

> There was such a degree of pressure being applied to me by the Fire Master and the officers that I was concerned, and my wife was concerned, in case I reacted in the wrong way. For example, I was stationed in the Central Fire Station in Ingram Street, and there was one appliance that went to every fire in the north of the city: every fire. Now

that's a lot of fires, and I was always allocated to the driving of the appliance which meant that when I was on duty I was on the go from the time I went on duty to when I came off the next morning. Further, we had street fire alarms in Glasgow, each particular station having several street alarms in its area, and when I wasn't out driving they would ensure that I was called upon through the night to go and check all these alarms; to walk round the whole area testing these alarms. There is no doubt that this was a deliberate policy, to keep me busy, in the hope that they would get me to do something that would cause them to take disciplinary action against me.

By 'do something' I mean to breach the very strict codes of procedure and discipline. And of course I was leading an extremely busy life in the union. I was secretary of the Glasgow area committee, we wrote all letters by hand, and there was a very old duplicator; and I was also a delegate to the Trades Council. So between my union duties and 60 hours a week at work, I would go home to my two-room house in Bridgeton, with no hot water and an outside toilet and occasionally the roof down, or something happened, and the usual domestic problems. It was finally agreed between some of my colleagues and my wife and myself – union colleagues as well as my Communist Party comrades – that I should apply for a transfer, so in 1949 I applied for a transfer to the Lanarkshire Fire Brigade. Now the Lanarkshire Fire Brigade goes from Glasgow south to Hamilton and Motherwell. When I made the request for transfer I did not know that the Fire Master of Glasgow did not get on with the Fire Master of Lanarkshire. I also did not know that the latter had been a pre-war fireman in Glasgow and at one time a member of the union. Now the Lanarkshire Fire Brigade was a much poorer brigade than Glasgow in many ways; it didn't have the full-time professional stations the same as Glasgow. All Lanarkshire had was a series of huts in different towns, and they were looking for experienced men in their brigade. When I applied I put down my qualifications, where I had served, what training I had been through, and so on. I was

> interviewed by Alec Nisbet, the Fire Master, and his words at the end of the interview were, 'I don't know why Chadwick's letting you go.'

Enoch moved into a brand-new house in Cambuslang provided by the fire authority, and his wife was delighted. It was not long, of course, a matter only of weeks, before Enoch was elected area secretary for Lanarkshire. In general it was not a well organised district, with a lot of part-time firemen, but when Enoch asked to see the Fire Master on union business the latter refused to see him. Enoch had not been asked any questions at his interview about the union, but Nisbet must soon have appreciated why Glasgow had let Enoch go. The Lanarkshire was a friendly brigade, Nisbet himself was a decent man, quite different from the Glasgow Fire Master, but he must have thought that Enoch was going to disrupt his area. It took a fair amount of intervention not only by Hasson, the Scottish regional organiser but by John Horner – who knew Nisbet personally – before relations with Enoch were established on a proper footing; in the end, because Nisbet was a reasonable man, Enoch was able to develop a satisfactory working relationship with the senior officers. 'I was with him until he retired,' Enoch said, 'and we were on first name terms.' Enoch had a nice anecdote about Chadwick, the Glasgow Fire Master. In the late 1960s, when Enoch was president of the FBU, he was invited to speak at the Chief Fire Officers' Conference in Harrogate. Chadwick, now long retired, had also been invited as a former senior member of the service. Enoch was having a drink in the bar with some Chief Officers and Chadwick came up and said, 'I was responsible for helping Enoch in his career.' Enoch replied, 'You were, there's no doubt about that.'

Lanarkshire stretched from the outskirts of Glasgow through large rural areas almost to Dumfriesshire. There were a very few professional firemen before the war. When the fire service was returned to local authorities in 1948 in Lanarkshire it was really a matter of building a fire service from scratch. There were about 400 professional firemen when Enoch moved into the region, and many difficult problems were emerging – as was the case all over the country, it must be added. Although the National Joint Council for Local Authority Fire Brigades had come into being in 1948, Scotland was not yet part of it. The problems were centered around hours of work, pay and working conditions. The local authorities still remembered the pre-war days when firemen used to paint street lamp posts and do repairs to local authority property and now they were expected to provide police rates of pay for firemen who were professional and not part-time labourers as well.

The issue reached the point when an increase of something like 35 shillings was going to be required to bring firemen into line with the police. This was around 1950. The employers offered a consolidated increase, including rent allowance, of 15 shillings. Rates of pay were on a national basis. The union rejected the 15 shillings and then organised a national 'Spit and Polish' demonstration whereby firemen would attend fires, but would not do any of the cleaning involved. This was the first national movement of this kind the union had initiated, and it was not an easy time for the national leadership. Their problem had always been to instil a sense of union solidarity into their members, most of whom had never previously been in a union. As Enoch said:

> It was extremely difficult to get across, bearing in mind that the persons they were speaking to were persons who had been accustomed to obeying orders, they were ex-servicemen, and they had been accustomed during the war to be told what to do and to obey what to do.

One very important episode was the London demonstration of November 12, 1951, which the union organised in support of its demands. Firemen came from all over Britain, and the Scots brought a pipe band:

> We asked for as many people as were off duty. It was only those whose watch was off duty that could get away because they still had their sixty hours per week; so we filled buses and trains in getting people to London in

> uniform. All wore their uniforms and we had this pipe band from Glasgow, and the pipe band started the parade in Euston Road. It was coming down in torrential rain, and we marched to Hyde Park; the water was running off us, and we had the gathering addressed by the general secretary and a number of prominent people from the trade union movement, including Ted Hill of the Boilermakers and Bryn Roberts of NUPE. I don't think I can recall any of the Labour politicians, but we had a very, very good feeling amongst the lads. We brought them back to the Royal Hotel in Southampton Row to dry out the pipe band in the boiler house before we sent them back to Scotland.

In the lead-up to the 'Spit and Polish' demonstrations the union agreed to go before the Industrial Court. John Horner represented the Union, and Sir Lynn Ungoed-Thomas, a KC and Labour MP, spoke for the employers. All in the union were convinced that they had a very good case, and Horner was able to show that the employers had over-estimated the costs of the consolidation by about £500,000. In the event, the Industrial Court in January 1950 consolidated pay and allowances, thus destroying pay parity with the police, a judgement that astounded the members of the FBU:

> It was devastating. The members did not believe that you could go to a court and present such an excellently documented case and show that the employers had made errors in their calculations, very substantial errors, yet have the court come down by a majority in favour of the employers. The union wasn't blamed. Who was blamed, in fact, was the system that we lived under that provided for that. There was no backlash against Horner. As a matter of fact, Horner was constantly congratulated for the quality of the case that he presented.

The Fire Brigades Union faced many problems in the 1950s after this pay award. Hours of work were among the most intractable. The local authorities in general were always looking for ways of keeping their costs down. In some parts of the country they introduced a day-manning system whereby the fire station was manned by professional firemen only during the hours of daylight. The crews lived close to the stations and had bells in their houses, while those who lived further away were provided with free bicycles by the authority. It was a system that was favoured by many men, not least because every time they were called out during the night they were paid a fee. The union was against this system, because it was equivalent to the continuous duty which had been in operation before the war. There were other authorities operating the two-shift system, and there was also the system of the members being on duty for 24 hours and then off for the next 24 hours. This variety of working hours was not conducive to the sense of solidarity the union was attempting to develop, but it met considerable opposition to change from its own members. The 24 hours on and 24 hours off, as well as other variations of the two shift system, encouraged moonlighting which Enoch insisted was widespread, not only in Britain but in many if not most of the fire-fighting services round the world. The union's aim 'was to move the fire service towards a 48 hour week, and ultimately, towards the same hours as other manual workers'.

One interesting generalisation that emerged from the interview with Enoch was the considerable difference between the attitudes of different local authorities. That is hardly surprising, but Enoch went on to make the point that there was remarkably little difference between Labour and Conservative authorities:

> In the 1950s there were eleven fire authorities in Scotland, and in England and Wales there were almost 125 separate authorities. You can well imagine all the various local authorities meeting in their own county borough premises and having the Chief Fire Officer come along and speak about the need to purchase a new fire appliance or to spend money on training or installation of standardisation of hydrants. Now this leads me to the question you were asking about Labour authorities. I did not find many

> Labour authorities who either had the knowledge or the understanding to speak on the subject of the fire brigade since it was a comparatively new organisation that they had taken on board. The new councillors who had been elected in the post-war period relied very heavily on the chief officer and the treasurer or the county clerk or the town clerk and, therefore, when they were suddenly confronted with those bills ... they obviously baulked at that through a lack of political maturity and understanding of what in fact was expected of this modern fire service ... There was very little difference, if any, between Labour and Conservative boroughs. There were one or two authorities which were extremely helpful to us, Birmingham and Coventry for example ... Only one or two authorities were quite helpful in supporting the general direction which the union was trying to steer this new, post-war modern fire service. But by and large, when they had received advice and guidance from the Chief Fire Officer, they said to the council, our men are perfectly happy in that day-manning station, go and see them, and we have just renewed the new Raleigh bikes for them and even allow them to ride the bikes off duty, and we are giving them a bit of a reduction in the rent and we are paying them every time they go to a fire, ask them if they are happy or whether they would like to go into this city brigade with two shifts.

It was during the 1950s that Enoch began to move towards the centre of union affairs. He was elected Scottish national chairman in 1954. There was a good deal of press attack at this time against Communists in the trade unions, the *Daily Mail* being especially prominent. Enoch left the Communist Party in 1956 following the secret speech by Khrushchev and the Soviet invasion of Hungary in the autumn of the year, as did John Horner. Enoch was emphatic that he never adopted an anti-Communist position, or that he found political hostility against him from those who remained Communists:

> I never came across any colleague of mine who had been a member of the Communist Party becoming part of an anti-Communist group or, in any way, hostile to others. I found them to be most understanding and I always had the same degree of relationship.

Enoch was elected from 1954 to be a delegate to the Scottish Trades Union Congress, and in 1960 he was elected to the executive council of the union. That meant he was now involved in national matters and he also became a member of the National Joint Council. He was also elected a delegate to the TUC and to the Labour Party. He continued to live in Scotland and was still a serving member of the Lanarkshire Fire Brigade. There was no problem about obtaining the time off for his union activities, and in 1963 he added to his other responsibilities election to the General Council of the Scottish TUC. At the time he went on to the General Council he was the only lay member. All the rest were full-time officials and politically the congress was on the right. He remained on the General Council until 1978, and was president in 1968, the year that Barbara Castle introduced *In Place of Strife*.

John Horner resigned from his position as general secretary of the union in 1964 in order to enter the House of Commons at the general election of that year. Enoch decided to stand for election in his place:

> In 1964 when John Horner resigned and the union decided to sponsor him, there were nominations requested from the branches and I was nominated by a number of branches from all over the country and there was also Tom Harris, he was the assistant general secretary, as was John MacDonald, my colleague from Scotland, and there was Terry Parry. There was a lot of internal conflict on the executive as you will see when you come to read the minutes. There was also the question of whether I was eligible to stand because of what I had said in my election address, and there was a great deal of hostility by a number of people on the executive in regard

> to my person. Eventually the ballot took place, and Terry Parry was top; I was second with 2,000 votes below him. Tom Harris got 3,000 (2,000 fewer than me) and Johnny MacDonald got 2,000. I think some people thought I was a new boy on the executive, and I should not have run; I should have allowed Terry to have the post. I don't think it was political, although there were one or two groups on the executive who certainly did not share my politics.

Almost as soon as the election of the general secretary had been settled the position of the president of the union became open; and there was further considerable dissent about Enoch's candidature. The arguments against him were entirely procedural in respect of the union rules. There were, in Enoch's words, 'mountains of correspondence' but at the ballot he was successful. In the interview in which these matters were discussed Enoch was several times asked whether the opposition to him, in both elections, was in any way related to his known left-wing political views. His answers were not always clear cut, largely, it may be suggested, because these events took place a long time ago, and Enoch was not perhaps willing to rake over very cold ashes. The executive at the time was in political terms to the right of Enoch. That is quite clear, and the general conclusion that seems reasonable to offer is that political opposition did play some part in what, for the most part, were rather involved procedural matters. Much more important for the historian of the union is that relations between the new general secretary and the new president were close and co-operative from the beginning. Enoch was most emphatic on this important matter. He also maintained that during the years he was president, from 1964 to 1977, he and general secretary Parry were broadly able to carry the executive council with them, and no faction or clique established itself.

The post-war years saw large changes in the role of firemen in society. Originally the fireman was someone who put out fires, but has become a multi-purpose public servant with a wide range of skills to cope with the hazards, accidents and catastrophes of an increasingly complex society. Before John Horner retired from the position of general secretary the union published a forward-looking programme which accepted the rapidity of technological and social changes and which set down proposals for the training of firemen in the coming years. *A Service for the Sixties* was its title, and it not only insisted upon the importance of continuous training for a changing technology, but it also underlined the union's demands that firemen must have the old jobs of cleaners and polishers removed from their duties. At the time when Enoch became president in 1964 cleaning toilets and windows, polishing brass and so on were still daily tasks for the firemen on duty. The changes did not come until the late 1960s, and it was a phasing-out process rather than a once-and-for-all change. Here is Enoch's account of these changes:

> It was in 1965 that the union was able to persuade the then Home Secretary, Roy Jenkins, of the need to transform the Civil Defence Training Unit at Moreton-in-Marsh into a Fire Service Technical College which is now world renowned. The college services firemen from all over Britain, and from all over the world, so that was a tremendous step forward in that particular period and it took place against a background of very severe economic constraints on public expenditure. So Moreton-in-Marsh stands as a credit to that decision taken by Roy Jenkins as the Home Secretary in the building of such a fine, excellent college for the fire service. By the late 1960s the union had been able to persuade both the National Joint Council employers and the respective local authorities that firemen must be technically trained to give advice to industry, and to everyone in the fire area regarding prevention and safety; and that the duties they had previously been engaged on, such as the cleaning duties, should be the work of people specifically employed for those purposes.
>
> The union is responsible for education courses for our members to acquaint them with the role of the union, and also with the various organisations and bodies which the

union serves on to improve the quality and the technology of the fireman and his trade. There is a national school once a year, held at Wortley Hall near Sheffield and there are a series of weekend schools throughout the various regions.

Enoch Humphries retired at the normal age of 55 both from the presidency of the union and from the fire service. His last years were the troubled prelude to the 1977 strike, and his retirement, because of his 55th birthday on 25 September 1977, took effect just before the Recall Conference which took the momentous decision to embark on a national strike. 'It was quite clear to me,' Enoch said, 'in the last few months before I was due to finish that there were all the signals, which in firemen's language, were ready "for a good blow-out".' When Merlyn Rees, who was Home Secretary, came to the annual conference in the spring of 1977 Enoch told him in clear and unequivocal terms that there was trouble brewing. Enoch was speaking to Rees not only as the Home Secretary, but in a comradely way as a member of the Labour Party. Sir Kenneth Holland, the Chief Inspector of the Fire Brigades, was telling the Home Secretary the same things, and Holland, so Enoch said, 'had got a very close ear to what we had to say'.

The problems over hours of work and pay went back many years. On the question of hours, the union had been constantly in battle with the employers who wanted to return to the system of duties that prevailed before the war. And then in the 1960s the reorganisation of London government with the establishment of the Greater London Council brought major problems for the fire services: the constant problem of recruitment, the quite marked variations in conditions between different boroughs, a considerable turnover of lay officials, all against a national background in which unrest was increasing steadily.

We had been negotiating in 1965 and 1966 on pay and hours, and we had made considerable progress. By the middle of 1966 we were finalising the details of the work of many months on the National Joint Council. The Council was scheduled to meet on 21 July 1966 to endorse formally all the options and proposals to improve pay and towards a reduction of hours. On 20 July, the day before this scheduled meeting we received an urgent call from the Home Secretary to come and see him at the House of Commons. When we arrived at his room on the afternoon of the 20th, we noticed that the employers' side of the National Joint Council were leaving by another entrance. When we met Roy Jenkins he said: 'I'm afraid I've got some bad news for you. It's about your pay discussions and negotiation. The government has no direct representation on the National Joint Council for local authority fire brigades, which is composed of local authority representatives from all over the United Kingdom along with the employers' officials, and the union on the other side. Then Roy Jenkins intimated that the Prime Minister had just made a statement a few minutes earlier to the effect that there was now what they called a standstill. A White Paper had been issued which indicated that there were to be no pay increases for anyone who had not had their agreement ratified by the date on which the pronouncement was made, namely the 20th. We immediately protested in the strongest possible terms that he was aware of the discussions that had been taking place, that he had been kept abreast by the local authority organisations, and that he knew the NJC was due to meet less than 24 hours away to ratify the agreements. He simply said, 'Well, the state of the economy is such that that's where you are placed at this particular stage.' It was understandable that the fire service and the union and its membership were in a serious state of discontent as to the way they had been treated. It wasn't until the latter part of that year that we were informed our case had been referred to a new body called the Prices and Incomes Board. We then embarked on feeding the new board with a great deal of detail and explaining the basis of all our discussions on the National Joint Council.

The Report of the Prices and Incomes Board came the next year, 1967. It recommended a very meagre improvement in pay for firemen, and that there should be introduced a bonus shift. This shift gave firemen the option of working eight hours longer which would then bring their duty system up to 56 hours per week. The union's policy had been to campaign for 48 hours. We had a special conference on the bonus scheme proposal which voted to operate the scheme. Individual brigades were to ballot to see if their members agreed to accept the scheme. Clearly the reason why the members voted for the bonus shift was to get more money. They had been deprived of any pay increase for almost two years. By the time we reached 1969 we were again involved in negotiations with the local authorities, and once again the unrest was widespread. Especially in the London Fire Brigade, where the demand for a strike was growing, and where, in fact, a breakaway organisation was being threatened. At this time there were changes in the London representation on the executive. When one of our new colleagues was welcomed by me at an executive meeting a resolution from the London membership was introduced which called for the operation of Rule 37, by which the union was to be dissolved and some unspecified body set up in its place which would be more militant and achieve some of the aims the union had failed to win over the previous years. It was made clear that many London members were sickened by the way they had been treated over a number of years, and that responsibility for this lay with the leadership of the union.

So there was a real build-up as we moved into the 1970s. Labour was defeated in the June 1970 election and we had a new Home Secretary, Reginald Maudling, whom we met quite soon after his appointment; and after a lot of meetings and argument he agreed to set up an independent enquiry. There was a lot of argument about the composition of this enquiry. The chairman was to be Sir Charles Cunningham, who had been Permanent Under-Secretary at the Home Office, and whom we knew well, and we believed that he would try to do a job for the fire service. Then the Home Office and the employers argued that the other two members should be 'independent' and that it should not be a matter of the union submitting nominees. Our response to that was that the only place you could find independence was Regent's Park Zoo, so we weren't having any of that; and we went for Will Paynter, recently retired from the general secretaryship of the NUM. The report of the Cunningham Committee recommended successive increases in pay and successive reductions in hours of work down to a 44-hour week. And then Robert Carr replaced Maudling at the Home Office and the Heath government imposed economic constraints, and several of the agreements and conditions of the Cunningham enquiry were put into cold storage.

The growing concern among firemen about these developments expressed itself especially in the Glasgow area. The Glasgow firemen had decided not to go for the bonus shift and they were getting a fair amount of regular overtime. But although there was a high level of unemployment in Scotland adequate numbers of men were not being recruited into the Glasgow fire service, and the men were working far too long. Glasgow was a very high-risk fire area, and the firemen in Glasgow put in for a plus payment. They called it a travel allowance. The authority refused the demand; the firemen had a ballot and decided they were going on strike. The union nationally became involved, because it was not in the union's interest to see different rates in different places. And then the Glasgow corporation conceded the travel allowance – something in the region of £2.48 per week. This so shocked and surprised our members in Glasgow that they said, 'Well if we can get £2.48 for threatening a strike, what are we going to get if we actually do strike?' So, lo and behold the members in Glasgow went on strike for one week in 1973. It was an exceptionally successful strike, and the Glasgow public was wholehearted in its support for the firemen. The army was brought in. The union then called a national delegate conference in the Beaver Hall in London, which had a very heated debate about where the union was going, and by an overwhelming vote we called on the lads in Glasgow to go back. Not surprisingly this was not taken very well by our colleagues in Glasgow, but they did return after a week's stoppage and we then became involved in national negotiations.

Then came the return of the Wilson government in 1974, and the introduction of an incomes policy in 1975 which provided for a maximum of 10 per cent. We had been through all this before, and when we came into 1976 there had developed serious divisions throughout the union. There was a split on the executive. My colleague, Terry Parry the general secretary, was a member of the General Council of the TUC, and he argued on the executive for support for the TUC incomes policy. I opposed this. The executive voted eight to seven in favour of the TUC and the government. This was before our Annual Conference in 1976 which was to be held at Bridlington, and I explained to the executive that in view of the circumstances I could not present the president's address to the Conference in the normal way. This caused some concern among members of the executive because it had never happened before. At the Conference the general secretary introduced the report on behalf of the executive, and when the vote came it was an endorsement of the executive's recommendations. It seemed to me extremely strange, since those brigades which endorsed the government's incomes policy were in contradiction to what they themselves had been demanding. London, in fact, did endorse the statement.

I think what happened between the conference of 1976 and 1977 was a continuation of the deep frustration which the members had in terms of what we had been going through for the past twelve years, from 1964 to 1976, with various forms of government involvement in the question of firemen's pay and conditions, directly and indirectly. Now I'm not sure as to whether the position would have been altered had the decision of 1976 been a different

> one, but it certainly would have put the union leadership in a different situation in relation to the employers. It had seemed to me by the time we came to the 1976 conference, that we had all been together so closely and intimately at fairly regular intervals that the men were saying this is another old story. I could sense a degree of explosiveness that was going to develop inside the fire service from parts of the country, like the South-East of England and East Anglia, and parts of the East Midlands, which normally would not have been thought of as militant.

Enoch then turned to his last conference as president, that was attended by Merlyn Rees.

> I have always been a person involved in international matters. I believed in close associations with countries all over the world to bring about a better understanding and to create closer contacts. At the Conference we had invited some comrades from the Spanish trade union movement; and we also had along Mrs Allende, the widow of the president of Chile, who had been assassinated a few years earlier, because we were also much involved in the question of Chile. When the Conference finished we had received an invitation to send either the general secretary or myself to Australia as the guests of the Australian Fire Service, and the executive decided that I should represent them in Australia, and should also meet some of our American colleagues on the way back.
>
> I made an especial effort to see that Merlyn Rees attended this 1977 conference. He was at first going to send someone else, but I wanted to make sure that when I left office no one would be able to say that it was a pity that I hadn't acquainted the Home Secretary with the ways things were developing. So I pushed for him. He came from the conference of the Police Federation and there was a great deal of unrest in the police force at this same period. I had met, along with Terry Parry, officials of the Police Federation on many occasions to talk about matters of mutual interest, and the coppers certainly conveyed the

view that they were being left behind in terms of what was taking place.

When Merlyn Rees spoke to the conference he said a lot of nice things about the firemen, but he never said anything about the things that really mattered. He said nothing at all because obviously that meant someone had to find the necessary resources to provide for the additional manpower that would be required. I spoke to him after the conference when we spent the evening together and told him that the flashpoint was pretty close.

After I had returned from Australia and the United States I attended the TUC annual conference, and I knew that the fire service was going to have problems. But I had retired under the age limit scheme before the Recall Conference of November 1977 which took the decision to call a national strike. I didn't attend the Recall Conference, thinking it better that I kept away. The FBU now had a new president.

I was extremely surprised that the Recall Conference had taken the decision to strike, even though there was no doubt at all that the problems were accumulating fast. But the 1976 Conference had voted for the TUC's document; and as I said earlier it was the areas that traditionally were not militant which came out for the strike. It made me wonder whether the strike would, in fact, materialise, since putting their hands up was one thing but actually going on strike was another. There was, of course, a hurried series of meetings between Merlyn Rees and company to try to avoid the starting of a strike, and I could see that Terry Parry was having a very, very difficult time. We spoke to each other on many occasions, for he had a new president with whom he had not worked over many years as he had with me. He had therefore to be the main and often the only spokesman. He was on the General Council of the TUC and had associated quite closely with Jack Jones, who was the architect of many of the proposals which Terry himself had supported. It was all very difficult and he was trying very hard to get the government to respond, but Merlyn Rees was not able to move anybody, and

Callaghan, the Prime Minister, was a very hard man in the situation.

I think there was no doubt at all that Callaghan and his government have to take responsibility for creating matters which forced our members to take some form of action. They had pushed them in to such a corner and had trodden them down so firmly that there was no other way out for them at all. I attended the gathering they had when they were lobbying the General Council of the TUC who were certainly not going to endorse support for the firemen. They were saying to Terry Parry, 'Well, you were part of the original decision to support the government's pay policy, and now you will have to handle your own problem, even though the boys have overturned you.' The real problem was that the dangers of firemen taking strike action are a very different matter from say that of dustmen. But as the weeks went by I could see the strength of feeling which was building up and the strength of feeling in the shire areas which I didn't believe possible. I had never believed they would be involved in that form of activity, but my God they were, and there was no indication of any kind of saying, well now we've had a day or two, or a week or two, let's pack it up. The strength of feeling was tremendous.

The other great development was the way the public had pushed the government aside and was on the side of the firemen. At the same time we were all very fortunate that during the nine weeks of the strike there were few or no fatalities that could be attributed to a lack of proper fire-fighting.

The main aim of the leadership was to get an agreement in a form of words that could be truly accepted. The public had to be made aware of the response from a government which was forcing the firemen to take a form of action unheard of in its lifetime. If that had been forthcoming from the Callaghan government then the strike could have been averted; but on all occasions when there were discussions with Callaghan and Merlyn Rees and Denis Healey and company, it was to the effect that we are not

> conceding anything to you, and that you, in fact, will go back to work in the same manner as you came out.

When firemen went back to work, it was with a feeling of victory.

> Quite naturally, after nine weeks of strike with no pay and with a pay formula that was going to take some time before it materialised, there was obviously some resentment in many parts of the country that they weren't getting something more positive right away. But at the end of the day, when they finally met in conference to decide what was on offer, and the executive council recommended that we pick that up, and emphasised that hours were going to be reduced, so a substantial number of people were to be brought into the service, and that we had a pay formula that is going to last, the vast majority of people agreed to accept that.
>
> There may have been a few disgruntled people about, but once the main items had been tidied up, and they had also set in motion certain machinery to deal with individuals who had not carried out the conference decisions, there were extremely minor matters in terms of the union getting back on the rails. I think the fact that we are meeting in this lovely building in Kingston gives an indication as to how quickly the union recovered from a very expensive nine-week strike. We didn't pay strike pay at all, but also there was no income from our members, and there was a great deal of expenditure incurred in servicing the members in travel, and meetings and so on.

Finally, Enoch spoke about the role and place of the Fire Brigades Union in society in general:

> We always had strong views about the role of firemen in society, and that is why we tried to insist that our work was evaluated in the same way as other public servants, such as the police. By virtue of the place of the FBU in the labour movement, and taking into full account our duties towards everyone in the matter of fire prevention and fire risk, and

our obligations to our fellow citizens when fires broke out, we were absolutely opposed to firemen becoming involved in matters of civil disorder, as happens in some other countries of Europe and elsewhere. There was no question that our fire appliances would be brought out in these situations. I think that there were a number of occasions when some Chief Officer and others would have liked to provide these sort of services. But because of the nature of the union, and the union's strong position accepted and agreed by our members, we were not going to be used for these purposes. We were an organisation that anyone could call upon for assistance.

When the current round of troubles started in Northern Ireland the Home Office suggested that fire stations should be secured in the same way as police stations, that was to barricade them up, and sandbag them and have people on guard duty and so on. We thoroughly refused. Roy Mason was the minister at that particular period, and we refused under any circumstances to have fire stations protected, even when there had been one or two minor incidents at fire stations. We said that if people want to destroy the fire appliances or to knock the building about, then they'll just have to do that; but we must have an open door so that any person can come in and seek assistance, and we will respond to that request for help. This is an important matter of principle, and in fact, there have been very few violent incidents directed against fire stations or our members. We serve both communities.

Notes

1. The reminiscences of Enoch Humphries were first recorded in a series of interviews conducted by John Saville in the early part of 1988. The tape-recordings were then transcribed, and the complete version can be read in the Library of Bradley House, the Fire Brigades Union headquarters, or in the Fire Brigades Union archive in the Brynmor Jones Library, University of Hull. This edited version has been agreed by Enoch Humphries. The text was written by John Saville, using Enoch's own words as much as possible, and the long quotations that are given are taken from the full transcription.

12 The Glasgow Strike

Jim Flockhart

Glasgow opposed the re-introduction in 1967 of the 56-hour week and was one of the few brigades in Britain not to return to the so-called 'bonus shift'. This was a thorn in the flesh of the executive council and other FBU senior officials. National officials were travelling, unannounced, round the Glasgow branches in an attempt to sway the membership, but unfortunately for them local officials were informed of this, and were following them round the branches challenging the case for the 'bonus shift'. A certain amount of resentment towards senior FBU officials was therefore developing among the membership.

Matters really came to a head at the end of June 1973 when a 'discussion document' was issued by the Firemaster to the local officials of the FBU. This document recommended re-introduction of the 56-hour week, and if this was not accepted a reduction in appliance manning standards was to follow. It also became clear that at least one senior FBU official had a hand in drawing up this document. Meetings were held in all the branches, and in many cases the document was received with disbelief, distrust, resentment and even hostility. At the end of August 1973 a meeting of the Glasgow area committee was called. The 'discussion document' was indeed discussed and finally rejected, and a letter was sent to the Firemaster informing him of this decision.

What the document had brought to the surface was the low pay, low morale and low recruitment of the Glasgow fire service. The brigade was 23 per cent short of its authorised establishment and the members were required to work a great deal of overtime to maintain appliance availability. Despite allegedly large sums of money being spent on recruitment, the drive to improve the staff shortage had failed. Throughout these discussions no one mentioned that no fewer than eight colleagues had been killed on duty the previous year and that this must have had a serious effect on morale and recruitment. The decision was that the only way to resolve the situation was to improve the pay of the Glasgow fireman. But how?

The Heath government of the day had a pay policy of £1 plus 4 per cent. The union nationally was due to settle on 1 October 1973 under Phase II of the government's incomes policy, and there was no sign that our national executive would do anything other than accept what was on offer. The previous year Phase 1 was accepted without challenge, the only exception being that Glasgow corporation, because of the firemen killed at the Kilburnie Street fire in August 1972, felt it was not justified in absorbing the remaining 48p per week of the 'undermanning' allowance until October 1973. It was also pointed out that the FBU executive would not support 'local plus payments'.

Having considered all these points, the local area executive decided that it could not just sit back and hope that things would improve. As Glasgow area chairman, I recommended that we aim for a minimum wage increase of £5 and plead Glasgow as a special case. This would be no easy matter given the government's pay policy and the attitude of our national executive. The area committee accepted this and the area executive gave the assurance that it would vigorously pursue our claim despite the difficulties that lay ahead.

A meeting was arranged with the Firemaster to explain the situation and a letter was sent to the Glasgow corporation's establishments committee. On 26 September 1973 the Glasgow area executive met the Glasgow corporation fire committee and, even though we knew its remit was not 'pay and conditions', we explained the grounds for our claim: high fire risk, fire fatalities, manpower shortage and increased workload. The fire committee stated that the Glasgow men had a 'wonderful case' and that it would do what it could to persuade the establishments committee to be sympathetic.

On 29 September 1973 the Glasgow executive met the establishments committee. The proposed absorption of the 48p per week undermanning allowance was discussed, together with the claim for £5 per week. The establishments committee said that its hands were tied due to government policy and there was nothing it could do. The area executive stated that it was very serious about the claim and that industrial action was not ruled out. The meeting broke up without any agreement.

A meeting of the area committee was called and the attitude at the meeting with the establishments committee was reported. It was the unanimous decision of the area committee that 'emergency calls only' action be called for from 8 a.m. on 1 October 1973.

On 2 October the area executive met the Glasgow corporation establishments committee and received an offer of £2 per week, to be absorbed when the NJC joint working party reached a conclusion on pay, and to be subject to approval by the Scottish Secretary of State. It was explained to the establishments committee that this would be unacceptable to the membership because the Scottish Secretary of State, as a member of the government, would not approve.

The area executive reported to the area committee the decision of the establishments committee. This was met with dismay, anger and calls for strike action. A heated debate took place and the area executive recommended that whilst industrial action should be stepped up it was important to try to keep the public on our side. Until then the media had, in the main, reported our case sympathetically, and we had to try to maintain that relationship. It would take just one fatality, attributable to shortage either of personnel or appliances, for the Glasgow FBU to be blamed. It was decided to implement industrial action in stages, with strike action as a last resort, but not ruled out, and only after all members had been consulted. The next stage of industrial action would be to insist on a minimum of five men on pump crews and bans on overtime, detached duties and operational personnel covering watchroom duties for sickness.

The president, Enoch Humphries, called a private meeting with the Glasgow area executive and pointed out the difficulties in which the FBU found itself, in particular in relation to the government's pay policy. He stated that he could not support any argument for a 'local plus payment', but would support a revised claim if it came within the 'conditions of service'. The area executive gave its view covering all the points previously mentioned. It was very clear that Glasgow was going to be out on a limb, so it was decided to pursue the claim for a travel allowance and a further meeting was arranged with the establishments committee.

Several formulae based on re-imbursement of travelling expenses were put forward and rejected; all required approval of the NJC. A figure based on a global brigade figure, divided and spread equally among the membership, was finally arrived at. This was £2 per week per person, and the 48p allowance would remain. This did not require approval of the NJC.

The area executive put this offer to the area committee which unanimously rejected it. The area executive decided that this was a matter for the whole membership to decide, so mass meetings were held which would allow dayshift and nightshift personnel to air their views. The membership overwhelmingly rejected the offer.

At this point the area executive declared that only the membership as a whole could decide what was acceptable and that in order to pursue the wage claim it needed to know the views of the membership. The area executive therefore decided to ballot the members to see whether they were prepared to take industrial action. A lengthy debate followed and finally a ballot paper was agreed.

The area executive reported to the area committee that in its view dealings with the Glasgow corporation had gone as far as they could go, and that the membership should decide whether to opt for its sole remaining weapon, all-out strike action. It was agreed that the ballot paper be circulated to all members and that these should be returned by 12 October.

By this time letters and telegrams of support were arriving from FBU members, branches, brigades and the general public all over the country. The most notable point in the messages of support from FBU members was their condemnation of the national executive for its lack of activity on the pay front.

A problem was beginning to emerge with the number of political organisations which were trying to board our 'wagon'. This was discussed by the area executive, and while it was agreed that we required all the support we could get, the involvement of too many political groups and factions could only cloud the issue at hand. It was decided, therefore, to ensure that, in as much as this was possible, the dispute remained a 'Glasgow fireman' issue.

On 11 October a telegram from the executive council was received by the Glasgow area chairman stating that the ballot was 'unconstitutional' and instructing the Glasgow area executive to proceed no further with the ballot. The area executive met and discussed this. It was agreed that matters had gone too far to be put into reverse, and in any case our commitment had been to pursue the matter for our members who had made it clear that was what they wanted. It was decided to continue with a slightly amended ballot, pointing out to the membership where it would leave us.

The result of the ballot was 424 against acceptance of the £2 offer, 125 for acceptance and 133 abstentions. This result was conveyed to the establishments committee, the FBU national executive, the Firemaster and the media. It was pointed out to all concerned that there was a possibility that the area executive would be removed from office, and if this was the case the area executive would still be prepared to serve the membership.

On Tuesday 16 October the full Glasgow area committee was summoned to a meeting with the FBU's national executive at the city chambers in Glasgow. A lengthy meeting took place in which both sides put their points of view, with the executive underlining the constitutional position. The general secretary, Terry Parry, then made a statement which was to astonish the Glasgow membership. He stated that 'the executive was not against militancy, but it had to be on matters which would attract public and trade union support'! It goes without saying that this statement dismayed the members of the area committee who were present. 'Does this mean we only take action on popular issues?' they asked in reply. The executive council demanded to know whether, if the Glasgow members instructed the area committee that they wanted strike action, that committee would act on such a demand? We adjourned to consider our reply.

Returning from the adjournment, the area committee chairman said that the committee would support their members if they decided on strike action and would lead them. The general secretary said the executive would declare its opposition, remove the area committee from office and support those firemen who remained at work. A member of the area committee stated that there might be mass resignations from the union, but the general secretary said the FBU could only accept members who abided by its rules. A member of the area executive then asked when the committee would be removed. The general secretary stated that this would be effective immediately the area committee accepted a strike decision from mass meetings.

The Glasgow area executive met after this meeting to discuss the situation. What astounded all members present were the general secretary's views on the circumstances in which militancy was permissible. The consensus of opinion was that the union nationally would never achieve a satisfactory wage rise as long as that attitude prevailed. A meeting was arranged with the area committee, and similar feelings – some more hostile – were expressed. It was decided to go ahead with the mass meetings arranged for 17 October.

At both mass meetings there was great reaction from the members about the general secretary's statement on militancy made on behalf of the national executive. There were calls for the general secretary and the national executive to resign, and also calls for a vote of no confidence in the whole national executive. The Glasgow area executive stated that it would be folly to pursue either of these matters, which could only detract from the issue at hand – the effort to secure a £5 per week increase for Glasgow firemen. Both mass meetings were unanimous in their confidence in the ability of the Glasgow area executive to represent them, and it was decided to go back to the Glasgow corporation to seek an improvement and to report back to mass meetings on 24 October.

A few days after the 17 October meeting a letter was received from the Glasgow corporation establishments committee reiterating that it was prepared to pay the £2 per week travel allowance plus the retention of the 48p per week, subject to confirmation by the joint secretaries of the NJC. This brought great anger and frustration from all members of the Glasgow area committee, as it clearly put all negotiations back to square one. It now seemed likely that strike action would be the only means left to force a change in attitude from the Glasgow corporation.

The area executive called for a further meeting with the establishments committee. At this meeting the ground was gone over again concerning the situation in Glasgow. Clarification was also sought relative to the position of area executive officials in the event of their being removed from office. The convenor of the establishments committee made it quite clear that it would not deal with anyone who was not an official of the FBU. It was also emphasised that the offer of £2 travel allowance plus 48p, with agreement of the joint secretaries, was as far as the establishments committee was prepared to go. The area executive stated that it would then have to withdraw, and that it could not be held responsible for the decision of the mass meetings, which had already been arranged, if the decision was to go on strike. As the area executive withdrew the convenor of the establishments committee had tears in his eyes.

All this information was passed to the president and general secretary, in particular the now ambiguous intent on the payment of the £2.48, as it clearly put the area executive in a difficult position in relation to their integrity and the forthcoming mass meetings. A further meeting of the area executive was arranged. Support was flowing in by letter and telegram from all parts of Britain, and this was a great boost to morale. Support was pledged by all members of the community, from pensioners to grass-roots trade unionists, and the area executive found this extremely moving. A great deal of criticism of the Glasgow corporation and our national executive was also received. The media was still reporting our case sympathetically, and it was agreed by all present that our support came from having always reported matters honestly and simply as they had happened, and that this must continue.

A meeting of the area committee was convened and an up-date of the situation given. It was agreed that all the facts be reported to the mass meeting exactly as they had happened. That evening, while the Glasgow area chairman was on night shift, he received a phone call from the president telling him that a private meeting had been arranged with the convenor of the establishments committee and asking him to attend. This was agreed. The chairman was taken from the fire station by an assistant firemaster to the home of the convenor. There the ambiguity of the last offer of £2.48 was discussed. The convenor gave the assurance that the £2.48 would be paid without recourse to the joint secretaries of the NJC. The chairman gave the assurance that the clarified offer would be put to the mass meetings already arranged.

The following morning the area executive met and discussed the new situation. The chairman was advised that he should not have attended the meeting on his own as this gave rise to suspicion. It was agreed that the matter be put to the mass meetings and the membership would decide. The question of strike action was discussed. It was agreed that any decision on strike action, be it for one day, two days, or indefinitely, would have to be organised by the area executive. To allow the membership to act independently would not only be letting them down but also lead to a shambles.

At the mass meetings on 24 October the full events of the happenings since the previous meetings were reported. On every occasion the national executive was mentioned there were calls for their resignation and others of 'no confidence'. The meetings were told that as far as the area executive were concerned we had gone as far as we could under the present circumstances. There were then calls for a vote on strike action. This was put to both meetings and the combined results for both morning and evening meetings were 485 for strike action and ten against.

The area executive on announcing the result were greeted with prolonged applause and cheers. The area executive informed the members that from the moment it accepted the strike decision it was deemed to be out of office. The membership accepted this, and also agreed that the area executive and area committee would now take over as the 'Glasgow strike committee'. In order to co-ordinate and unify the situation, the membership were told that strike action (which would be indefinite) would commence at 8 a.m. on Friday 26 October, and that all members, regardless of shift or annual leave, should report to their respective branches at that time. It was also agreed that the action would only be called off on receipt of an acceptable offer, and this when it was put to the whole Glasgow membership by the area committee or strike committee. The meeting was closed with calls for confidence in the 'Glasgow officials' and by the statement, 'at last we have leaders who'll fight for us!'

The area executive then met the president, general secretary and two senior Scottish officials and reported on the decisions of the mass meetings. The general secretary offered to clear up any ambiguity in the offer of £2.48, but the area executive informed him that at this stage it would be unacceptable. The area executive were then told that, as had been stated at the 16 October meeting, it and the area committee were removed from office, and arrangements would be made for officials to administer the Glasgow membership.

Late on the evening of 25 October the executive committee of the 'Glasgow strike committee' was called to a meeting in the St Enoch Hotel. This was a private meeting and a last ditch attempt to stop the strike going ahead. The resolve of the Glasgow officials to support their colleagues was again emphasised, as was the resolve of the national executive to oppose it. Lengthy debate ensued about the ambiguity of the £2.48, and at 2 in the morning of 26 October the following offer was put by the convenor of the establishments committee:

> Dear Sir,
> I confirm an offer of £2.00 travel allowance across the board and the retention of 48 pence.
> William Harley

The strike committee discussed this letter, but it was decided that, apart from being far too late, it was not an offer which would stop the impending strike.

On the day prior to the strike every member of the Glasgow fire service received a letter from the Firemaster 'instructing' personnel 'to report for duty at their home stations on Friday 26 October, at 0800 hours'. At 8 a.m. on the 26th the nightshift booked off duty. They were not relieved by day shift crews. A head count was carried out and reported to the Glasgow strike committee. The Glasgow firemen's strike was solid.

It was also reported to the strike committee that letters had been received from Len Murray, general secretary of the Trades Union Congress, and James Jack, general secretary of the Scottish TUC, condemning the action of the Glasgow members and urging them to return to work. The strike committee believed this was the work of the 'dirty tricks department' of the national executive, as the press knew about the contents before their release by the secretary or chairman of the strike committee. The opinion of the committee was that this was another attempt to sully the image of the Glasgow membership. Even on that first day of strike, however, the press was behind the firemen.

At a mass meeting arranged for that day the written offer of £2.48 was presented. The membership made it very clear that the offer was too little too late, and it was rejected by 500 votes to 40. The letters from the TUC and the STUC were read out and only served to strengthen the resolve of the Glasgow membership. The position of the army moving in to take over fire-fighting duties was also discussed. It was agreed that our fight was not with the troops and that it would not be in our interest to interfere with their operations, so, in order to maintain support, no Glasgow member should attempt to prohibit or impede troops carrying out their duties.

It was pointed out to the membership that as the area executive and committee had been removed from office and no longer were allowed to negotiate our main task should be to organise the strike, collect funds and speak to as many members of the general public and trade unions as possible.

The Trades Union Centre in Carlton Place, Glasgow, had been the main meeting place of the area executive and committee. Instructions had gone to the centre that as these committee members had been removed from office they should be denied the use of the premises as a meeting place or strike centre. This was obviously designed to stifle the strike committee and prevent it from operating effectively. To the credit of those who ran the social side of the centre, they made it clear who they would allow to use their building and we were given the full run of the premises and allowed to use it as a strike headquarters. They even had a phone installed for our use. The next few days were taken up by speaking at public meetings, to trade unionists at workplaces, students at colleges and universities, and to collecting and organising funds. The support we were getting from all sections of the community, both morally and financially, was very gratifying.

At this point mention should be made of the role played by the armed services and NAFO. We had made it clear that we would in no way interfere with the operations of the troops, or the remaining officers of the Glasgow fire service. The troops had moved into the fire stations with their Green Goddesses, as the operational fire appliances were considered too sophisticated for them. The remaining officers, 95 per cent of whom belonged to NAFO, formed themselves into the 'pathfinders', their main function to show the way to the fire and direct operations on arrival. This situation can best be summed up by a statement from General Sir Edwin Bramall:

> It was the first ever fire brigade strike in the UK. It had been condemned by the TUC and the Scottish TUC. There was little outside support, most important of all, 60 officers remained on duty, and the strikers announced that their pickets would not harass either their officers or those of other fire brigades or the troops. Nor did they. And on the services' side, there was ample warning to prepare and gather together the equipment, and there was also proper service expertise, particularly in the Royal Navy and RAF. The result was that 70 to 80 calls a day were coped with over a ten-day period; and it all ended in something approaching euphoria, with special letters of thanks and free beer all round.

This account is not entirely accurate, as there were a few extra 'car parks' when they left, but is, broadly speaking, correct.

The next main event was the recall conference in the Beaver Hall, London, on 29 October. Our strike committee was aware that it would be used to give the Glasgow officials a 'going over', but we had to attend in order to air our members' point of view. To say we were concerned about the reception we would receive from the delegates would be an understatement. It was with apprehension and trepidation that the four officials, Jim Flockhart, L. Nearin, D. Laird and Ronnie Russell, walked towards Beaver Hall. On turning into Beaver Lane we were met by a wall of firemen. The wall parted to reveal the lane, lined its entire length with firemen, four deep on either side, cheering and clapping; a most uplifting and humbling experience.

Once inside the hall we were witness to what was, in our opinion, one of the best stage-managed and manipulated conferences in the history of the Fire Brigades Union. The Glasgow delegates were given fifteen minutes to state their case, followed by an hour and a half debate, contributed to, in the main, by the general secretary speaking on behalf of the executive council. There were a number of incidents, both inside and outside the hall, which were attempts to disrupt the meeting, and to which the Glasgow membership was not party. In any event, the vote was 20,000 to 12,000 against Glasgow. This did not come as a surprise, and in fact the voting was better than we had expected.

On leaving the hall the Glasgow delegates were once again cheered and applauded until they left the area. The reception for the general secretary and president was entirely the opposite, and in fact they had to have police assistance. Again, it should be stressed that no Glasgow member played any part in this.

The delegates returned home and reported the decision to a mass meeting in Glasgow. The strike committee stated that it was prepared to continue to represent the Glasgow firemen and the decision of the mass meeting was to fight on. It was reported that a number of brigades had now gone on 'emergency calls only' until the Glasgow members had returned to work and the Glasgow officials re-instated. There were also many more letters and telegrams of support. These were greeted by much cheering and applauding and morale was high. There was further cheering when it was announced that thousands of pounds in financial support was flowing in from various supporting organisations and individuals. There was a call that Glasgow should withdraw from membership of the FBU, but this was ruled out as neither feasible nor desirable.

The next few days were again taken over by public meetings and meetings with other trade unionists. The press was still reporting the Glasgow situation sympathetically, much to the annoyance of certain senior union officials who had tried various smear tactics, not least that an 'extra 50p' would settle the strike.

An extract from a *Glasgow Herald* editorial at the time read:

> Since the strikers have their backs to the wall, being in dispute with both their employers and their union, they are not going to be amenable to logical argument. This dispute is long past the stage of logic and is now into the realms of emotion. What is needed now is something to take the heat out of the

> situation, and the only people who can do that are the leaders of the strike. They may be counting on some government intervention, discreet or otherwise, and if so they are wrong, for there is as much determination on the part of the government to ensure that the terms of their counter-inflation policy are not flaunted as there is at present on the part of the strikers to settle for nothing less than they have demanded.
>
> But the situation would not be so intractable if the strikers' leaders considered the position realistically and dispensed with their false hopes of intervention. In the short term they have no choice but to accept the maximum that is possible to offer, but in the medium term can surely look forward to a radical improvement in their pay and conditions. By continuing the strike they can only jeopardise this justified expectation.

This was the harshest criticism yet of the strike leaders and it was also wide of the mark. Back at the beginning we knew we had an excellent case and there was still no reason to change our mind, and we were aware that negotiations were being carried out. We also strongly believed that the strike had awakened the country as a whole to the injustice in pay and hours in the fire service and it would be a mammoth let down to many if we gave in now. Our determination to continue was as solid as ever.

Friday 2 November saw another day of talks and visits to factories and offices to spell out our case. Support for the Glasgow firemen was strong. That evening a call was received from the press that a major fire in the centre of Glasgow was being tackled by the troops and it looked as if they were having difficulty containing it. The press wondered if any firemen would volunteer to help. It certainly put us in a difficult position, but we had to make it clear that our claim was for a decent wage for firemen and this fire only highlighted the dangers of the job and the skills needed to tackle it. A number of calls from the press followed and we found ourselves in a tricky situation. The press even wanted the chairman to have his photograph taken with the fire as backdrop to plead his case.

A call was then received from a member of the Press Association stating that a wage rise had been agreed with the

FBU and that this was to be between £5 and £8. The chairman of the strike committee said that if this was correct then it would be raised with the membership, but we would have to wait for confirmation from our national officials. Our strike headquarters was suddenly deluged by journalists telling us about a deal that had been hammered out at a national level. We had to hold our silence as there were too many journalists in the building, but we still had no official word. John McDonald, a national officer of the FBU who had been sent to Glasgow as 'liaison officer', had been there two days. What his thoughts were during that period I do not know, but shortly before midnight he informed me that a pay rise had indeed been hammered out and that the £2.48 was still on offer, over and above. It would be impossible to describe the feelings of members of the strike committee on hearing this news, but suffice it to say that the bar was kept open late!

On Saturday 3 November the headlines in the press were '£9 for the Firemen'. Telegrams and letters of congratulation flooded into the strike headquarters. The Glasgow strike committee met in an atmosphere of euphoria and discussed the pay offer. It was decided to call a mass meeting the following day and put the offer to the Glasgow membership. At first we thought it would be difficult to muster about 600 members at such short notice when they were not at their normal place of work, but once again the press came to our aid and printed the time and place of the meeting in their news reports.

On Sunday 4 November the Partick Burgh Halls were filled with 600 firemen in very jubilant mood, clapping and cheering. It took some considerable time for the chairman to quieten down this excited, happy bunch before the report on the pay offer was given. Not a sound was heard during the reading of the report. Once the report had been completed, all hell broke out once again, and it took some time before order was restored. The pay offer was put to the vote. On this occasion it was easier to count the votes against: there were two. It was also agreed that the strike would end at 8 a.m. on 5 November 1973.

The Glasgow Strike

At approximately 7.45 on the morning of 5 November, the troops moved out of the stations. A certain amount of rapport had developed between the firemen and the troops during the past ten days and the firemen applauded them as they pulled out. At 7.58 the Glasgow firemen lined up for duty, and at 8 the Glasgow firemen's strike was over.

Thus ended two months of the most intense activity the union locally or nationally had ever known. During that period the Glasgow area committee and, in particular, the Glasgow area executive, had been under terrific pressure and at times severe strain. One member of the executive had resigned, but we always believed that we had a more than justifiable case and that is why we had to fight on.

What had started as a local issue had escalated into a national one. Not only had it made Britain's firemen aware that their pay and hours agreements were miserly, but it had touched the hearts of ordinary people and grass-roots trade unionists everywhere. If it had not been for the action of the Glasgow firemen, supported by many of their colleagues throughout Britain, and for the support of ordinary trade unionists in all areas of industry, many in defiance of their union leaders, and of ordinary people, including pensioners, the firemen's lot would have been £1 plus 4 per cent. In the case of a Glasgow fireman, he would have received £1 plus 4 per cent, less 48p.

The national executive of the FBU had signed and sealed the agreement of £1 plus 4 per cent. Only the Glasgow action had moved them to try and achieve something more realistic. The article in the 1973 November issue of *Firefighter*, under the title of 'Return to Sender', was in the opinion of Glasgow area executive, less than fair or honest. It wasn't a 'unique negotiating coup', it wasn't 'simple, but brilliant'; it was action by firemen that achieved it.

13 Unofficial Action on Merseyside

Bob Roxburgh

This short piece describes a little-known episode that took place in May 1977, some months before the national strike. At a series of meetings of FBU members throughout the brigade concern was being expressed that because we had a Labour government which most of us supported at the polls our national executive would be reluctant to carry out the call for strike action in the event of our claim for a just settlement being denied. It was also felt that a show of strength would help to convince our employers that the time for taking firemen's demands lightly had passed.

So it was decided that an unofficial work-to-rule be implemented throughout the brigade. Myself and another fireman were elected to lead this action.

The work-to-rule amongst FBU members was 100 per cent solid, and representation was made to our local FBU officials (who were opposed to the action because it was unofficial) to get a commitment from the executive to call for strike action if our claim failed.

The work-to-rule was effective for some time, when my colleague and I were called to the brigade union office where the brigade reps, including Terry Fields, laid down the law and pointed out that we had made our point, and that a continuation of our action would be looked on by some as a split in the union and could not help our negotiators. After a further series of meetings it was agreed to call the action off, and a date was given to the Chief Officer for a return to normal working. And then came the crunch. The Chief Officer decided to issue an order on a date before we had agreed to return to normal working, that any brigade personnel who did not return to normal working by 9 o'clock on his date would be sacked.

On this date senior officers were present on every station; at 9 o'clock members of the on-coming watch were individually called into the station office and given an ultimatum: return to normal working or go home. The reaction of the FBU members on Merseyside was fantastic and an indication of the response the national executive were to get in November.

Not one man accepted the Chief Officer's ultimatum and, after a series of phone calls was made around the stations, a mass meeting was called for 10 o'clock at waste ground in Strand Road, Bootle. At this never-to-be-forgotten meeting 1,000 firemen turned up and voted unanimously for all-out strike. The atmosphere and feeling of solidarity was tremendous. During the morning of that day the Chief Officer declared that all striking firemen had been sacked. Our response was that the strike would continue until all the dismissal notices were withdrawn. We called his bluff.

At 9 o'clock the following morning, on the instruction of the council leader, a Mr Thompson (Tory), the Chief Officer informed me, in front of hundreds of Merseyside FBU members, that the sacking order had been withdrawn and that he would accept our date for a return to normal working. Complete victory!

These events might not normally be included in the union's history because they were unofficial, but rightly or wrongly we felt at the time that we were fully justified in our actions. They were brought to an end by some wise counselling by our local FBU officials, notably Terry Fields, who, while agreeing with our sentiments did not agree with our actions.

14 The Strike in London

Paul Kleinman

At the time of the national strike I was stationed at Lambeth, London, as a crewman on the Fireboat *Firehawk*, Blue Watch. We had a FBU branch meeting on the pontoon about a week before the strike started. Our branch rep was Jock Lee. Terry Fordham, who was area secretary of the old 'B' Division, was also on Blue Watch and attended the meeting. I had only been on the boat about six months at the time, although I had been a member of the London Fire Brigade for nearly fifteen years. Prior to coming to Lambeth I had served all of my service in the 'F' division which took over from the LCC 'B', and I had been Branch rep at Poplar, Leyton and Millwall, and later went on to be rep at Lambeth, Peckham and Deptford. However, at that time I was only an ordinary branch member.

As is well known, London brigade had voted not to strike, but when it was announced by Jock Lee that the strike was definitely to go ahead we all accepted the situation, although at the time I think none of us really thought it would actually happen. Jock made it crystal clear that anyone who did not strike would lose his union card, and as there was a closed shop at the time this could mean the loss of his job. As we were all solidly behind the union I don't think this remark was really necessary, but we all understood why he had to say it anyway.

After the meeting finished, at about 7.30 in the evening I walked over Lambeth Bridge to get the bus home to Walthamstow from Victoria Station. On a fireman's pay at the time I couldn't afford a car as I had three growing children at home so my wife couldn't go to work. I could have got the underground from Vauxhall but the bus fare was cheaper. I remember wondering how on earth I would manage with no pay at all, as, like most firemen at the time, even those with working wives, I was heavily overdrawn at the bank nearly all the time. Still, I told myself optimistically, the strike wouldn't happen. No government, least of all a Labour one, would let a national fire brigade strike happen. Like nearly all London firemen I was forced to take on secondary employment. In my case I had a window-cleaning round, and the money I earned from this plus my fireman's pay just about kept my head above water, with the aid of my bank overdraft, although there was certainly not much left for luxuries.

Walking over Lambeth Bridge I was jolted from these maudlin thoughts by a strange sight. A huge convoy of Green Goddess fire appliances was wending its way towards what I now know to be Chelsea Barracks. I still didn't really believe the strike would actually happen, but I remember thinking that this was taking bluff to the very brink.

I was on rota leave the Thursday and Friday night before the strike started. This was due to the union securing the 48-hour week. We still worked two days, two nights and two days off, but every third week we had two days, or two nights, off. Before I went off-duty on days I was told to report to the pontoon opposite Lambeth fire station in plain clothing as the strike was due to start at 9 o'clock on Monday morning. I was wearing my best, and only, suit and overcoat and was sitting upstairs on the 38 bus, which had pulled over to let two fire engines go by. People on the bus remarked that firemen would soon be on strike but no one seemed unduly concerned and in the main seemed to be fairly sympathetic.

Before leaving for work that morning I said to my wife that I still didn't believe the strike would actually go ahead. My wife disagreed. 'You'll be home for lunch,' she said. I arrived at the pontoon at about 8.30. There was a crowd of firemen at top of the brow, plus an even bigger crowd at the fire station opposite. There was also a battery of TV cameras plus assorted sound crew, as this was the headquarters of the London Fire Brigade. As 9 o'clock approached I still could not believe it would happen. Like most men who joined at the time I did, I came from a military background and just could not see firemen striking or the government allowing it. I was wrong. On the stroke of nine, Red Watch walked off the station, the boat was chained up. We refused to take up our positions. The strike which I never thought would happen ... happened.

I have never been photographed for TV so many times. Cameras were everywhere. We were advised not to answer any questions from the press as it's too easy to be quoted out of context. After about an hour we worked out how we would organise the picket. The 'land crabs', as we affectionately called the firemen on the other side of the road, had large watches so for them there was no problem, but we on the river were a separate station, so we divided our watches into two, with the station officer and sub-officer on our watch. The agreement was that we would halve the duty system and we would have a 24-hour picket of one day and one night. It was cold and we made a little hut on top of the brow leading down to the boat and pontoon. As the other half of our watch was to be the first, I got the bus home with instructions to return that night. I arrived home and the first words my wife said to me were ... 'Your lunch is in the oven.'

That night I dressed in my warmest clothes. We had decided on our side not to wear uniform. We had a big notice on our side of the Embankment, 'TOOT YOUR HORN IF YOU SUPPORT US', and nearly every car, van, lorry, cyclist, motor cyclist and bus did so. Public support was magnificent. We made a giant thumb from a large piece of plywood and an old broom handle which we used to give a 'thumbs up' gesture, and our own morale and good humour was tremendous. The strongest support came from the licensed taxi-drivers who stopped to put money and bottles of whisky in plastic strike buckets which we had put out on a little table on the Embankment. As it was a freezing cold night we found an old dustbin which we turned into a brazier, and some friendly lorry drivers dropped off old wooden pallets for us to burn. We took it in turns, two at a time, to sit on the Embankment while the rest of us stayed in the cabins on the pontoon, where we drank hot coffee and whisky before doing our stint up top. Our conditions were quite grim compared with the 'land crabs', as they had a centrally heated fire station, but we were happier in our own company. By the morning, which soon came, I set off for the bus station tired but happy, thinking the strike would shortly be over, we would have a decent pay settlement, and peace would reign once more ... I couldn't have been more wrong.

When I arrived home I was tired. My wife wanted me to go out shopping with her, which I did. She tried to be very careful with money, trying hard to stick only to essentials, but it wasn't easy. Even in those days, everyday items which you normally take for granted, like cleaning materials, were beginning to look like an impossible luxury. Once we got home I was so tired I went straight up to bed in the middle of the day – something I had not done for years – and almost slept the clock round.

The next day I went to the Social Security office, as it was finally getting through that the strike might be prolonged. I had never, in all my life, been to one of these places before, so I was completely ignorant of the system. As I had to wait for several hours to be seen I got talking to some of the regulars. It was an education. Some of the stories I heard, and of the injustices involved, almost had me in tears, forgetting my own problems; but I must admit that one or two cases I heard almost had me boiling over with anger. There was a fit-looking man, who looked to be in his early forties, who hadn't worked for years, claiming he had a bad back. Judging from his conversation, though, his back didn't stop him from going to the pub every day and spending most of the rest of the time in the betting shop.

Any idea I may have had of the social services lobbing out buckets of money to 'work-shy loafers' were soon corrected, however, when my turn came to go to the little window. You have to know how to work the system really well to do this, if at all, and I didn't. It's not very easy to put your case through a glass partition. First I had to explain why I needed assistance in the first place and then list all of my regular out-goings on a sheet of paper, things like mortgage repayments, rates, gas, electricity, etc. The first clerk I saw was really quite a pleasant young lady, but half-way through our conversation she was replaced by an elderly looking old 'battle-axe' who explained that as I was a striking fireman I had already received a month's pay and that I would be receiving two weeks pay at the end of the month, because the strike had started on 14 November, I was not liable to anything for another four weeks. She said this was in response to a letter the department had received from the government as her department didn't know firemen were paid monthly. This was my first experience of government interference, and I went home empty handed.

The next problem ... how to survive another four weeks. I had a small window-cleaning round but without my fire brigade pay this wouldn't nearly be enough, especially as the two weeks' pay I would be getting at the end of the month would immediately be swallowed up by my overdraft. As I've said previously, my wife couldn't go to work because of the children, both my in-laws and my father were dead and my mother was a pensioner. The rest of my family and my wife's were true Tories, not very sympathetic to strikers, so we decided that come what may we would ask them for nothing. I couldn't even find another job because I had to do picket duty. I was in a fix.

Luckily for me there was a manual employment agency close to my home which specialised in casual drivers and various other unskilled labouring jobs. I possessed a heavy goods license as I was a brigade driver, so the first work I had was the occasional day of driving. The weather was foul so I was given all the lousy work the full-time drivers wouldn't do. I drove battered old lorries all over the Home Counties and even as far as Leeds, Grimsby and other Northern towns. I also worked for a lemonade company delivering door to door, and when there were no driving jobs available I worked at night as a labourer in the bottling plant. Not forgetting my window-cleaning round when weather permitted. And of course I still had to do my one day and one night's picket duty. I made a surprising discovery. I was absolutely exhausted at the end of the week, but one way or another I was actually earning more than I did as a full-time fireman plus my window-cleaning round.

As I was becoming a regular employee of this agency out of sheer necessity, I was several times offered full-time employment, because I was a hard reliable worker, even if I say so myself. I loved being a fireman, but I must admit that if the strike was indeed to drag on for ever, as both the government and the union threatened, I think the time would have come when I would have had to resign and start another career.

Meanwhile, back to the picket line. As I had extensive experience of being a branch rep before I served on the fireboat, I was nominated to attend the daily meetings which took place at the National Union of Seamen's office next to Clapham fire station. As I didn't have a car I was usually given a lift by one of the 'land crabs' who sent a rep of their own. Jock Currie, an instructor at the training centre, was then a regional official; he chaired the meeting and told us all the latest developments. He said at the very beginning of the strike, and he was proved to be so right, that if the strike lasted more than ten days or so we would lose it.

A strange thing happened. On our section, in a way we actually started to enjoy the strike in a strange sort of way. Most of my colleagues were slightly older than me and had no family commitments or their wives worked. A couple of them were licensed taxi-drivers or they had profitable part-time businesses. The rest, like me, had managed by casual work to sort out their personal finances, at least for the time being, so money was not a pressing problem, so we began to enjoy the close sense of comradeship – us against the world – that none of us had ever experienced before.

Of course, not all firemen on strike were as fortunate as us. None of us had very large mortgages, because we had all been in our homes for a number of years, or were council tenants, and all of us lived in the London area where casual work was readily available. Many were the stories we heard of really serious financial hardship, of men being forced to sell their possessions and in the worst cases even their homes. I must admit I never met anyone in quite that predicament, either from the river service or the land station over the road. Apparently it was the men from the provinces who were hit hardest because there wasn't much casual work where they were.

One tale I did hear, although it may be apocryphal, was that two firemen from Poplar fire station took a lorry up to Leeds as temporary drivers. On seeing a group of firemen huddled round a brazier outside a fire station, they dismounted from their lorry and approached them.

'How are we doing lads?' they inquired.

'What do you mean WE?' asked the Leeds firemen. When the London firemen explained what they were doing, the anger they engendered was so great they literally had to run back to the lorry to avoid being beaten up. No prizes for guessing why.

As the strike dragged on into the third and then the fourth week we were getting a little impatient for signs of a breakthrough. After all, we kept telling ourselves, every industrial dispute is settled eventually. Although, as I have already stated, none of us on the *Firehawk* was really hard up, we knew that this state of affairs couldn't last indefinitely. Apart from the fact that we were working much harder, there was always the worry the casual work would dry up, but more importantly we were all firemen and wanted desperately to carry on with our chosen profession.

One morning we heard on the wireless that there was a big fire at Poplar hospital and that firemen from Poplar fire station had left the picket line carrying breathing apparatus sets in their private cars and had put the fire out. It was a particularly nasty fire, started in the basement by a mentally deranged patient, and the army, who had no breathing apparatus, wouldn't have stood a chance without the help of regular firemen. Surely, we thought, now the government would see sense and settle. Once again we were wrong. This looked like becoming a fight to the finish. Many were the stories heard on the picket line of the army completely messing up fires, and where they did succeed in putting out a fire causing a lot more damage than necessary. It seemed obvious to us there was a deliberate news black-out on fires, but of course these were only suspicions and we had no means of verifying them.

When the strike started, as I've already said, the public were with us almost to a man. Our radio on the pontoon was tuned permanently to LBC which was nearly all 'phone in' in those days and was a good guide to public opinion. However, as the strike was now entering its sixth and seventh weeks there seemed to be a change. I'm not saying public opinion was reversed, but more and more of the calls pointed out that firemen got free uniforms, had their shoes repaired for nothing, had a wonderful pension scheme, had free dental and optical treatment, unlimited sick pay, security of employment and so on and so on. Every time we tried to phone and point out that all these so called perks didn't rule out the fact that we were still, at the end of the day, very poorly paid for a disciplined service where from time to time your life was in great danger or you stood more than a fair chance of being permanently maimed, we found the lines were engaged or no more calls on the firemen's strike were being accepted. We all wondered exactly who was phoning LBC with all this information anyway. Perhaps they were government *agents provocateurs*.

One more thing that didn't help was that a peace agreement was in the process of being concluded between Israel and Egypt, and the powers that be considered, rightly or wrongly, that this was more important than striking firemen.

Morale, as far as I could see, was excellent. I have never before or since seen such determination to see things through. But I must admit cracks were beginning to appear. Several of the land crabs resigned to take up other employment, and even on the fireboat one of our men, who suffered very badly from deteriorating eyesight, worked a quick medical discharge. We heard stories of real hardship from provincial firemen, and one station, West Wickham I think it was, went back to work. A mass picket was organised with firemen travelling in coaches to get there, but to no avail. Other stations around the country were also drifting back to work, probably more out of hardship than conviction, but as I've said the great majority were still prepared to sweat it out.

The National Association of Fire Officers (NAFO) voted four to one not to strike and many of their members helped to train and direct the army, and much bitterness ensued when we heard this. There were a few 'scabs' on the FBU side as well, and there was also a fireman from the land station who proclaimed that as he wasn't a union member he wouldn't strike, and no amount of persuasion would make him change his mind. I must admit that, to our collective shame, his locker was broken into and all his firegear, as well as his private property, was thrown out onto the Albert Embankment, much to the delight of passing tramps. Men like him and NAFO were more than balanced by officers who left NAFO, joined the FBU and went on strike like the rest of us.

Marches were organised. One we attended had its rallying point in Hyde Park and we had a whip round to get a taxi but the taxi-driver, to his credit, refused to take the fare.

When the strike started, relations with the police were good. Indeed one constable at our station put on a picket's armband, probably against all orders, and stood on our line. By the time the strike had been on for a few weeks, however, we noticed that the police were starting to keep their distance, and were even in some cases becoming a bit hostile. For instance, they made us remove our brazier from the wide pavement, although it posed no danger to the public, and we also had to remove our little table with the collecting bucket. They also kept a discreet distance from our picket line and were no longer so chatty. They were probably acting under instructions.

We each received at our private address a letter containing details of the government pay offer. Some were quite acceptable, like the introduction of the 42-hour week, others, like no victimisation of scabs, we didn't like. The 'upper quartile' which is in use to this day seemed quite good, but the bottom line was that we still had to go back to work for 10 per cent, which is what we were offered before the strike started.

One day we marched to TUC headquarters near Russell Square for a lobby. Several leaders of other unions made speeches supporting us, but we heard that the General Council had decided not to throw the whole weight of the trade union movement behind us because we were fighting a Labour government. No words of mine could picture the sense of betrayal we all felt. It was becoming obvious to even the most militant of us that there was no way we could win this dispute without the help of other unions, yet here was the 'parliament' of the union movement withdrawing its support. We tried to organise a 'sit in' but were stopped by the police, who by now were even more hostile. Perhaps this was due to the fact that there were a great many extreme 'lefties', members of the Communist Party and the even more extreme Workers Revolutionary Party, masquerading as firemen. The extreme left had muscled in on our strike from day one, and had even recruited some firemen to join their movement. Every day they brought their newspaper, *News Line*, onto our picket line. One item which attracted particular attention was a daily article, 'Diary of a Fireman', purporting to be events happening on the picket line and about the strike and politics in general. From the style of writing and use of words, however, none of us thought it really was written by a fireman.

The strike was now nearing its end. Cracks were starting to appear all over the country. Every day the wireless brought news of more and more fire stations going back to work. It was obvious we would have to settle soon or face ignominious defeat.

We had our meeting along with the land crabs in the drill yard at Lambeth fire station. Even though defeat seemed inevitable we voted almost to a man to continue the struggle. The rest of the country voted to go back to work, so paradoxically London was out on a limb. We started by voting against the rest, by voting not to strike, and ended by doing the reverse.

On the night of the 'surrender' a few of us from the boat walked to the Home Office at Queen Anne's Gate with John (Lew) Lewis and Terry Fordham. Lew said that when he saw the document in its original form he was near to tears, but it was watered down to make it a bit more acceptable.

The rest is history. But what would happen when we returned to duty? What would happen to the 'scabs' and non-strikers? And what would the reaction to the senior officers who supported them be? Many hours were spent on the picket line in the dark days leading up to the end of the strike. There were all sorts of threats, from total snubbing to outright physical violence. I myself swore never again to speak to NAFO station officers on the land side or to the one fireman on the whole station who didn't strike.

And what did happen? Not a lot. I didn't speak to the station officers, but they were both soon transferred to other stations anyway. The one fireman? I'm not the sort to completely snub someone forever. I didn't. I won't say I ever completely forgave him. No one did. But time is a great healer and most firemen are not vindictive types. There were a few half-hearted attempts to expel 'scabs' from the FBU, but I don't think the leadership was that much in favour, I don't know why, and to the best of my knowledge no member was actually expelled from the FBU.

Senior officers? What could we do? They didn't live on stations. Most who aided the army or didn't strike were not members of the FBU anyway. Also, although photographs were taken of senior officers working at fires during the strike, the photos were not widely circulated, so not many knew who they were. Some senior officers, to their credit, were striking with us. At the end of the day, it would be fair to say, in London, that they got away with it. I'm not so sure this applied to the more tightly knit firemen's communities in the rest of the country, and there were stories of firemen leaving the service on pension because of so called nervous debility brought on by their so called 'treatment'. Management might transfer officers to get them out of trouble, but this obviously didn't apply to firemen.

The bottom line. Was it all worth it?

At first glance, no. We were offered the 'upper quartile' shortly after the strike started. We went out the doors for 10 per cent. We returned with 10 per cent, so you could say we lost. Not quite true. The 'upper quartile' is a good deal, and to this day has preserved peace in the fire brigade.

When the 42-hour week was actually introduced in 1979, we had to suffer the loss of 42 front-line fire appliances and one fireboat, that based at Greenwich, went completely, and the other, Lambeth's, which was mine, was transferred, along with all its crew, to Lambeth land station. We were split up among the four watches, as Green watch was newly created. The union wasn't very keen on all the losses of appliances, but such was the enthusiasm to get on the 42-hour week, with four complete days off after each tour, that it simply had to go along with the loss.

What of the future? Well, up to the time of writing, the upper quartile agreement still holds, although every year the employers threaten to end it. My brigade, London, is going through, and has indeed gone through, many great changes, all of which are too well known for me to chronicle here. I myself have retired from operational service, having failed the eyesight test on my medical, but am still employed by the brigade as non-operational. There is a rumour, probably no more, that the brigade wants to get rid of all men who were on strike. There is no evidence to support this but I must admit that with the passage of time there certainly is a huge reduction of serving '77 strikers.

I will end by trying to answer the question I have been asked many times. If I had known then what I know now, would I still have done it?

I can't really answer this question, there are so many 'ifs and buts', but in retrospect I think we lost more than we gained. We might possibly have had the upper quartile and the 42-hour week by now anyway. What we lost, and this is only my personal opinion, is union credibility.

Up to the time of the strike, we, as a union, won victory after victory, by the mere threat of the possibility of a strike. The strike was our big punch, our strongest weapon. Once it was used, and it was a bitter pill for us to swallow, that society as we know it didn't collapse, we had lost.

We still have the disputes procedure, which is good, but once the nation saw the return of a Tory government, with a whole succession of anti-union laws to follow, the chances of another strike occurring, are, in my opinion, remote. Of course, as I say, no one can foresee the future, and maybe if the economic state of the country worsens and conditions become intolerable, it may happen. I hope and pray this doesn't happen as this would affect society as a whole and not just the fire brigade.

I am still an active member of the Fire Brigades Union and look forward with optimism to the future. I am convinced that we can put the past behind us and we can all move forward to a new era of co-operation and understanding, and that not only firemen, but all working people, will benefit and live their lives to the full in health, peace and prosperity.

15 The Strike and the Executive

Pete Rockley

Driving alone through the night from Eastbourne to Nottingham gave me ample opportunity to contemplate the events of the past few weeks before the Eastbourne conference that had set the date for the first firemen's strike. Certainly as a 'freshman' executive councillor I felt I'd been thrown into the thick of it.

To be honest, neither I nor the vast majority of my colleagues had expected either the strike vote or the naming of the strike date. Although, to be realistic, the rank and file had become very tired of 'enquiries' and somewhat disillusioned with the executive.

To the best of my recollection, the Eastbourne Conference had been called to inform the membership of the results of yet another enquiry, the 'McCarthy Report'. At a previous executive meeting some days before I had listened to Terry Parry's presentation of this report and had found little in it to appease a disgruntled membership. Although, I repeat, a strike was the furthest thing from my mind.

I duly reported back to the East Midlands membership and found that the word McCarthy had used, 'benchmark', was the only thing of substance in the report. This word 'benchmark' indicated that firemen should have a special place in society and not classed with any other workers – but where?

My first meetings with the members were dominated by pay, many of them waving their pay packets and demanding some kind of action. But no one had seriously contemplated strike action – to sit on their 'arses', as it was described, yes – but didn't they pay you for that? I remember as my drive home progressed racking my brains to think when the executive had lost the Conference and, more importantly, failed to read the danger signs.

Jack Haworth from Manchester had made a valid contribution at the EC meeting before the Eastbourne Conference, in which I remember him saying, 'The lads are prepared to go all the way, either with EC backing or without it.' 'You mean strike, Jack?' the general secretary asked. 'Yes, yes,' Jack replied, 'Strike is what I mean when my members qualify for family income supplement, that for many of them was the last straw.' The president went around the table; most of us agreed with some kind of action, but I only remember Big Jack saying a strike was the only alternative. After what seemed an eternity the EC cobbled together a resolution asking for more time – more time to meet the employer – more time to use that 'benchmark' excuse to extract more money. But now historically we know that was futile and it was bound to fail. The members at the Conference rejected other resolutions and to me appeared to be drawn inevitably to a strike resolution. In the words of one EC member, the Conference was 'highjacked' from the executive by weak leadership.

Yes, Terry did ask 'Would you let children burn?' and a large section of the Conference heckled him for it – but to redress the balance, it must be said that once the decision had been taken Terry accepted full responsibility and I believe he led from the front. A man of ailing health, he had great qualities as both a negotiator and an experienced leader, and the now famous compromise 'upper quartile' was due to Terry and the employers' secretary.

As my long journey home continued, my thoughts turned to my district secretary who had just a few days to go to retirement, and the young fireman at my station who had used my name on his application form for a large mortgage. I thought of my Northern Ireland colleagues who obviously had the most difficult decision to make. My thoughts turned to Lincolnshire, a very rural brigade, and the firemen who lived in tied housing slap-bang in the middle of the community they were there to protect.

I remember that at times like these you automatically turn to experience and the strong minded, and to me this came in the form of Bill Deal of Essex (later to become one of the greatest presidents of our union). I asked Bill what he thought of the situation? And Bill in his characteristic East London accent said, 'Well Pete let's whop it up em.' Did I really need this as a 40-year-old rookie? But Bill's words became more relevant as the weeks progressed. 'Whop it up em' meant solidarity, and solidarity is what we got. I was amazed at the response we got from our members – they marched out of the stations and quickly organised their picket huts. There were very few abstainers and virtually no drop-outs. At Christmas of course, the members were under pressure, particularly those with mortgages and family responsibilities. But we always punched home the same sermon: we came out together and by God we'll go back together, and this always worked.

During December 1977 the Prime Minister was visiting Derby. Both the FBU and the Police Federation were granted a meeting. I arrived there just before dinner with two of my regional officials. To my surprise, there were about 200 firemen and police to picket 'Big Jim'. As he passed me he was escorted by two senior police officers, one of whom had his cap tipped over his eyes by someone in the group. 'Tell your lads to back off,' the officer barked at me. 'All my lads are in uniform,' I replied, 'and the man that did that isn't a fireman,' I said. The Prime Minister intervened and said, 'Come along gentlemen, let's get on with it.'

I remember the meeting very well, armed with so much documentation: wage league tables, wage slips, DHSS family support slips, even letters from Chief Fire Officers; and the Prime Minister read the lot, and after our twenty-minute talk, he looked me straight in the eye and said, 'Yes you have a good case, and I agree we've had a belly full of enquiries into the fire service – but we have taken a Cabinet decision: across the board a ceiling of 10 per cent, and I don't intend to weaken. The public may support you,' he went on, 'but I stand or fall on this principle of arresting inflation. Your case will no doubt be just as relevant in the next period of pay bargaining.' Jim Callaghan gave me a look that convinced me there was nothing left to be said. He certainly was the most determined person I'd ever met. 'I stand or fall,' he said, 'that no one will beat the 10 per cent this year.' As he reached for his glasses I noticed his clean cut suit with what appeared to be J.C. repeated in the pin stripe, very tiny letters going throughout the suit. As he left us behind, I turned to my Derbyshire rep. and asked 'The J.C. on his suit, does it stand for Jim Callaghan?' 'No,' my Derbyshire wag replied, 'it means Jesus Christ!'

During the strike the response from the retained crews was fairly good, particularly in view of the fact we barely had time to consult them. However, in some areas it was patchy. One area was the border between Nottinghamshire and Yorkshire, where some miners were allegedly reporting for duty. We rang the Nottinghamshire president of the NUM and got a favourable response. However, he suggested that we should also ring the Yorkshire president. This we immediately did and found Arthur Scargill at the end of the telephone. Arthur didn't like putting a blanket ban on his members, saying we really should contact each individual pit branch secretary. When we asked if he would follow up our request, he seemed very reluctant to be involved.

However, it must be said that other members of the NUM executive gave us magnificent support. But one stood out more than any other, and that was Joe Whelan. He took up the stand as determined as any fireman and devoted himself to make sure his members obeyed the FBU line. Joe was a magnificent trade unionist who will always be remembered in the East Midlands.

Christmas came with me at Westminster trying to catch a few Midland MPs before the recess and finding only one there. Sitting on a cold marble slab in the Palace of Westminster I saw some of the employers come out of a side room. An embarrassed silence occurred before one came over to me. 'We may have something to offer Peter,' he said, 'but it may be jam tomorrow.' What came immediately to my mind was disappointment that we were not going to break the 10 per cent barrier.

As I left parliament snow began to fall. Christmas 1977, seven weeks into the strike and it's jam on the table. I took the underground to St Pancras only to see the last train to Nottingham winding its way out of the station. Six hours to wait for the 5:30 the next morning. After an uncomfortable night at the station I looked a terrible sight arriving at 7.45 the next morning. I was met by my local officials off the train. 'Good lord,' my chairman said, 'If they see you looking like this they'll think we've lost the bloody strike.' I was quickly taken to the station wash-and-brush-up and miraculously provided with a clean shirt, and off to meet the night shift picket going home. I remember saying, 'Keep it up lads, we're going to win,' and thinking, 'But it may be jam tomorrow.'

The two weeks following Christmas were for me the most testing of the strike. There were some doubts, particularly at small stations. I would hastily call a general meeting and plead for solidarity, and with the classic 'we all came out – we'll all go back' gained valuable time.

And that crucial time gave us two important factors – obviously the firemen's pay formula which was beginning to evolve, and a document leaked to me informing councils that troop deployment had to be paid for in full. This was an unacceptable cost for some metropolitan authorities, and there was actually talk of scaling down the troops because of the costs – it was a gift from the gods and it undoubtedly put great pressure on the employers. So in the end it was a close thing and I believe Bill Deal was right, the last ace was played by the government on our behalf and it was a devastating blow.

'Merlyn Fiddles Whilst Britain Burns', captioned the large print of the Home Secretary, reproduced in its thousands. It was impossible to turn a corner without seeing the poster. It was certainly stuck on most buses in Derby.

However, contrary to popular belief, Rees was desperately trying to end the strike. He was a close friend of Terry Parry and in my dealings with him at the Home Office he would seize on any worthwhile proposal. One that was suggested was that we be granted the 42-hour week in name only, and work the 48-hour week until the formula caught up with the wages. This, together with recruitment, meant that in eighteen months we could genuinely work the 42-hour week and receive the formula. Merlyn took this idea to the Cabinet but was over-ruled. I believe, however, that Rees was largely instrumental in persuading the government to finance its part of the 42-hour week.

By January 1978 we had all been introduced to the upper quartile and had secured as part of the settlement the 42-hour week. Terry Parry couldn't afford another reversal of groundswell opinion, so each EC and regional member was brought into special session with instructions to brief the membership at general meetings and to recommend acceptance. This was done with overwhelming support from I believe eleven of the fourteen regions. The subsequent conference at Bridlington really was a foregone conclusion because sincerely it was an incredibly generous deal and quite plainly a victory. But brigades were not voting as regions and as at recall conference, each individual brigade had its say, and although the votes were overwhelming, some brigades felt betrayed that we had struck to beat the 10 per cent and had not achieved this. This was illustrated on the streets outside the conference where a crowd of 200 were demonstrating against the return to work. I knew there were genuine feelings like this in Strathclyde, Merseyside, London and Essex. As news of the return to work was reaching them, the snow began falling and their chants got louder. What looked like a 30-foot banner was unfurled. 'No Surrender', it said, and although a few hot heads did attack Terry Parry, I felt that the majority had been our company commanders during the nine-week campaign. At the hotel a bruised Terry Parry said to me, 'Peter, just think what they would have done to the employers.'

I remember looking at the now famous, snow-covered picture of the 'No Surrender' message some years later and thinking, 'This could well go down in history.' I accept that there was violence directed at members of the EC, particulary Terry Parry, who had suffered greatly in his health. And yet in my heart of hearts I knew these demonstrators, wrong as they were, somehow had to let it out: the genuine bitterness and frustration that was evident in many people's minds.

It certainly became a strike with the popular support of the membership and there was a groundswell of support even though there was no ballot. Activists sprang forward like mushrooms, organising pickets, collections, food distribution and so on. And although the executive had suffered a defeat at Eastbourne, the activists never made a serious challenge to our union. They appeared to be dedicated in serving the union only, and not other causes. And as far as I know the executive remained in secure control. I was amazed to see these activists demand from the membership total loyalty to the leadership and rigidly kept in that framework.

The strike was successful, no doubt about that, but what amazed me was when it was all over those people who had been the leadership's main critics, and were in a position to challenge, never did. And within a short space of time they melted back into the broad membership. It was back to normal for the structure of our union. One such member, very active during the strike, came on to the executive many years after and I asked him this question. Came the reply, 'It was never our policy to seek high office in any union,' and in any case, he added, 'The strike made bloody heroes of you, who was I to seek bloody heads.'

16 The Strike in Scotland

Bill Craig

As an activist in the union since 1957, I was a delegate to the Eastbourne Conference from Central Region, within the Scottish area. The Scots delegates I believe were very clear in their minds, the time had arrived for firemen to act and stop using kid gloves against quite ruthless employers and an equally stupid Labour government.

The night prior to Conference the Scots delegates in company with our very good friends, the Liverpool delegation, spent hours in a variety of hotel rooms persuading our brothers and sisters that the union's leadership were following the wrong path, pursuing the wrong line. A false loyalty to the Labour government was in fact denying firemen decent wages, decent hours, thus it was vital the executive council should be overturned.

The next day the Standing Orders Committee was very busy as brigade after brigade queued up to support the resolution calling for 'All-Out Strike Action'. EC members tried very hard indeed to influence people to swing back behind the EC line. If I remember correctly there were five or so different resolutions down for discussion.

Suffice to say each in turn was disposed of. The president and general secretary were decidedly unhappy as it became clearer and clearer that the last resolution to be discussed was the Vital All-Out Strike. Terry Fields, the Liverpool lads and we Scots knew in our bones the EC was going to be defeated.

They were, and the vote was a resounding victory for firemen, a victory that led to nine weeks of the hardest work most union officials had ever been involved in. The train back to Scotland was joyous; at last we were going to fight.

The Scottish district committee met early, and every brigade in Scotland was visited by the chairman (myself) and secretary (Jackie Cunningham) to explain the reasons for the strike vote. Our task was to persuade the doubters that the union was serious and that the wage policies of successive governments had restricted progress in improving firemen's earnings. We were considered an easy target, and now 14 November 1977 was to be the day that firemen started the fight-back.

We watched and waited. Any discussions taking place did nothing to beat our resolve.

Just ten minutes after the strike started at 9 o'clock on 14 November 1977 I was able to report that every fire station in Scotland was occupied and the strike was on. The Glasgow Trades Council kindly gave the union facilities, officials were constantly on the move, supporting, cajoling and, more importantly, in many instances assisting members through the maze of DHSS forms and the problems caused by their rules. Money was of course a major problem, and each brigade committee and the Scottish district had a responsibility to raise funds to help out members where extreme hardship arose. I might add that the rules to qualify were strict and firmly applied.

The government under Callaghan had, of course, totally misread the public's attitude, and it became clear very quickly indeed that the armed forces could provide only a very basic form of fire cover and many were the stories of firemen leaving picket lines to ensure that there was no risk to life at nearby fires. The spirit and comradeship of all union members were apparent from the earliest days. Equally apparent was the fantastic support of wives and girlfriends, Mums and Dads.

In Strathclyde the officials at all levels were superb in their organisation and their selfless dedication to the cause. Jim Flockhart, Ronnie Scott (the union's vice-president), R. Robertson, Chalmers, Patton, Len Nearin, Campbell, Tierney, the McLennan brothers and so many others too numerous to recall, all gave magnificently of themselves, as did the officials in all areas of Scotland. The Napiers, Mick Jones, Jack Cunningham (the Scottish secretary) and all the others from the Lothians, Fife, Tayside, Dumfries, Highland and Grampian. Names like Andrew Keddie, Bill Inches, Jake Dunn, Jake Munro, Davidson, Dick Robertson and Alex Sutherland all spring to mind.

It is, however, very important to remember all the members who rose to the occasion and put themselves in the firing line for the duration of the strike and returned to their usual type of union involvement when the strike was over.

Perhaps one of the most moving moments was the 'All-Scottish' demonstration to Glasgow Green. Thousands of firemen and their families gathered in Blytheswood Square with bands and banners. Proudly they played and proudly the banners flew. The public made the day ... they applauded, they poured money into the lads' buckets ... they even left the pubs to cheer us on and give us cash! At Glasgow Green Mick McGahey inspired us with his oratory. Jimmy Milne, general secretary of the STUC, and others prominent in the movement, also fired our enthusiasm.

All in all, the Scots stood firm, and a wee song to the tune of 'Flower of Scotland', was born:

> The firemen of Scotland
> When will we see their likes again
> That went on strike for a wee bit more than ten
> And sent him homeward ... proud Callaghan's army
> TAE THINK AGAIN.

Yes, there were tales too numerous to tell. My favourite is of police leave being cancelled in Dumfries for a firemen's demonstration when in fact the march that day was in Dundee! The story goes that the phone-tappers were deliberately misled by naughty union officials.

The period of our strike is obviously an important area of our history, and it should never be recorded without thanking the hundreds of trade unionists, the rank-and-file brothers and sisters who worked, who gave financially to help the FBU. Nor should it pass without comment on the diabolical attitude of the TUC. Their two-vote majority against the motion in support of our union's struggle was an absolute disgrace and typical of the right-wing majority of that organisation.

Yes, there were those who supported us. Ray Buckton of ASLEF, in particular, was a friend indeed. Ken Gill and others who knew that the working class struggle was important and that employers and governments will walk all over working people unless a united front is presented.

Nothing has changed. The Labour Party and the trade union movement has abandoned the working class, and until the spirit of '77 is reborn we stand alone.

And, of course, the old maxim still applies ... Divided we fall. As Thatcher so easily demonstrated.

17 Fighting a Labour Government

Alistair Spence

After fifteen years of being a fireman, facing cutbacks, pay and conditions being eroded, I found myself in a position where, in spite of the opinions of the union's general secretary, the executive council and their hangers-on, I voted to close the station doors. This, after much soul-searching and great consideration. This strike was against a Labour government whose ideas were far removed from socialism.

I felt a great animosity towards the general secretary, who up to the last minute was saying to the Home Secretary, 'Never mind Merlyn. I'll keep them talking.' Then we the membership, who are the union, voted to strike, Terry Parry almost had a fit and promptly lost interest in us. We did the thing alone, the general secretary and the EC acting like a drag anchor. I felt a very deep anger at Jim Callaghan, Merlyn Rees and their cohorts. When I went home after my stint on the picket line, one or other of them was on the television condemning us. Being pretty volatile and having perhaps too short a fuse, before I knew what I was doing I had the coffee table in my hands ready to fling it at the set. I am very lucky in that I have a very supportive wife who was able to cajole me into putting down the table. Radio Rentals would have kicked up hell anyway.

It must be borne in mind that the government had instructed the DHSS (as if they needed such encouragement) to clamp down hard on striking firemen. At that time a qualified fireman went to the unemployment office to see what he would be worth if he was unemployed, having four children, he was told that he would be worth £54 per week, his counterfoil from his pay slip read approximately £47 odd. I did not then, and still do not, subscribe to the view that £54 was too much for an unemployed man, but I did and still do believe that £47 was too little for a qualified fireman after a 48-hour week. These figures are imprinted in my brain. I also felt and still do feel anger at a government which could tell troops that after some home training by NAFO members, some of whom were in day-duty jobs because they did not come up to the standard operationally, they were considered suitable for firefighting duties. I can never forgive the TUC, the majority of whose union executives rejected our call for support.

When Willie Whitelaw went skipping over hose lines run out by the troops I was disgusted that the Labour Party (the working man's party) had united with the Tories against our cause.

Some time after the strike, from which, let no one tell you any different, we were starved back, I was introduced to Ken Cameron. I said that I hoped that he had more guts than his predecessor. He informed me that Terry Parry had been a brave man. On reflection I had to agree. Anyone who could consistently sell out his membership to the politicians (of whatever hue) and risk their ire and ill temper must indeed have guts.

On the first morning of the strike, at around 9.15, a gentleman passing by in his car tooted his horn. Taking this to be encouragement we all waved back. He gave us a V sign and shouted, 'Get back to your F.....g work you lazy bastards.' Now fifty yards up the road is a set of traffic lights which were set at red. As his eyes were on us and not on the road he collided with four stationary cars. He naturally received a standing ovation.

As I stood on the picket line with my fireman son, my youngest was settling in at primary school and my middle son was sitting for his A and O levels. It could not have been easy for them as I was at that time very easily raised to anger.

To this day I am convinced that the Labour Party was pursuing Tory principles and that the populace were thinking that if we were to be ruled thus it might as well be by the real McCoy. I know for a fact that many firemen voted for Maggie in 1979 (not me I hasten to add) and the rest is unpleasant history.

It should be considered by one and all that the first strike is the most difficult to undertake. The second and subsequent ones are a lot easier to implement. I hope and pray that we never have to descend to such depths ever again. I have begun to understand the feelings of my older ex-colleagues, the real 'old hands', who said to certain individuals, 'I fought a war for you c..ts and you take this stance.'

After the strike and in subsequent years I have said virtually the same thing to younger men who in their striving for promotion, leave the union and join our sister organisation, and I get ill-tempered when they say that the strike was before their time and did not affect them. The union has on many occasions felt the rough edge of my tongue and no doubt will do so again in the future, but leaving it will not solve the problems. Staying in as I have and going on strike gave me and them a better standard of living, and I would encourage any waverers to do and think likewise.

18 Manning the Picket Line

John Curran

My earliest recollections of the pending industrial action to be taken by the firemen of Britain (as we were then called), as a fireman with just under two years' service, was the growing unrest and anger particularly among the older 'hands' at the declining wages and conditions of the members of the service.

Day-shift after day-shift, night-shift after night-shift, the same discussions, the same arguments. We have been treated as doormats for far too long, now is the time to stand up and be counted, now is the time to use the ultimate weapon, now is the time to strike. How could we live with our consciences? How could we stand by and watch people die? How can we stand by and watch people's homes burn? The full range of discussion and argument; the despair and anger that it was a Labour government that we were about to take on.

I am to this day absolutely certain in my own mind that none of us embarked on the course of action that we did take without an awful lot of soul-searching and thought. Will it split the membership? Will the public understand? And will they support us in our fight?

I vividly remember finishing my shift at 8 o'clock in the morning of 14 November and along with the rest of my watch immediately forming a picket line in front of my home station (with some trepidation, I should add). The lights of the TV cameras, the flashbulbs of the press, what were we letting ourselves in for? My fears and doubts were, however, very soon dispersed, as all the vehicles that went past were honking their horns and their drivers and passengers were giving us the thumbs-up in a gesture of support. All the pedestrians walking past the picket lines uttering words of support and encouragement; it seems the first battle of the war has been won, the public are behind us. Maybe I have stretched the truth just a little, there were the odd one or two who gave us the odd victory sign!

At home that night I recall watching the evening news and seeing that the strike action was solid up and down the country and indeed the public support for our action seemed every bit as solid.

On the second day on the picket line the first questions being asked by all the lads was whether there had been any serious incidents during the night? No, thank God. The feelings of the lads were that this would be a short-lived strike, the government would have to succumb to public pressure. A feeling I hasten to add that was soon to be reinforced by the arrival on the picket line of one Jim Sillars, ex-fireman and a Labour MP (present day SNP Member of Parliament), complete with media entourage. 'Don't worry lads,' he said, 'I have been lobbying around parliament, you will be back at work by the end of the week.' It must be said we all felt very encouraged by his remark coupled with the support we had received so far.

As the days began to run into weeks and the reality of the situation began to dawn, we were in for a long hard struggle. Rallies were taking place up and down the country, the battle cry was, 'What do we want? 30 per cent! When do we want it? NOW!' The resolve of the men grew stronger and stronger, day after day manning the picket lines with the vast majority of the public voicing their support. However there was the odd abusive person. I recall one occasion when, after attending a rally in Dundee we were walking back to our bus and an elderly gentleman crossing the road and approached us with the remark that he hoped all our mothers would burn to death. I am glad to say that none of my party rose to the bait.

My next recollections are of Christmas approaching, money being really tight, people having mortgage arrears and everyone wondering how we were going to cope with supplying the families with Christmas dinner, presents for the kids and so on. Again the support of the general public was superb, with people coming up to the picket lines not only with financial support, but with donations of food and drink and all sorts of things, which was a great morale booster. Somehow we managed to cope and Christmas and the New Year were past.

The strike was now drawing to a close. I recall at the last meeting held in my own area at the Aberdeen Trades Council offices, a vote was taken on whether or not to continue our strike action and the result was a resounding 80 per cent in favour. Unfortunately this was not the case up and down the country and a return to work was agreed.

The question now was how were we going to work alongside the NAFO members who had scabbed on the rest of us during the strike? After all, part of the agreement for the return to work was that there was to be no victimisation of these people. After spending nine weeks manning picket lines in the freezing cold and without any money coming in, and the fact that these scabs were going to benefit from everything that we had gained from our action, it would seem to be asking a lot from our membership to pretend that nothing had happened.

19 The Long Shadow of the Strike

James Alexander

I was serving at Kilmarnock fire station on that fateful morning in 1977. I was then a Sub-Officer, aged 39 and had two children aged eight and five. I was due on duty at 8 o'clock. The bell sounded for roll call and everyone – the watch going off duty, the new duty watch and all off-duty personnel – walked out onto Titchfield Street. The strike had begun.

I had been in service for fifteen years; before joining I was in the 2nd Battalion of the Scots Guards for three years; before army service I had completed a five-year apprenticeship as a baker. I had never been involved in strike action before and here I was being forced out on strike by a Labour government! Despite that I still vote Labour. Even now I find it weird to remember how many (especially newish) firemen believed the strike would be over within 48 hours. They didn't believe the government would depend on the army for so long and let us rot freezing on pavements all over the country.

A neighbour of mine was serving on local authority 'night watch in case of fire', making extra money like many others did. He had the cheek some time later to ask me to contribute towards the cost of repairing the large fence which he erected to divide our properties. I was extremely polite.

We walked out of the station to be met by the on-duty police superintendent who told us that as long as we behaved ourselves there would be no problems, and hoped the dispute would not last long. 'Just doing his job', as we all said, and a few days later he was back kicking up hell because we had a dummy of Merlyn Rees hanging by a noose to the front of the station. Those poor army lads were on a hiding to nothing, though they did fortunately save some lives, but as for property, that was a joke. The government was obviously not concerned about that either. Cost in the first week? Millions!

Fire calls in our area, which would normally have had the Green Goddess passing the station were soon taken on alternative routes to avoid the screaming from my friends on picket lines, men who only a few weeks before would never have felt the venom of hate and frustration towards brave young untrained men doing our job so badly we didn't know whether to laugh, cry or feel sick, or to feel extreme anger and hate for a government which was supposed to represent the ordinary working man.

The local authorities were very shrewd in making all of us sign a non-violent or Coventry-style pact towards NAFO members or anyone else who did not support the strikers.

I am now retired through injury, and after all this time, I am sad to say, I will never forgive those officers who did not support us. They really did believe they had the right to guide the army, they were afraid some people would die because the fire service was not available. Did NAFO really believe we did not care? I will never forgive those who left the union to join NAFO simply hoping that would save them from another strike. If NAFO had supported the FBU, there would have been no guidance to the army, an army without guidance cannot find its way and the government would have lost.

My wife said to me yesterday, 'You know Jim, I reckon it took us four or five years to get over the strike financially speaking.' I replied, 'Margaret, I will never get over the strike.' The bitter feeling is now going away, only like now while I write does the memory of it all come right back, smack into view like it was only yesterday.

Our station janitor was new on the job at the time of the strike, though sadly he has now passed away, and 'wee

Francie', god bless him, made big pots of soup and tea, cooked everything for us on the picket line during those freezing weeks. It seemed to be freezing or raining every day during the strike, and the hot brazier in front of the station was great. Fuel for the fire came from floors of empty shops and houses opposite the station which were shortly supposed to be knocked down. This provoked another row with the police because entry to these buildings was not allowed.

The public support was tremendous, and all types of food were handed in; money was gathered and sent on to be shared out to help all involved. All types of support came in from around the town and across the country. As always, our wives were miraculous in their achievements.

Support from everyone was needed. Support from the TUC was sadly not forthcoming, it seemed they didn't want to go against a Labour government.

1977 was a very bad year for me personally. My father died in September 1977, seven hours after I went on duty at 6 o'clock one evening. My father had been a miner all his life, he supported the miners' union and the Labour government and would have supported me at a time when I needed his support most. My father would have said the union was correct. The union members did themselves proud. The outcome was an obvious success.

Appendices

Appendix I

A Service for the Sixties

The introductory statement on behalf of the executive council by general secretary John Horner is reproduced below. This statement was the main pivot of the debate on *A Service for the Sixties* at the annual conference at Rothesay in 1960.

A Service for the Sixties launched the FBU's campaign for a new and highly trained technical fire service. The task was, as the union conceived it, 'to change the service into a modern fire protection – fire fighting force'. To this end the document insisted that firemen be given 'up-to-date conditions of employment in keeping with the skilled profession they pursue'. This meant the introduction of the 48-hour week, as a step towards further improvements in duty systems, and the establishment of pay scales commensurate with the skilled job of fire-fighting and thus capable of attracting good quality recruits.

A second strand to the modernisation of employment conditions was 'the jettisoning of useless housemaid's work'. *A Service for the Sixties* was sweeping in its condemnation of station work, of 'charring', which still occupied the major part of a fireman's duty period. Routine chores would be replaced by the extension of fire inspection and fire prevention duties to the entire fire service.

Finally, the document called for the establishment of a directorate of training, 'responsible for training from recruit level to that of station officer and above'.

In conjunction with sections on the rank structure and

discipline of the service, and on the management of the service at Home Office and local authority level, *A Service for the Sixties* subjected every aspect of the fire service to a penetrating and 'no holds barred' criticism.

Following John Horner's introductory statement, and debate on the document, *A Service for the Sixties* was put to conference by the president, Terry Parry, and adopted unanimously by the 291 delegates present, representing every brigade in Great Britain and Northern Ireland.

Introductory Statement on behalf of the Executive Council by John Horner, General Secretary

The document, 'A Service for the 'Sixties', is a programme of development for Britain's fire brigades. It is not put to this Conference, to the fire service or to local government as a blueprint for the future service. We do not suggest in this document that we have been able to examine all the aspects of our present service, and the deficiencies and defects which have to be remedied. We do believe that the document will, given the support of this Conference and with subsequent discussion throughout the union, initiate in the entire service a refreshing examination of the present state of our service and what has to be done if that service is to face the challenge of the next decade.

Nobody believes, surely, that the ambitious programme which is set out here is going to be achieved in the space of a few months. It is going to take long, persistent agitation and activity on the part of this union if we are going to form the sort of service which we think is in the best interests of the men who earn their living therein and in the best interests of the people whom we serve.

In the document, Mr President, which I think is one of the most ambitious ever produced by the union, we make two assumptions. We assume that in the next decade there will be no war. Quite clearly, if that assumption proves to be false, there will not be a service in the sixties, because there will be nothing to serve in the next decade!

Our second assumption is that there is no major economic recession. We make it perfectly plain in the document that the economic position of Britain is still very delicately balanced. In this 'affluent society', one should not forget the large number of people who are now defined as the 'casualties of the welfare state', the old people who have remembered us today in their telegram; the sick, the injured; the underpaid. This so-called affluent society for Britain is basically the result of the fact that over the last few years the terms of world trade have been slightly in our favour. The terms of world trade, if they turned against Great Britain in its present precarious situation, could bring about a state of society which would hardly be called affluent, except for a number of people who, because of the fact that it remains a capitalist society, would be able to safeguard themselves against the economic ills of any recession.

That being said, Mr President, we say that with rational planning of our resources, sound political action, a progressive trading policy, particularly with the swelling demands of the new socialist countries, full employment can be guaranteed and a rising standard of living maintained. The trade union movement will do its job. We shall be part of that joint effort.

With these two assumptions, we ask a question: 'What do the sixties hold for firemen?' We are a trade union and it is not our job primarily to solve the problem of the administration of the fire service. People pay this organisation two shillings a week in order to get better conditions of employment, higher pay, a shorter working week, better pensions. This is why they pay two bob a week to the Fire Brigades Union and not, basically, for the union to produce blueprints as to the sort of service local authorities should provide in the future.

The executive council in presenting this document, however, takes the view that in this unfolding period, unless the Fire Brigades Union gives a lead and has a constructive policy upon which it can build up unity in the service, changes will be introduced into brigades which need not necessarily be in the interests of the men who earn their living in those brigades. We have seen one very significant intimation of the sort of changes which certain people have in mind.

A Modern Service

Last year at the Annual Conference at Southport you, Mr President, presented the Conference with a document on cadets. Since that Conference we have had a number of discussions in the Central Fire Brigades Advisory Council on the cadet proposals. I would not like to say how far we have got as a union in beating down proposals which are basically reactionary, basically opposed to the best interests of the service as we see them, and certainly fundamentally opposed to the conception of this trade union which is to build a better service based upon better conditions of employment for *all* the men in the service.

If Britain's economy continues to expand, even at this modest figure – and we put in the document that Britain in its economic expansion is proportionately behind the ratio of industrial expansion in many Western European countries, let alone behind the socialist countries of the world – if this expansion continues, if constantly new technical processes are introduced into industry, if, as we must to maintain our position in the world, we continue to expand our exports, if automation is to come, and indeed it will come, and if the cost of industrial fires is going to increase, as they will with these fantastically expensive automated processes, then the role of the fire service is going to be even more significant, its contribution to the country's economy is going to be even greater. Questions are being asked by some authorities – 'Shall we be able to find in the service today men of the necessary administrative calibre and technical efficiency to fill the senior positions of the service of the seventies?'

Many people in local government have taken the view that it is not possible for those senior posts to be filled from the present day human material that we find in the fire service. Hence the proposal for the cadet system. Somehow or other, they say, we have to import into the fire brigades men of a different calibre, men of a higher education, men with potential administrative qualities which you cannot expect to find among the rank and file firemen of the sixties. By this means we shall be able to have in a fire service in the seventies some men of a sufficiently high technical standard to fill the senior positions, ensuring for industry the necessary protection for the very expensive machines and industrial processes.

We believe that those who subscribe to that point of view are betraying not only the future interests of the fire service but are turning their backs on, and betraying, the interests of the present day firemen and officers both in this organisation and in the National Association of Fire Officers. I make that point because we have been appalled to learn that in the higher ranks of the National Association of Fire Officers there is a support for this idea of the introduction of a two-tier system of entry and a cadet corps designed to fill the senior posts of the future.

We start off from an entirely different footing. We do not in this document seek to gloss over what we regard as the grave deficiencies of our present-day service. We do not say that everything in the fire service is wonderful. When HM Chief Inspector of Fire Brigades says, as he does so often, 'We have the finest fire service in the world,' neither the Chief Inspector nor anybody else is deceived. Because we have not got the finest service in the world. In many parts of the country we have got a ramshackle fire service. We indicate some of its deficiencies in this document.

We say, however, that if the union's lead is followed it will be possible to transform this fire service of ours into an effective instrument which will be able in the period which is opening before us to meet the new challenge, to accept new responsibilities. And to do it on a basis of a transformed, modernised fire service in which modern conditions of employment are granted for the men therein, in which the new and higher technical and administrative standards we are seeking to achieve, will be won not by the introduction of a privileged group from outside but on the basis of an elevation of the *entire* fire service. It is going to be a man-sized job.

In the introduction to this document we refer to incidents which have happened in these last two or three months. We mention the fact that in Glasgow when those nineteen men lost their lives, they lost their lives in circumstances in which we, as firemen, and I choose my words carefully, can take no pride. We have nothing but admiration and pride for our comrades of the Glasgow brigade. Only firemen can fully appreciate, and only people who have seen the ruins of that Glasgow whisky warehouse can understand, the magnitude of the job of fire-fighting which our Scottish comrades put in on that terrible night. (*Applause.*)

Firemen can understand what those circumstances were. Almost the entire first attendance was wiped out. There was no fire-fighting being done, there could not be, when the job was getting away, when the men who were there were well-nigh overcome with fumes and with the horror of that situation. And yet if you go along Cheapside Street on Anderston Quay today you can see Harland & Woolf's still standing; you can still see the liquid oxygen store almost a hand's breadth away from the bottling department where the firemen stopped that fire.

We say in this document that when all is said and done, at the end of it fire-fighting comes down to this; that a small number of men will go into a darkened, smoke-logged building not knowing what they are going to meet, having faith in each other, in the long run prepared to risk their lives to save the lives of other people. In the long run, no matter what transformation we effect in the fire service, fire-fighting in its final stages remains just that. And we do not forget it.

But think of the situation in Glasgow. If this had happened in another more populous part of the city, if the liquid oxygen had gone, who knows what disaster would have followed? And the day after, the President and I were involved in arguments about what authority the fire brigade had for these places. Did they have any authority? Nobody is quite sure. Arguments ensued between the fire brigade and the Customs and Excise. Everybody has been concerned, quite rightly, with radiation hazards. We have done a lot of work on radiation hazards, as you have read in your report. We have not lost nineteen firemen over radiation hazards, in circumstances which the union considers must be the subject of the most searching examination. (*Applause.*) It is a reflection upon our service, and the President was quite right. You just cannot catalogue the deficiencies of the service without saying what is the responsibility of the union.

We quote Smithfield. Two years ago, in the very heart of the metropolis, in the basement of the central building of the Smithfield Meat Market two firemen lost their lives. Their fire station was at the top of Farringdon road, just up the hill. They did not know the danger existed; they walked to their deaths in that catacomb, in the terrible basement spreading over acres of Smithfield Market. And we are supposed to protect the *population* against fire.

Men are told again and again that they cannot go out on fire inspection, they cannot leave their station to examine their risks; there is too much station work to be done. These are the facts, and we have all accepted this in the past.

We say in this document that we are glad that some of the most dreadful – I can hardly call them fire stations – these abortions which are still propped up, that bespatter our countryside, known as fire stations (100 years old, some of them), we are glad indeed that bit by bit they are being replaced by modern fire stations.

It is my pleasure from time to time to go round to the opening of new fire stations. I am proudly shown the hundreds of square feet of windows and the hundreds of yards of polished floors, and I say 'I'm appalled at this.' I went to one station and the chief officer told me, 'We think this is a memorial to your work. The last time you were in this town you said so many things about the old station that it helped us immensely in getting a new one. What do you think of it?' I said, 'I think it's terrible.' He said, 'What will satisfy you?' (*Laughter.*)

What has this got to do with a modern fire service? Why are we condemning firemen to spend so many of their hours keeping these white elephants polished and shining? What has it got to do with today's fire service? We say in this document that we want a fireman's job in the sixties to be transformed. We want firemen to get off their knees! We want firemen to be firemen in the real sense; we want firemen and officers alike to remember that the job of protecting Britain against fire, the job of reducing the economic losses which our country suffers because of fires which each year are mounting, can only be done if we really modernise this fire service from the ground up. And that does not mean introducing cadets. That means starting at *recruit* level.

When we saw the programme of instruction for the Brighton cadets we thought it was excellent – first class; two years' instruction, covering all the main aspects of fire service administration and fire-fighting as we know it today. We said, 'We're for it. We want this programme. That's fine. We want this programme to apply to every new entry into the fire service.' They said, 'Oh, we can't afford that. This is only for a few people. How can we afford to bring all recruits in and teach them this? We say in this document that the public would be appalled to learn that so thin are we on the ground with fire-fighters that very often we cannot even afford to send people away on courses, because that would deplete the fire-fighting strength. We can't afford this training, say some authorities.

Our reply is that Britain cannot afford not to train its fire-fighters in this way!

When we won the new Factories Act for this fire service, with the assistance, as we readily concede, of our friends in the Parliamentary Labour Party, we brought the fire service on to the ground floor of industrial fire protection for the first time. We were then forced to consider how to implement these new, very limited, powers which the fire service have got. This would need training; this would need instruction; this would need an increase in establishment. We have got to get more officers, more men qualified and trained in fire prevention and fire inspection. I can tell you that on the Central Fire Brigades Advisory Council at the last hour, after the Bill had gone through parliament, the County Councils Association representatives attempted to apply the new legislation in such a way that very little progress would be made at all. They could not see how our fire service could afford the increases in personnel, the additional officers that we have got to promote, if we are going to apply the new Factories Act.

For the Entire Service

It is necessary for someone in the service constantly to be giving the lead. Who can give this lead? One organisation can lead this service through the next decade, and that is the Fire Brigades Union. Why? We are an organisation which represents *all* ranks; we welcome Ted Jones on to the executive council. We are happy to see among the delegates here today station officers, not coming as members of the Officers' National Committee but as duly elected delegates from their own areas. This is a fine thing. (*Applause.*) We are able to speak for the entire fire service. While we have no illusions about the size of the job we are tackling I think we should also recognise that what we have been saying this last year or so is already creating echoes in the minds of people who are not in our union. Certain chief officers are being won over to the conception, the progressive conception, of the sort of service that we want to create. They are being held back; they are being held back by the restrictive economies about which you spoke, Mr President. Consider the new duties of the fire service in respect of industrial fire protection. What a contradiction! The new officers who are going to be promoted in order to give effect to the new Factories Act, for industrial fire protection duties, will have to have their salaries paid largely from the domestic ratepayers. And not from the industrial and manufacturing interests of this country. It is a contradiction upon which I think our union will have a great deal to say as this work develops.

We speak for the entire fire service. When we criticise the

fire service as we do here, when we make pungent comments about how the service is run, we do so because we are entitled to do so. Indeed we are more entitled to do so than anyone else. We ask for a transformation of station routine, for the removal from station duties of all the menial chores that so overshadow and dampen the spirit of firemen. We present a different sort of future. Young men come up to us with three or four years' service saying, 'Well, this is what I've been waiting for.' I was at a meeting when a young chap came up to me and said, 'I was going to give the service another year and then I was going, but what I've heard from the FBU gives me hope. When we make these propositions we make them as a union which embraces the entire fire service.

We do not disregard the help that we have got in certain matters from the Chief Fire Officers' Association. But who fought and won the battle of manpower? There are in Scotland here fire masters who to their shame – and they are not very far from this building – have accepted decisions of their fire brigade committees which will condemn the people in their areas to an inferior standard of fire protection. And they have not said a word. They do not mind the FBU coming in. 'That's good, John,' they say, 'You make the pace.' OK, we will make the pace. I know full well that among many of the NAFO there are good, honest, station officers and others who are supporting the FBU's general plans.

Why Discipline?

When we talk about a new relationship between officers and men in this section, *Rank upon Rank*, what are we after? We are after a modern fire service, and there is so much in our service today which is so deeply rooted in the past that it ought to have been cleared out many, many years ago. We make the daring proposal, the revolutionary suggestion, that men earning their living in the fire service, if they have got to wear a uniform, ought to wear the same uniform! What a dreadful thing! What *is* this rank that we have in our service? Men are foremen, men are managers – that is what officers really are – managers in uniform. We say with great seriousness, and we are not joking, that our fire service is rank-ridden. (*Hear, Hear!*)

People say, but you have got to have discipline. Of course you have got to have discipline. Do you know why you have got to have discipline? Because in the long run four or five men together have to go into that darkened, smoke-logged building and risk their lives, and they have to depend upon each other. The only possible justification of any so-called discipline is that that team of men is a unit, interdependent, confident that the other chap will back you up; that you have confidence in the officer that when he says do a thing he knows what he is saying – and you do not get that sort of confidence by just 'Yes, Sir' and 'No, Sir' – 'Three bags full, Sir'. (*Applause.*)

That is why we are asking for a new look at this aspect of our Service.

The Home Office

In this document we deal not only with the service as such, but we deal with how the service is administered, and we have a particular section on the Fire Service Department at the Home Office. We have for many years allowed to pass by without comment the deficiencies which in our view exist in the administration of this service of ours.

On Monday night of next week your union representatives will be meeting eminent Harley Street consultants who have been helping this union. We shall be discussing with them the creation of a proper medical service for the fire service. A proper medical service for the fire service – in the year 1960! No one has got the statistics illustrating how many firemen die from coronary thrombosis, or from other heart ailments. No *single* doctor in this country has a comprehensive knowledge of what a fireman's job is. That is a reflection upon this union, but not only upon this union. We had to fight the case which is reported in the Annual Report of the sub-officer suffering from angina: an operational sub-officer collapsed from angina and was then permitted by the medical officer to return to duty with this medical certificate: 'provided he does no work which gives him a pain across the chest'. Last year when Manchester had that series of big fires, this sub-officer was sent to one of them to act in a 'supervisory' capacity. Can you imagine sending an operational sub-officer to a fire telling him to do no work giving him a pain across the chest? Twenty-four hours later that man was a dead man.

The fire authority gave his widow an 'ordinary' pension. The union said she was entitled to a 'special' pension. The fire authority under the pension scheme had to take the opinion of a medical practitioner. The only one they could take was that of the last doctor who saw him, the one who signed the certificate. The question was put to him, 'Do you think that the sub-officer's duties as a sub-officer would have aggravated the coronary conditions from which he was suffering?' The answer had to be 'No', for obvious reasons. We had to go and see the chairman of the committee and argue and plead until we got a 'special' pension for his widow.

What gratification do we get out of that? We in the union want people to treat the fire service seriously. We want them to understand that we are no longer prepared to stand to one side and see the 140 fire brigades which combine to make a great service treated in this extraordinarily nonchalant and slap-happy way.

On Monday night it will be the union here consulting with eminent medical men, trying to find a way to bring about in Britain's fire service what has been existing in Continental fire services for many years – a medical service. I mention this as one example of the sort of deficiency or gap in our general administration about which we have a great deal to say in this document.

There is no independent research undertaken by the Fire Service Department. They have no means of doing it. We talk about the seven years that we have been looking for a lightweight uniform. A number of us on this platform have been doing a bit of research, independent research, on lightweight uniforms – we have got browned off, tired waiting for official results.

This report you have in your Annual Report this year, these statistics and these graphs that have come out of the Department of Scientific and Industrial Research, have only been produced because of the very biting criticisms which you representatives put before the Advisory Council last December. This flapping around for a new breathing apparatus set – in the hands, as we were for years, of a single monopoly! We are a fire service. They are spending £100,000,000 in trying to get a rocket off the ground! They cannot spend £500 in helping to evolve a new breathing set for firemen. But men die ... men die! We had a member die in Middlesex with BA and we have never really discovered how it came about. That man was suffering from an obscure cerebral condition because of loss of oxygen.

We are saying that you are never going to elevate this fire service unless you can force upon the government their responsibilities through the Fire Service Department. We do not agree that our members are second-raters. We agree that our members are getting browned off. The sort of service where the station officer is more concerned, as unfortunately is the case in some stations, with seeing that the windows are polished and the floors are polished when the DO comes round. (*Applause*). What has it got to do with the modern fire service? How does that stop a whisky warehouse blowing up and killing nineteen men? Clerkenwell Fire Station (not that you could ever do much with the Clerkenwell Fire Station) has got nice doors, has it not? – not done, incidentally, by firemen. The brass is polished. But then a mile down the road, there is a fire risk unknown to the brigade which kills two men. It is in this sense that the sixties will demand a transformation of this service if we are going to make it a *real* fire service.

Faith in Firemen

Our faith in firemen. The President talked about cynicism yesterday, and there is cynicism in our ranks: 'We are not interested in a service for the sixties; what about my public bank holiday leave?' 'Flannel'. 'What has it got to do with the FBU?' 'Why does the FBU not get on with the main job?' We have heard remarks like this in recent weeks. The executive council says that, in the sixties, the job of transforming our service into a modern fire service will be part and parcel of our job of transforming the conditions of employment of the men in that service. The 48-hour-week, of course, must come and come quickly. You cannot have in the sort of service that we are seeking to build the relics of a past age. You must break this tradition of long hours in the fire service. Members say, 'What does this mean? What shift system? Does it mean we're going to lose the beds?' I will say this – really sticking my neck out – you are not going to make a modern fire service of it until you get rid of the beds! (*Hear, hear and applause.*)

We are talking about increasing pay. We have had a modest increase of pay. We have got a figure which is about equal to the average earnings in industry. Can we be content with that? Of course we cannot. But other people have got ideas about the sort of service where the great multitude of men who earn their living in the fire service are on a sort of glorified labourer's rate, and there is a higher strata, the administrators, the technicians, the officers, the supervisors. They will be on a different basis. The level of their conditions of employment will be infinitely superior to that of the men who are told, 'Get in there'; 'Get that branch in there': 'Come out of there'. That is not the sort of fire service we want to build in the sixties. We want a fire service where we are drawing fully upon the human material which we know exists in the service, a reservoir of human material waiting to be tapped. Some members say, 'What's the FBU up to? Has it lost its senses talking about refresher courses? Who the hell wants a refresher course? I know all about fire fighting. Good Lord, it might mean going down to Moreton in Marsh or some place like that!' It is because we have this faith in our membership, that they will understand that only the union can give this lead, that we are asking you seriously to consider this document, 'A Service for the Sixties'.

Appendix I

We welcome constructive criticism. The more criticism we can have and the more searching examination you can help us to make of these problems, the greater will be our pleasure. We do believe that this 1960 Annual Conference of the Fire Brigades Union, Mr President, must mark a new era, when the FBU fully comes into its own as the only organisation which can make the fire brigades of Britain a modern fire service – and our job one well worth having. (*Applause.*)

Appendix II

Chief Officials of the Fire Brigades Union

General Secretaries

G. Gamble	1918-22
J. Bradley	1922-29
P. Kingdom	1929-39
J. Horner	1939-64
T. Parry	1964-80
K. Cameron	1980-

Presidents

A. Odlin	1939-44
J. Burns	1944-59
T. Parry	1959-64
E. Humphries	1964-77
W. Barber	1977-79
W. Deal	1979-86
S. Fitzsimmons	1986-91
R. Scott	1991-

Assistant General Secretaries

H. Short	1939-46
J. Grahl	1946-56
T. Harris	1957-74
R. Foggie	1974-82
M. Fordham	1982-

Appendix III

Total Membership of the Fire Brigades Union, Whole-time and Retained Personnel (selected years)

1935	2,386
1939	3,150
1940	66,500
1941	71,500
1946	15,293
1950	18,580
1960	23,810
1970	31,993
1980	41,053
1990	47,801

Appendix IV

Fire Service Statistics Establishment for Whole-time Personnel (selected years)

	Great Britain
1918	3,200
1939	6,600
1943	130,000
1947	18,606

	England and Wales	Scotland
1950	19,422	1,722
1960	21,484	2,281
1970	24,812	3,218
1980	35,693	4,359
1990	35,902	4,689

Appendix V

The Fire Brigades Union and its Solicitors

John Saville

William Henry Thompson – known as Harry to his friends – was born on 15 October 1885 in the north Lancashire town of Preston. His father was a grocer, two uncles were solicitors, and young Harry was articled, qualifying as a solicitor on 1 April 1908. He first worked for a firm in the Potteries.

Exactly when Harry Thompson became influenced by radical ideas and politics is not known, but he lived at a time when young people like himself were greatly influenced by the writings of Bernard Shaw and H.G. Wells, and a host of lesser known personalities. The Independent Labour Party and the Marxist Social-Democratic Federation were beginning to establish themselves in most parts of Britain. There was a radical flavour in the air, and the years just before the outbreak of the First World War witnessed a massive industrial unrest. During the war Harry Thompson declared himself a conscientious objector, and when he was called up for military service at the end of 1917 he refused to be conscripted and served eighteen months in various prisons. By this time he had many friends and contacts within the labour movement, and it was while he was in prison that he began corresponding with his future wife. Joan Beauchamp, a woman of high moral integrity and sharp intelligence, was parliamentary secretary of the No-Conscription Fellowship, largely but not entirely a pacifist organisation. They met after Harry was released from prison, and they married in August 1921.

After the war ended – Harry himself was not released from jail until April 1919 – he concentrated mainly on legal work connected with the labour movement. His first major political case was as solicitor to the Poplar Borough Council when it took its famous stand against the burden of poor rates upon the poorer boroughs of London and, as a result, 30 Labour councillors went to prison, George Lansbury among them. Harry Thompson was a central figure throughout. He began his own practice in the same year with offices at 27 Chancery Lane. He had a staff of two, and during the next decades his reputation grew steadily as he became the leading expert in the country on workmen's compensation. He was also a founder member of the National Council for Civil Liberties in 1934, and much of his London work in the 1930s was defending members of the anti-fascist movement subject to police prosecution for their actions against Mosley and his Blackshirts.

When John Horner was elected general secretary in 1939 of a near moribund organisation he was 27 years old: a young man of enormous energy, a striking intellect with a very quick capacity for learning but with precious little experience of the trade union movement. The union he took over came to have offices in Chancery Lane, and when the bombing of London started in the late summer of 1940 a considerable part of Chancery Lane was destroyed one night. W.H. Thompson took over spare rooms in the new head office the union found. Horner already knew W.H. Thompson. As the former records in his memoir in this volume, John and his future wife Pat had enrolled as evening students – this was before the war – at a Quaker educational settlement where W.H. and his wife Joan were well known among the circle of pacifists and progressives who managed and taught in the settlement. John and Pat's favourite tutor was Fred Parsons, a close friend of W.H. – he called him Harry, which Horner never did – and Fred Parsons was the father of Owen, who is quoted below, and Henry, who became well known for his work in the Labour Research Department.

Appendix V

The association between W.H. and Horner was perhaps the most important stroke of luck enjoyed by Horner in these very early years. As he himself has written:

> In those days I was the most privileged of union secretaries, for I had in the room just above my head, the sharpest of intellects, the most liberal of minds and the possessor of the widest experience in trade union law. He taught me procedures, constitutions and rules. He drafted the amendments necessary to launch our AFS section.

There are innumerable examples of the importance of W.H. Thompson to the history of the Fire Brigades Union during the war years. When, for instance, the National Fire Service was established in the summer of 1941, Herbert Morrison, the Home Secretary, told John Horner and John Burns (the FBU president) that FBU members were now no longer employees of local authorities and that the government was giving serious thought to the application of the 1927 Trade Disputes Act to the FBU. Strictly applied this could mean insisting on the FBU dissociating itself from the TUC and the Labour Party, as the civil service unions were obliged to do. When Horner consulted W.H. Thompson the latter said it was 'bluff' and explained to John Horner what the arguments were. With these Horner then went to see Sir Walter Citrine, general secretary of the TUC, and Citrine said that he would take action. He did, and soon Morrison was explaining to the House of Commons that the Trades Dispute Act would not apply to the newly established National Fire Service.

W.H. Thompson's contribution to the development of the FBU during the war years was a major source of strength, but his health was deteriorating and it was not helped by the very serious injuries his wife sustained from a flying bomb explosion. Harry Thompson died on 4 August 1947, by which time his staff numbered 70 and were the leading solicitors for the British trade union movement. Harry Thompson's life and work was summed up by Owen Parsons who worked for the firm for eleven years from 1935:

> Fundamentally, Thompson believed in using his great skill and knowledge and courage as a lawyer in the interests of the oppressed against the rich and powerful, on behalf of injured workmen against insurance companies, on behalf of tenants against landlords, on behalf of trade unions and trade unionists against employers, on behalf of political demonstrators against the police, on behalf of the citizen against the bureaucrat, in short on behalf of the poor against the wealthy, on behalf of the mass of people against those who sought to govern and control them.

* * *

There were two sons of Harry Thompson, Robin and Brian, and both in due course became solicitors and joined the firm. Robin became an articled clerk immediately following the death of his father in August 1947. The firm was still a tenant of the FBU with five or six rooms at the top of First Avenue House, 52 Bedford Square. At the time of W.H. Thompson's death Henry Shramek was acting as principal of the firm. Shramek was already a solicitor when he joined the AFS. He became a leading member of the FBU regional council for the London Civil Defence Region. His legal training and dedication to the FBU led to his forming and training a team of 'accused friends' from among union members which won a healthy respect from senior officers who administered the strict disciplinary code which accompanied the creation of the National Fire Service. When Shramek was demobilised he was immediately taken on by W.H., in large part as a result of the reputation Shramek had won as the outstanding authority on NFS Statutory regulations. He was to play an important part in the business of the firm during the years immediately following W.H.'s death.

The FBU has continued to use the services of the Thompsons throughout the post-war years. The firm grew steadily with branches all over the United Kingdom, and in the 1960s Robin and Brian divided the branches between them and set up as independent firms. They both continued to cover all the work of the FBU, the decision to use one or the other being largely a matter of geographical location. In the Robin Thompson group Arthur Charles was the main person responsible for FBU work. His wife, Jessie, was Horner's personal secretary for many years. Arthur Charles retired after 26 years' service in 1975, and at a presentation made at the FBU Annual Conference in that year he made a very interesting speech which deserves commemoration:

> ... When I joined W.H. Thompson's back in the dim and distant past they said to me: 'Look, there is a little union here, the Fire Brigades Union. Will you take it over? You will never do any work for them, they never have any trouble. It is another union you act for and that is it.' We all know how different that is today and I am very, very proud to be amongst friends and I am very proud to have played a part in building up the history of the legal work of this union and, what is far more important, putting your union on the map in the league of the world trade unions.
>
> I am sure you won't mind me saying that you are a small organisation. We act for large organisations from the AEUW upwards and downwards. This union historically has played a very, very great part in making industrial history. I heard Dick Foggie tell you about the success of damages and so forth over the years. That is all very fine but I would like to retire thinking that W.H. Thompson never did another case for the Fire Brigades Union because every case I have been involved in, from the £5 claim to the £50,000 claim, as Dick said, means pain and suffering. Only last night I was told of another tragedy. We have done an awful lot to prevent accidents. We made brigades realise that if they do not work properly, if they do not devise a safe system of working, people are going to be injured and it is going to cost money; and I think that many types of accident that I was brought up with back in the 1950s have now disappeared. Those accidents do not happen. Why? Because the work you have done as a union, and the work behind the scenes I have been proud to do for you, make the courts say: 'This shall not be. If it is, you will pay money.' And even insurance companies are hurt most when they have to pay money. My object of working for you and working amongst friends has been to cut out accidents. I do not thrive on accidents. It is no satisfaction to me to earn a salary because somebody has been killed and left a wife and kiddies. I would rather think the fireman is not injured and none of my work is ever necessary.
>
> I would also at this stage like to pay tribute to the help I

> have had. If I have ever had any success at all, it has not been all my effort, it has been the work from the top to the bottom of this organisation. Of the unions I act for, I get more help, support and co-operation; far more important is that I get more encouragement, from the rank and file right at the bottom of the organisation. When I ask them to do something for me they do it to the best of their ability and as soon as they possibly can, and they do something for some poor unfortunate individual lying on his back in hospital ... I am going to be around for a little while because – and I say this very sincerely – I could not bring myself to give up the Fire Brigades Union. I would have retired last year but I just could not bring myself to give up this union. I am called the fireman's friend. I wanted to live up to that and think whoever takes over from me is able to carry on where I left off and achieve as much for you as I have been able to. Thank you all.

Arthur Charles did not in fact finally retire from Thompsons until March 1981, when he was 71 years old; and after a long illness he died on 9 December 1987. His work at Robin Thompsons was largely taken over by Andrew Dinsmore.

The Labour Research Department has shown that in 1989 the FBU Legal Assistance Scheme received over £5 million in compensation. The Labour Research Department surveyed 36 trade unions and the FBU was shown to be the top performer. Compensation to the union averaged £105 per member, more than £12 per head compared with the union in second place. As Ken Cameron commented in the July 1990 issue of *Firefighter*:

> 1989 was the best year ever for the FBU Legal Assistance Scheme, and Thompsons, the union's solicitors, are to be congratulated on the magnificent job they have done for our members. It is also a fitting tribute to Dan Riddell that the legal department achieved so much in his last year.

It remains to add that the efficiency, competence and success of the Thompsons are not only the result of the close and helpful association with the FBU at all levels, but that over the decades it has been their legal expertise which has persuaded the courts to interpret the existing law relating to compensation and claims of all kinds in liberal and sympathetic ways. Further, the tradition that was established from the years of the Second World War of the FBU constantly campaigning on safety questions as well as on adequate financial compensation for its members has never faltered, and is as vigorous and lively as ever. We should never forget what is owed by the whole union to the early collaboration between John Horner and W.H. Thompson.

A Note on Sources

Contributors have given guidance to the primary and secondary sources used, in the notes at the end of each chapter. There seems little point in listing all the items drawn upon. It may be useful, however, to list the most essential archives and materials used in this study of firemen's trade unionism.

The FBU has no large body of materials, as a result of the blitz, which destroyed the Chancery Lane office, and, irony of ironies, of a fire at head office in the 1950s. However, Bradley House, the Union's head office in Kingston-upon-Thames, does hold *Reports of the Annual Conference of the FBU* for the years 1936-37, 1940 and 1946 to the present (with the exception of 1955-56), and copies of the Union journal, *Firefighter*, from 1945 onwards. The minutes of executive council meetings are also available from the late 1940s to the present.

For the London Fire Service, there is no better source than the documents in the Greater London Record Office: LCC Fire Brigade, LCC/FB/GEN, LCC/FB/STA and LCC/FB/WAR; LCC Clerks Department, Fire Brigade Committee, LCC/CL/FB and LCC/CL/ESTAB. See also LCC/MIN.

For the National Fire Service, the reader should consult Home Office papers in the Public Record Office: HO/186 and especially HO/187.

Finally, readers should be aware of Terry Segars, 'The Fire Service: the Social History of a Uniformed Working-Class Occupation' (Essex University PhD, 1989), which examines the subject from the mid-nineteenth century to the 1940s, with an appendix on more recent times.

Notes on Contributors

James Alexander is a fireman at Kilmarnock fire station.

Victor Bailey, formerly a Research Fellow of Worcester College, Oxford, is Professor of Modern British History at the University of Kansas. He is the author of *Policing and Punishment in Nineteenth Century Britain* (1981) and *Delinquency and Citizenship: Reclaiming the Young Offender* (1987).

Kenneth Brown is Professor of Economic and Social History at Queen's University, Belfast. He won the Royal Historical Society's Whitfield Prize for his biography of *John Burns* (1977). His other publications include *Essays in Anti-Labour History* (1974), *The English Labour Movement 1700-1951* (1985) and a *Social History of the Nonconformist Ministry in England and Wales* (1988).

Bill Craig is a retired executive council member of the FBU. He was chairman of the Scottish district committee during the national strike.

John Curran is a fireman at King Street fire station, Aberdeen.

David Englander is senior lecturer in European Humanities Studies at the Open University. He is the author of *Landlord and Tenant in Urban Britain, 1838-1918* (1983), co-editor of *Culture and Belief in Europe 1450-1600* (1990) and co-author of *Mr Charles Booth's Inquiry: Life and Labour in London 1886-1903* (1992).

Jim Flockhart, now retired, was Glasgow area chairman of the FBU at the time of the 1973 strike.

John Horner joined the London Fire Brigade in 1933. He was general secretary of the FBU from 1939 to 1964, and Labour MP for Oldbury and Halesowen, between 1964 and 1970. He was a member of the Select Committee on Nationalised Industries and is author of *Studies in Industrial Democracy* (1973).

Enoch Humphries joined the National Fire Service in Glasgow in 1946. He was president of the FBU from 1964 to 1977, and member and sometime president of the General Council of the Scottish TUC. He has been a member of the Employments Appeal Tribunal and the Greater Glasgow Health Board.

Graham Johnson has taught courses in social and labour history at Hull University. He completed a PhD in 1988 on 'Social Democratic Politics in Britain, 1881-1911'. He has contributed to the *Dictionary of Labour Biography* and is currently writing a book on the Social Democratic Federation.

Paul Kleinman, former crewman on the fireboat *Firehawk* and still serving in the London fire brigade, was a branch representative of the FBU for many years.

Pete Rockley, now retired, was a member of the executive council of the FBU for the East Midlands from 1976 to 1988.

Bob Roxburgh, a retired firefighter, used to work for the Bootle and Merseyside fire brigade.

John Saville is Emeritus Professor of Economic and Social History, Hull University. He was a founder member and sometime chair of the Labour History Society and is a member of the Council for Academic Freedom. His books include *Ernest Jones, Chartist* (1952), *The Labour Movement in Britain: A Commentary* (1988) and *1848: The British State and the Chartist*

Movement (1989). He is also co-editor of three volumes of *Essays in Labour History* (with Asa Briggs), *The Socialist Register* (with Ralph Miliband), and nine volumes (to date) of *The Dictionary of Labour Biography* (with Joyce Bellamy).

Terry Segars has been a member of the executive council of the FBU since 1980 representing East Anglia. He completed a PhD in 1989 on the social history of firemen. He is the author of 'Working for London's Fire Brigade, 1889-1939' in Andrew Saint (ed.), *Politics and the People of London: The London County Council, 1889-1965* (1989).

Alistair Spence, now retired, was a station officer at King Street fire station, Aberdeen.

Name Index

Name Index

Name Index

Subject Index

Subject Index

Subject Index

Subject Index

Subject Index